Jesus
in the
Nag Hammadi Writing

Jesus

in the

Nag Hammadi Writings

Majella Franzmann

T&T CLARK
EDINBURGH

T&T CLARK LTD
59 GEORGE STREET
EDINBURGH EH2 2LQ
SCOTLAND

First published 1996

ISBN 0 567 08526 0

British Library Cataloguing-in-Publication Data
A catalogue record for this book is available from the British Library

Printed in Great Britain by Bell & Bain, Glasgow
Bound by Hunter & Foulis, Edinburgh

For Michael Lattke

Preface

This study was begun during the first of two periods of research as an Alexander von Humboldt Fellow in Germany. I am extremely grateful for the wonderful generosity of this Foundation and their continuing support. I owe a debt of gratitude to those who acted as my host professors during both research periods, especially to Luise Abramowski, for the seventeen-month period of research in Tübingen 1992–3 which saw the foundations of the work established; and to Hermann Lichtenberger in Tübingen and Hans-Joachim Klimkeit in Bonn who shared their resources with me for the second two-month period in 1995 that enabled the final details to be completed. Many others in Germany deserve heartfelt thanks for hospitality and for giving up precious time to speak with me about the project and make helpful suggestions: Martin Hengel, Otto Betz and members of the Theological Faculty in Tübingen, with special thanks to Monika Merkle and Dorothea Epting; Kurt Rudolph in Marburg, Peter Nagel in Bonn, and Hans-Martin Schenke and Karl Wolfgang Tröger in Berlin. That these scholars made suggestions should not be taken to indicate that they are in agreement with what I have written in this study. I take full responsibility for the work and the opinions expressed in it.

Colleagues in Armidale, Peter Forrest and Mary Dolan, made my second period of research in Germany possible by their generosity with teaching assistance. Josie Fisher undertook the mammoth task of helping with the final editing and proof-reading, and Frances MacKay and Kathryn Hedemann made helpful editorial comments on draft chapters. Jeff Hodges arrived in Armidale just in time to make some last minute suggestions, especially with regard to several of the Coptic passages.

I dedicate this work to Prof. Michael Lattke (University of St. Lucia, Brisbane, Australia), *Doktorvater extraordinaire*, mentor, colleague and friend.

M. Franzmann
University of New England
November, 1995

Contents

Introduction

The Nag Hammadi writings (sometimes called the Coptic Gnostic writings), which consist of a total of fifty-two tractates (twelve of which are duplicates), were discovered in late 1945 in the Nag Hammadi region in Egypt.[1] As with the Qumran writings discovered also in the mid-20th century, these texts are of immense significance not only for the study of the religions of the Graeco-Roman world, but also for the history of development and ongoing self-understanding of three world religions, Christianity, Gnosticism, and Judaism.

I propose in this study to chart in the Nag Hammadi texts the constructions of the character Jesus, especially as that character is active within the earthly context. In doing this I hope to present a systematic outline of material within the various strands of the traditions of interpretation about this character during the early centuries CE. The idea of using the Nag Hammadi texts for Jesus research is not new; nevertheless it remains a radical perspective for the academic study of Christian origins and the early development of Christianity. This is easily indicated by the paucity of scholarship on the subject.

The primary focus of this study is Jesus' contact with the world: his entrance into the world; the kind of world he comes to; his being and nature; his role in the earthly context especially as revealer; his friends and enemies; his struggle with the archons who control the world; the close of his "physical" contact with the world. His experience within the world is set within the broader context of heavenly origin and destiny, although I have not made the investigation of the heavenly context a priority of the study.

The study is not an attempt to present one picture of a single Jesus, not an attempt to produce a unified christology of the Nag Hammadi writings, even if that were possible. Rather it is an attempt to summarise the variety of portraits of Jesus with an emphasis on common themes. The questions I ask of the character will always be necessarily limited, simply because I have chosen one particular focus rather than another, but I hope to cover the major aspects of the character. Not all the texts have material explicitly relevant to all the questions. Sometimes information can be inferred, but not always. Where

---

[1] Hedrick (1986) provides a good introductory summary to the Nag Hammadi material (preceded by a helpful bibliography). The major bibliographical contribution on the Nag Hammadi writings stems from Scholer 1971 and the supplements to that work that have appeared in *NT* since that volume. Scholer's arrangement of the material is more helpful than Giversen's (1963b; simple alphabetical arrangement by author). For an overview of the work on Gnosticism in general including bibliography, see the ongoing studies of Rudolph (1969/71/72/73/85/90) in *ThR*; and also Berger.

there is no explicit material, and none can be inferred, this does not mean that the subject was not important to the community. Not everything of importance to the community is necessarily dealt with within each individual text.

In order to outline various aspects of the figure of Jesus and to make comparisons across texts, it is necessary to use passages without being able to situate them within their particular textual context. The analysis cannot be done without this, though it is dangerous since individual categories are always qualified by the total picture of Jesus found in the entire text. Thus two texts which describe the birth, taking flesh and crucifixion of Jesus, may attribute different meanings to these events and present different understandings of the Jesus figure.

The study will use all those writings in which the figure of Jesus appears, even when scholarly opinion regards Jesus as no more than a convenient symbol attached to a text as a secondary accumulation. Here of course we come up against a number of complications such as the diversity of the texts at Nag Hammadi, and the question of whether the texts are Christian or non-Christian. However, it must suffice for the study that in the final event we have a collection of texts that are basically Christian in orientation (i.e. have a focus on the person of Jesus Christ) and it is the interpretations of the Jesus figure within the entirety of the collection and a comparison of these interpretations which is of interest here.

I have made no attempt to outline a possible dating for the works I am studying, and neither do I think that it is necessarily important in the first instance. A community can use both old and new texts without differentiating between them by this aspect. Thus a community which uses the canonical gospel texts may make no dating distinctions between Mark's Jesus and John's Jesus, taking them both as the one person. So also with the Nag Hammadi texts: a community could just as easily make no distinctions between Thomas' Jesus and the Jesus of Tri. Trac., taking them both as the one figure.

Technical Preface

1. Texts Used in the Study which Follows

The study investigates every occurrence of a Jesus figure in the collection of texts. The character Jesus or Jesus (the) Christ or Christ occurs in Pr. Paul, Ap. Jas., Gos. Truth, Treat. Res., Tri. Trac., Gos. Phil., Orig. World, Thom. Cont., Ap. John, Gos. Thom., Gos. Eg., Soph. Jes. Chr., Acts Pet. 12 Apost., Treat. Seth, Apoc. Pet., Teach. Silv., Ep. Pet. Phil., Melch., Testim. Truth, Interp. Know., Val. Exp., On Anoint., On Bap. A, On Bap. B, On Euch. A, and Trim. Prot. Within this group of texts, Pr. Paul and Orig. World have a Jesus figure who appears only within the heavenly context and are therefore of limited interest to the study since few categories are covered with regard to Jesus in the earthly context (see Chapter II, "The Jesus figure confined to the heavenly region").

A Jesus figure is not named explicitly but can be inferred from the context in Exeg. Soul, Dial. Sav., 1 Apoc. Jas., 2 Apoc. Jas., and Great Pow. A question remains over the presence of a Jesus character in Hyp. Archons, Apoc. Paul, Zost., Apoc. Adam, and Paraph. Shem. Since I have decided not to include these texts in the discussion, I present arguments for their exclusion here briefly.

1.1 The Hypostasis of the Archons

There is no Jesus character mentioned and the only possibility for identifying one implicitly would be in the character of the true man within a modelled form (ⲡⲣⲱⲙⲉ ⲛⲁⲗⲏⲑⲓ[ⲛⲟⲥ ⲟⲩⲱ]ⲛⲍ ⲉⲃⲟⲗ ⲍⲛ̅ⲛⲟⲩⲡⲗⲁⲥⲙⲁ) (96.33–34) who comes at the end of the ages to teach the Gnostics, to anoint them with the chrism of eternal life, given him from the undominated race (97.1–5); or the Son who appears with the Father in the final paragraph, of whom it is said that he (is) over the all (97.18–19). Layton seems to put both characters together as a composite in his list of the Dramatis Personae, in which he places "the All-Powerful or True Man, the Son of God who will come at the end of time to manifest the Spirit" after the Father of Truth and the Holy Spirit of the Father of Truth (1974, 389).

Barc comments that this use of the man of truth, especially the description of his action in 97.1–20, is a Christian rereading of the function of Eleleth in 93.11–13, but does not go further to identify who the man of truth is (1980, 128). Bullard makes a link from the true man in this text to the true man in Orig. World 164.11 and 171.24 (113 fn. 406).

1.2 The Apocalypse of Paul

Many scholars consider the small child who appears in the text to be (the risen) Jesus.[1] This figure acts primarily as guide and interpreter of the action for Paul as he ascends through the heavens. The text is not concerned with a Jesus within the earthly context.

1.3 Zostrianos

The child of the child, Ephesech, occurs as the revealer on p. 13, and this may be a reference to a Jesus figure. However, there are no explicit references to any Jesus figure in an earthly context.

1.4 The Apocalypse of Adam

There are one or two possibilities for finding a Jesus figure implicitly in this text. In 76.8–9, the character of the Illuminator appears who is said to redeem souls from the day of death (76.15–17). Thereafter the text describes a man who will perform signs and wonders in order to scorn the powers and their ruler (77.1–3) and against whom the ruler will arouse great wrath (77.7–9). It is unclear whether the Illuminator and the man are the same[2] or separate characters.[3] The description of the (holy) spirit coming upon them both may provide the connection (77.16–18; 80.15), yet 77.14–18 may well be interpreted as suggesting that they are separate. The powers will not see the Illuminator (77.14–15) but they will punish the flesh of the man upon whom the holy spirit has come (77.16–18).[4]

With regard to a possible Jesus figure for the purpose of the present study, certainly the description of the suffering in the flesh of the man upon whom the holy spirit has come seems at first glance to be a strong reference to the baptism of Jesus and his subsequent suffering at the hands of the archons. Yet within the descriptions by the various heavens concerning the Illuminator, the seventh heaven speaks of him being a drop who came from heaven, brought down by dragons to caves where he became a child, and a spirit came upon him, and he was brought to the high place from which he had come forth (80.9–20). This passage presents a much closer connection therefore *within*

---

[1] See, e.g., Böhlig and Labib 1963, 15; Rudolph 1965, 360; Haardt 154; Murdock and MacRae 48; and Stroumsa 79. W.-P. Funk identifies the child as the Spirit: "...seine Rolle beider anschließenden Himmelreise ähnelt stark der eines Deuteengels, er wird jedoch nicht als 'Engel', sondern stets als 'der Geist' (gelegentlich auch 'der heilige Geist') bezeichnet" (1989, 629).

[2] Those who assume that the Illuminator and the man are the same character, Jesus or Jesus Christ include H.-M. Schenke (1966, 31), Haardt (158–9), and Daniélou (1966b, 292).

[3] Of those who interpret as two characters, Beltz sees the man as possibly Jesus, so that he is not the Illuminator, the redeemer, but rather a prophet (1974, 162).

[4] Orbe refers with this passage to Lk 1:35; 3:22 and Jn 1:32f (1965, 170); see also Evans et al. who concur for Lk 3:22 and parallels, but also cite Matt 26:67; Matt 27:26–50; Lk 22:63–66; Jn 18:22; 19:1–3, 16–37; and parallels, for the first part of the verse (260).

therefore *within* the text to the former passage about the man and the spirit, with no hint of a Christian tradition as its background.[1]

1.5 The Paraphrase of Shem

The Saviour is identified in this text as Derdekeas (1.4; 8.24). In his introduction, Roberge sums up the section comprising 30.4 – 40.31 in this text as "the baptism of the Savior and his ascent on the occasion of his crucifixion" (Roberge and Wisse 339).

Most scholars interpret the action in 32.5–15 as the baptism of the Saviour, Derdekeas, by the demon. Certainly in 31.17–19, Derdekeas speaks of his future appearance "in the baptism of the demon". This may be what is described in 32.5–15 although there are no details concerning what the demon actually does. The reader is told of Derdekeas coming down to the water, the conflict between him and the whirlpools and flames of fire, followed by his rising from the water in the light of faith and the unquenchable fire. Wisse states that the idea of a baptism of the Saviour is contrary to the negative view of baptism in the text (cf., e.g. 36.25–29; 37.14–25), and that the passage simply refers to the Saviour descending to and ascending from the realm of darkness (1970, 137). This seems quite feasible since there are a number of passages in the text which refer to characters coming down to the water or rising from the water without any context of baptism (e.g. 16.1–3, 17–19; 23.21), with one passage actually referring to Derdekeas (21.13–14). I must therefore conclude that baptism is not certain but possible.

There is nothing in the text itself to suggest the canonical traditions about the baptism of Jesus, yet the baptiser is invariably identified by scholars as

---

[1] Christian motifs are identified in the text by Daniélou ("la mission de l'Illuminateur et la conversion des peuples, sa désignation comme Logos, son origine divine et son incarnation; les allusions à une maternité virginale; le fait qu'il accomplit 'des signes et des miracles'; il souffre dans sa chair; de nombreuses allusions sont faites au baptême; les disciples de l'Illuminateur 'reçoivent son nom sur l'eau'" [1966b, 292]); H.-M. Schenke (the Holy Spirit 77.17f; the flesh of the redeemer 77.16–18; the holy baptism 84.7; 85.24f; the name 77.19; 83.5f [1966, 31]); and Kasser (the third kingdom which speaks of one born from a virgin womb, cast out of his city with his mother, brought to a desert place where he was nourished, and his reception of glory and power [78.18–26] may be that of the Christ [1965, 92 n. 49]).

Böhlig is more inclined to think that the source of the text lies in pre-Christian traditions, with the references to baptism (receiving the name on the water) going back to Jewish baptism developments (Böhlig and Labib 1963, 90, 93; see also MacRae 1965, 33 on Is 43:1f; 49:10; 41:17f). MacRae asserts that there is an "absence of any explicit or clear borrowings from the Christian tradition". For him, the passage concerning the Illuminator-redeemer is "a sort of Gnostic midrash built on the Deutero-Isaian Servant Songs, with other details from the whole context of Deutero-Isaiah". He gives more precise details: the name φωστήρ (Is 42:6; 49:6); the relation to knowledge/*gnosis* (Is 53:11; cf. 43:10); the role of the saviour (Is 49:6; 53:11f); being loftier than the powers (Is 52:13f); the Holy Spirit came upon him (Is 42:1); as an object of wrath (Is 53:3); his deceptive appearance (Is 52:14); and his physical sufferings as punishment (Is 53:5) (1979, 152).

John and the baptised as Jesus.[1] However, the description of the activity of the demon and of his final "fixing" goes far beyond what might be said of John the Baptist. The only point of contact for the two figures is the (possible) activity of baptising. If indeed the polemic in the text against baptism refers to the activity of the mainstream Christian church (see, e.g., Fischer 1975, 261; cf. *contra* Fischer, Dubois 1986, 152–3), then the demon could be either John or Jesus, yet even the target of the polemic cannot be identified clearly as mainstream Christian church, or the followers of John, or some Jewish or Jewish-Christian baptising group. If, after all, there is an allusion to the baptism of Jesus by John intended, then it is simply used to enhance the myth already there concerning Derdekeas (see, e.g., Sevrin 1975, 91).

There seems to be some confusion concerning the question of the crucifixion of the Saviour. Roberge speaks at one point of the ascent of the Saviour "on the occasion of his crucifixion" (Roberge and Wisse 339), then later speaks of the attempt of Nature to seize the Saviour which fails, so that Nature only manages "to crucify Soldas (that is, the terrestrial Jesus)" (341). He is clearly referring to 39.28–32, where Nature is described as wishing to capture Derdekeas and about to make fixed/establish (ⲚⲈⲤⲀⲢⲠⲎⲤⲤⲈ) Soldas, the dark flame (39.28–30).[2] The question is, what exactly is Nature doing with Soldas?

This is the only use of the verb πήσσειν (a late form of πήγνυμι) in the Nag Hammadi corpus (Siegert 286). That the verb can be used in conjunction with σταυρός to indicate crucifixion or setting up a cross can be seen from the example in Lampe of Cyril of Alexandria's *Commentary on John* Bk XII, 1046 (πήξατε τὸν σταυρὸν [Migne PG 74, 633]) (1080b).[3] However the fact remains that there is nothing in the text to indicate that it is crucifixion which is taking place. The activity of fixing may well be akin to that described in Gos. Eg. (III 64.3–9/IV 75.17–24) where the powers of the thirteen Aeons are fixed/nailed and established. I would therefore conclude that there is no solid basis for arguing that Soldas is crucified.

One final point here. Roberge states that it is the terrestrial Jesus who is crucified (i.e. Soldas = Jesus),[4] and that the demon who baptises Jesus is John the Baptist (Roberge and Wisse 341). In his recent article, Roberge identifies the demon Soldas as the "l'enveloppe terrestre du Christ céleste, c'est-à-dire

---

[1] Sevrin, for example, suggests that the myth here without a doubt makes allusion to the baptism of Jesus, that Soldas resembles John, and that the whole scene is best explained by Jesus plunged into the Jordan by John (1975, 90). Orbe suggests that it is the baptism of Jesus, even though the names of John and Jesus have been omitted (1976, 1: 504). Evans et al. also refer to canonical passages on the baptism of Jesus (293).

[2] Krause translates, "Sie war im Begriff, Soldan, die Finsternis-Flamme, fest zu machen" (1973, 85). Wisse has, "She was about to fix (to the cross) Soldas who is the dark flame" (Roberge and Wisse 357).

[3] See also Passow II,1: 905b–6a, where nails are included among those objects which may be used in conjunction with the activity of fixing described by the verb. Roberge also mentions these possibilities (1992, 384–5).

[4] See also Fischer: "Soldas scheint... ein verschlüsselter Name für Jesus zu sein, mit dem sich der himmlische Christus (= Derdekeas) verbindet" (1975, 266).

de Derdekeas"(1992, 385). However, the demon who baptises is identified as Soldas (30.32–33). Thus the demon who baptises and Soldas who is fixed by Nature must be one and the same character.

The various aspects of the activity of the figure of Derdekeas which may appear close to the activity proposed for the Christian Christ (see the summary in Wisse 1970, 135 and Sevrin 1975, 87) are those which can be used to link Derdekeas to other Gnostic saviour figures. In the end, I agree with those who hold that the work is at basis non-Christian Gnostic (see Wisse 1970, 140; Bertrand 156; and Sevrin 1975, 88).

The texts which will constitute the basis for the discussion in the study are as follows:

I,2	Ap. Jas.	VI,1	Acts Pet. 12 Apost.
I,3; XII,2	Gos. Truth	VI,4	Great Pow.
I,4	Treat. Res.		
I,5	Tri. Trac.	VII,2	Treat. Seth
		VII,3	Apoc. Pet.
II,1; III,1;		VII,4	Teach. Silv.
IV,1; BG, 2	Ap. John[1]		
II,2	Gos. Thom.	VIII,2	Ep. Pet. Phil.
II,3	Gos. Phil.		
II,6	Exeg. Soul	IX,1	Melch.
II,7	Thom. Cont.	IX,3	Testim. Truth
III,2; IV,2	Gos. Eg.	XI,1	Interp. Know.
III,4; BG 3	Soph. Jes. Chr.	XI,2	Val. Exp.
III,5	Dial. Sav.		
		XIII,1	Trim. Prot.
V,3	1 Apoc. Jas.		
V,4	2 Apoc. Jas.		

2. Versions of Texts Used and Damaged Texts

2.1 The Apocryphon of John

There are four versions of the text of Ap. John, two shorter versions (III,1 and BG 2), and two longer (II,1 and IV,1). The better preserved of the latter is II,1 and this text has been used predominantly in this study.

---

[1] All references to the Ap. John in the following work will be to II,1 unless otherwise noted.

2.2 The Sophia of Jesus Christ

Till comments on the versions of this text: "Die beiden Texte der Sophia Jesu Christi... stimmen bis auf Kleinigkeiten überein." (1955, 52). I have worked here basically from Codex III, supplementing from BG 8502,3 where necessary, especially for the missing pages (109–10) and those badly damaged (117–19) in Codex III.

2.3 Damaged Texts

One of the problems with texts like Gos. Eg. and Val. Exp. are their damaged state in many places (and the corresponding tendency of scholars to make conjectures and thereafter treat the conjectures as if they are actually there in the manuscript), which makes interpretation extremely difficult in many cases. Studies on both these texts rely heavily on other sources for their interpretation. Unfortunately because of this method, the text itself appears on occasion to take second place to, or to be adapted to suit, the other sources when it does not accord with what the scholars expect from the perspective of the other sources.

3. Two Notes on Problems with Terminology

3.1 Terminology Used for Jesus/Christ

As the work proceeded I became more and more aware of the rather easy and inattentive way in which scholars sometimes use terms to refer to the Jesus or Christ figures in the texts. Frequently one reads remarks about "the risen/resurrected Christ" as the revealer figure in texts where there is no explicit reference to a resurrection, nor to death prior to resurrection.

It becomes clear that scholars have to be much more careful about terminology so as not to be overly influenced by the sort of theological images or terms which we have from the canonical texts which may not always be appropriate to these texts. New categories or ways of description become necessary but the process of finding the new terms brings its own problems. When, for example, there is reference to a Jesus figure who does not experience suffering, death, or resurrection before return to the realm above, then we need a designation for such a figure that approximates "Jesus/Christ post-earthly context but not yet post-earthly contact". He is no longer "the earthly Jesus", since he has completed a first stage of departure from the earthly context in which he has been involved. Yet he has not returned finally to the region above, so he is not yet totally "the heavenly Jesus" in a spatial sense, although he may well be and always may have been the heavenly Jesus in a spiritual, or original sense. If he has not been described as dying or rising, then he cannot automatically be referred to as "the risen Jesus".

3.2 Gender Exclusive Language

The Nag Hammadi texts use gender exclusive language for the most part, taking the masculine as norm. I have no doubt that women who listened to or read the texts could have understood themselves to be included as audience, even with a text like Teach. Silv. in which the teaching is addressed to "my son". However, the texts are not unambiguous, and I do not believe that it is always the case that women should be thought to be included automatically under the normative masculine. In Thom. Cont., for example, which is certainly an extreme case, women are only mentioned in the text in negative terms as those who are partners in polluting intercourse (144.8–10), and I would doubt that women are at all included in the community addressed as "you" (pl.) by the Saviour in this text.

I could have chosen to use inclusive language by substituting third person plural forms where masculine singular references occurred in the text and rearranging sentences accordingly. For the most part I have not done this, since I consider that such a process distorts the emphasis on the individual which is crucial to Gnostic understandings of how salvation is achieved.

Abbreviations

1. Nag Hammadi Texts

1 Apoc. Jas.	The First Apocalypse of James
2 Apoc. Jas.	The Second Apocalypse of James
Acts Pet. 12 Apost.	The Acts of Peter and the Twelve Apostles
Allogenes	Allogenes
Ap. Jas.	The Apocryphon of James
Ap. John	The Apocryphon of John
Apoc. Adam	The Apocalypse of Adam
Apoc. Paul	The Apocalypse of Paul
Apoc. Pet.	The Apocalypse of Peter
Asclepius	Asclepius 21–29
Auth. Teach.	Authoritative Teaching
BG	Codex Berolinensis 8502
Dial. Sav.	The Dialogue of the Saviour
Disc. 8–9	The Discourse on the Eighth and Ninth
Ep. Pet. Phil.	The Letter of Peter to Philip
Eugnostos	Eugnostos the Blessed
Exeg. Soul	The Exegesis on the Soul
Gos. Eg.	The Gospel of the Egyptians
Gos. Mary	The Gospel of Mary
Gos. Phil.	The Gospel of Philip
Gos. Thom.	The Gospel of Thomas
Gos. Truth	The Gospel of Truth
Great Pow.	The Concept of our Great Power
Hyp. Archons	The Hypostasis of the Archons
Hypsiph.	Hypsiphrone
Interp. Know.	The Interpretation of Knowledge
Marsanes	Marsanes
Melch.	Melchizedek
Norea	The Thought of Norea
On Anoint.	On the Anointing
On Bap. A	On Baptism A
On Bap. B	On Baptism B
On Euch. A	On the Eucharist A
On Euch. B	On the Eucharist B
Orig. World	On the Origin of the World
Paraph. Shem	The Paraphrase of Shem
Plato Rep.	Plato, Republic 588B – 589B
Pr. Paul	The Prayer of the Apostle Paul
Pr. Thanks.	The Prayer of Thanksgiving

Sent. Sextus	The Sentences of Sextus
Soph. Jes. Chr.	The Sophia of Jesus Christ
Steles Seth	The Three Steles of Seth
Teach Silv.	The Teachings of Silvanus
Testim. Truth	The Testimony of Truth
Thom. Cont.	The Book of Thomas the Contender
Thund.	The Thunder, Perfect Mind
Treat. Res.	The Treatise on Resurrection
Treat. Seth	The Second Treatise of the Great Seth
Tri. Trac.	The Tripartite Tractate
Trim. Prot.	Trimorphic Protennoia
Val. Exp.	A Valentinian Exposition
Zost.	Zostrianos

2. Publications

The following abbreviations are taken from Schwertner, except for those marked *. These are either my own construction or used by the relevant publication.

ADAI.K	Abhandlungen des Deutschen Archäologischen Instituts, Kairo: Koptische Reihe
AGJU	Arbeiten zur Geschichte des antiken Judentums und des Urchristentums
ABRL*	Anchor Bible: Reference Library
ANRW	Aufstieg und Niedergang der römischen Welt
AThD	Analecta theologica Danica
AThR.SS	Anglican Theological Review: Supplement Series
ATLA	American Theological Library Association
BA	Biblical Archeologist
BAC	Biblioteca de autores cristianos
BASPap	Bulletin of the American Society of Papyrologists
BAW.AC	Bibliothek der Alten Welt: Antike und Christentum
BBA	Berliner byzantinistische Arbeiten
BBB	Bonner biblische Beiträge
BCNH.E*	Bibliothèque copte de Nag Hammadi: Section "Études"
BCNH.T	Bibliothèque copte de Nag Hammadi: Section "Textes"
BEThL	Bibliotheca Ephemeridum theologicarum Lovaniensium
Bib.	Biblica
BIMI	Bible and Its Modern Interpreters
BTB	Biblical Theology Bulletin
BT(N)	Bibliothèque théologique. Neuchâtel
BZNW	Beihefte zur Zeitschrift für die neutestamentliche Wissenschaft und die Kunde der älteren Kirche
CBCo	Cahiers de la Bibliothèque Copte
CBQ	Catholic Biblical Quarterly
CCen	Christian Century

CR.BS*	Currents in Research. Biblical Studies
DGMFT	Dissertationes ad gradum magistri in Facultate Theologica ... Louvain
EdF	Erträge der Forschung
EHS.T	Europäische Hochschulschriften: Reihe 23, Theologie
EK	Evangelische Kommentare
ET	Expository Times
EThL	Ephemerides theologicae Lovanienses
FF.F*	Foundations & Facets. Forum
FF.RS*	Foundations & Facets. Reference Series
FKDG	Forschungen zur Kirchen- und Dogmengeschichte
GoPe	Gospel Perspectives
Gr.	Gregorianum
HeyJ	Heythrop Journal
HR	History of Religions
HThK.S	Herders theologischer Kommentar zum Neuen Testament: Supplementband
HTR	Harvard Theological Review
ICA	Initiations au christianisme ancien
JA	Journal asiatique
JAC	Jahrbuch für Antike und Christentum
JAC.E	Jahrbuch für Antike und Christentum: Ergänzungsband
JBL	Journal of Biblical Literature
JR	Journal of Religion
JRSt	Journal of Religious Studies
JSNT	Journal for the Study of the New Testament
JSNT.S	Journal for the Study of the New Testament: Supplement series
JThS	Journal of Theological Studies
MSSNTS	Monograph series. Society for New Testament Studies
NHMS*	Nag Hammadi and Manichaean Studies
NHS	Nag Hammadi Studies
NT	Novum Testamentum
NT.S	Novum Testamentum: Supplements
NTA	Neutestamentliche Abhandlungen
NTS	New Testament Studies
NTTS	New Testament Tools and Studies
OBO	Orbis biblicus et orientalis
OLZ	Orientalische Literaturzeitung
OrChr	Oriens Christianus
OrChrA	Orientalia Christiana analecta
OCP	Orientalia Christiana periodica
PG	Patrologiae cursus completus. Accurante Jacques-Paul Migne. Series Graeca.
PIOL	Publications de l'Institut Orientaliste de Louvain
PTS	PatristischeTexte und Studien
RestQ	Restoration Quarterly
RevSR	Revue des sciences religieuses
RSR	Recherches de science religieuse
RThPh	Revue de théologie et de philosophie

SBB	Stuttgarter biblische Beiträge
SBL.DS	Society of Biblical Literature: Dissertation series
SBL.MS	Society of Biblical Literature: Monograph series
SBL.SP	Society of Biblical Literature: Seminar papers
SHR	Studies in the History of Religions
SJTh	Scottish Journal of Theology
SR	Studies in Religion/Sciences Religieuses
SRivBib	Supplementi alla Rivista Biblica
StAC*	Studies in Antiquity & Christianity
StOR	Studies in Oriental Religions
StTh	Studia Theologica
SWJT	Southwestern Journal of Theology
TBT	Theologische Bibliothek Töpelmann
Tem.	Temenos
ThD	Theology Digest
ThLZ	Theologische Literaturzeitung
ThR	Theologische Rundschau
TRE	Theologische Realenzyklopädie
TU	Texte und Untersuchungen zur Geschichte der altchristlichen Literatur
UTB	Uni-Taschenbücher
UUA	Uppsala universitets årsskrift
VigChr	Vigiliae Christianae
VIOF	Veröffentlichung. Institut für Orientforschung
WMANT	Wissenschaftliche Monographien zum Alten und Neuen Testament
WUNT	Wissenschaftliche Untersuchungen zum Neuen Testament
WZ(H)	Wissenschaftliche Zeitschrift der Martin-Luther-Universität Halle-Wittenberg
WZKM	Wiener Zeitschrift für die Kunde des Morgenlandes
ZÄS	Zeitschrift für ägyptische Sprache und Altertumskunde
ZNW	Zeitschrift für die neutestamentliche Wissenschaft (21, 1922ff:) und die Kunde der älteren Kirche
ZRGG	Zeitschrift für Religions- und Geistesgeschichte
ZThK	Zeitschrift für Theologie und Kirche

3. General

cf.	compare	i.e.	that is
diss.	dissertation	ref.	reference
ed./eds.	edition or editor/s	rev.	review/revised
e.g.	for example	vol./vols.	volume/s
esp.	especially		

I

Nag Hammadi and Jesus Research

In this first chapter I examine the broad issues related to a study of Jesus in the Nag Hammadi writings, locating that study within Jesus research in general: First, how have people studied Jesus up to this point and how do they understand what they are doing in such study? Second, what are some of the major issues for people who study Jesus? Third, how have these issues influenced investigations of the Nag Hammadi writings? Fourth, how does the present project relate to these issues?

1. Jesus Research

"The historical Jesus is 'in the news,' both in the scholarly world and in the much broader world of the public," writes Marcus Borg (1994a, ix).[1] That is clearly so, but what is not at all clear is which particular historical Jesus is considered newsworthy. As far as the public is concerned, there is a broad spectrum of interest, from those wanting good scholarly work made available for the non-specialist, to those who are captivated by works of a more sensational or polemical nature, which often make some reference to non-canonical material.[2]

As far as scholars are concerned, studies on the historical Jesus do not constitute a new phenomenon. Current studies are actually referred to sometimes as the "Third Quest", previous stages being identified as the Old Quest (1778 to 1906) and the New Quest (beginning with Käsemann in 1953), and its

---

[1] There are a number of good summaries of the recent Jesus research: e.g. especially Telford, and also Charlesworth 1988, Chapter 1: "Research on the Historical Jesus in the Eighties" (9–29). Kümmel gives a summary of the continuing debate concerning the historical Jesus in the first section of each of his reports on Jesusforschung: 1965/66, 16–46; 1975; 1981, 318–34; and 1988. As Kümmel constantly indicates, there is now great difficulty in keeping all the literature in view. Overviews such as provided by Baumotte's anthology can be helpful.

[2] Macklin's *The Secret Life of Jesus* is a good example of the latter. Schneemelcher refers rightly to such popular works as "Machwerke": "Sensationslust und Geschäftssinn verbinden sich dabei oft mit antikirchlichen Ressentiments" (Hennecke and Schneemelcher 1989, 1: 72). John Dart's *The Jesus of Heresy and History* is a curious mixture of popular material and worthwhile scholarly information. Although patchy, it is vastly superior to works like Macklin.

fragmentation.[1] The period from 1921 to 1953 witnessed a paradigm shift, generally characterised as the No-Quest Period (led by Bultmann and the form critical school). While there are those who are wary of announcing a Third Quest different from the New Quest, nevertheless there is certainly "a revitalization movement" in Jesus Studies (Telford 61).

There appear to be two major trends in the current quest. On the one hand there are those like Hofius (1978 and 1991; extending the earlier study of Jeremias), and the members of the SBL Jesus seminar who continue the earlier search for the very words (and sometimes deeds) of Jesus.[2] On the other hand there are those who define the quest in terms of looking for the earliest developments of traditions about Jesus. Among the latter, J.G. Williams explains his focus in the following way: "When I speak of Jesus or the historical Jesus, I have in mind the 'earliest tradition,' that is, Jesus as remembered and constructed in the early years after his death particularly in the Palestinian Jewish context" (7).

The trends are not quite as clear cut as they might appear. In a recent study, Meier attempts to differentiate between the "real" Jesus (who he says is unknown and unknowable) and the "historical" Jesus ("a modern abstraction and construct ... whom we can 'recover' and examine by using the scientific tools of modern historical research" [1: 22, 25]).[3] Yet by using a scientific historical method, Meier continues to investigate the possible historicity of the words and deeds recorded of Jesus, in an attempt to find that material which provides the partial overlap between the historical Jeus and the real Jesus (2: 4).

2. The Question of Valid Sources for Jesus Research

While scholars involved with these two differently focused concerns in the quest may differ in their views of what constitute valid research methods (e.g. the debate about the worthwhileness of the criteria for historicity), many of the same scholars are united in their response to broader questions, such as: What are valid sources for study, either of the "real" Jesus or of the interpreted Jesus of the early traditions? More specifically, are the apocrypha valid sources? Are texts which are not "gospels" valid sources? What constitutes a "gospel"? Are the canonical gospels unique sources for the study of Jesus?

---

[1] See Telford 55–61 and Reumann 502. See Lattke 1979 for an earlier summary, and Lattke 1978 for a useful bibliography of Jesus research.

[2] The work of the Jesus seminar is reported through the voting charts in *Forum* (from vol. 6 in 1990), and has reached a high point in Funk, R.W. et al.

[3] See, similarly, Carlston 2–3. Keck perhaps implies much the same idea: "the historical Jesus is the historian's Jesus, not a Kantian *Ding an sich*" (20).

The revival of interest in Jesus research raises once again the question of sources. The controversy about valid sources finds a good example in James Robinson's experience at a session of the annual meeting of the Society for New Testament Studies in 1984. In a 1988 article, Robinson describes how he attempted to have the saying of Jesus in Gos. Thom. Log. 17 recognised as a parallel to 1 Cor 2:9, and thus included in the primitive Christian Jesus tradition used by Paul.[1] He argued that the exclusive investigation of canonical materials for the tradition used by Paul is arbitrary from a purely historical point of view (1988, 47–48).

Robinson's point was eventually accepted, but the publication which resulted from this session shows no change with regard to his point, although changes with regard to other points have been made.[2] Robinson comes to the conclusion that some New Testament scholars are consciously or unconsciously avoiding opening "a Pandora's box – which is precisely the significance of the Nag Hammadi Codices for the study of the historical Jesus!" (48).

However one defines the goal of the present quest, the discussion of valid sources to be used is not new. In his 1909 study of the life of Jesus in the apocryphal gospels, Bauer warns that scholars can seriously overestimate the meaning which the canonical gospels had in the early stages of the Christian tradition, simply because of the way in which these gospels were "successful" in powerfully influencing which interpretations of the life of Jesus came to have sway in the growing tradition. Bauer contends that, apart from the minorities who rejected all or part of the canonical gospels and replaced them with others, even in orthodox circles the four canonical gospels did not always command absolute sway as descriptions of the life of Jesus (1–2).[3]

Bauer was not successful to any degree in persuading scholars to include the apocrypha as source material for research on the historical Jesus or in early Christianity. Some sixty years after Bauer, Koester laments that research on the historical Jesus continues to be limited to the synoptic Gospels with the occasional use of Johannine material, the apocryphal gospels

---

[1] Patterson (1991) investigates the writings of Paul in relation to the sayings tradition in Gos. Thom. For a broader treatment of New Testament sayings in non-canonical material, see Charlesworth and Evans, 483–9 (the Agrapha) and 491–532 (Apocryphal gospels). For Nag Hammadi specifically, see Evans et al.

[2] Walter has made no change subsequently in the English translation.

[3] Bauer illustrates his point by reference to Clement of Alexandria and Origen, both of whom treasured the Gospel of the Hebrews, Clement also considering that the Gospel of the Egyptians belonged really to the history of Jesus (2). See also Gamble's more recent discussion of the history of the New Testament canon, especially "The Gospels" (208–12). Some years after Bauer, Dunkerley, who does not seem to have known the former's work, appeals in somewhat less scholarly fashion, "It seems strangely lacking in imagination and insight to suggest that the tradition about Jesus had become fixed and settled by the time the Gospels were written, and that there was nothing else to be learned about him outside that tradition" (11).

being seen only as secondary alterations of the canonical gospels (1968, 203–11), or as "the fictional elaboration of the four gospels", as R.J. Hoffmann puts it (143).

Although it would seem to be the usual scholarly procedure to keep as broad a context as possible for any field of study, Koester is right to point out that this has not been the case generally speaking with the study of Christian origins and particularly with the study of its founding figure. The failure to take other sources into account has led to a narrow and false view that Christianity was a very stable and homogeneous entity from its inception and that the only "true" or historically accurate traditions about the founder, Jesus Christ, were preserved by those who became the dominant mainstream group.[1]

Some ten years later, Koester calls attention once again to the problem of "deep-seated prejudices" reflected in the attitude of New Testament scholars towards the apocryphal writings (1980, 130), yet scholars continue to ignore the exhortation. There is little or no reference to non-canonical material, for example, in recent work in Meier, Green and Turner, and Charlesworth 1988. In the latter case, only Gos. Thom. in the Nag Hammadi texts is seen as essential for the historical Jesus quest (83–90).[2] Fredriksen's study makes no mention at all of any non-canonical text, even in the final chapter, "Jesus of Nazareth in Christian Tradition" (205–15).

Like Bauer before him, Koester points out how much poorer is the view of the history of earliest Christianity when seen solely from the perspective of the canon:

> This history was much richer than the canon would suggest, and in theological terms it was more controversial and more interesting, because the 'Living Jesus' spoke in many different ways to different people who confessed him as their Lord. The historian must never solve this problem by using the labels 'orthodox' and 'heretical,' nor should responsible Christians and theologians try to do that any longer today (1988, 76).

Of course, Koester and others have not escaped criticism. Charlesworth and Evans voice their reservations that "the priority that Crossan, Koester, and others have given to the various agrapha and apocryphal gospels is questionable and in our estimation borders at times on being uncritical" (532).

---

[1] I use "founder" for Jesus in the broad sense to describe him as the one who provided the initial impetus for what later became a new religion as distinct from a sect within Judaism. Thus Jesus is not a founder in the same sense as Muhammad or the Buddha.

[2] Meier's second volume contains more detailed argumentation against using Gos. Thom. (on the grounds of dependence on the canonical tradition) than his first volume. The fact that the abbreviations for the Nag Hammadi texts are listed in full in the second volume (2: 1058) is misleading. Only Gos. Thom. is cited, as a quick glance at the index bears out.

Although Charlesworth and Evans state that the agrapha and apocryphal gospels should be given "due consideration", Evan's later work is much more critical, suggesting that the only credible material for Jesus research "ultimately derives from the canonical Gospels themselves" (1995, 17). He makes extensive criticism of Crossan's work, and rather polemical remarks against some staff and graduates of Claremont and Harvard and the "influential coterie of American scholars", especially the "Jesus Seminar and its sympathisers" (26–40).

That Claremont and Harvard should be singled out is not surprising. Subsequent to his story about his experience at the 1984 SNTS conference, Robinson presents a brief overview of the impact of the Nag Hammadi material on New Testament studies concerned with the historical Jesus. He suggests that American scholars are more open to including the apocryphal writings as source material for that quest than are European scholars (1988, 48–50).[1] This is quite well illustrated in Marcus Borg's interesting summary of his personal experience from the 1960s to the present, and the clear view one gets from his article of the North American perspective and the changes between the 1960s and 1980s/1990s (1994b, 16–29). As Borg rightly indicates, "German voices" are no longer the dominant ones in historical Jesus research for North Americans, with the exception of Gerd Theissen (29).

That scholars from these two geographical areas are quite strongly divided cannot be denied,[2] but to separate them in such a fashion can also be overly simplistic. There are differences broadly speaking in the area of methodology emanating from both sides of the Atlantic,[3] but there are also significant groups of scholars on both sides whose hermeneutical stance differs radically from their compatriots. One has only to compare in general the approach of those engaged in Religionswissenschaft in Germany with that of the New Testament scholars in the theological faculties of the same country, or the radically different hermeneutics of evangelical scholars in North America and scholars like Robinson himself.[4]

---

[1] Evans also divides scholarship between those he characterises as the more theologically oriented Germans and the more historically minded American and British (1995, 457–8). That the field is still poor with regard to the use of extra-canonical source material even within American circles can be seen in Telford's summary, where only Crossan and James Robinson rate a mention as major figures (48).

[2] Of course, this is true of more geographical locations than North America and Germany. The divided situation is not helped by some scholars' apparent lack of awareness of (or perhaps lack of interest in) what is happening on the other side of the Atlantic. McDonald's overview of historical Jesus research, e.g., presented in 1978, makes minimal reference to American scholarship (162). By contrast, Kümmel's reports over the years in the *ThR* present a very balanced picture of *Jesusforschung* from both sides.

[3] Hollenbach reports on the use in American historical Jesus scholarship of a social science methodology which is less preferred in Europe (1983 and 1989).

[4] Johnston presents a helpful overview of "polyform" evangelical hermeneutics.

In the light of this kind of evidence it is hard to accept Evans' assertions that the so-called Third Quest "is not driven by theological-philosophical concerns" (1995, 10–13). Perhaps the quest may not be driven quite as *explicitly* by these concerns as it once was, but it is is certainly erroneous to claim that "the related concern to find a Jesus relevant for the Christian kerygma seems also to have receded" (11–12).[1] (I consider the question of the kerygma below.) On this point it is worthwhile to note an earlier statement by Lattke that continues to be relevant to the debate about theological concerns:

> Ob das Frage- und Erkenntnisinteresse dabei schon vom Ansatz her *theologisch* ist oder nicht, spielt *zunächst* keine Rolle. Doch wer sich vermeintlich positivistisch und objektivistisch bloß der vergangenen historischen Gestalt nähern will, wird wenn er offen genug ist, rasch merken, daß *Jesu Wort* und *Jesu Verhalten* *un*theologisch sich überhaupt nicht erschließen. Leben, Farbe und anthropologischen Sinn bekommt Jesus von Nazareth erst im Kontext der Theologie. Und insofern wird die historische Frage zu einer nicht nur theologisch motivierten, vielmehr auch inhaltlich theologischen Frage werden (1979, 293).

3. Apocryphal Gospels and Jesus[2]

Some have heeded the appeal to include apocryphal material in the discussion of gospel genre, whether that be apocryphal writings in general, or more specifically the Nag Hammadi gospels.[3] (The question of whether certain Nag Hammadi writings belong to the apocrypha is considered in the final section

---

[1] Evans cites three differences between the previous Quests and the Third Quest, under the headings of 1) myth and miracle; 2) historical value of the Gospels; 3) theological apologetics (1995, 2). Although by contrast Telford deals with theological issues of the quest (62–5), he fails to consider adequately theological motivations which may have been academically limiting. In a most interesting recent essay, Koester goes well beyond the idea of theological motivations to discuss Dieter Georgi's contention that the quest for the historical Jesus is tied to bourgeois consciousness and that the work of Weiss and Schweitzer should be seen in the context of the "Burgher-Dämmerung" beginning in the period before World War I (Koester 1994a, 538–9). Koester concludes: "... certain factors that dominate the consciousness of this Western world will continue to prejudice the results" (539). Evans criticises Koester for suggesting that the current Jesus research is driven by theological concerns (1995, 457–9).

[2] For primary text collections in translation, see Hennecke and Schneemelcher; Cameron 1982; Layton 1987; and Robinson, J.M. 1984/1988. Weidinger is a good example of those semi-popular collections which are not helpful from a scholarly perspective. For a general introduction to the New Testament Apocrypha, see Wilson 1989. Wilson 1978a contains an excellent bibliography of primary sources and secondary literature (357–62); Charlesworth 1987 also offers useful bibliographical material.

[3] See, for example, Corley "Part Three: Seminar on Gospel Genre" (195–262). The articles in *Semeia* 43 (1988), "Genre, Narrativity, and Theology" are useful, especially Talbert. See also the summary in Frankemölle's section, "2.2.4. 'Evangelium' in den apokryphen Schriften" (42–52).

below.) However, given the ongoing work of Koester and equally vocal attempts by other scholars to have the apocrypha included in the discussion of "gospel", it is interesting to note the extent to which some scholars disregard this material.

3.1 What is a Gospel?

With few exceptions within recent work devoted to gospel genre, scholars either fail to mention the apocrypha at all (e.g. Cantwell; Dahl; Dihle; and Thatcher), or make a footnote or two to Gos. Thom. (e.g. Stuhlmacher 1991b, 7), or they mention the apocrypha briefly only to dismiss them (e.g. Keck 117; Kee 1977, 271; Stanton 1989, 125–35; and Sanders 64–5). In his otherwise marvellous summary of the research on "gospel" as a literary and theological *Gattung*, Dormeyer is not concerned with the place of the apocryphal gospels within that discussion, except for a brief mention of Koester's early (1968) work (144). One gains the impression from such studies that the apocryphal material need not be taken seriously when dealing with "gospel".

A similar approach can be found in recent works whose titles appear to promise a breadth of scholarship. Aune's study, *The New Testament in Its Literary Environment*, uses only the four canonical gospels as the basis for the discussion of gospel genre (17–45). Grant's *Jesus after the Gospels: The Christ of the Second Century*, takes for granted that "gospels" comprise the four canonical gospels only.

The investigation of the apocrypha is limited here to the issue of their status as gospels and proper material for Jesus research. Perhaps the issue itself is misguided, given Perkins' perceptive comment: "The most radical question this research poses is not about the plurality of primitive 'gospels' but the sense in which Christian orthodoxy affirms that there is 'one Jesus'" (1991, 441).

3.2 Are the Canonical Gospels Unique Sources for the Study of Jesus?

Why is there such reticence with regard to the apocryphal material? Two points are basic to the discussion, even if they are not always explicitly discussed: the concept of the uniqueness of the so-called Christ-event (death and resurrection of Jesus) as the originating event of the Christian tradition, and the concept of the uniqueness of the canonical writings in which the kerygma of that event is to be found (with the related concepts of inspiration and the authority of the canonical writings).[1] An affirmative stance on these basic points can lead to the restriction of where one may validly look for material

---

[1] See the summary in Koester 1990, 24–6.

about Jesus and, secondly, can underline a negative attitude to the nature and status of the non-canonical texts about Jesus. The discussion of "gospel genre" is often found in association with these points.[1]

The concept of the uniqueness of the canonical writings within Christian writings and the apocrypha in general, rests on the belief that the kerygma is contained properly in the canon. This is often taken to lead logically to the concept of the historical uniqueness of the canon and the literary uniqueness of the canon. The first point has been put in question by scholars like Bauer and Koester, as outlined above.

3.2.1 The Literary Uniqueness of the Canon

Many scholars consider the apocrypha to be of a different genre, form and content from the canonical gospels.[2] Although there is no real agreement as to what this distinctive form might be, there seems to be a decided preference for narrative. To give just two examples from more recent studies, Burridge holds that the canonical gospels have generic features such as narrative or chronological and geographical settings (250), and Bauckham defines a gospel as a work "which recounts all or part of Jesus' earthly life and teaching (including his appearances on earth between the resurrection and the ascension)" (286b).[3]

Koester, on the other hand, proposes that even the canonical gospels do not have a distinctive unifying form, and that their different literary forms are influenced by the theological standpoint of each writer concerning the interpretation of Jesus.[4] Thus he proposes to define "gospel" not by literary genre but by what is contained therein about Jesus of Nazareth: gospels are "all those writings which are constituted by the transmission, use, and interpretation of materials and traditions from and about Jesus of Nazareth" (1990, 46).[5] In more recent (1994b) work, he outlines three different genres of gospel: passion narratives as the Christian cult story (includes Gospel of Mark and Gospel of Peter); catechisms (including the Sermon on the Mount); and

---

[1] Borg's overview of Jesus study in North America recognises two other areas of discussion: Jesus and eschatology, and Jesus' relationship to his social world (1991, 1–2; and 1994a, 18–9).

[2] See, e.g., Guelich 175.

[3] Gero classifies gospels in general as "connected narrative accounts of Jesus", whether they be called gospels or not (3970–1).

[4] Mark is a passion story; Matthew and Luke are biographies, though Luke is closer to that by his further use of the journey report; Matthew resembles a church handbook; and John is closest to the form of a gnostic revelation book (Koester 1983, 296).

[5] The definition is reminiscent of Bauer's understanding of "gospel", which he says allows for the inclusion of apocryphal works: "Evangelium bedeutet für uns eben nicht allgemein verehrtes heiliges Buch, sondern 'Leben Jesu'" (1), although even here narrative appears to be a focus.

sayings of Jesus (Gos. Thom., the Synoptic Sayings source, Dial. Sav., Gos. Mary, "and other so-called Gnostic gospels").

Koester also argues against literary uniqueness of the canon by outlining a number of the characteristic literary forms of the sources used by the canonical gospels (the Synoptic sayings source, the miracle stories source for the first part of Mark, John's Semeia source, the parable source of Mark 4, the apocalyptic prophecies of Mark 13, and the birth legends), which reappear in several of the apocryphal gospels. Moreover similar literary characteristics may be found in contemporaneous genres like the wisdom book, the dialogue, and aretalogy (1990, 45–47).

3.2.2 Canonical Uniqueness and the Apocrypha

The concepts of the historical and literary uniqueness of the canon have meant more often than not that the apocrypha are viewed solely from the perspective of the New Testament. The centre point is the canonical tradition under which all else must stand in question. This perspective may prevail even when the scholar is not necessarily negatively disposed towards the apocryphal material. One sees this attitude, for example, in Wilson's introductory remarks to the New Testament apocrypha:

> It is not surprising that interest in this field of study was comparatively slight: the material, after all, is secondary to the NT and does not add much to the information there contained, nor does it belong to the mainstream of the development of Christian theology... In point of fact, the significance of this material lies in quite different directions, not in its contribution to the history of doctrine or the development of theology but in the glimpses it affords into trends and tendencies in popular Christianity of the early centuries, and also in the fact that it provides an insight into what can happen when imagination ranges uncontrolled, a standard of comparison by which to measure the relative sobriety and restraint of the books recognized as canonical, especially the Gospels (1989, 429).

In an earlier article, Wilson had indeed seen some theological significance in the (Nag Hammadi) apocryphal material, suggesting that it provides

> ...a reminder of the variety and vigour, and the complexity, of early Christian thought and belief. It represents the culmination of one line of development, not perhaps the most important one for those who stand in the 'orthodox' tradition but nevertheless one which some people at least found meaningful (1982, 290).

Indicating an awareness of this problem of perspective, Cameron introduces the studies on the apocryphal material in *Semeia* 49 with the assurance that "[n]o attempt has been made to restrict our inquiries to the usual, tired question of the relationship of these gospels to the writings of the New Testament. Instead, each text is investigated as a document worthy of study in its own right" (1990, 1). This is a reply to what is regarded by some scholars as the tyranny (to borrow a term from Hedrick 1988) of the New Testament over the apocrypha. More specifically this is the tyranny of the canonical gospels (or perhaps better, the tyranny of New Testament scholars or scholars of the canonical gospels), with the result that the apocryphal writings are only seen as worthwhile documents for what light they might throw on New Testament studies.

A second outcome of this concept of uniqueness, and an example of a more subtle "tyranny", occurs where the questions brought to bear on the apocryphal writings are mostly questions which are derived from New Testament text study, where questions about Jesus in the apocrypha are posed from the point of view of Jesus in the canonical gospels (as, for example, with Tuckett or even to some extent with Bauer). Whether this is done within the quest for the historical Jesus or not, the results may be the poorer for the limiting perspective brought by one set of works and its prevailing interpretations over another.

> ...the canon controls both how the past is reconstructed, as well as the very substance of the reconstruction itself. In regard to Jesus of Nazareth, a myopic approach to the study of the Jesus tradition has ensured the dominance of the synoptic Jesus (Hedrick 1988, 2).[1]

Finally in this section I mention one aspect of the argument about the value of the canonical texts or the apocrypha which is not often explicitly discussed. Some scholars on both sides of the debate make subtle use of the concept of time: i.e. earlier is better since earlier is truer; closer in time to the historical Jesus means closer to the truth about the historical Jesus. On the one hand, there may be an emphasis on the canonical gospels as prior to the apocrypha and therefore of more worth in looking for the historical Jesus. On the other hand, there may be a somewhat similar attitude among those working with the supposed Q or the Gos. Thom. or the apocrypha in general in order to find a tradition stratum prior to the canonical gospels. Koester, for example, indicates some writings (the Synoptic Sayings Source [Q], the Gos. Thom., the Unknown Gospel of Papyrus Egerton 2, Dial. Sav., Ap. Jas., Gospel of Peter)[2] which he considers to be "at least as old and as valuable as

---

[1] Koester identifies this issue of the canon as the first within what he calls the "three borders which had been erected traditionally in order to protect the integrity of New Testament studies: (1) the border between New Testament and the history of ancient Christianity; (2) the treatment of the New Testament as if it were not a part of early Judaism; (3) the investigation of the New Testament and early Christian literature as a phenomenon distinct from Greco-Roman culture and religion of its period. All three borders are artificial" (1991, 472).

[2] See Kirk for criticism of Crossan's and Koester's positions on the Gos. Pet. in relation to the canonical gospels.

the canonical gospels as sources for the earliest developments of the traditions about Jesus. ...significant witnesses for the formation of the gospel literature in its formative stages" (1980, 130). Arguments about dating are not necessarily unhelpful, but care should be taken with some arguments which are based more in confessional conviction than in scholarly reason.[1]

3.2.3 The Uniqueness of the Kerygma

Perhaps the most difficult of the concepts is that of the uniqueness of the kerygma of the Christ-event[2] contained in the canon which is taken to provide the basis of the uniqueness of the canonical gospels as "gospel".[3] Out of this concept, the test question for the apocryphal gospels has been and remains predominantly: Is there a passion narrative or a passion-resurrection narrative? Those who want to include the apocrypha and the supposed Q in the discussion of gospel have to deal with this question in one way or another.[4] In the work on Q, for example, one finds a number of reactions to the question:[5] those who suggest that Q is really closer than it might appear to the unique kerygma of the Christ-event, arguing that there is actually a

---

[1] This is not the case with Tuckett who presents a critical investigation of the work of Koester, arguing that the appeal to agreements between Q and Gos. Thom. as the basis of an underlying wisdom gospel are unconvincing. For Tuckett it is possible that sayings of Jesus in Gos. Thom. which show parallels with the synoptic tradition in Q may witness to a post-synoptic development of the tradition (1991, 359). Arguing from the basis of Q itself though is seen to be another question entirely which Tuckett mentions but does not discuss (359–60). For a recent study on Gos. Thom. and Q, see McLean.

[2] Most often understood as the kerygma of the death-resurrection of Jesus. A distinction should be made, however, between the historical event of the death of Jesus and the metaphor of the "resurrection" which builds on this event.

[3] Against this view, Koester has argued most recently that 1) it is not possible to claim that Mark was attempting to transform the oral kerygma ("gospel") into a literary document; and 2) there is no evidence that writers of the second century who first used the term "gospel" in reference to a written source had any awareness of the kerygma-character of this literature (1990, 29). See also Koester 1957 and 1984 for the use of the term εὐαγγέλιον in the Apostolic Fathers.

[4] Thus Kloppenborg writes: "If Q functioned like the intracanonical gospels, serving as the guiding theological statement of a particular community or group of communities, it is necessary to ask what significance the Sayings Gospel attached to Jesus' death and resurrection" (1990, 71). Interesting for the whole discussion is the recent shift in "status" for Q with the terminology moving from "Q source" to "Sayings Gospel Q" (Kloppenborg 1993, 9). Perhaps in the light of Horsley's latest work on the genre of Q as a series of discourses, the use of the term "sayings" should also be rethought (1994, 737). For detailed studies on Q, see Hoffmann, P., Schulz, Kloppenborg 1987, Jacobson 1987 and 1992 (especially Chapter 3), Van Segbroeck et al., Vol. I, Part II (361–688), and Piper.

[5] See Kloppenborg 1990 for a summary of earlier positions with regard to the lack of a passion narrative in Q.

primitive framework there for interpreting Jesus' death;[1] or those who argue that the absence of a passion narrative does not rule out Q's knowledge of the death and resurrection of Jesus;[2] and those who assert that the very form of Q rules out the inclusion of a passion narrative.[3]

Some of the study on Q argues strongly against the concept of the uniqueness of the kerygma of the Christ-event, raising serious questions about the *sine qua non* of that kerygma in the *Urgemeinde*. This work emphasises both the priority of Q and that it contains no interpretation of Jesus' death as a saving event.[4] Instead there is another kerygma at work in Q, focused on the reign of God rather than on Jesus (Lührmann 94–6; Kloppenborg and Vaage 6). For Q, Jesus is Wisdom personified, or a wisdom/cynic sage, the Lord of the logia, "a revealer figure without any appeal to an 'Easter' mythologem" (Mack 1990b, 10).[5]

Similarly there are scholars who argue that the kerygma of the canonical gospels is not to be found in Gos. Thom. Mack, for example, proposes a process of mythmaking in Gos. Thom. that provides the link with Q ("from Jesus as a cynic sage to Jesus as the revealer of esoteric knowledge about salvation"), and has no relation to the myth of the resurrected Christ (1990b,

---

[1] Kloppenborg writes: "It is not simply a matter, then, of Q's silence in regard to the pre-Markan passion account (if there ever was one), but of the use of a quite different explanation of suffering and the conceptualization of suffering and vindication in corporate terms. In Q we seem to be at a very primitive stage of theologizing the experience of persecution. Jesus' fate evidently was not yet an issue which required special comment" (1990, 81). Schweizer finds a somewhat different sense to the presentation of "the Passion" in Q: "Die Erfahrung der Kreuzigung schlägt sich nieder in der Aussage von der Ablehnung Jesu und seiner Jünger (14,27 'Kreuz') und des dadurch bedingten Leidens... Die Passion soll gelebt, nicht (als soteriologisch verstandene Heilstatsache) erzählt werden" (1987, 698). See also Mack 1988, 86 and 1992, 212; Smith 1990, 134–8; Seeley; and Gnilka 139.

—[2] Thus Dormeyer: "Der Tod Jesu wird als Prophetenschicksal verstanden..., das im Endgericht geahndet wird. So endet Q mit Logien vom Kommen des Menschensohnes... Die (biographische) Existenz ist über Tod und Auferweckung hinaus auf das Wiederkommen zum Gericht verlängert und akzentuiert" (189).

[3] Sato argues from his contention that Q belongs to the genre of a prophetic book: "In keinem Prophetenbuch des Alten Testament wird über den Tod des Propheten berichtet" (383). But cf. Kloppenborg: "It is tempting to argue that the absence of a specific treatment of Jesus' death in Q is a function of the genre of Q as a sapiential document. Sapiential collections normally do not concern themselves with the death of the teacher. But it must be kept in mind that Q is very far from being 'timeless wisdom' like Proverbs..." (1990, 82).

[4] Mack 1990b, 6. More recently, Kloppenborg writes: "The discovery of the *Gospel of Thomas*, however, showed that it was quite possible for a Gospel to lack narrative – including the passion narrative – and to locate the saving significance of Jesus elsewhere" (1993, 11).

[5] For the identification of Jesus as Sophia especially in Q, see, e.g., Robinson, J.M. 1975, Koester 1980, 113, and Kloppenborg 1990. Gnilka holds that Q contains Logia "in denen Jesus in die Nähe der Wiesheit gerückt, doch nie mit ihr identifiziert wird. Das geschieht erst auf einer späteren Überlieferungsstufe, etwa im Matthäusevangelium. In Q wird Jesus in Relation zur Weisheit als großer Weiser gesehen." (139). Downing characterises Q as a sort of Life of a Philosopher, with most significant similarities to Cynic material.

12).[1] After comparing the tradents of Q and Gos. Thom.,[2] Mack concludes that the roots of both traditions may be found in similar Jesus movements, "that were not impelled ideologically by events associated with his death" (11, 18). In a more recent work, Mack continues the argument:

> This means that the death of Jesus, though known and possibly reflected upon by his Q followers, was not seen as an intellectual offense unbecoming the Messiah, was not regarded as a founding event, was not observed as a martyrdom for their cause, was not invested with vicarious significance, and was not interpreted by means of sacrificial mythologies. The Q people were not kerygmatic Christians (1991, 19).

This kind of argument questions many of the previous givens in the study of early Christianity. As a result, Mack calls for a revision of what are presently understood as essentials in the history of Christian origins (including an apocalyptic Jesus and an indispensable resurrection), if we are to move some way toward understanding the experimental nature of that early history (1990a, 169).[3]

The "pandora box"-like quality of the situation referred to by Robinson becomes clear with this thesis and with the implications as worked through by Mack: "Extra-canonical texts result in extra-canonical Jesuses. The wider lens now being used to search for Christian origins brings myths and movements into view that were erased in that process of selective 'memory' we call canonization" (1990a, 169).[4] If the apocryphal gospels are regarded as "real gospels" along with the canonical writings, then it is necessary to treat seriously, at least from the scholarly historical perspective, the interpretations of Jesus to be found in them. These gospels must contain equally valid indications of what was happening in the process of the formation of Christian traditions in the early centuries. It is no longer possible to assume uncritically that the historical Jesus is the one most closely aligned to the canonical Jesus.

---

[1] Similarly, J.M. Robinson investigates a possible "Q trajectory between John and Matthew, on which a major sapiential deviation and a re-apocalyticizing may be plotted" (1991, 190). Horsley (1991) takes a contrary stance to the theory of a primary saptiential layer and secondary apocalyptic layer, suggesting that Q is *logoi propheton* instead of *logoi sophon*. Mack (1992) deals with the idea of Jesus as "prophet-but-not-quite" within a recent work that continues to emphasise Jesus as wisdom sage in Q. Perkins asserts that "Reconstructions of the historical Jesus that fail to take this radical wisdom eschatology into account, but presume that they can begin with the apocalyptic orientation of Q, are on weak historical grounds" (1991, 434).

[2] See also Robinson, J.M. 1986.

[3] See Perkins' (1993b) critical review of Mack's work.

[4] If Mack does not mean primarily when one reads now, as Michael Lattke points out (in conversation 3.5.92) this should read rather "extra-canonical Jesuses result in extra-canonical texts".

Almost twenty years ago, Gager drew attention to this problem with regard to the study of the historical Jesus:

> What documents are most likely to yield reliable information about
> Jesus? In theory, the answer should be that any reported saying or
> deed, no matter what its present literary setting, merits at least initial
> consideration. In practice, the answer has been that only the Synoptic
> Gospels qualify, despite the existence of numerous noncanonical Gos-
> pels and the occurrence of isolated sayings in other types of litera-
> ture... Here, then, is a serious question of method. On what grounds
> can one justify this drastic reduction in the number and type of pos-
> sible sources, especially with respect to the noncanonical or apocry-
> phal Gospels? The answer would appear to lie in the canonical status
> of the Synoptics. Their religious authority as sacred scripture has
> been extended to cover their historical authority as well (245).[1]

In summary then, the basic problem encountered in expanding the basis
for the discussion of the figure of Jesus to the apocryphal writings appears to
be the relativisation thereby of the canonical material. First, there are no
documents which provide objective historical detail about the life of Jesus the
Jew from Nazareth. Second, there are many interpretations of this figure to
be found in canonical and non-canonical texts. Third, all of these texts must
be considered when searching for the early stages of interpretation of this
person. Such a process undercuts decisively the concept of uniqueness, at
least in a scholarly historical sense, with regard to the canonical gospels.

For some scholars, the question may be in the end not so much one about
sources but rather a personal question. Can one work on the basis of the relative historical equality of canonical and apocryphal gospels in reconstructing
Christian origins and at the same time confess the uniqueness of the canonical
gospels? It is not intended here to discredit scholars who confess the uniqueness of the kerygma of the Christ-event, but such a confessional standpoint
cannot be the starting point for historical enquiry, nor can it be used as a foil
against questions which are felt to come too close to the heart of the kerygma.[2] It is an entirely different matter to undertake the historical research in

---

[1] Many concur with Gager: e.g. Hedrick 1988, 1; Gero 3995; Robinson, J.M. 1994, 39;
and Polkow 336–7. Jonathan Smith discusses a similar problem with the term "unique" used
in relation to the so-called Christ-event. For Smith, difficulties occur when scholars of early
Christianity illicitly transfer ontological claims about this event to the level of historical claims
about the "radical incomparability of the Christian 'proclamation' with respect to the 'environment'" (1990, 38–9). Smith's earlier study on canon has gone a considerable way to putting
the problem of the authority extended to the canonical scriptures into some reasonable perspective by investigating the way in which the process of canonisation works in the ordinary
socio-political setting (see especially 1982, 48).

[2] Mack voices a suspicion "that the scholarly quest for the origins of Christianity has, in
effect, been driven by the Christian imagination" (1988, 8), and that the claim for the uniqueness of Christian origins (especially with regard to the resurrection) is a result of a confessional stance which effectively blocks the investigation of the myth of Christian origins (3–9).

an honest and critical manner, allowing all the historical sources, and then to make a confessional choice for the kerygma of the canonical gospels.

4. The Issues Applied to the Nag Hammadi Writings

The key questions which have been posed for those who want to use the apocrypha as sources for Jesus research, have also had their influence on the investigation of the Nag Hammadi texts. In this section I will outline the response to two questions: Do the Nag Hammadi texts belong to the apocrypha? Are any of the Nag Hammadi texts gospels?

4.1 Do the Nag Hammadi Texts Belong in the Apocrypha?

Can we include the Nag Hammadi texts, or some of them, within the New Testament apocrypha? This question is not uncomplicated and hinges in part on whether certain of the Nag Hammadi works are Christian or non-Christian Gnostic.[1] Another question entirely relates to whether the texts are

---

[1] Tuckett cites as non-Christian: Disc. 8–9, Pr. Thanks., Asclepius, Plato Rep., Eugnostos, Thund., Steles Seth, Zost., Norea, Marsanes, Allogenes (1986, 14). Berger's list comprises: Norea, Zost., Allogenes, Steles Seth, Marsanes, and Hypsiph., with Eugnostos as either pre-Christian or dechristianised (526). Böhlig includes Eugnostos, Paraph. Shem, Steles Seth, Zost., Norea, Marsanes, Allogenes, Hypsiph., and adds Apoc. Adam although suggesting that this text is somewhat debatable (Böhlig and Markschies 1994, 180). Tuckett's Category III (Christian texts where Christian elements are more deeply embedded) includes: Teach. Silv., Exeg. Soul, with Auth. Teach. as debatable (42–57). Pr. Paul and Apoc. Paul are cited earlier in the study as Christian (15). Sent. Sextus is poorly preserved but thought to be Christian (16). Judgment is left open on whether Paraph. Shem and Apoc. Adam are Christian or non-Christian (17–21); see similarly Berger (526). Tuckett reserves a separate category for texts which he considers are more clearly Gnostic, but one assumes that he must mean *Christian* Gnostic as he lists the texts exclusively as Valentinian: Gos. Truth, Treat. Res., Tri. Trac., Gos. Phil., Val. Exp. (57–83). The gnostic character or otherwise of the Nag Hammadi texts is of course a further related question, especially with regard to Gos. Thom. (see, e.g., Grobel 1962 and Richardson). It is as well to keep in mind for the Nag Hammadi material in general what Wilson suggests with reference to Gos. Thom.: "Here an important distinction must be drawn: there is no question that it can be read as a gnostic book, but does this mean that it is of gnostic origin, written by a Gnostic and intended to be understood in gnostic fashion?" (1989, 439).

For the most extensive argument against the categorisation of Nag Hammadi texts as non-Christian, see Pétrement, especially "Chapter XII: The 'Apocryphon of John'" (387–419) and "Chapter XIII: On the So-Called Non-Christian Works Found at Nag Hammadi" (420–61). The question of whether certain Nag Hammadi writings witness to the pre-Christian origin of Gnosticism is not necessarily related to this first question of the christianisation or not of Nag Hammadi texts, as Krause states: "It does not follow, however, from the absence of Christian material that these must be of pre-Christian origin" (1983, 187; see also Wilson 1989, 436).

For an overview of the meaning of "Gnosticism"/"Gnostic", see Tardieu and Dubois 21–37; Rudolph 1983; and Wilson 1978c.

Gnostic or non-Gnostic, or perhaps with just a hint of Gnosticism, and so on.[1]

There are certain sub-sections to the question of Christian or non-Christian, concerning principally those writings where no Jesus figure is to be found, but where perhaps a number of possibly related figures such as Christ, Saviour, the Word, or the Son appear,[2] or writings where symbolism occurs which could be (but is not necessarily) Christian.[3] Equally important is the debate concerning whether some texts are fundamentally non-Christian and have been subsequently Christianised to varying degrees.[4] Within the latter texts, should a Jesus figure occur, the character is often considered as a secondary addition, perhaps even a cynical addition by the Gnostics to win Christians to their group. These texts are not considered valid sources for Jesus research since the texts are not Christian in even their first intention.[5]

---

[1] This is not an easy question for many of the texts. The sort of disagreement to be found among scholars can be illustrated by Gos. Truth. Till remarks, "Das darin zutage tretende Weltbild ist sehr einfach und steht dem orthodoxen Christentum sehr nahe. Die charakteristischen gnostischen Elemente sind sozusagen nur in Spuren vorhanden" (1959, 168). On the other hand Grobel writes, "Apart from its blurred mythology the meditation is unmistakably Gnostic in thought and feeling – Gnostic in a wide enough sense to include some underlying presuppositionss in Paul, John, Deutero-Paul, and Ignatius" (1960, 24–25), and Ménard concurs that it is an "ouvrage gnostique et valentinien" (1972, 2).

[2] See, e.g., the debate over whether the Saviour figure in the Apoc. Adam is related to Jesus or not (Berger 526).

[3] With regard to the use of the symbolism of baptism, Berger questions whether the water baptism in Paraph. Shem is only meant as Jewish baptism (526). Abramowski argues for Zost. as a "hidden" Christian work ("'Zostrianus' kann demnach nicht als genuin nichtchristliches gnostisches Produkt gelten, sondern nur als eins, das nichtchristlich scheinen will"; 1983, 2) from the imagery of baptism "in the name", together with an apparent knowledge of the New Testament, and the concepts of repentance and renunciation of the world in association with baptism (1–4).

[4] See Krause 1983, 190–1 for an overview of the debate over these texts between himself, Doresse, and Tröger, as well as a proposal for a set of objective criteria by which to judge which texts are Christianised. The three scholars agree only on including Soph. Jes. Chr. and Ap. John (188). Tuckett lists as texts where the Christian elements are peripheral and probably secondary additions: Ap. John, Hyp. Arch., Orig. World, Soph. Jes. Chr., and Gos. Mary. The inclusion of Gos. Eg. and Trim. Prot. is debatable (1986, 22–42).
   Less frequently the opposite concept of a dechristianising of previously Christian texts can be found. Thus Wisse writes: "Just as there are cases of christianization among Nag Hammadi tractates, it is also conceivable that there was a process of de-christianization going on in gnostic circles, particularly at a relatively late date when the gnostic sects were losing the battle against the orthodox Church and were moving away from Christianity" (1970, 135).

[5] On Ap. John, Pearson writes: "The commentary (on Gen 1 – 6) has been editorially modified, in a rather clumsy manner, into a dialogue between Jesus and his interlocutor John. ...when we remove from the Apocryphon of John the apocalyptic framework at the beginning and the end, together with the dialogue features involving the ten questions put to Christ by his interlocutor John, we are left with material in which nothing Christian remains, except for some easily removed glosses" (1986, 19–20; brackets mine).
   The problem can be complicated by virtue of the type of writing. Hedrick suggests, e.g., that contradiction occurs in Gos. Eg. with specifically Christian imagery or with passages where the figure of the Christ appears (1981, 255). However, given the possible confusion also over the figure of Seth, it may be more the case that the text *in general* is confused rather

In writing on Soph. Jes. Chr., Perkins comments on the usual (tacit) assumption made by scholars when they speak of some texts at Nag Hammadi under the category "Christianised":

> The question that I am raising strikes at the heart of what we intend when we speak of a Gnostic text as having been Christianized. Most of us... have written and spoken about this process with at least the tacit assumption that such Christianization was aimed at the conversion of Christians to Gnosticism. I do not wish to suggest that that assumption is necessarily faulty. But my reflection upon the peculiar shape of that process in SJC suggests that we might also entertain another possibility: a Christian-Gnostic might feel compelled to portray Christ as greater than all the non-Christian, Gnostic redeemers, much as the author of the <u>Gospel of John</u> portrays Jesus as transcending all the religious symbolism of mankind. Perhaps it is not non-Gnostic Christians who need to know the truth about the structure of the pleroma and the plan of the Saviour, but non-Christian Gnostics such as the author of Eugnostos...? (1971, 176–7).

We must be careful with the kinds of presumptions and categorising that inform such a debate about the nature of Christian texts. Above all we should be wary of the tendency to try to make clear categories such as Christian, Gnostic, non-Christian, heretical and orthodox, as if the entire range of early Christian movements, including the Gnostic Christian movement, were clearly identifiable and relegated to orthodoxy or heterodoxy from the very beginning.[1] Second, caution is advised with the view that inserting or taking out Christian symbols can presuppose a Christian, or non-Christian or post-Christian intention. Perhaps the most we can say is that there are certain symbols in the writings that point to certain early Christian traditions.

Because of the presence of so many Christian Gnostic writings within the Nag Hammadi collection, we must understand the community which possessed the texts within the broad range of groups calling themselves Christian. But what kind of Christians? How could one community have ascribed with any degree of serious commitment to so many seemingly different ideas? The question itself of course may not be a particularly helpful one. There may not have been such an emphasis in the community on distinguishing so clearly the demarcation lines beloved of modern Western scholars, and yet on the other hand, as we shall see in the final chapter, the communities from whom the texts originated were often at pains to distinguish themselves

---

than the so-called specifically Christian sections. This article provides a good summary of the contradictory nature of many of the Nag Hammadi texts.

Care must be taken with studies in which Nag Hammadi texts are said to only contain peripheral or secondary additions of Christian material. Sometimes the investigation is hindered by too much dependence on the question of relationship with the synoptics rather than a good discussion of Christian elements *per se* (see, e.g., Tuckett 1986, 22–42).

[1] See Pearson 1991b, 464.

clearly (sometimes with vehemence) from other groups who also called themselves Christians.

In response to the main question of which texts may be included in the apocrypha, Schneemelcher defines New Testament apocrypha generally as "...Schriften, die in den ersten Jahrhunderten der Kirchengeschichte entstanden sind und die durch Titel oder Gattung oder Inhalt in einer bestimmten Beziehung zu den neutestamentlichen Schriften stehen" (Hennecke and Schneemelcher 1989, 1: 52).[1] He affirms that the relationship will be different for individual apocryphal texts. Within the first volume one finds several Nag Hammadi texts: Gos. Thom., Gos. Phil., Gos. Mary, Dial. Sav., Ap. Jas., 1 Apoc. Jas., 2. Apoc. Jas., and Ep. Pet. Phil. Other works are mentioned but not analysed (Gos. Truth, Soph. Jes. Chr., and Ap. John), since in each case it is held that the "gospel" elements are secondary additions to the text, or that the title "gospel" does not really apply (Gos. Truth).

4.2 Are Any of the Nag Hammadi Texts Gospels?

Which of the Nag Hammadi texts may be categorised as a gospel? It is generally pointed out that most of the Nag Hammadi texts which use the title "gospel" are so designated in subscriptions, which makes it less certain that they were initially intended to be regarded as gospels.[2] Cameron too suggests the unreliability of the title "gospel" in these works as an indication of genre, defining gospels as "texts that present sayings of and stories about Jesus" (1982, 17). Meyer proposes that for Nag Hammadi texts such as Gos. Phil. or Gos. Eg. the title "gospel" indicates "their general character as 'good news,' regardless of the actual gattung (sic.) of the text" (1990, 162–3).[3]

The theories regarding gospel genre by Gero, Burridge, and Bauckham which we dealt with in the first section of this chapter would exclude much of the Nag Hammadi material. Burridge concludes that these texts do not represent a distinct literary genre and should be seen "as part of the tertiary stage of reinterpretation and sophistication away from the basic generic pattern of βίοι Ἰησοῦ" (250). Koester also excludes some texts from consideration as gospels (Gos. Phil., Gos. Truth, Gos. Eg., Soph. Jes. Chr., and Ap.

---

[1] Wilson follows Schneemelcher's definition, but suggests that the definition must be treated with some flexibility so as to take certain other "fringe groups" of related texts into account (1989, 434). However he is rather vague about which Nag Hammadi texts may or may not be included in the category of New Testament apocrypha.

[2] On the use of the term "gospel" in the Nag Hammadi writings, see Koester 1990, 20–3.

[3] See, similarly, Guelich 205, and Lampe and Luz 403. Unlike the majority of scholars who proceed from the canonical gospels to a comparison with the Nag Hammadi material, Evans studies the paradigm in what he calls non-Christian texts (Paraph. Shem, Apoc. Adam, and Gos. Eg.) and concludes: "What would appear to be the case is that the non-Christian (which could conceivably be pre-Christian) texts have provided the paradigm that has become the basis for the Christian Gnostic *Gattungen* 'gospel' and 'apocalypse' attested in the Nag Hammadi library" (1981a, 411–2).

John, as well as Pistis Sophia and the Two Books of Jeu), and excludes others such as Soph. Jes. Chr. and Ap. John because of the use of a Jesus figure as a secondary stylistic device (1990, 47).

5. Previous Studies of Jesus in the Nag Hammadi Writings

Academic studies of Jesus in writings outside of the canon have been few. They include the previously mentioned work by Bauer in 1909 (unfortunately too early for many of the important manuscript finds during this century), Stegemann's 1934 study of the figure of Jesus in the Coptic magical texts, Dunkerley on the non-canonical Jesus in 1957[1] and Bruce in 1974. More recent work includes that by Meier, whose study of the historical Jesus seems at first to allow for all the available ancient records which deal with the figure of Jesus, but the major Gnostic texts are disregarded because they are not independent of the New Testament (1: 123–39; 2: 332–3). In contrast to Meier, Crossan's (1991) work on the Jesus figure makes extensive use of the Gos. Thom. and the Gospel of Peter, although still based for the most part on the canonical gospels. Crossan obviously owes much to the earlier scholarship of Koester and to the increasing influence of the American scholars associated with the Jesus Seminar of the Society for Biblical Literature.

Apart from these monographs there have been articles, principally on the Nag Hammadi texts: Arai (1963, 1964a and 1964b) on the Jesus of the Gos. Thom., on the christology of the Gos. Truth, and on the understanding of Jesus within Gnosticism in general; James Robinson (1982), on the resurrection appearances of Jesus from the Gnostic sources;[2] Evans (1981a) and Porcarelli with brief general studies of the Jesus figure in the Gnostic writings. The only significantly lengthy work is Partrick's thesis which covers in detail the Jesus figure in Gos. Truth, Treat. Res., Gos. Thom., Gos. Phil., and Soph. Jes. Chr.[3]

6. The Present Study in Light of the Issues

In this final section, I return to the key points and issues discussed above and suggest how the present study relates to them.

In the first section of this chapter I identify two strands of current historical Jesus research, i.e. study of the "real" Jesus and study of early traditions

---

[1] Although the Nag Hammadi texts had been discovered some ten years earlier in 1945, Dunkerley makes no reference to the find. Given the early history of the Nag Hammadi material, this is understandable. See Robinson, J.M. 1979.

[2] See the criticism by Craig.

[3] See Chapters III to VII, 71–142.

about Jesus. I would suggest, however, that these are not two different enterprises. Both the material about the "real" Jesus and the early traditions are interpretations. Even if one could go back to "the very words" or "the very deeds", these are still reported by others, contextualised according to certain narrative formats, and given a particular theological flavour by their placement within larger works which emphasise some theological themes and concepts rather than others. Although couched in narrative, they are just as much a part of the early traditions of interpretation of Jesus as material couched in more explicitly philosophical or theological language and format.

The majority of texts which I will study have Jesus as their central character. It is true that some Nag Hammadi texts appear to use the figure of Jesus (and disciples) only as a secondary framework for a revelation which has little or no relationship to traditions from or about Jesus which we have from canonical sources.[1] Nevertheless, even these texts must be taken seriously since, as Perkins suggests in the quote above, even they can represent an attempt at Christian theologising. The authors of these texts used Gnostic material upon which to theologise, much as the author of the Gospel of Matthew used texts from the Book of Isaiah as a basis for his reflection on Jesus.

We could ask the same question of the Jesuses in the New Testament as for the Christian Gnostic texts: Is there really any relationship between these Jesuses and a Jew called Jesus who lived and was crucified? Of course, to ask the question of the Gnostic writings in the first place implies that there is an historical Jesus somewhere to be found (perhaps within the canonical writings) and that we are more likely to find him where texts seem to be more "purely" theologically motivated.[2] Who can suggest under which theologically interpreted Jesus figure we might find the Jew Jesus?

The principle applies to more than the Nag Hammadi writings or the apocrypha. The entire range of early Christian movements, including the Gnostic Christian movement, needs to be recognised as contributing historically to that broad non-homogeneous phenomenon known as earliest Christianity. As I have stated above, it is misleading to relegate certain sections of the earliest Christian movements to "heresy" as if they were always so identified from the beginning as being clearly outside the acceptable limits of an "orthodox" tradition. When "heterodox" is used in retrospect to describe the Christian Gnostic interpretations of Jesus, the judgment is made from a confessing

---

[1] Jeremias, e.g., understands the use of "gospel" for the Gnostic gospels, "weil sie als 'frohe Botschaft' Offenbarungsweisheit vermitteln wollen, die meist in langen Reden dem auferstandenen Herrn in den Mund gelegt wird" (24).

[2] Kloppenborg and Vaage, with reference to Horsley 1989, 69, within a criticism of a number of Bultmann's terms with reference to the primitive community, write: "...if the terms 'mission' and 'missionary' imply that only 'religious' concerns were at stake – an assumption which is obviously lurking in many of our treatments of early Christianity – then these should perhaps be abandoned as descriptions of what Jesus' earliest followers were doing" (12).

interpretive perspective, based on a choice made from conviction for one interpretation out of the many offered.

A good example of the distortion which a misguided confessional stance can bring to the research enterprise is found in Grant's study of the Christ of the second century. For Grant, christology is essentially to be derived from the canonical Gospels. Gnostic christology is subsequent to that and best derived from what the early Church Fathers have to relate rather than from the Gnostic texts themselves. One can only wonder in disbelief at the methodological perspective from which Grant can write: "In spite of the exciting and valuable Gnostic documents recovered from Nag Hammadi in Egypt, the basic starting point for the study of the Gnostics has to lie in the earliest criticisms by Christians who wrote against heresies" (41).[1]

The study in the next chapters will be an attempt to present a description of the Jesus/es one finds in the texts of Nag Hammadi. I see this as a valid investigation of the historical Jesus since the texts belong to one strand of the many interpretive traditions about him.[2] I will not be discussing the broader question of the relationship of the Nag Hammadi texts to an "orthodox" strand. As noted above for the apocrypha in general, a considerable amount of the work on the Nag Hammadi codices has been, and continues to be, devoted to finding possible links between these texts and the canonical gospels.[3]

---

[1] For the weakness of the book with regard to Gnostic studies and in general, see the review by Perkins (1992). For the opposite argument that the primary texts are of more worth than any secondary readings in the Fathers, see Krause 1975c, 79–80.

[2] The study may have something to offer to the programme for the historical Jesus quest as outlined by Batdorf, especially his third section: "...we need as participants in the quest (1) to abandon the myth of objectivity, (2) to formulate for public inspection what our personal hermeneutic prejudices are, (3) to formulate for public inspection the total image of Jesus on the basis of which our investigations proceed, and (4) to make explicit how personal bias and total Jesus image are related to each other and to the canon's insistence on reading the story of Jesus in its totality" (212).

[3] Many studies of the Nag Hammadi texts investigate links with the New Testament. Evans et al. is a comprehensive study of all possible biblical parallels or allusions. Within this research in general, as could be expected, Gos. Thom. has attracted the most attention, in particular with regard to the study of sayings of the historical Jesus; see e.g. Jeremias, Hofius 1978 and 1991, and Callan. Patterson suggests three further areas of common ground between Gos. Thom. and the synoptics: a) wisdom sayings; b) social radicalism; and c) parables (1990, 628–36). His most recent work provides an overview of the history of research and scholarly positions on the relation of Gos. Thom. to the Synoptics (1993, 77–90). Davies also provides a summary of the scholarly positions and comments that the emerging American consensus is that Gos. Thom. is independent of the Synoptics and compiled mid-to late first century (663). J.M. Robinson provides an outline of recent research and the three major themes of discussion at the moment: the relationship of Gos. Thom. to the Synoptics; the meaning of the apocryphal gospels in relation to the canonical gospels; and the different interpretations of the early Jesus traditions (1994, 39).

On the significance of the Nag Hammadi Codices for the study of earliest Christianity, Perkins refers to the importance of the texts for raising questions "about the adequacy of our models of religious syncretism in early Christianity" (1991, 441). More recently Cameron has suggested that the challenge of Gos. Thom. lies "in the larger issues it raises for determining the questions we ask, evidence we need, arguments we make, and theories we employ to reconceive the history of early Christianity. It is difficult to avoid the suspicion that *Gos.*

This has found its most recent advocate in Tuckett (1986).[1] While this is helpful and one area of study that is certainly to be encouraged, one cannot escape the impression at the same time that the Nag Hammadi texts will somehow gain more credibility if they can be shown to have a firm relationship with the canonical texts.[2]

The format of Tuckett's work most closely approaches what I want to do here in the first instance, although the approach to the content of the writings will be from a different perspective. Tuckett investigates the relationship of the Nag Hammadi material to the "orthodox" tradition, specifically with reference to the synoptic gospels. He moves beyond the usual comparison of sayings to a discussion of narratives concerned with the birth of Jesus, his baptism, miracles, crucifixion, and so on (1986, 3–4). I will also be dealing with the same passages, but my questions will not be posed from within a paradigm for the life of Jesus already established by the canonical gospels. In other words I want to take off the blinkers of a pre-constructed figure of Jesus from the canonical perspective.

Wilson writes that "none of the Nag Hammadi 'gospels' is a gospel in the traditional sense: they contain no account of the life and ministry of Jesus, or of his death and resurrection" (1989, 433). He may not have intended it so, but his perspective from the outset is a negative one; that is, we begin with the consideration of what the Nag Hammadi gospels are not. Moreover, the discussion above on the nature of Q indicates that it may be unnecessary to ask questions of the apocryphal writings from the point of view of the kerygma (of the Christ-event) contained in the canonical writings.

Inappropriate questions can lead to inappropriate conclusions or can mean that one simply does not see data that is there to be considered. Thus I will not ask, "Is there a passion narrative in this text?" but rather, "How does the life of this character conclude?" or "How does this character close his contact with the earthly realm?"

I want to be clear at the outset about what sorts of questions I am asking of the texts and within what perspective I am doing that. I am aware of the danger of limiting the text by the sorts of questions I am asking, but one has to begin somewhere or remain silent. As Crossan points out, it is possible to

---

Thom. has been treated in isolation, if not actually ignored, by most biblical scholars because its account of Christian origins does not square with the conventional picture gathered from the writings of the New Testament... To take *Gos. Thom.* seriously, therefore, is to situate it intertextually within the spectrum of early Christian history, and that means we must revise our understanding of Christian origins" (1991, 388–9).

The investigation sometimes moves in the opposite direction. Thus Koester (1986) argues from Gnostic texts to propose traditional sayings of Jesus behind the speeches in Jn 8.

[1] See also his earlier articles (1982 and 1984).

[2] That the research on the Nag Hammadi writings is not wholly centred on their relevance to canonical material is indicated by Pagel's outline of a number of directions of study (xxxi–xxxvi).

reconstruct almost any picture of Jesus one wishes, because of the nature of the texts themselves.[1] The diversity of the picture is the first given of modern historical Jesus research and this has to be coupled with the plurality of the ancient interpretations (1988, 122–3).

The greatest challenge while carrying out such research is to be constantly aware of how the initial questions change in the process of engagement with the texts. All I can do is try to be aware constantly of the ongoing subjective play of myself as interpreter and the text which is both shaped by and shapes/reshapes my questions. I have pointed out above that the Third Quest is not without its theological (and perhaps political) motivations, despite how individual scholars may think otherwise about their enterprise. I have no illusions that this is not also the case with my study. In the final analysis, I am aware of the possibility that at the most fundamental level, the answers I find may be chosen for their aesthetic appeal, where the patterns of symbol and meaning find their most satisfying reflection deep within my own psyche.[2]

---

[1] From a different perspective, see Blair's rather negative suggestion that, "Every theologian today makes Jesus a figure in the pattern of his own problems, or cuts him down to the dimensions of his own capacity for believing" (264).

[2] This is perhaps similar to what Batdorf means when he writes of the rooting of scientific study "in a very personal orientation to reality" (205).

II

Origin and Entrance of Jesus into the Earthly Context

There are a number of moments of origin and entrance into the earthly context for Jesus which can be differentiated. In this chapter I am interested above all in identifying the first moments of origin and his entrance into the earthly context. The first moment of origin, above all, takes place in the heavenly region and either concerns the coming into being of Jesus or the character from whom Jesus derives eventually for the purpose of earthly activity. The second major moment of origin concerns Jesus within the earthly context, but there may be a number of moments preceding that, specifically concerning the number of forms which Jesus takes on and strips off prior to, during, or at the conclusion of his descent into the earthly region.

After the earthly region has been entered, Jesus may depart and re-enter. In Chapter VIII, I investigate the ways in which Jesus may close his contact with the earthly region. Generally speaking this is only the first departure of Jesus. Many texts present Jesus as a revelatory figure who has re-entered the earthly context, after the events by which the first contact closes. Some texts posit a number of departures and entrances or appearances for this revealer, generally ending with a type of final ascension to the heavenly region. The texts give no information of where Jesus remains before the final ascension, although one can presume that it is generally the heavenly region. Thus in Ap. John 1.30–32, prior to the appearance of the revealer, there is a description of the heavens opening, light appearing, and the earth shaking – the typical language of heavenly appearances in the human realm. Finally there are also possibilities for extra appearances once the Jesus figure has returned properly to the heavenly region.

In summary, the "earthly" Jesus of the Nag Hammadi texts has a heavenly origin, whether that be explicitly stated as a sending forth from that region, or whether we are told that he has a relationship with some other character in that region and thus we must assume a certain closeness to that character within that region before his movement into the earthly realm. The origin of Jesus becomes a little more complex when we are dealing with a character composed of multiple aspects in which part of the character may have an earthly origin and part may have a heavenly origin.

1. Heavenly Origin

Origin in the heavenly region may be expressed firstly in personal or impersonal terms. When expressed in personal terms there is usually imagery of parenting (father and son) or emanation or perhaps germination (the Lord as a seed of the Truth in Treat. Res. 44.35), usually from the highest God, variously named as Father, Light, the Great Power and so on. This highest God may actually be named as the sending agent, as is the Father in Ap. John 1.22–24; 4.17–18; Acts Pet. 12 Apost. 6.18–19 and Ep. Pet. Phil. 137.28–30, and the Light (= the Infinite [96.19]) in Soph. Jes. Chr. 93.8–9; 106.5–7; 107.11–14. Jesus is actually named as the son of the Father who sends him in Interp. Know. 14.28–30, but it does not seem to be a necessary corollary that such is always the case.

For those texts which speak generally of the relationship of Jesus to the highest God, mostly with the metaphor of father and son, one may assume that Jesus finds his origin in this character and moves into the earthly context out of, but still within, this relationship. Thus Treat. Res. 44.21–23; Tri. Trac.114.22–28; Gos. Thom. Log. 61; On Anoint. 40.12–13 ; and On Euch. A 43.36–38 speak of Jesus' relationship to the Father/God. Great Pow. 40.26–27 presents the Saviour as the man who will come into being who knows the Great Power, but it is unclear whether this knowledge implies heavenly origin in the Great Power.

In Treat. Seth we read that Jesus Christ comes from the assembly of the house of the Father of Truth (50.7–13), the assembly which came together upon the places of the Ogdoad before the foundation of the world (65.33–37), which at first seems to imply origin on a lower level than the highest God. However being in the assembly is equal to being in the Father, as later in the text we are told that Jesus has been in the bosom of the Father from the beginning (70.5–6), in the place of the Sons of Truth and the Greatness (70.6–8).

Within this section, Teach. Silv. must stand alone as a special case since here Christ is described as god who becomes man (110.18–19; 111.4–6; 103.34 – 104.1). Of course one must be careful since the allocation of the term "god" does not necessarily imply equation with the highest God. In his function as Word, the Christ is described as coming forth from the mouth and the heart of God as the first-born (112.33–35). He is a light from the power of God, an emanation of the pure glory of the Almighty, the spotless mirror of the working of God, image of his goodness, Light of the eternal Light (112.37 – 113.7), alone begotten by the Father's good pleasure (113.11–13)... He is the Son, the image of the Father (115.19).

Origin may also be expressed in impersonal terms as "from above", or "from above the heavens", or "from the place of Truth", and so on (Treat. Res. 44.33–35; Treat. Seth 52.1–3; and Gos. Phil. 73.23–27).

Some texts give little detail concerning the origin of Jesus but one can sometimes assume a heavenly origin. Thus, for example, in Apoc. Pet. one assumes from his function as revealer, his association with the Light, and his exaltation above the heavens, that his origin is in the heavenly region, from the Father.[1]

The activity of descent can also be an indication of heavenly origin. Sometimes the descent is with reference to a starting point as in the third section of Trim. Prot. where Protennoia descends from the Light as the Word or Christ into the region below, the world of mortals (47.31–32), or there may be no starting point explicitly named as in Ap. Jas. 8.37; 9.2, 8–9; 10.19–20; 10.28–29;13.9–11; 14.37–41; Val. Exp. 35.17–24; and 1 Apoc. Jas. 28.7–16; 2 Apoc. Jas. 46.10–23; 59.19–21.

There is sometimes a question concerning the final destination (the human/ earthly realm or farther on to the Underworld) of the Jesus figure who descends. The question is not as simple as it appears since the human condition or the world is often compared to the condition of death and the human body may well be Hades in microcosm. I deal with this question further in Chapters III and VIII. Whatever the ultimate destination, the fact remains that the descent is from the heavenly region.

Occasionally the Jesus figure simply appears in the earthly context as in Gos. Truth 20.23. Here one can only infer an origin in the heavenly region from the following verses which speak of his being drawn down to death even though clothed with life eternal (20.28–30).

Summing up then we can say that, in general, the texts speak of an origin for the Jesus figure in the heavenly region or from the highest god or Father. Though this is a true statement, it is also misleadingly simplistic. This will become clear in the individual texts, when we investigate the way in which the heavenly region is constructed. It will also be apparent in outlining the various levels of complexity of the system of relationships within which the highest god and the Jesus figure function. It will be necessary therefore, if only briefly, to consider this heavenly context which is also an important background for understanding the figure of the "earthly" Jesus.

By heavenly context, I mean the heavenly structure out of which the Jesus figure proceeds or within which he functions, either prior to descent into the earthly region and/or subsequent to ascension from that region. For the most part, this means an investigation of the working of relationships, which I propose to deal with on an increasing scale of complexity, beginning with those texts which have little more than a few statements about the relationship of Jesus with the highest god/Father or perhaps with some few heavenly figures, progressing through to those texts which comprise a fully developed and complex heavenly system of relationships. Of course, the lack of a

---

[1] Havelaar uses 70.21–25 to suggest that Jesus is related to the Father as the revealer is related to the source of revelation (166).

complex system in the first series of texts does not necessarily imply that the author or community of origin did not know such a system.

1.1 Jesus in Relation to the Highest God/Father

This first section includes two texts which refer to the Jesus figure in relation to the highest God/Father with no details of further relationships. In Acts Pet. 12 Apost. 8.31–32, the character Lithargoel, who is the heavenly Jesus who retains the wounds of crucifixion,[1] is described as the son of the great king (= the Father). One assumes a similar filial relationship for Jesus with the Good, the king (145.14) in Thom. Cont.[2]

Ap. Jas. presents both heavenly and earthly aspects for the Jesus figure, whose description of what awaits him in the heavens subsequent to his departure includes taking his place at the right hand of the Father (14.30–31). That there are also other beings, perhaps angels, present in the heavenly region is implied by the fact that hymns also await him in the heavens (14.29–30).

Several texts contain a further aspect of some minimal description of the heavenly context:

– Treat. Res. contains a reference to the restoration of the Pleroma by the Son of Man (44.33–38).

– In Gos. Thom. Log. 19, Jesus refers to the five trees in Paradise, which implies that he has knowledge of, or perhaps access to, this heavenly Paradise. Apart from this, Jesus is described as "the living Jesus" or "the living one" (Prologue and Log. 52, 59, 111), which implies that he has a heavenly nature. (See the discussion below in Chapter IV.)

– Apoc. Pet. makes a number of references to the relationship between the Father and the Saviour as the one who reveals him. A cosmological system is presumed by the activity of the archons in the events of the passion of the Saviour and their influence on the heretics.

– 2 Apoc. Jas. presents three key heavenly figures – the Father, the Lord who is his Son, and the Demiurge who is the creator of heaven and earth (58.2–6) – but the relationship of these figures is not described in any detail. We are told that the Lord was the Holy Spirit and the Invisible One who did not descend upon the earth (58.16–17). The latter description perhaps refers to the Lord's union with the highest God, in that he came as

---

[1] I am following H.-M. Schenke's interpretation of the clothing of Lithargoel as he appears earlier as the pearl seller. Apart from the golden belt which is a sign of his angelic identity, "das übrige dürfte biblizistische Phantasie sein und die Bekleidung des Begrabenen meinen, während Füße, Hände und ein Teil der Brust wohl eigentlich nur deswegen frei sind, daß man die Wunden des Gekreuzigten sehen können soll" (1973, 14; see also 1989b, 373).

[2] Jesus is related with truth and light in Thom. Cont., but it is not clear from the text that the latter are intended as characters in their own right.

an image of, or as one who shares the nature of, the Invisible One who did not himself come upon the earth.[1]

1.2 Jesus in Relation to Multiple Heavenly Characters

I move now to investigate texts with a more complex system, that is, with multiple heavenly characters. With reference to Jesus, a number of variations occur: there are sometimes multiple heavenly characters of which one is Jesus; there may be multiple manifestations of one character who is Jesus; there may be multiple manifestations of one character and one of these manifestations may be Jesus. The latter two categories are not always easy to differentiate.

On the simplest level are those texts which describe a relationship for Jesus and the highest God and perhaps one or two other characters of importance within a structure which may also include the negative characters of the archons or a Demiurge.

Ep. Pet. Phil. presents Jesus Christ in relationship with the Father as his child/son (133.25–26; 137.27; 139.26–27) and implicitly as one who shares in the nature of the Father ("God Jesus", 133.7–8). These two characters are set in opposition to the Mother who produces the Arrogant One. From him come the powers of the cosmos who are strangers to the pre-existent Father (135.8 – 136.5). The Mother is also responsible for the fall of the seed which Jesus came down to save (136.16–18).

In Interp. Know. the Son exists in the presence of the Father, the Logos and the height (10.23–25). In a very damaged section of text, it appears that the Logos must be differentiated from the Saviour as his wife/spouse (?) (3.26–28).

Testim. Truth and 1 Apoc. Jas. may also be included in this section. In the former, within the heavenly realm, the Son of Man is associated with Imperishability, the God of Truth, who is the highest God (41.5), to be seen in opposition to the God of the Genesis account who is depicted as a malicious envier of Adam (47.14–30). The activity of dividing carried out by the Word of the Son of Man presumes a heavenly structure including angels (40.25–29; 41.2–4). Similarly in 1 Apoc. Jas., the Jesus figure (the Lord) is intimately connected with the highest God, He-Who-Is, of whom he is an image ⲉⲓⲕⲱⲛ (25.1). Both are unnameable (24.20–23). A further structure is implied by the positive relationship between the Lord and Sophia (35.18–19) and the negative relationship between him and the twelve archons or hebdomads and their subordinates, the seventy-two heavens (27.18–24).

---

[1] W.-P. Funk holds also that here the highest God is meant "so daß die Konsubstantialität zwischen Vater und Sohn den Inhalt der zweiten Hälfte des Satzes ausmacht: Er, der Herabgekommene, war eins mit dem Höchsten, der niemals herabkam und -kommt." He makes further reference to Jn 10:30; 17:11, 22 (1976, 159).

We can complete this section with Teach. Silv., in which the place of Christ within the cosmological order is presented simply in the list of those who are said to be difficult to comprehend, beginning with God, then Christ, the Spirit, the chorus of angels, the archangels, the thrones of the spirits, the exalted lordships, the Great Mind (116.21 – 117.3).

1.3 More Complicated Texts: Jesus under a Number of Designations and in Relationship to Other Heavenly Characters

We move now to texts which are much more complicated in their descriptions of the relationships associated with the Jesus character. In general we can say that the texts contain some detail on Jesus under a number of designations and in relationship to, but not equivalent to, other heavenly figures.

I begin with Gos. Truth and Trim. Prot. which are unusual among these texts (as Perkins indicates at least for the former [1990, 71]),[1] by their identification of the Son and the Word/Logos, who otherwise is placed much lower in the cosmic hierarchy.

1.3.1 The Gospel of Truth

In Gos. Truth 24.7–9, we find the formula: "... into the Father, into the Mother, Jesus of the infinite sweetness" (ⲁⲍⲟⲩⲛ ⲁⲡⲓⲱⲧ ⲁⲍⲟⲩⲛ ⲁⲧⲙⲉⲉⲩ ⲓⲏ(ⲥⲟⲩ)ⲥ ⲛ̄ⲧⲉ ⲧⲙⲛ̄ⲧ⟨ⲁⲧ⟩ⲁⲣϩⲁⲍ̄ ⲛ̄ⲧⲉ ⲡⲓ<.ⲗⲁ6). This is either a trinity of persons or Jesus appears in apposition to the Mother[2] (if one does not accept the suggestion of Orlandi that the word "Jesus" here is more probably a badly inserted gloss [54–5]). F.E. Williams comments on the unclear syntactical position of Jesus, and suggests that Jesus may be intended to be seen in apposition with the Word which is the subject of the paragraph (1985b, 71; see also Arai 1964a, 75 fn. 2). The formula could also be interpreted in the light of the following paragraph where a connection is made between the Father, the Holy Spirit, and the Son (24.9–14).

Both interpretations serve to link Jesus and the Word/Son who came in fleshly form (30.27–32; 31.4–8) and make it less likely that Jesus appears in apposition to the Mother. Moreover there are a number of connections to be found between the activity of Jesus and the Word/Son: both reveal the Father (18.24–29; 24.14–16), proclaiming what is in his heart (20.39; 31.9–11); both carry out major revelatory activity, bringing knowledge within the places of ignorance and terror/oblivion (18.16–19; 20.34–39; 30.15; 31.30–

---

[1] See also Schenke, H.-M. 1959a; Till 1959, 168; Giversen 1959; Grobel 1960, 22; Arai 1964a (in his summary of the contents of the text, for example, he gives the title of 23.18 – 29.9 as "Jesus als Wort des Vaters", 15); Ménard 1972, 38; and Attridge 1986, 250–1. The most recent work on the text as a whole suggests that the Jesus figure is probably distinct from the other revealer figures (Attridge and MacRae 74–75).

[2] H.-M. Schenke asserts that the mother is Sophia, who is also the thought of the Father from which the Logos comes forth (1959a, 16 n. 7).

31; 32.36–37); both give life (20.13–15; 31.15–16; 32.20–21) and oppose Error (18.21–24; 31.21–27); both are connected with the way, the Son as the way, Jesus as the one who shows the way as a guide (18.19–21; 31.28–29); both are searched for (18.11–16; 31.31–32).[1]

Above all, the connection of the Word/Son and Jesus is clearest through their relationship to Truth and the Father. The Son is the way (31.28–29) and the name of the Father (38.7 – 40.23; the name in truth, 39.1; 40.5–6);[2] the Truth is the way (18.19–20) and the mouth of the Father (26.34–35); Jesus is the Truth (16.31 together with 18.11–13) and he shows a way of truth (18.19).[3]

Finally it should be noted that Jesus, the Son and the Word all have imperishable bodily existence (20.29–32; 26.7–8; 30.27–32; 31.4–6). Moreover, the body which the Father's love made over the Word (23.30–31) might well be the book which Jesus puts on (20.24).[4] Thus the Word may be the body of Jesus as in Gos. Phil.

1.3.2 Trimorphic Protennoia

The Son, Logos and Christ are identified as the same character within the text (37.4–5; 38.22).[5] He is the third of the existences (with the Father and the Mother) of the Voice who is Protennoia (37.22), originating as the Word from the Voice (37.5–6, 23–24), the speech from the Mother (46.8–9), proceeding from the height (37.6). He is the Perfect Son (38.17, 22; 39.12–13), the Son of God and Aeon of the Aeons (38.24–27), a male Virgin by virtue of a hidden Nous (= Silence) (46.21–22).

---

[1] F.E. Williams includes the shepherd metaphor used of the Son in 31.35 – 32.30: "The interpretation of the shepherd imagery here follows the tendency already evident in John 10:11 to equate Jesus with the Good Shepherd" (1985b, 92; see also Evans et al. 36). Attridge and MacRae stress the aspect of hiddenness assigned to Jesus and the Son: Jesus is the hidden mystery (18.15) and the Son is hidden in the Father (24.13–14) (1985a, 74), but "hiddenness" is also a quality of the Father (37.38), so it is too broad a category to be used on its own to indicate the equivalence of Jesus and the Word/Son.

[2] See Mortley on Jesus as the name for the Father. Thomassen concentrates on the concept of name in general but also on the idea that the Name is given to the Son and at the same time the Son is the Name, meaning the equation of naming and generation (1993, 146).

[3] Dunn comes to the same conclusion but by the study of 26.23 – 27.3 (163–4). See also Arai 1964a, 98; and Strutwolf 163.

[4] The book was written in the thought and mind of the Father and was within the Father's incomprehensibility before the foundation of the All (19.36 – 20.3). The Word is called thought (37.12–13) and the first to come forth (37.15–16).

[5] Commenting on the addition of the name Christ to references to the Son (38.22; 39.7), G. Robinson writes: "This addition does not serve any apparent purpose other than to identify him with the pre-existent Christ. Christ has no function of his own in the text. It may also be noted from other Sethian texts that this seems to have been the simplest way to 'Christianize' a gnostic text externally" (43).

1.3.3 A Valentinian Exposition

From the Father, the Ineffable one, who is a monad (22.19–25) or a dyad together with Silence (22.25–29),[1] the Son comes forth who is his hypostasis (24.23–24), his revelation, his goodness, his descent and the All (22.31–36; see also 24.24–26), the Monogenes (24.33–34), the Father of the All and the Mind of the Spirit (23.36–37). His syzygy is Truth, and thus they complete with the Ineffable One and Silence the first tetrad (39.20–24). This figure is to be differentiated at least from Jesus, who is his image (39.15–24).

The heavenly Christ is described as possessing four powers: separator, confirmer, form-provider and substance-producer (26.23, 31–34; 27.32); that is, creative powers. This activity of separating and forming, which is not described further in the heavenly context, parallels the creative activity of Jesus with the seeds of Sophia (37.32–38).[2] He is sent forth by the Aeons to establish Sophia (26.22–24), who has fallen from her position in the Pleroma because of acting without her syzygy (34.23–31; 36.32–38).[3] We are told that this correction will only occur through her own Son (= Christ),[4] who alone has the fullness of divinity (33.28–32).

---

[1] Pagels emphasises the absolute solitude of the Father as Monad: "Silence is interpreted specifically as the tranquility in which he reposes (22,22–23) in the absence of any companion" (Pagels and Turner 1990b, 97). The tetrad of Father, Silence, Son/Monogenes, and Truth appears to suggest otherwise; that is, that Silence is the syzygy of the Father, as the Truth is of the Son.

[2] On the other hand, Thomassen identifies this figure as the Limit, noting that the powers would normally be those of the Son, or Christ, or Logos-Saviour (1989b, 230–1). Pagels also interprets as the Limit who, as a Saviour with Christ, re-establishes Sophia, Christ expressing the healing and restorative powers of Limit (Pagels and Turner 1990b, 99, 101): "Since the activity of Limit prefigures that of Christ, the latter development of his soteriological powers accords with the statement that Sophia's correction 'will not occur through anyone except her own Son'" (101). In a very damaged passage, Limit appears also to have powers of separation and confirmation (25.22–24). Although the text of p. 26 is also damaged, I would argue that here it is Christ rather than Limit who is described, subsequent to his being sent forth by the Aeons.

[3] According to Ménard, Sophia's syzygy is Jesus or the Logos Christ-Jesus, but the Logos must also be logically her Son, if Ménard interprets 33.32–35 as a reference to the incarnation of the Logos (1985, 5–6). (According to the text, the syzygy of the Logos is Life [29.27–28, 30; 30.30–31] and the union of these two is in parallel to the union of the Ineffable One and Silence, for whose glory they exist [29.30–33].) According to Pagels the syzygy of Sophia is "Desire" or "the will of the Father" (Pagels and Turner 1990b, 93), but Sophia's syzygy in 36.27–28 is said only *to exist in* the will of the Father, since the will of the Father is that nothing should happen in the Pleroma without a syzygy (36.28–31). In the notes to the text, Pagels and Turner designate Jesus as the syzygy of Sophia, although with reference to Hipp. *Ref.* VI.36.1–3 (1990b, 163), so it is not clear whether they mean this to be the interpretation of this text as well.

[4] Thomassen prefers to read "his Son" (the Son of the Father or perhaps the Son of the Pleroma as a collective entity) rather than "her Son" in 33.30, stating that the pronoun is not able to be read clearly from the manuscript (1989b, 233). *Contra* Thomassen, Pagels and Turner assert that the "ᴄ of ⲡϣ̄ⲏⲣⲉ has been written over ч" (1990b, 163). Although Thomassen is right with regard to 33.30, in so far as the pronoun cannot be read with any degree of certainty (at least from the Facs. Ed.), I would read ⲡⲉᴄϣⲏⲣⲉ in 33.37, which would lend weight to the argument for ⲡᴄϣⲏⲣⲉ in 33.30 (Facs. Ed. XI, 1973, 39).

Both Ménard (1985, 74) and Thomassen (1989b, 232–3) agree that Christ (or Christ-Jésus for Ménard) is the Son of Sophia. Pagels simply equates the Son (of the Father) with

Arguing from other Valentinian sources, Thomassen writes: "...it does not agree with the other sources to make the son of Sophia, or Christ, as distinct from Jesus, the Saviour... the Saviour in *Val. Exp.* carries the name Jesus... Thus the descending Saviour probably is, here as in other Valentinian documents, Jesus, who incorporates the totality of the Pleroma" (1989b, 233). It is necessary to question how Thomassen manages to identify Jesus with the Son of the Father or the Son of the Pleroma. Apart from that, Jesus is certainly a Saviour in this text, but the Christ has a part to play independently from Jesus and in this sense can also be taken as a Saviour, since it is through him that Sophia is brought to the knowledge of who she is and the need for repentance and return.

The only possibility I can see for equating Jesus with the Son of Sophia is from 39.20–24 where, in a very damaged passage, Sophia may be presented in parallel to the complete One, the seeds with Silence, and Jesus with Monogenes. If the restorations are correct, and this passage is taken to its logical conclusion (not always a safe method with the Gnostics!), then there may be grounds for suggesting that Jesus is the Son of Sophia, as the Monogenes is the Son of the Ineffable/complete One. If the final reuniting of Jesus with Christ (39.29–30) is to be interpreted as a reunion with the heavenly figure of whom he is the image, then it is possible that the Monogenes and Christ are the same character. Thus Jesus is to be differentiated in one sense from Christ/Monogenes but is also to be seen at the same time as intimately connected with him as his image.[1]

1.3.4 On Baptism A and On the Eucharist A

On Bap. A and On Euch. A should be considered in close association with Val. Exp. which they follow in the codex. On Bap. A presents "our Lord Jesus Christ, the Monogenes" as the revealer of knowledge (40.32–35). As Colpe points out, there is no differentiation between the two characters, yet the text goes on to speak of "these" and "walking in them" and "they are those of the first baptism" (40.34–38), which, as Colpe remarks, seems to separate the Lord and the Monogenes again (1974, 113). Either "these" (ⲛⲉⲉⲓ) refers to two characters, Jesus and Christ,[2] or it refers to the content of the summary of knowledge, as Pagels and Turner interpret by the insertion of "(items)" in the translation (1990b, 143).[3]

Pagels and Turner edit On Euch. A 43.36–38 as follows: ⲡⲉ]ⲁ̣ⲩ ⲛⲉⲕ ϩⲓⲧ̅ⲛ̅ ⲡⲉⲕϣⲏ[ⲣⲉ ⲁⲩⲱ] ⲡ̣[ⲉ]ⲕ̣ⲙⲓⲥⲉ ⲓ̅ⲏ̅ⲥ ⲡⲭⲣⲏ[ⲥⲧⲟⲥ] (1990b, 149).[4] Jesus

the Son of Sophia and names him Christ, without any information about the grounds for the equation (Pagels and Turner 1990b, 93, 163).

[1] *Contra* Ménard who appears to recognise only one character, the Logos who is the Christ-Sauveur-Jésus (1985, 83).

[2] Ménard interprets ⲛⲉⲉⲓ as referring to the Aeons (1985, 86).

[3] In the notes to this passage, however, they appear to read two characters, referring to Jesus Christ as the psychic manifestation of the Saviour (1990b, 170).

[4] Ménard has [ⲙ̅ⲛ̅] where Pagels and Turner read [ⲁⲩⲱ] (1985, 62). The space available would seem to call for ⲁⲩⲱ (Facs. Ed. XI, 1973, 43).

Christ is clearly the offspring of the Father, but is he also the Son? If the reconstruction of 43.22–23, "your son, Jesus Christ" is correct (see Ménard 1985, 62 and Pagels and Turner 1990b, 148), then there is no question of the identification of Jesus Christ as both Son and offspring.[1]

1.3.5 The Dialogue of the Saviour

Dial. Sav. is the simplest example of those texts in which the Jesus figure is not equivalent to the Logos, or at least in which a decision cannot be made as to their equivalence. We find a clear relationship between the Lord, who is also the heavenly Son,[2] and the Father. The relationship can be inferred from the statement that the community bases its assurance that the Father will hear them upon the fact that the Father has heard the only-begotten Son (145.17–18). The character of the Logos also occurs, who is the body of the Father among men (133.18–21) and we might be inclined to presume that the Logos is therefore equivalent to the Lord, but there is no suggestion of this in the text. Indeed there is no reference to a relationship between the Lord and the (First) Logos, who acts in relation to the creation of the cosmos and also in relation to humankind, in a way that is strongly suggestive of the activity of the Logos in the Johannine prologue (133.10–13; 133.19–21; 145.11–14).[3]

1.3.6 The Gospel of Philip

With reference to Gos. Phil., Rewolinski comments: "While the stance of the GPh with regard to God and God as Father is relatively clear, the posture of the Son, the Logos, Jesus (and) Christ is as complex as the several designations used to describe the nature and function of the Son" (76). The designations Jesus, Christ, Son and Saviour are all references to one and the

---

[1] Rather oddly, after making such a reconstruction for 43.22–23, Ménard interprets 43.36–38 as referring to the three figures of the Father, the Monogenes and Jesus-Christ (1985, 90).

[2] See Krause 1977a, 25. There is no information about the Son as a heavenly figure.

[3] *Contra* Koester and Pagels, who state that there is no evidence in this text for the use of the canonical gospels and that the dialogue source should be dated "certainly not later than the gospel of John" (15–16). However, the following three passages are impressive when taken together:
    133.10–13: the Word established the cosmos and he was in it (ⲁϥϣⲱⲡⲉ ⲛ̄ϩⲏⲧϥ̄) (Jn 1:3, 10, 14).
    133.18–21: the Word comes forth in [the body] of the Father among men ([ⲡⲥ]ⲱⲙⲁ ⲙ̄ⲡⲓⲱⲧ ϩⲓⲧⲛ̄ ⲛ̄ⲣⲱⲙⲉ) and is not received (Jn 1:10–11, 18).
    145.11–14: the Word comes forth to the abyss (= the earth) in silence with a flash of lightning, giving birth, and the archons cannot overpower it (Jn 1:5, 9, 12–13).
    I am surprised that Perkins has not included this within her section on the Johannine prologue in Chapter 8 "Jesus as Word" (1993a, 109–21). Evans et al. make no reference to the first passage, but note Jn 1:11, 13–14 for the second, and Jn 1:5, 13–14 for the third (236–7).

same character.[1] All of these manifestations, except for the Saviour (the term appears only once), are described as having some contact with the earthly realm and the heavenly realm. However, the Son remains mostly within the context of the heavenly realm, specifically in relation to the Father (54.5–10; 74.22–24), but also in relation to the Holy Spirit with the Father (59.11–18 and 67.19–20). The most problematical of all the designations is the Logos, and it seems as if this character might be intended primarily as a character in its own right.

At first, 84.8 ("The Word said, 'If you know the truth, the truth will make you free'") appears to offer the best possibility of equating the Jesus figure and the Logos, if the intention is to replace the designation for the speaker in Jn 8:32 (Jesus) with an equivalent designation (Logos). However, one finds that John the Baptist as the speaker in Matt 3:10/Lk 3:9 has been replaced in similar fashion by the Logos in 83.11–13 ("That is why the Word says, 'Already the axe is laid at the root of the trees'"). Perhaps in both cases, the use of the Logos is a general reference to the word of scripture. Wilson takes a middle course and makes a distinction between the two, using "logos" for 83.11–13 and "Logos" for 84.8 (1962, 185–6).

80.4–5 might also be used to make the equation between Jesus and the Logos, depending on how one divides the Coptic text. I would read the text as preserving a kind of parallelism: This is Jesus Christ... Therefore he is blessed... For this (is) the Logos. (ⲡⲁⲉⲓ ⲡⲉ ⲓⲥ ⲡⲭⲥ... ⲉⲧⲃⲉ ⲡⲁⲉⲓ ⲟⲩⲙⲁⲕⲁⲣⲓⲟⲥ ⲡⲉ... ⲡⲁⲉⲓ ⲅⲁⲣ ⲡⲗⲟⲅⲟⲥ). However, Kasser (1970, 100), H.-M. Schenke (1989a, 170), and Layton and Isenberg (203) read ⲗⲟⲅⲟⲥ as the subject of the following verb, in which case the equivalence of Jesus Christ and the Logos is less certain.

We find also that the Logos is presented as the flesh of Jesus (57.7), a kind of heavenly garment of glory which must hide itself in certain circumstances so that Jesus can be seen (58.2–3). The Logos is also the flesh of the perfect, since they have put on the Perfect Man, whereby their flesh is the true flesh of Jesus (57.15–16). In this way the Logos appears more as a wide-ranging element of heavenly influence which Jesus, and the perfect through him, possess rather than as a character equivalent to Jesus. That the Logos is an

---

[1] Within the text, there is reflection on the names of Jesus: Jesus, Nazarene, Christ. Barc considers that the names represent three different manifestations of Jesus corresponding to three groups of beneficiaries of his activity: he appears as Jesus in the Pleroma, as Christ to humans, and as Nazorean to the angels (1982, 369). Barc argues principally from 52.35 – 53.14 that the three interventions of Christ are directed at the three categories of being of the strangers (= the powers of the Pleroma), the soul (in the middle), and the good and evil ones (= the humans) (370–1). The theory is open to question on at least two points. First, where Christ's coming is spoken of in the text, in each case it is in terms of a coming into the world (ⲕⲟⲥⲙⲟⲥ). Although the text does not explicitly say where the soul is, the description of Christ laying down the soul from the day the world came into being suggests that it is in the world that the soul has been laid down. The text also speaks of Jesus' coming to the whole place (= the cosmos), to crucify the world, and to bring food. Thus both the Christ and Jesus are active in the same sphere. Second, I would be more inclined to interpret the strangers as the Gnostics in the world, since this is so often the use of the term in a positive technical sense in the Gnostic writings in general (see Chapter IX).

element capable of relating is clear from 78.34 – 79.1 (if one becomes the Logos, then the Logos will mix with this person), and 79.5–10 (the person who becomes an animal cannot be loved by the Logos).

1.3.7 The Tripartite Tractate

At first glance the text presents three levels in which three distinct Son-Saviour figures can be identified: the Son of the Father in the highest level, the Saviour of the Logos below the second limit (although he originates between the first and second limits), and the earthly Saviour.

The Son in the highest level comes forth from the Father, and subsequently he and the Father produce the heavenly Church (48.21–33). He is the "man of the Father" (66.12), and the light raised up by the Father (62.33 38), so that the Father might be revealed (63.17–19). His names in part bear out this function: revelation, illumination, wisdom, life, power, the word of the unutterable (66.13–29). He is in union with the Aeons ("they wear him while he wears them" [63.12–13]) who exist for his glory (59.15). In his "stretching out" he produces a foundation for the pleroma (65.4–9).

Following the fall of the Logos, and the intercession of the second Logos who is produced from what is perfect in the first Logos (86.8–9), the Father, the Aeons, and the second Logos join in harmony to bring forth the beloved Son who reveals the countenance of the Father (86.28–32; 91.33–34), who is accompanied by an army who are themselves the countenance of the Aeons (87.20–23). He puts himself on the Totalities as a garment (87.1–2), and gives them a foundation (87.5), but is also described as containing all the Totalities (past, present and future)[1] within himself (87.34–36). He is also a garment (91.34–35) and food for the pleroma (spiritual powers) of the Logos (91.35–38). He is an organising and founding agent, directing the organisation of the universe according to the authority given to him from the first (88.4–6).

As with the first Son, this Son is described primarily as revealer and as the light and life-giver in his activity on behalf of the the fallen Logos and of his offspring (87.3–4; 85.29–30; 88.8 – 89.8). That he is ultimately a revealer figure can be seen from the two summary statements concerning his activity: "Thus he began and effected his revelation" (88.6–8); and "Thus he made himself manifest to him" (88.26–27). His names are: Saviour, Redeemer, well-pleasing One, the Beloved, the one to whom prayers have been offered,[2] the Christ, the Light of those appointed (87.7–10) but the most important name is Son "since he is the knowledge of the Father..." (87.13–16).

Within the earthly realm, the Saviour appears in flesh. He is the Son of the unknown God (133.16–19), an image of the unitary one (Saviour) who is the

---

[1] Thus the Totalities also represent the heavenly Church and the earthly elect.

[2] Thomassen translates with "le Paraclet" (1989a, 139), and Attridge and Pagels note that the phrase probably translates the Gk. παράκλητος (342).

Totality in bodily form (116.28–30). "The Father had foreknowledge of him, since he was in his thought before anything came into being" (125.24–27). This figure too is accompanied by a heavenly army or bodyguards who take on a body and soul (115.29–34).

Much work has been done on the activity of the three Son-Saviour figures by Attridge and Pagels, but these scholars regard the figures as distinct from each other, carrying out parallel activity and referred to by the same name of Son by a principle of analogous predication because of the analogous functions which each carries out (183, 340). However, they also seem to assume the equivalence of the Saviour of the Logos and the Saviour in the earthly realm (436).

I am more inclined to see the three Son-Saviour figures as manifestations of the same character, the first-born and only Son of the Father (57.18–19), before whom there was no other (57.15) and after whom no other Son exists (57.16–17). The structure of heavenly and earthly regions then should be viewed in a vertical fashion with the same character of the Son occurring on all levels, rather than as three individual horizontal planes with parallel activity by three individual Son-Saviour characters.

The cosmic system in which the Son operates in three manifestations is a metaphor of the human condition in its three possibilities of pneumatic, psychic and hylic nature. The Father brings forth firstly the Son and thereafter the Church, but the heavenly Church represents the origin and final destination of the Gnostic elect who have within them the three possibilities of pneumatic, psychic and hylic natures, just as the powers which the Logos brings forth are pneumatic, psychic and hylic, and finally human beings also.

Finally we should note that the Logos who exists as the last of the Aeons to be brought forth (76.13–16) is not the same figure as the Son but is the recipient of salvation by the action of the Son. However, he is patterned after the Son, being a founder, creator and revealer, though only by images and shadows of what is (77.10,16–17; 83.18–21; 91.9–17; 96.3–6; etc.).

I will deal finally in this section with those texts which present a number of relationships for the Jesus figure in the heavenly context: first, relationships with individual characters who are not the more conventional such as Son, Saviour, Logos, and so on, but rather those which are less frequent in the Christian writings in general (Barbelo and Seth); and secondly, relationships within a heavenly group.

1.3.8 The Apocryphon of John

In the final section of the Apocryphon, dealing with the descent of the revealer into the Underworld, the revealer, who is Jesus after the first closure of the earthly context, refers to himself among other designations as the perfect Pronoia of the all (30.11–12), the remembrance of Pronoia (30.34–35), the perfect Pronoia of the pure light (31.11), the thinking of the virginal spirit (31.12–13), the root (31.16). The first and third designations make the link with Barbelo/Pronoia, but the second and fourth designations (30.34 35; 31.12–13) refer not to the virginal spirit Barbelo herself but to the remembrance of her and to her thinking. If the revealer is not Barbelo herself, then he may be connected to her in the sense of being a development out of her as Mother; that is, as the Son/Christ who proceeds from the Father and Barbelo.[1]

However, when one investigates the figures of the Christ and Barbelo within the text as a whole, there are no really strong links between the revealer and either of these figures. What little connection there is, seems to imply a closer link to Barbelo than to Christ, which may be summarised as follows:

– both the revealer and Barbelo are referred to with triple-form descriptions: the revealer as child (BG 21.4), old man (2.4), and a third form which is impossible to identify because of the corruption of the text of II,2 at this point;[2] Barbelo as the thrice-male, thrice-powerful, thrice-named androgynous one (5.4–11).

– both have a possible relation with Sophia: the revealer refers to Sophia as "our sister" (23.20–21); the consort of Sophia is the Spirit who appears to be the male aspect of Barbelo (9.25 – 10.7).

– the descent of Barbelo into the abyss and the shaking of its foundations (14.24–34) is similar to the descent of the revealer into Hades and the subsequent shaking of its foundations (30.16–32).

– Barbelo is also involved in revelation about the way of descent and ascent for humans (20.9–28).

– Barbelo too appears in the image of a human form (14.18–24), which the Christ figure does not. Apart from the trickery narrative (19.15–33), he is involved totally within the heavenly region, in the creation of powers and their establishment.

---

[1] The earlier self-designation of the revealer as [Father], Mother and Son (2.13–14) is of no help here. In the context of the ensuing revelation, it may imply an external manifestation of the triad of Father, Barbelo and Christ.

[2] Regarding the identification of the third form, Till has "Einheit" (ογ[ΜΝΤΟγ a]) for BG 8502, II 19.6 (1955, 82). With reference to Codex II, Krause and Labib suggest "ein Kleiner" (ⲍΜ) (1962, 111), Giversen (following Till?) has "unity" (ⲟγ a) (1963a, 49), Wisse has "servant", presumably from ⲍ aλ (1988a, 105), Layton (following Krause and Labib?) has "young person" (1987, 29), and the most recent work of Waldstein and Wisse has "servant" (17). Whatever the term, logic would suggest that it be the third of the three forms for the revealer (2.8–9). It is tempting to look toward the later self-designation of [Father], Mother and Son (2.13–14), but it is difficult to see how the manuscript may be read as Μ aaγ or even Cⲍ ΙΜⲈ, since there is room after the ογ for perhaps two letters before a final a or λ (Facs. Ed. II, 12). The suggestion of a final Μ (as for ⲍΜ) seems unlikely since the right hand vertical stroke which is visible for the final letter is slanted and the scribe in this manuscript writes the final vertical stroke of the Μ straight.

1.3.9 The Second Treatise of the Great Seth

The Christ is the third member of the heavenly triad with the Father and the Mother/the motherhood. His relationship of union with the Father is stressed by the phrase, "...the Father who is I" (59.17–19). That this is union rather than equivalence is clear from the statement that Jesus Christ has been in the bosom of the Father from the beginning (70.5–6). Regarding relationship with the Mother, we read simply that he is in the spirit and the truth of the motherhood (67.28–30).

Jesus Christ includes himself as a member of the house of the Father of Truth, the heavenly assembly (the Sons of Truth [70.7]; the Sons of Light [60.19]), from whom he comes (50.1–13). This group is itself in positive relation to the Father: he is "our Father" (49.22) and they are found grouped with him when the text speaks of the false witness spoken against the Man (= the Father) and against the whole greatness of the assembly (52.34 – 53.1).[1] The Spirit too is a friend to Christ and this group (49.18–19).

Sophia, who emanates the form Sophia-Elpis for her work directed at the region below, is spoken of positively within the text in general. In relation to Christ, he refers to her as "our sister – she who is a prouneikos"[2] (50.27–28) and asserts that he alone is her friend (70.3–5).

The heavenly powers arrayed against the Christ are the archons belonging to both Yaldabaoth (also called Cosmocrator, Demiurge, and Hebdomad who sets himself up as Father over against the true Father [64.18–26, 32–33, 37–38; see also 53.30–31]), and to Adonaios (52.17–30; 53.12 – 54.14). The latter character is not presented in a totally negative light, since the Christ states that Adonaios knows him because of Sophia-Elpis (55.7–9).[3] The angels who are in the control of the archons (and presumably divided between the Seraphim and Cherubim [54.34]) are also arrayed against the Christ. This is perhaps most subtley expressed in the emptiness of their laughter as opposed to the triumphant laughter of Christ (53.31–34; 54.1–4, 13–14).

---

[1] *Contra* Painchaud who interprets the false witness against the Man and the assembly as an allusion to the false witness given by the Sanhedrin against Jesus in Matt 26:59–61 (1982, 92–3; see also Evans et al. 296). There is some confusion here, since in his introduction, Painchaud identifies the Man with the Father and not with the Christ (2). The following line in the text makes it clear that the Man and the Man of Greatness who is the Father of Truth are the same character, and that this is the Father (see Gibbons 1972, 183; and 1973, 243). I would rather interpret the false witness in a similar way to the false witness of the Cosmocrator (i.e., that he is the only god). Here the false witness is by those who think (wrongly) that Sophia is the whole greatness.

[2] *Prouneikos* has been traditionally translated and understood as "whore" (but see Pasquier's study). If the term is to be used here in the sense of "whore", perhaps she is so characterised because she acts without the consent of the highest god or of the heavenly assembly when she makes preparations in the world (50.25 – 51.13; see Gibbons 1972, 15), or perhaps as Sophia-Elpis she is a whore by virtue of her union with Yaldabaoth (68.28–31).

[3] Bullard and Gibbons have "Adonaios knows me because of hope" (365) which does not properly appreciate the role of Sophia-Elpis (see also 52.21).

1.3.10 The Gospel of the Egyptians

The relationship of the Jesus figure to Seth is fairly clear in the passage dealing with the baptism of Seth. Seth undergoes baptism in a Logos-begotten
body (III)/has baptism of the body, through [the] Logos-begotten one (IV),
which he prepared "in a mystery" (ϩⲚ ⲞⲨⲘⲨⲤⲦⲎⲢⲒⲞⲚ) for himself through
the virgin (III 63.11–13/IV 74.25–29).[1] This baptism that "surpasses the
heavens" is established through Jesus, "he whom the great Seth has put on".
Thus Jesus is the means by which Seth moves from the heavenly to the
earthly region and we might speak of a Seth-Jesus character. The connection
between Seth and Jesus is further emphasised by the statement that Oroiael is
the place where the great Seth is, together with Jesus who possesses the life
(III)/Jesus of the life (IV) (III 65.16–17/IV 77.12–14).

Other relationships of the Jesus figure are not so easily identified, complicated by the difficulty in general of the text, as Böhlig warns, "Der Inhalt ist
durchaus nicht eindeutig..." (1967, 5). The major area of investigation cen-
tres on the hymn section at the conclusion of the text.

There seems to be general agreement that the hymn section may be divided
into two parts (III 66.8–22/IV 78.10 – 79.3 and III 66.22 – 68.1/IV 79.3 –
80.15). Böhlig and Wisse suggest that Jesus may be addressed in the 3rd, 4th
and 5th strophes of the first part (200–2), but this is not at all clear. One does
not find there ⲒⲎⲤ or ⲒⲤ as in the second part, but rather ⲎⲒ or ⲒⲎ. It seems
more likely that the five strophes of the first part of the hymn are actually
addressed to the five seals of baptism or are somehow connected with five
moments of sealing (see Turner, J.D. 1994, 144; or five moments of
immersion, see Sevrin 1985, 141) in a baptismal rite. Certainly the first
strophe is addressed in part to the living water (III 66.11/IV 78.13; see also
III 64.10–12/IV 75.25–27).[2] It seems probable that the triad Iesseus-
Mazareus-Iessedekeus, which is the living water, actually represents a play on
the names "Jesus" and "Nazarene" combined with a reference to Jn. 4:14;

---

[1] With the connections between Jesus and baptism, and the activity of Seth and the virgin
in producing the body of Jesus, the text brings to mind the Jesus of Gos. Phil. (the baptism
and birth of Jesus in the Bridal Chamber from the Father of the all and the virgin who came
down). See the discussion below.

[2] H.-M. Schenke sees the connection between the seals and baptism but does not make the
link to this part of the hymn: "In den rätselhaften Fünf Siegeln..., möchte ich meinerseits eine
Bezeichnung der höchsten 'Fünfeinigkeit' vermuten, insofern als jeweils bei der Anrufung
ihrer Namen im Ritus der Taufe der Täufling mit einer σφραγίς versehen wird" (1979, 18).
(That Schenke should not have included the highest Spirit within the five is indicated by
Böhlig with reference to III 63.2–3/IV 74.14–16 where the Spirit is named together with the
five seals [1989a, 352].) Sevrin identifies the first part of the hymn as a separate (first) baptismal hymn (he treats both parts of the hymn as baptismal [1985, 117–38]), and concludes:
"L'Hymne entier est donc adressé à une entité pléromatique qui appartient aux cinq sceaux et
se confond probablement avec eux..." (124). For Sevrin, the hymn is baptismal because of
its context ("Depuis la description de l'oeuvre de Seth... la thématique baptismale est présente
dans toutes les pièces rassemblées") and because of the address to the tetrad Iesseus-
Mazareus-Iessedekeus-the living water, which he refers to as a "formule rigide, apparaissant
dans divers contextes mais certainement liée au rite baptismal" (125).

7:37–38, but it may well be that at this stage of the transmission, the connection is no longer made to the original source of inspiration.[1]

If the first part of the hymn is addressed to the five seals, however, there is a problem. The names used in the hymn do not correspond to Böhlig's suggestion as to who make up the five seals, namely the thrice-male child, Juël and Esephech (1989a, 352; see also 369). There would be one correspondence if we accept Sevrin's proposal that the glorious name (III 66.12) may be a reference to Esephech (1985, 123).

The second part of the hymn may also have a connection with baptism by virtue of the imagery there: the name which is upon the speaker (III 66.22–24/IV 79.3–8); the intermingling of the speaker and the one addressed who is now known or comprehended by the speaker (III 66.27 – 67.2/IV 79.12–14); the reception of an armour of grace (only IV) and of light (III 67.2–3/IV 79.14–16) so that the speaker has become light (ⲁⲉⲓⲢⲟⲨⲟⲉⲓⲚ) (III 67.4). The action of stretching out the hands may indicate a formal liturgical action (III 67.6–7/IV 79.17–18).[2]

Böhlig and Wisse understand the ones addressed in the second part of the hymn to be first the primal God, then the Mother, and finally Jesus[3] (202–3). If the suggestion is correct that the hymn is baptismal (see further in the text, the incense of life which is in the speaker which he has mixed with water [III]/baptismal [water] [IV]; III 67.22–24/IV 80.9–11 [text damaged]), then one might expect that Jesus or Seth-Jesus is the one addressed throughout. When we consider the concepts associated with Jesus in the final section of the hymn, we can suggest parallels with the imagery of the first section: the speaker's comprehension of Jesus (III 67.13–14/IV 79.25–26 [text damaged]); and the imperishable name of Jesus (III 67.21–22/IV 80.8 [text damaged]).

There are a number of difficulties with identifying Jesus or Jesus-Seth as the addressee of this entire second part of the hymn. Most importantly, it can be objected that the first character addressed in this part is designated as self-begotten (ⲁⲨⲧⲟⲅⲉⲚⲎⲤ) (III 66.24), and that this cannot refer to Jesus or Seth-Jesus. Yet the text as a whole is often contradictory when it comes to such designations of characters. Thus one could point to the contradiction that the Word is said to be self-begotten and yet also the son of the great Christ. Secondly, the connection of the light imagery with Jesus (III 66.27 – 67.4/IV 79.12–16) may be weakened by the strong association of the primal God with the Light in III 40.15 – 41.4/IV 50.4–15. Finally there is the

---

[1] See Evans et al. for these Johannine references and Rev 7:17; 21:6; 22:1, 17, as well as references from the Hebrew scriptures (226).

[2] Böhlig comments on the two hymnic sections: "Damit wird in dem Text sein liturgischer Charakter deutlich, der ja schon aus dem Amen hervorgeht" (1989a, 350–1), but although the "amen" occurs once within the body of the text and three times within the concluding sections of the text (III 55.16; 69.5, 17, 20), it is not found within the hymnic sections.

[3] Sevrin identifies the one addressed as the Logos, and suggests that the appearance of the name Jesus in the hymn produces incoherence by the identification of Jesus with the Logos (1985, 129–30).

appearance of the Mother in III 67.4–5, although since this sentence does not occur in IV, it can be fairly easily treated as an addition in III.

If Böhlig and Wisse are correct that the hymn addresses the primal God (Father), the Mother and Jesus, then it would be possible to postulate a relation between Jesus and the Son, although this link does not appear explicitly in any other place in the text. From the information already to hand in the text, Jesus is the "son" in a certain sense of Seth, but Seth does not appear in the hymn text, unless of course the Father-figure here is Seth and the Mother, the virgin. This is probably taking the interpretation too far, but on the other hand if the context of the hymn is baptism, and the baptism of Seth (on which the Gnostic baptism is based) takes place in the body which is Jesus, who is prepared by Seth through the virgin, then there is a certain logic to this idea.

Finally one should note that the colophon contains the formula: ⲓⲥ ⲡⲉⲭⲥ ⲡⲱϩⲣⲉ ⲙⲡⲛⲟⲩⲧⲉ ⲡⲥⲱⲧⲏⲣ ⲓⲭⲑⲩⲥ (III 69.14–15), which links Jesus and Christ, but often the colophons have very little to do with the content of the text, having been added at some stage by a copyist. Within the text itself, the Christ may have some association with Seth but has no connection with Jesus.

I would conclude that the Jesus character in the text has a relationship only to the great Seth and only indirectly through him to other heavenly figures. There is no direct link to the Christ or the Word as the Son of the Christ or to the thrice-male child.

1.3.11 The Sophia of Jesus Christ

It is not easy to differentiate the various characters of the cosmological system in Soph. Jes. Chr., in order to ascertain to whom the revealer corresponds or to whom he is linked. On the one hand, the author uses some titles and descriptions ("Father", "Man", "Saviour", and so on) for a number of characters. As H.-M. Schenke points out:

> Die Lektüre der SJC ist zunächst schlechterdings verwirrend. Dazu trägt nicht unwesentlich der Umstand bei, daß oft nicht ohne weiteres deutlich ist, welches Wesen mit einem Pronomen oder einer bestimmten Bezeichnung gemeint ist. Man muß es bei der Interpretation jeweils mit einer Deutung versuchen und sehen, ob man mit ihr durch die ganze Schrift hindurchkommt (1962b, 267).

Moreover, the situation is complicated by the fact that the author seems to have adapted Eugnostos without being careful of the resulting inconsistencies with his other source material.

Within the text there are a number of heavenly figures designated as Saviour and one as Christ, apart from the heavenly Saviour who is the revealer in the text (hereafter referred to as the Saviour Revealer). Those designated as Saviour are the Unbegotten Father, God, Son of God (100.2) or the Unbegotten, God (BG 92.13); the First-Begetter Son of Man, who is the son of the Immortal Androgynous Man and his consort, the great Sophia (BG 108.6); and the Saviour whose consort is Sophia Pistis, who is the male aspect of the great androgynous light created by Son of Man (= Son of God) and Sophia Agape, Mother of the All, who is his consort (106.20–21).

The First-Begetter Son of God is also called Christ (104.22).[1] The use of the term in BG 112.15–17, within the list of aeons "...Christs, Christs of Christs..." where Codex III has "...lords, lords of lords..." is meaningless and simply indicates the slavish way in which the copyist of the former text changed each occurrence of ΠⲀΟΕΙⲤ to ΠⲈⲬⲤ.

The question of interest here is which if any of these characters is equivalent to the Saviour Revealer, and to which character/s he may be related. As Perkins has indicated, the character designated as Saviour whose consort is Sophia Pistis is not the Saviour Revealer (1971, 167). The Saviour and Pistis Sophia belong to the third Aeon while the Saviour Revealer is always found in connection with the highest level of the Forefather or of the lesser level of the Immortal Androgynous Man. The self-descriptions by the Saviour Revealer place him three times (93.8–9; 96.17–18;106.5–7) in direct contact with the Forefather, the Light for whom he is the revealer. A fourth time he speaks of himself as coming from the Immortal Androgynous Man (First Who Was Sent) also for the purpose of revealing the Forefather (118.15–17). The latter origin makes less sense in the context of the total action of the text since the Saviour Revealer also speaks of himself as saving Immortal Man from the bonds of the robbers (BG 121.13–17).[2]

Krause's proposal that there is only one Saviour figure (1964, 221) brings an incredible complexity to the interpretation of the text, as he attempts to show how the Saviour moves from the level of the third emanation to the first and even to become equated with the highest God. Krause begins with the relatively clear system of the three emanations which are three Aeons

---

[1] Perkins refers to this passage but sees it as a designation of the Immortal Man, equating the First-begotten and the Immortal Man (1981a, 596). The text clearly speaks of the the first-begotten androgynous son (= Christ) who results from the reflection of First Man, Begetter with the great Sophia, his consort. Thus the Christ results from Immortal Man rather than being identified with him.

[2] Given the fact that the Saviour Revealer speaks of himself as rescuing the Immortal Man or even of his being sent by Immortal Man, the proposal by Good that the Saviour Revealer is to be identified with the Immortal Man seems to make little sense (34). She gives BG 94.11 and 95.4 as reference, but neither passage makes such an identification clear.

How the Immortal Man comes to be in the bonds of the robbers is not clear. Perkins comments, "...we have no indication in the description which we have been given of the activities of Sophia and the Immortal Man that they are in any predicament which would require such redemption. On the contrary, they are portrayed as having the situation well in hand" (1971, 168). However, 101.9–12 implies that the Immortal Man descends to save and awake from forgetfulness what has been trapped in the power of the robbers. In this case, it would mean that he has been somehow caught during this activity and the Saviour Revealer has come to save the one who is intended first as the Saviour, Immortal Man. (This may be why Immortal Man is called the First Who Was Sent, implying that there is another or others to follow.) Thus Immortal Man seems to have a parallel fate to the drop of Light which comes from his consort Sophia and is also trapped by the robbers.

containing the Immortal Man, the Son of Man Progenetor and Sophia, and the androgynous Light whose male name is Saviour and who is also the son of the Son of Man. This system is revised so that the first Aeon is given to the second emanation; that is, to the Son of Man. Subsequently the Immortal Man receives the function of Saviour, the Saviour is then equated with Christ (BG 106.11; 114.14), and finally equated with the highest God (BG 92.13f/III 100.2). Krause sums up: "...das bedeutet, daß in der Sophia Jesu Christi der als dritte Emanation entstandene Soter (BG 102,15ff) gleichzeitig mit der zweiten Emanation, dem 'Sohn des Menschen = Protogenetor' (BG 108,2ff), gleichgesetzt wird, er den ersten Äon (BG 108,1/11) erhält und als erste Emanation ihm die Funktionen des Soter (BG 94,11ff) übertragen werden, er mit Christus gleichgesetzt wird, ja sogar mit der höchsten Gottheit (BG 92,13f)."

Perkins' proposal of the identification of the Saviour Revealer (she calls him "Christ") with the First father is more helpful (1971, 170–1). "He (the author) tells us that no one knows the highest God except those to whom he is revealed through Christ" (175). Perkins supports her proposal with BG 91.12. It is not at all clear that this passage should be taken together with the saying that no one knows the highest God except those to whom he is revealed through the Saviour Revealer (BG 83.17–18:[1] 126.4–6), but the combination of the image of the First Father as the mirror-likeness of the Forefather with the revelation activity of the Saviour Revealer certainly adds weight to the proposal that the Saviour Revealer is to be equated with the First Father.[2]

Two further points should be investigated before making this equation however. First, we must consider the continuation of the passage concerning the race over whom there is no kingdom:

III, 99.24 – 100.4

...ⲱⲁⲩⲙⲟⲩⲧⲉ ⲉⲣⲟⲟⲩ ⲇⲉ ⲛ̄ϣⲏⲣⲉ ⲙ̄ⲡⲁ.....ⲏⲧⲟⲥ ⲛ̄ⲉⲓⲱⲧ ⲡⲛⲟⲩⲧⲉ ⲡⲉ...ⲏⲣ ⲡϣⲏⲣⲉ ⲛ̄ⲡⲛⲟⲩⲧⲉ ⲡⲁⲓ̈ ⲉⲧⲉ ⲡⲉϥⲉⲓⲛⲉ ⲛ̄ⲙ̄ⲙⲏⲧⲛ̄

...they are called the sons of the Un[begotten] Father, God, [Saviour], Son of God, this one whose likeness is with you.

It is not clear exactly whose likeness is with those being addressed, whether the likeness of the Unbegotten Father who is the Saviour, or the likeness of the highest God whose son is the Unbegotten Father.

---

[1] Perkins has "BG 8s, 17f." (1971, 181 fn. 21).
[2] I am strongly reminded here of Jn 14:6, 9. See also Thomassen on the name of the Father given to the Son, and the naming of the Father as Forefather (1993, 145–9).

BG 92.11–16 has

...ⲱⲁⲩⲙⲟⲩⲧⲉ ⲉⲣⲟϤ ⲁⲉ ⲡⲁⲅⲉⲛⲏⲧⲟⲥ ⲡⲛⲟⲩⲧⲉ ⲡⲥⲱⲧⲏⲣ
ⲛ̄ⲛ̄ⲱ̄ⲏⲣⲉ ⲛⲧⲉ ⲡⲛⲟⲩⲧⲉ ⲡⲁⲓ̈ ⲉⲧⲉ ⲙⲛⲧⲁϤ ⲉⲓⲛⲉ ⲛⲙ̄ⲙⲏⲧⲛ̄

...he is called the Unbegotten, God, the Saviour of the Sons of God,
this one who has no likeness with you.

If Codex III is the correct reading, what does it mean? Is it a self-reference in the third person (see Krause 1964, 219) to the presence of the
Saviour Revealer either as the likeness of the First Father (or Unbegotten
Father, according to Codex III) or as the likeness of the Forefather (= the
First Father)? Is it a reference to the continual presence which is also
described of the Immortal Androgynous Man, the interpreter who was sent,
who is with them until the end of the poverty of the robbers (101.9–15),[1]
assuming of course that the Saviour Revealer is not the Immortal
Androgynous Man, nor that the Immortal Man and the First Father are the
same figure.

The Immortal Man is also described as the First Who Was Sent, an immortal in the midst of mortal men (93.21–24). He is not explicitly described as
the likeness of the Forefather or the First Father, but he does appear when
the Self-grown Father (= Forefather) decides to have his likeness become a
great power (101.4–8), so he certainly has a connection with this character.
When one considers the possibility of the Immortal Man being present for
mortals as the likeness of either the Forefather or the First Father, one difficulty appears to be that, at least in his earthly context, the Immortal Man is
said to be psychic, which is the reason that he is trapped in the poverty of the
robbers until the end of the time of chaos (BG 121.6–13). Being such a likeness while being psychic would seem to me to be incompatible.

The second and final passage to be considered is 103.22 – 104.4 in which
Bartholomew asks whose son is the one designated "man" and "son of man"
in the gospel. The answer is that Christ, First-Begetter Son of God, whose
consort is Sophia Agape, is the son of the Immortal Man, the First Man,
Begetter, whose consort is the Great Sophia. From this answer and from the
other conclusions reached above as regards the Christ and the Saviour
Revealer, it seems that the figure who appears in the gospel as the son of
man, that is the Christ (or at least some earthly manifestation of the Christ),
is not the same as the Saviour Revealer. However, this is at least an indication
that the Christ figure in the text has some relationship to the earthly realm.
That he is a lesser figure is clear from the final categories of "judgment":
knowing the Son of Man, which appears to be the same as having a defective
knowledge of the Father, only leads to a dwelling-place in the Eighth rather
than with the Father, whereas the Saviour Revealer brings the true revelation
of the highest God.

---

[1] Perkins understands the interpreter as the Christ sent by the Immortal Man (1980, 95).
BG 121.6–13 seems to make it clear that it is the Immortal Man.

There is one final detail to note. The archangels and angels created by the Christ (104.22 – 105.2) and by the aeons (113.3–5) do not belong to the higher levels of the cosmos (see Helderman 1982, 259, 262). In the introduction to the revelatory dialogue, the Saviour Revealer is described as appearing in a likeness which resembles a great angel of light (91.12–14). The fact that he also comes from infinite Light should make it clear that he is not to be regarded literally as one of the angels but that the initial description of him is in keeping with the common description of the appearance of a heavenly being in the earthly region.

In conclusion, although no definite statement can be made, of all the characters designated as Saviour (at least according to Codex III), the First Father who is the likeness of the Forefather would seem to be closest to the description of the Saviour Revealer. If it is also taken into consideration that the Saviour Revealer speaks of himself as sent from the Forefather and as revealing the Forefather, then it seems he must be differentiated from the Forefather rather than equated with this character as Krause suggests.

1.4 Jesus Confined to the Heavenly Region

The final texts under consideration present a Jesus figure who is basically to be viewed in the heavenly context. The connection to the earthly context is by virtue of helping believers in some way or as the object of human prayer. There is no activity of descending and being within the earthly context in some physical or quasi-physical or present way. However, it is necessary to differentiate between texts which deal with a Jesus figure who is heavenly subsequent to resurrection or ascension (where it is not clear if this figure was always heavenly or whether being in the heavenly region is the result of his earthly existence) and a Jesus figure who is heavenly and has never been truly in touch with the earthly context.

1.4.1 The Prayer of the Apostle Paul

The Jesus of this text is a heavenly Jesus. The only sure reference to him occurs in A.14.[1] It is unclear whether Jesus is addressed in the prayer in the 2nd person, since he appears in this reference in the 3rd person. At first glance it seems possible that "through Jesus Christ..." (A.13–14) is parallel to "through the Son of Man, the Spirit, the Paraclete of [truth]" (A.16–18), but seems thereafter less likely since the next parallel phrase is "through the evangelist" (A.21), unless Jesus is also intended by this term. Either all three phrases refer to Jesus Christ (see Mueller 1985b, 3) or there are three levels of intercession: first Jesus Christ, followed by the Spirit who is also the Son of Man or Paraclete, and lastly an evangelist, whom Layton suggests is Paul (1987, 303).

---

[1] Mueller speculates that the angelic image of the psychic God in A.30–31 is also the Christ (1985a, 7; and 1985b, 4).

1.4.2 On the Origin of the World

A Christ figure occurs in two passages in connection with Sabaoth, the son of Yaldabaoth, and the character is only found in connection with the heavenly realm of Sabaoth. The first occurrence is found in association with Sabaoth's creation of a heavenly mansion, throne, and congregation (105.23–29),[1] the second with reference to the souls which are manifested to Sabaoth and his Christ (ⲘⲚ ⲠⲈϤⲬⲤ) (114. 17).

A question remains over the figures of the immortal man of light/the Adam of Light/the true man (103.19–23; 108.7–10, 20–21; 115.7–9, 21–23; 117.10–12, 28–30; 120.17; 122.19–20; 123.23–24) and the Saviour (unless they are the same character) (124.33), or the Logos (125.14–19), or the Unbegotten (127.5–7) as other possibilities for the Jesus figure. If this is so, then there is some interest in earthly contact and presence in the activity of these manifestations of the Jesus figure, most particularly in the description of the human likeness within the light which confronts Yaldabaoth (108.7–10).

1.4.3 Melchizedek

Apart from the opening line of the tractate (Jesus Christ, Son [...], possibly "of God"; 1.1), the three other specific references to Jesus Christ in the text are all within the context of the heavenly realm.[2] 6.2, 9–11 presents a list of heavenly beings, within which Jesus Christ is named after Barbelo and Doxomedon and prior to the chief commanders of the luminaries. Tacked on at the end of the list is the formula, "through Jesus Christ, the Son of God, whom I proclaim". In 18.4–6, which is unfortunately damaged, there may be the designation "Commander-in-chief of the All" (ⲠⲀⲢⲬⲓⲤⲦⲢⲀⲦⲎⲅⲟⲤ ⲘⲠⲦⲎⲒⲢϤ) for Jesus Christ.[3] This appears at the end of a similar listing of heavenly beings in doxology form, so it may be possible that Jesus Christ should also appear within the list after Doxomedon in the lacuna at 17.3–4.

---

[1] There is some debate as to whether there are one (Israel-Christ) or two (Israel and Christ) figures created by Sabaoth. H.-M. Schenke (1959b, 252) and Böhlig and Labib (1962, 53, 55) interpret as two characters. Bethge and Wintermute interpret as one character, Israel: "...and (also) having another name, 'Jesus the Christ,'..." (166), but both more recent translations by Bethge, Layton and the Societas Coptica Hierosolymitana (1988 and 1989) assume two characters: "and a firstborn called Israel... and another being, called Jesus Christ" (1988, 176).

[2] Apart from these references, there are two references to a Saviour in Melch. 4.7 and 14.4, who may be the earthly appearance of this character. I deal with these texts in Chapter IV.

[3] See also Böhlig and Markschies 185.

2. Earthly Origin

Together with the origin in the heavenly region, one must also consider the movement of the Jesus figure into the earthly region.[1] We have noted that there may be a description of descent, but there is also the question of how Jesus manages to make contact with those who are in the earthly context (human beings, the human soul, the seeds which belong to Sophia, and so on), or how he contacts or avoids contact with the archons whom he meets along the way to the earthly region. Often within the process of descent, he is described as taking on various shapes or likenesses or garments while passing through the various heavenly levels, either to avoid contact (invisible in a garment of glory) or to remain unremarkable (in a similar shape), until at last he takes on a human shape, or appearance, or flesh (see, for example, Teach. Silv. 103.34 – 104.1). This concept will be investigated in Chapter IV. In this section, the focus is the idea of entry into the human context via a human agent (human parent/s), or via an event (activity at the Jordan, perhaps baptism).

As one might expect, at least in view of the canonical tradition, in general the problem with human parentage is more to do with a human father than with a human mother. Thus an earthly mother is often viewed positively. In Gos. Phil. Jesus' mother Mary is one of his three intimate female companions who always walked with him (59.6–11). In 2 Apoc. Jas., James' mother is said to have suckled the Lord and James, and thus the Lord calls her "my mother" (50.18–21). In a damaged section of text, James' mother seems to state that the Lord is James' brother by his father (ⲡⲥⲟⲛ [ⲍ ⲁ] ⲡⲉⲕⲉⲓⲱⲧ ⲡⲉ) (50.23). It seems most unlikely that here James' physical father Theudas is meant (44.18), but that rather they are both sons of the heavenly Father. The Lord asserts in a later passage that James' father is not his father, but "my father has become a father to [you]" (51.19–22).

Earthly familial ties are viewed negatively in Gos. Thom. (for example, Log. 105: "He who knows the father and the mother will be called the son of a harlot"), including negative references to his mother and his brothers (Log. 79; 99).[2] The references to his father seem always to imply the Father in heaven, except for Log. 101 (text corrupt) which appears to present earthly and heavenly "parents" in contrast.

---

[1] Two texts contain the idea that the coming of the Jesus figure into the earthly context has been foretold. In 1 Apoc. Jas., the Jesus figure himself has spoken from the heavens, prior to the revelation proper, about his destiny (29.8–11), and in Tri. Trac., the coming of the Saviour is proclaimed by the Hebrew prophets (111.6 – 112.14), who, unlike the Greek philosophers or the Hebrews in general who have been influenced by the hylic and psychic powers (108.13 – 113.5), have been influenced by the Saviour himself (113.5–11). They are the mouth of the Saviour (113.17–18), and gave an account of his flesh which was to appear (114.3–4).

[2] See Trevijano. The author also includes material from Gos. Eg., Gos. Truth, Tri. Prot., Soph. Jes. Chr., Gos. Phil. and Hyp. Arch.

A number of texts refer to the conception and birth of Jesus in the earthly context: Tri. Trac., Gos. Phil. and Testim. Truth.

2.1 The Tripartite Tractate

In Tri. Trac., the Saviour is described as the one who will be begotten (113.32–33; begotten in life,115.18), letting himself be conceived and born as an infant in body and soul (115.9–11). This appears to be a second stage of "parenting", since the text has already spoken of the conception of the flesh of the Saviour by the spiritual Logos (114.4–14).[1] In this second stage, on the one hand, he is conceived without sin, stain or defilement (115.15–17), on the other hand, he takes upon himself the smallness (= death) to which humankind had descended when they were born in body and soul (115.6–8).[2] There is no further information on the process of the conception and birth, and whether one or two human parents are involved.

2.2 The Gospel of Philip

The concept of dual parentage occurs clearly in Gos. Phil. where the virgin Mary is named as mother (55.23–24; 59.7).[3] In clear (polemical) reinterpretation of the tradition found in the canonical scriptures, the text states that she did not conceive by the Holy Spirit, for women do not conceive by other women (55.23–27; the Holy Spirit or Sophia Achamôth is clearly a female character in the text).[4]

That Mary's virginity is not in relation to Joseph may be seen from the following section in 55.33–36 where, although the text is fragmentary, the writer seems to argue that, if Jesus had not had two fathers, an earthly and a heavenly, he would not have said, 'My Father who is in heaven', indicating the heavenly one, but simply 'My Father'. Thus, his earthly father is Joseph, whose offspring or 'seed' (ϬΡΟϬ) he is (73.9–15).

---

[1] In this way it is the opposite of the double parenting in Gos. Phil., for example, where earthly parenting takes place first, followed by heavenly parenting at the baptism.

[2] Attridge and Pagels consider that the text "is concerned to show how, in his incarnation, Christ transcends human nature and so prevails over suffering and death", citing the earlier work of A. von Harnack (1910. *Lehrbuch der Dogmengeschichte*. 4th ed. Tübingen: Mohr, 286) to say that the characteristic of Gnostic Christology is not docetism but the doctrine of the two natures (186). Strutwolf also interprets this text as non-docetic (172–3).

[3] "The designation 'virgin' covers only her relation to the powers, not her relation to Joseph, and is not primarily a physical, but a spiritual expression" (Gilhus 1985, 92–3). For Mary as undefiled by the powers, see 55.27–28. Gilhus rightly makes a comparison here between Mary in Gos. Phil. and Norea in Hyp. Arch. 92.2–3, 18 – 93.2. In an earlier study, Partrick makes the comparison to Eve and her seduction by the serpent (124). Strutwolf interprets the description literally as a sign that the writer is affirming the virgin birth ("Jungfrauengeburt") (176).

[4] This leaves a question mark over the possibility of Adam's birth from the union of two virginal females: the Spirit and the virgin earth (71.16–18). Buckley argues for the positive presentation of 'gender symmetry in parentage' in the text, and suggests that if Jesus had two mothers, he would be seen in a negative light, similar to Adam (1988, 4180–1).

The concept of a set of heavenly parents for the Christ is found more clearly in 71.8–11, in the description of Jesus' body (cωмα) coming into being from the union of the bridegroom and the bride, the Father of all and the virgin "who came down", Sophia-Achamôth, in the great bridal chamber (71.4–13).[1] His rebirth (the one who was begotten before everything is begotten again) is within the context of his baptism at the Jordan in which he is also anointed and redeemed (70.34 – 71.2).[2] He is begotten anew as the Christ from the virgin to rectify the fall of Adam at the beginning (71.18–21). He is the Perfect Man, the Word who is Jesus' body (55.12; 57.7; 80.4–5),[3] who has existed from the very day that the world came into being (53.8–9).

1. *The Father of All.* There are two identities possible for the Father of All. First, he may be the Father, since one reads later in the text of the gifts which the Father gave the Son/Christ in the bridal chamber because he was anointed (the resurrection, the light, the cross, and the holy spirit; 74.18–22). Second, he may be the Christ, or the Saviour as H.-M. Schenke (1960, 53 nn. 10, 11), Sevrin (1974, 160), and Partrick 121 suggest. If Jesus receives the Christ as his body at his rebirth and thus becomes the Christ, just as each Gnostic does, then it may well be that, like each Gnostic, he is begotten again through the Christ and the Holy Spirit (69.4–7). Certainly in Val. Exp., the Son, the Monogenes, is called the Father of the All (23.36–37).

Although I agree this is a possibility, I have some difficulty with the argumentation, especially of Sevrin (1974, 160). He states boldly: 'On peut sans peine identifier le Père de Tout au Saveur', and supports his statement by citing in a footnote the passages given by Schenke (Adv. Haer. I, 4, 5 and Exc. Theod. 43, 2). Sevrin then admits that these passages do not speak of the Father himself but rather of being clothed in his power. Another citation from Adv. Haer. (I, 6, 4) follows, which indeed speaks further against his interpretation by describing the Saviour as begotten out of the All rather than being Father of the All. The final statement limps: 'Quoi qu'il en soit, la thématique d'union mise en oeuvre exclut le Père, le premier éon.'[4]

---

[1] Widengren cites a text from the songs of Narsai in which there is a dialogue between Jesus and John the Baptist on the occasion of Jesus' baptism at the Jordan (114–5). The images of bridal chamber and wedding feast are strongly connected with the baptism, although in this case it is Jesus who is the bridegroom. That this image in reference to Jesus had a fairly wide usage may be seen from Stegemann's citation of a Coptic magical text from the 4th/5th century: "Jesus! Heiliger! Heiliger Paraklet! Heiliger Unsichtbarer! Heiliger Bräutigam! Heiliger Pantokrator!" (21).

[2] Wilson, on the other hand, sees the passage as referring to five different stages: the divine origin, the incarnation, the anointing (Mk 14:3f or Jn 19:39f or perhaps the anointing with the Spirit at the baptism; Evans et al. include both possibilities [160]), deliverance from the grave, and the deliverance of others (1962, 1450).

[3] There is no differentiation intended between Jesus and the Christ after the event of Jesus' rebirth. The fact that the Christ is said to be Jesus' body does not imply that he is thereby an 'extra' added on to the person of Jesus. The text itself states that to put on the Christ as one would put on clothing, is to become Christ (67.26–27; 75.21–25). There are also passages in which either the two names of Jesus and Christ are used together (80.1–2) or where the same activity is postulated for both Jesus and the Christ (55.12–14; 73.23–27).

[4] Thomassen's study on the Son as the name of the Father (1993, esp. 146–9) seems to present a better basis for the argument.

2. *The Virgin 'who came down'*. I have already identified the virgin described in this passage as the Holy Spirit, Sophia-Achamôth, as do Schenke, H.-M. 1960, 53 nn. 10, 11 and Sevrin 1974, 160. Janssens (1968, 109) works backwards from Schenke's identification of the Father of All as the Christ to suggest that the virgin is Sophia-Mary Magdalene, who was the companion of Jesus (see also Sevrin 1974, 161–3). There are statements in the text that Mary Magdalene is the one whom the Lord loved more than all the disciples and he kissed her often, which implies that he loves her more because she is one who sees while the disciples are blind and in darkness (63.32 – 64.9). This easily leads to the idea of Jesus and Mary Magdalene as a syzygy.

First, the activity of kissing must be seen in relation to the kiss by which the perfect conceive (59.2–6). Mary Magdalene and Jesus conceive (the perfect?) in this way, so that Mary is not barren in comparison to Sophia who is barren and mother of the angels (63.30–32). Second, the fact that Mary is able to see means that in seeing Jesus rightly she is able to be united with him (64.4–10), because to see the Christ is to become him (61.30–31). With the equivalence of Jesus and Christ, there is a certain parallel to be inferred between the syzygies of Jesus-Mary Magdalene and the Christ-Holy Spirit.

Wilson (1962, 146), Orbe (1976, 1: 433–4), Trautmann (1981, 269),[1] and Ménard (1988, 202) assert that the virgin is the virgin Mary, understanding the writer to be attempting to unite the two concepts of birth at the Jordan through the Spirit (this is more expicitly expressed by Ménard) and birth from the virgin Mary. This requires of course, at least for Ménard, that the Spirit and Mary are equivalent, a concept also put forward by Barc (1982, 374–5) through a rather complicated line of reasoning. Proceeding from an investigation of the three names of Jesus (Jesus, Nazarene, Christ),[2] Barc proposes that this process of naming Jesus has something to do with uniting the divided Spirit, Sophia.[3] With regard to the passage concerning the three Maries (59.6–11), Barc suggests that the mother Sophia has three titles to correspond to her three divisions (the one in the Pleroma who sends the spirit; the spirit herself; the soul to whom the spirit is sent) but one name – Mary.[4]

---

[1] In her article on parentage in the Gos. Phil., Trautmann compares the parallel representations of Joseph and the Father of All as gardeners: Joseph's planting (the cross) brings death and the Father's brings life (274). Buckley finds this treatment of Joseph too negative: the plantings of each of the characters bring both death and life (1988, 4177–8).

[2] See the discussion earlier in this chapter.

[3] The division occured as follows: 1) Sophia, separated from the Son, became the sterile Mother of the angels; 2) the Demiurge breathed the soul which came from Sophia into Adam; 3) to protect this soul the mother Sophia sent her spirit into the world with the consent of her consort (Christ).

[4] This idea combined with the concept of the three names of Jesus is very close to the previous proposal from Orbe: "A las tres Marías – madre, hermana y esposa del Señor – correspondían en el Señor, probablemente, tres aspectos" (1976, 1: 254). Partrick identifies the three women as the earthly consort, Mary Magdalene, the heavenly mother, Sophia, and sister Sophia-Achamoth: "Thus the traditional historic context of Jesus' life and ministry reveals itself in this particular way as stuff of an allegory of a Gnostic cosmology" (128). Pagels interprets the three as "images of Christ's spiritual syzygos in her triple manifestation, respectively, as holy spirit, Wisdom, and as his bride the church" (1988, 202).

Si le Fils a revêtu trois noms (Jésus – Nazaréen – Christ) c'est pour rendre à l'Esprit divisé son unité symbolisée par un nom unique, celui de Marie (375).

Thus Barc sees equivalence between all three Maries, Sophia, and the Spirit. There are more than enough difficulties with the logic of this argument, but one simple difficulty at least may be indicated from elsewhere in the text. In 55.23–27 the author's statement that no woman can conceive of another woman, implies clearly that Mary and the Holy Spirit are seen as two separate characters.

Thus in Gos. Phil. we have a concept of two sets of parents, the earthly parents Mary and Joseph, and the heavenly parents, the Father of All and the Holy Spirit, which double parentage of course could serve as a basis for teaching about the two natures.

2.3 The Testimony of Truth

Testim. Truth also presents a concept of dual entry into the earthly realm for the Jesus figure. In this case the first entry by human birth involves only one human parent, and the second entry that takes place at the Jordan is not described explicitly in parenting imagery.

The text states clearly that Christ is born of a virgin and takes flesh (39.29–31),[1] his birth contrasted with that of John the Baptist. Where John is begotten by the Word through the woman, Elizabeth (in a womb worn with age; 45.12–14) (45.6–8), Christ is begotten by the Word through the virgin, Mary (45.9–11). Christ passed through (ⲁϥ̇ⲝ̇ⲱⲃⲉ) a virgin's womb (45.14–16),[2] and, after conceiving and giving birth to the Saviour (45.16–17), she was found to be a virgin again (45.17–18).

Earlier in the text, we read that the Son of Man came forth from Imperishability (30.18–19) and came to the world by the Jordan river (30.20–22). At first sight this appears to be a reference to the baptism of Jesus at the Jordan,[3] but both the Jordan and John the Baptist are perceived in negative terms: the Jordan as the power of the body and the senses of pleasure (30.30

---

[1] The character is not identified, but it could be assumed that this is Christ on the basis of 45.9–11.
[2] See Tardieu.
[3] See Orbe 1976, 1: 504.

– 31.1), its waters as the desire for sexual intercourse (31.1–3),[1] John as the archon of the womb (31.3–5).[2]

Baptism for the Son of Man is not described and, indeed, is unthinkable given the interpretation of John and the water.[3] Thus I cannot agree with Mahé who writes of the Son of Man coming into the world "en passant par le fleuve du Jourdain... implicitement comparé à une matrice dont Jean-Baptiste est 'Archonte'... tandis que les eaux symbolisent le désir sexuel" (133).[4] Perhaps Mahé means to say that Jesus passes through the Jordan in the same way as he passes through the womb of the virgin Mary, without appearing to experience any effect of that through which he passes. I would contend that the Jordan is presented too negatively to make this interpretation possible. The womb of Elizabeth is clearly unworthy in contrast to the virgin's womb, because Elizabeth has experienced sexual intercourse. If the Jordan represents the desire for sexual intercourse, then as a womb it is closer to that of Elizabeth than that of the virgin. Thus I agree with Koschorke who affirms that the Jordan does not touch the Son of Man (1978b, 93, 122).[5]

---

[1] Interestingly, the only other texts that come to mind as linking the Jordan with sexual desire or potency are the two variations of a legend reported by Drower of 'Nisbai's conception of John the Baptist by drinking water from the Jordan (1962, 100). Note the similar concept in *ATŠ* II,32 (Drower 1960) where the water from the *jardna* in the Mandaean priest's phial is said to be semen. The legend concerning John's birth is substantiated in part by *JB* 115,10–18 (Lidzbarski 1915; ref. by page and line number) and *HG* 5,2–5 (Drower 1953; ref. by page and line number).

[2] Koschorke makes the connection from John as the archon of the womb to Lk 7:28 (John as the greatest born of woman) in contrast to the Son of Man who has his origin in heaven and makes an end of carnal begetting (see the similar contrast of son of woman – son of man in the Pseudo-Clementines), and from there to the contrast between the generation of Adam and the generation of the Son of Man (1978a, 99 n.19; 1978b, 99). The naming of John as the archon of the womb suggests a connection to the baptism of the demon mentioned in Paraph. Shem 31.17–19. In the same text, 32.5–15 (Derdekeas' coming down from the heavenly region to the water, where there is conflict between himself and the whirlpools and flames of fire, followed by his rising from the water in the light of faith and the unquenchable fire) could be linked to the opposition of the Son of Man to the powers of the Jordan in Testim. Truth.

[3] Prior to the first description of Christ's birth from a virgin, within a damaged section of text, there is reference to the Holy Spirit coming down upon him, and the word "dove" appears in the following line (39.26–28). Both editions of the text make restorations which imply the baptism of Christ at the Jordan by John (Giversen and Pearson 1981b, 142–3; and Koschorke 1978a, 103), although the words "Jordan", "John", and "baptise" do not occur. It could just as easily be proposed that these verses refer in some way to the conception of Christ, although the use of the word "dove" may take us closer to the synoptic tradition concerning Jesus' baptism (Mk 1:10; Matt 3:16; Lk 3:22) or John's tradition, without baptism, regarding the coming of the Holy Spirit upon Jesus to which John the Baptist witnesses (Jn 1:32). Evans et al. give all of these references (368).

[4] Rudolph also presumes baptism for Jesus here (1975, 211).

[5] One difficulty remains in that John bears witness to the descent of Jesus (30.24–25). This could be interpreted as the descent of Jesus into the Jordan or the descent of Jesus as a heavenly figure. It is followed immediately by the reference to the power which comes down on the river. Either Jesus is a heavenly figure connected in some way with the coming of the power, or his entry into the Jordan is an entry between the waters since they have been turned back (Josh. 3; see also Ex. 14).

The entry of the Son of Man into the world is by a victory over the powers represented by John and the river, as may be seen by the turning back of the Jordan (30.22–23).[1] John sees the power which comes down on the Jordan and knows that the dominion of carnal procreation has come to an end (30.25–30). Later, within a very damaged section of text, the Son of Man is possibly described as having been manifest through the bubbling fountain of immortality (72.25–27), so that one may contrast further the Son of Man and this heavenly water or fountain with John and the waters of the Jordan.

Thus both Gos. Phil. and Testim. Truth attest to two moments or stages of entry into the world for the Jesus figure. However, the two texts are to be understood differently. Gos. Phil. presents a real human birth for the Jesus figure, whereas in Testim. Truth Jesus merely passes through the virgin Mary, by which action one assumes that nothing of her human nature really affects him. Thus for Gos. Phil., it could be said that the second stage at the Jordan represents a further empowerment for the Jesus figure, by which the earthly and heavenly aspects of the Jesus figure are merged, but this is not the case for Testim. Truth.[2]

It remains to suggest how the two stages of the Testim. Truth may be understood. It may be a simple case of two analogous descriptions of the entrance of Jesus via the Word or Power into the world: the Word comes down through the virgin Mary and Christ is born; the Power (Holy Spirit?) comes down on Christ at the Jordan and the Son of Man enters the world.[3] On the other hand, one must not overlook the text's earlier interpretation of the figure of John and Jesus. If John is the archon of the womb and Christ is the heavenly Son of Man, does the virgin Mary also have some kind of meta-human or cosmological function? The text does not go this far, and it may be a little naïve to suggest that the two descriptions of the origin of the Son of

---

[1] Note the similar reaction of the Jordan in *GR* V 192,16–23 (Lidzbarski 1925; ref. by book, page and line number) at the baptism of Mandā dHaijê by John the Baptist. (Koschorke cites the parallel in general as *GR* 190–192 [1978a, 98 n.15] ; Giversen and Pearson give *Ginza* pp. 192 and 178 [1981b, 125]). When John is unable to stand because of the swirling waters, Mandā dHaijê causes the waters to flow back and John to stand in the middle on dry ground. *GR* IV 144,29 – 145,10 also narrates a reaction of the Jordan at the heavenly baptism of Hibil-Zîwā before his descent into the world of darkness. When the Jordan sees the radiance, light and splendour of Mandā dHaijê, and the olivestaff of living water, it begins to play and leap and swirl about (145,2–4), and it must be commanded to be still so that Hibil-Zî wā can be baptised (145,5–10). Here however, baptism actually takes place and is viewed positively.

[2] *Contra* Mahé who investigates 45.12–18 and 30.18, 20–22, 26; 31.4–5 and asserts the polymorphic nature of the Son of Man: "'la Puissance'... qui descend alors sur la personne visible de Jésus, est manifestement semblable au Christ supérieur des Valentiniens" (133). I agree with Koschorke who sums up his understanding of the interchangeability of the various designations, Jesus, Saviour, Christ, Son of Man, and Power, as follows: "sie bezeichnen nicht, wie in der valentinianischen Gnosis, die unterschiedlichen Wesensstufen in dem einen Himmelwesen" (1978b, 98; see also 98 n. 13).

[3] Both Pearson (Giversen and Pearson 1981b, 105) and Koschorke (1978b, 121) see a link between the birth from a virgin and the (according to them) baptism of Christ. Koschorke finds the same meaning at the basis of both actions: "Jesus blieb der Sphäre 'fleischlicher Zeugung' (30,30) fern. Es ist allein dieser – einheitsstiftende – 'pneumatische' (50,1f) Sinn, der für TestVer zählt..." (1978b, 92; see also 99).

Man and Christ respectively can be taken on the same level, allowing for simple comparison.

Conclusion

In this chapter the origin of the Jesus figure has been the focus, both in its heavenly and earthly phases, and the way in which he moves into the world. Entrance into the world takes place in a variety of ways, including changing shape and taking on flesh. It is now necessary to investigate briefly the kind of world to which he comes.

III

The World to which Jesus Comes

In order to understand the world to which Jesus comes, it is necessary to ask how the world is viewed in the various texts and how the people who inhabit it are to be understood as the beings with whom the Jesus figure will be or has been in contact. Specific references to the world as regards geographical landmarks and the specific setting of the activity of the Jesus figure will be discussed in conjunction with the general activity of the Jesus figure within the earthly realm in Chapter VI.

1. Perspectives on the World

Although in general one can say that the world is viewed negatively in the texts, this statement must be further qualified. The world may be viewed negatively because it is inherently evil, or because it has been imperfectly (perishably) created, or because it is where the evil powers have their domain of influence, or because for the sake of salvation it must be renounced, and so on, or it may be a combination of any of these. In many texts there is no straightforward statement concerning the inherent evil nature of the world.

One of the most frequent concepts is of the world as inherently evil by virtue of its creation by the Demiurge rather than by the highest God. For 2 Apoc. Jas., the earthly perishable world is the place of sojourn (63.1–2, 10–11), the creation of the Demiurge (58.2–6), to be seen over against the Light (62.21–24). In Gos. Phil., the world is made by the Demiurge who is perishable. It is essentially a mistake, since the Demiurge wanted to create it as imperishable, but it could not be, since he himself was not imperishable (75.2–11). Although this is a negative view of the world, in this text the world is not the most evil place. In the three-fold division – the world, the middle and the resurrection – it is the middle which is the really evil place for it is death (66.7–23).

The world is also viewed negatively because of the activity of negative powers within it. In 1 Apoc. Jas., Jerusalem is the place of persecution, not only for Jesus but also for James, because it is the dwelling place of a great number of archons (25.18–19). In Treat. Seth, the entire history of the Jews has been influenced by the Hebdomad, Yaldaboath, who controls them. This is summarised in the text in a kind of "counter-litany" (Gibbons 1973, 251) of counterfeits who think they are stronger than the Christ and his brothers/the fellow members of his race, although indeed none of them know the Christ and his kindred (62.27 – 64.1; see also the further passage 64.18 – 65.1). For Dial. Sav., the world is also a place of wickedness (132.7–9), but this would not be the case if there had been one of love or goodness among the archons (142.6–9).

The evil of the world is also apparent in its ignorance, including ignorance of the Christ (Treat. Seth 64.13–14). Those who inhabit the world and belong to it are ignorant, whether that be the archons or human beings (Thom. Cont. 138.19–21).

Despite the negative categories used, some texts speak of the origin of the world in a more positive way. Thus in Treat. Res., we learn that this world was formed from a little piece which broke off from the Pleroma (46.35–38). Similarly, in Dial. Sav., the initial establishment of the cosmos is viewed positively, having been established by the Father for himself (129.20–21; 144.9–10) and full of good things by his command (130.11–22). There are also aspects which link both regions: there are powers above and below to be overcome (text damaged; 129.10–11; 131.6–7); what supports the earth is that which supports the heaven (133.3–4). There is also a positive way of viewing earthly existence within the world: "If one does not stand in the darkness, he will not be able to see the light" (133.23 – 134.1).

Gos. Thom. too seems to offer some positive statements about the presence of Jesus in the physical world, at least in terms of the imagery used, despite a generally negative view throughout the rest of the text. Log. 77 speaks of Jesus as present in the split wood and under the stone; Log. 113 describes the kingdom of the Father as spread out upon the earth (ⲕⲁⲍ).[1]

Although it has a positive view of the beginning of the world, Dial. Sav. sets up a clear dualism between heaven and earth. Heaven is above and the earth is below (131.13–15). Seen from the edge of heaven and earth, heaven is an exceedingly high place and the earth is the abyss below (135.4–7), and in the latter is fire and something fearful (135.10–11). Certainly one of the strongest ways of referring to the world as negative or deficient is to compare it with the region above: the world is the place of deficiency, envy and strife, the region above is the place of unity and perfection (Gos. Truth 24.20–26); it is perishable as opposed to what is immortal from the region above (Soph. Jes. Chr. 106.9–14; see also 97.24 – 98.9); it is a visible world

---

[1] "Erstaunlicheweise ist die Welt, die das ThEv andeutet, eine Wohlstandswelt, die der unseren nicht so fremd ist. Aber wenn wir über diese Eigenart des ThEv weiter nachdenken, wird uns deutlich, daß sie eigentlich doch nicht erstaunlich ist. Eine Wohlstandswelt hält den Menschen besonders fest in ihrem Griff, fester als eine Welt der Armut und bitterer Not" (Haenchen 1973, 208).

and people in it are visible, while the Pleroma is invisible and Gnostics must have faith in the invisible things that belong to it (Thom. Cont. 138.27–34; Soph. Jes. Chr. 98.13–20).

Within the understanding of the aspect of visibility, one often finds the concept of the world as illusory. In Treat. Res., this world (= this place or this element [49.33]) which can be seen is illusory (48.13–15). It is the sensible world as opposed to the intelligible world (46.35 – 47.1) or the Aeon (47.5–6), marked by corruptibility and change as opposed to incorruptibility (resurrection) and standing firm (48.20–33). Thus the visibility of the world is linked to its perishability and its inevitable fall into corruption (Thom. Cont. 140.19–20; 141.14–15).

In these passages from Thom. Cont., there is powerful imagery of corpses and tombs for the world, just as in Gos. Thom. Log. 56; 80. Even more, it is possible that some texts present the world itself as the equivalent of the Underworld or the world of death (see the discussion in Chapter VIII). Tri. Trac. 118.17–19 states that the triple division of humankind into pneumatic, psychic, and hylic conforms to the triple disposition of the Logos from whom they come. This reinforces the idea that the cosmos and the powers which inhabit it represent really a macrocosm of the human being – it is cosmology based on anthropology. The descent into Hades is a descent into the last level of the material aspect of the human person or the human world. (I deal with this question for Teach. Silv. and Testim. Truth in Chapter VIII.).

Such a concept is supported clearly by Ap. John 30.32 – 31.25 where the imagery associated with humans is totally concerned with the powers of heaven and the powers of the world of darkness (= the prison which is the body). Poirier also finds the concept in Trim. Prot. 36.4, where Protennoia declares that she descended into the middle of Hades. Poirier concludes that her descent is really into this world in which the Gnostics live (202–3). "Pour l'auteur de la PrôTri, c'est ce monde qui est l'Enfer, le dur Tartare où sont enfermé ceux que la Prôtennoia reconnait comme ses 'membres' et sa 'part' et qu'elle vient délivrer. Dès lors, il était tout indiqué de décrire ce lieu dans les termes mêmes qui étaient couramment utilisés pour peindre le séjour de la Mort" (203). Thus in Ap. Jas. 13.20–25, is the curse which Jesus has placed himself under "for your sakes", the condition of human existence, as F.E. Williams suggests (1985b, 32), or is it the curse of death?

Because of all these aspects, the world must be renounced, whether that is seen in terms of renouncing what it has to offer, such as riches or possessions (e.g. Gos. Thom. Log. 110), or whether it is seen in terms of renouncing the body (e.g. Gos. Thom. Log. 22, 37, 79, 114), which is a microcosm of the prison of the world. The body can be so aligned with the world in sexual activity and procreation that one turns away from the Light and is not able to pass by the archons into the heavenly region (Testim. Truth 30.2–18). One is only able to struggle against the passions (38.29 – 39.1) if one has known Imperishability (31.13 15), and this knowledge comes only by the renunciation of the world and the subduing of desires within oneself (41.4–13; see also 42.23 – 45.6). The whole process of salvation rests on the two foundations of knowledge (of oneself and of Imperishability) and renunciation (of the world and the Law which rules there) (see also Gos. Thom. Log. 111).

2. Perspectives on Human Beings

2.1 Types of the Individual Human Being

2.1.1 Three-Part Description: Spirit, Soul, Body

Generally speaking, the texts have a basic view of the human person as a combination of three facets – spirit, soul, and body (see, e.g., Treat. Res. 45.39 – 46.2).[1] The spirit is the highest function and that aspect of the human being which has its origin in the heavenly region or which links it with the Pleroma. The body is basically a prison which keeps the soul and spirit confined in the earthly context.

The soul seems to be viewed mostly as caught somehow between the spirit and the body, both of which have an influence for good or evil upon the soul: "For it is the spirit that raises the soul, but the body that kills it..." (Ap. Jas. 12.5–7). However, the soul is essentially good, a precious thing, according to Gos. Phil., which came to be in a contemptible body (56.25–26). It is like a pearl cast into mud, which always has value in the eyes of its owner no matter how its circumstances seem (62.17–19, 21–23).[2]

The division of three aspects is not always neatly outlined in the texts. Thus in Testim. Truth, one finds questions about the nature of the soul and the spirit (42.1–2), a reference to the corruptible flesh (42.5–7), the term NOYC (in the damaged text in 41.17), and a contrast between ears of the body and ears of the heart (29.7–9).

---

[1] See esp. Strutwolf's detailed study on the three-nature teaching in Valentinian Gnosticism (104–54).

[2] Layton and Isenberg are the only ones to read the statement concerning the pearl in the mud in the positive: "it becomes greatly despised" (164). The negative makes more sense, especially when one considers the parallel statement "nor if it is anointed with balsam oil will it become more precious" (62.20–21).

2.1.2 Three-Part Description: Mind, Soul, Body

In this second section, it seems clear that mind and spirit are interchangeable in their concept. One finds this three-part description in Dial. Sav. and Teach. Silv. In Dial. Sav., the mind is not a prisoner while the soul is, which must be saved from the "blind limbs" (NIKW[λ]ON ṄBλλє) (121.23–24). Once again the soul is trapped between mind and body: while the body causes weeping on account of its works which remain, on the other hand the mind laughs (126.22–23, text damaged).

Teach. Silv. has a rather more complicated structure, describing the human being as a mixture of body, soul and mind,[1] each of which corresponds to a race of humankind (92.15–33; see the section, "Types of human beings...", below). The process of mixing means falling from virtue into inferiority (92.33 – 93.3). A divine soul in the earthly context shares both in God and in the flesh (93.24–31; 108.25–27) so that a person lives continually in a situation of contention (reason vs animal life/death [107.17–25; 108.8–16]), while being exhorted to live according to the mind and not the flesh (93.3–5).[2] What the person needs is strength of mind and soul by which he can struggle against passions and wickedness and pride and jealousy and ignorance and so on, which are death and fire leading to an animal's life (84.16–26; 89.12–14; 93.5–7; 104.31 – 106.1).

2.1.3 Two-Part Description: Soul, Body

Both Ep. Pet. Phil. and Gos. Thom. speak of the flesh or body and the soul. However, Ep. Pet. Phil. may also imply possession of a spirit where the apostles/community are exhorted to strip off what is corrupt (= the body) (137.6–9), and to gird themselves with the power of the Father (= the Spirit) (137.26–27). Gos. Thom. uses the terms within the formula of woe in Log. 112: Woe to the flesh that depends on the soul; woe to the soul that depends on the flesh.

Whether human beings are described as having two or three aspects, what remains constant is the negative status of the body or flesh. We will investigate this aspect in more detail below.

---

[1] The heart is also mentioned briefly: God formed the soul for the human heart (92.27–29); the malicious man harms his own heart (97.5–6).

[2] Although bodily existence represents a constant conflict or tension between mind and animal life, the text gives the impression that the mind which shares in the bodily existence is not in such an oppressive state of imprisonment as described in some of the other texts. The text relates that in its actual being the mind is in the body, but in its thought it is not in any place because it contemplates every place (99.22–28; cf. the similarities with the teaching about the being of God; 99.30 – 100.13; 100.31 – 101.10).

2.2 Types of Human Beings within the Total Group of Humankind

2.2.1 Three Types

Tri. Trac. presents a good outline of the division of humankind into three types (ΟΥϹΙΑ): the spiritual (†ΠΝΕΥΜΑΤΙΚΗ) (118.16), who are like light from light and spirit from spirit (118.28–32); the psychic (†ΨΥΧ‹ΙΚ›Η) (118.16), who are like light from a fire (118.38–39); and the material (†ϨΥΛΙΚΗ) (118.17), who are dark and shun the shining of the light because they are destroyed by it (118.17–19).

As mentioned above, Teach. Silv. describes three races of humankind to correspond to three aspects of the human being. The earthly race are those of the body and from earthly substance (matter); the formed race are those of the soul and are the thought of the divine; the created race are those of the mind who are the image of God (92.15–33). Movement from one race to another was a result of falling: the mind which is male (see also 102.15–16) fell into a male-female entity which, having cast out the mind, became female (i.e. became psychic [the soul is the wife of the mind, 92.30–31]). When this element was cast out, the result was something not human, something of a fleshly, animal nature (93.7–21). I shall deal with this aspect further in Chapter IX.

2.2.2 Two Types

It is not common to find a deviation from the concept of a three-fold division of humankind. In Val. Exp. 35.30–37, Jesus is described as separating the passions surrounding the seeds of Sophia and then allocating the better ones to the spiritual and the worse ones to the carnal, and Thomassen (1989b, 233) rightly comments on the surprising lack of a psychic category in the division.[1]

Both Gos. Phil. and Interp. Know. describe two basic types of human beings, with the common theme that the Gnostic is contrasted with those given up to animal nature. For Gos. Phil. there are animals, slaves and defiled women on the one hand, and on the other, free men and virgins. Animals belong to what is below or outside; human beings, and spirit, and logos, and light belong to what is above or within (78.32 – 79.13). Interp. Know. states that the one who is lost (the one who is the seed of the female, 11.28–30), is related to the crafty one ([Ε]ΠΙΒΟΥΛΟϹ) and is from the beasts (11.25–26).

---

[1] Pagels and Turner suggest that there are psychic seeds apart from those created from Sophia's passions, which are brought by the Saviour to the place of the creation, citing 37.28–31, 36–38 (1990b, 165), yet the texts cited have no relation to such a situation. In fact the two-fold division is further emphasised in the first passage and subsequently in 38.27–33. The authors are apparently influenced in their interpretation by what is described in *Exc. Theod.* rather than this text itself.

2.3 The Body/Flesh

This category deserves further consideration, since it will be important for understanding the earthly "existence" of the Jesus figure in the following chapter. Here it will only be possible to give some summary statements with examples from the texts. Some examples have already been given in the section above on the types of human beings. There is a great deal of description about the human body or flesh in the texts and it could easily be a study in itself.

As already noted there is an opposition between spirit and body. This opposition is played out further in texts which use the imagery of death and life/resurrection for the effects of these elements within earthly human existence. Gos. Phil. takes the concept further and speaks of two types of flesh, one being carnal flesh and the other the flesh of Jesus, which the pneumatic experiences as the spirit and the light which are a ⲗⲟⲅⲟⲥ in the flesh (= the flesh of Jesus which is the ⲗⲟⲅⲟⲥ). It is necessary to rise in this flesh (i.e. the flesh of Jesus), since everything exists in it (57.9–19). It is the perfect man or living man which the person puts on at baptism (75.21–25; see also 76.22–29), whereby after chrismation one is no longer a Christian but a Christ (67.26–27).[1] I look further at the clothing metaphor applied to flesh below.

The link between the flesh and death is outlined in a number of interrelated images. First there is the strong description of the body as a grave of the archons (Soph. Jes. Chr. 119.1–2).[2] The indwelling of the archons of course means that the body is a place of corruption and perishability (e.g. Interp. Know. 6.30–33; Treat. Res. 47.18–19; 2 Apoc. Jas. 63.10–11; Ep. Pet. Phil. 137.6–9; Great Pow. 47.6–7). Teach. Silv. speaks of the death experienced by those in the flesh who lead an animal life. Such a life results from passions and wickedness and pride and jealousy and ignorance and so on, which are death and fire (84.16–26; 89.12–14; 93.5–7; 104.31 – 106.1) and this type of life is in opposition to reason (107.17–25; 108.8–16). Believers are exhorted to raise their dead (i.e. those under the influence of animal life/the body), and give them life (106.17–20).

The body or the flesh is also viewed as a prison or bonds which must be broken or cast off (see, e.g., 1 Apoc. Jas. 27.5–6; and Interp. Know. 6.33–34). Interp. Know. describes believers as bound in nets of flesh by the Demiurge (6.28–29). In Thom. Cont., the elect are exhorted to watch and pray so

---

[1] Wilson certainly understands Gos. Phil. to refer not to the physical rising in the flesh but rather to rising in the flesh of Jesus. However he finds problems with the statement concerning the rising "in this flesh, in which everything exists" (1962, 87–9). However, that this is not the flesh of the human being, is clear from 56.13–15 which concerns Christ who has everything in himself, whether man, or angel, or mystery, and the Father.

[2] Till explains the graves of the archons as the human body "in dem durch die Wirkung der irdischen Gewalten ('Räuber') der Tropfen aus dem Lichtreich begraben ist" (1955, 249).

that they do not come to be in the flesh, but rather come forth from the bondage of the bitterness of this life, the sufferings and passions of the body (145.8–16). Being in the body is a source of suffering and death (Ap. Jas. 5.6 – 6.18; 1 Apoc. Jas. 32.19–21), and distress (Dial. Sav. 126.22–23, text damaged). Believers must disregard the flesh (Ap. Jas. 5.6 – 6.18). They must not fear the flesh (which leads to its mastery) nor love it (which leads to being swallowed by it and paralysed) (Gos. Phil. 66.4–6). The right thing to do is to destroy it (Gos. Phil. 82.26–30).

Being in the body/flesh is variously described as a state of ignorance or blindness ("blind limbs", Dial. Sav. 121.23–24; the bond of the flesh = blind thought, 1 Apoc. Jas. 27.1–4) or being in darkness. In Testim. Truth, engaging in the sexual activity of the flesh means turning away from the Light (30.2–18), and for Interp. Know., serving the powers results in a state of ignorance of the true Father, and of being in such a state of darkness that the person calls many "father" (9.35–37). In Great Pow., those who know the speaker (the Great Power?) will enter into immeasurable light where there is no one of the flesh nor the wantonness of the fire to seize them (46.6–12; see also 47.13–14). In Thom. Cont. we read that the bitter fire of the passions and lust also binds and blinds people (139.32–42; 140.19–37) and they do not love the light (= Jesus; 139.25–31). Such people will perish in the concern for this life and the scorching of the fire (141.12–14). Finally being in the flesh is also clearly stated to be sinful (2 Apoc. Jas. 63.10–11; and Interp. Know. 21.33–34).

These descriptions have implications for human salvation. Ap. Jas. states that none of those who have worn/carried the flesh will be saved (12. 12–13). Likewise in Dial. Sav., the Lord tells Matthew that he cannot see the place of life as long as he is wearing/carrying the flesh (132.11–12), but he will attain rest when he lays down these burdens (141.3–6). For Thom. Cont., those who love the fire and are servants of death and rush to the works of corruption are deprived of the kingdom (141.29–31). Melch. states that even in this world anyone in the flesh does not qualify as a recipient of the revelation (27.3–5).

Much of the writing about body/flesh makes use of the imagery of clothing and stripping. The body/flesh is often referred to as a garment (e.g. "the garment of condemnation"; Interp. Know. 11.27–28), or as something which must be stripped off (Ep. Pet. Phil. 137.6–9). One of the most extensive uses of the imagery is found in Gos. Phil. which combines the imagery of clothing and nakedness with the discussion of salvation. Those who wear the flesh which is on them are naked, and this human flesh and blood will not inherit the kingdom (56.26 – 57.1), since no one can go into the king naked (58.15–

16).[1] Thus one must strip off human flesh before entering the kingdom (66.18–20). What will inherit the kingdom is what belongs to Jesus and his blood, since the flesh and blood of Jesus (= the Word and the Holy Spirit) are food and drink and clothing for those who have received them (57.1–3). Thus one needs to be clothed in the true flesh (Christ's flesh) in order to enter the kingdom.[2]

The link between the flesh/body and sexuality is a major theme in a number of works. The problem with sexuality appears to focus on the fact that birth into the world is a birth into death and corruption. One who has birth will perish, one who has a beginning has an end, and one who has a human form is the creation of another and is thus under the rule of another (Soph. Jes. Chr. 94.17–24; BG 84.15–17). This point is discussed further in the section on femaleness below, but a few passages will serve here to make the position clear. Thus Soph. Jes. Chr. states that sexual activity ("unclean rubbing"), which results from the fearful fire in the fleshly part of human beings, is the means by which the Gnostic is entrapped in forgetfulness by the archons (108.10–15; see also Thom. Cont. [passim]). The perfect ones who receive the revelation of the Father of the All (95.20), are not begotten in this usual way ("by the sowing of the unclean rubbing") but rather by the First Who Was Sent (93.17–24).

In Testim. Truth, the victory of the Son of Man over the carnality of the Jordan and John indicates clearly from the beginning the anti-flesh, anti-sexuality tenor of the text (30.20 – 31.5). The defilement of the Law, which is the opposite of the undefiled Truth/the Light (29.22–24, 26 – 30.1), is seen in terms of the command to marry and to multiply (30.2–18). The document condemns the sexual practices of certain groups, including the act of begetting children (58.2–4), and intercourse while breast-feeding (67.30–31). Sexual activity and the love of Mammon go together, since the father of Mammon is also the father of sexual intercourse (68.6–8; cf. the father of the flesh as the Demiurge in Great Pow. 38.19–20, 24). The one who renounces both of these belongs to the generation of the Son of Man, as opposed to the generation of Adam (68.8–11). Gnostics are conceived or reborn by the Word (40.2–4), who assists in separating them from the error of the angels (41.2–4).

This idea of spiritual begetting is echoed in Teach. Silv., which asserts that the illumination of the mind takes place inside the bridal chamber which is the opposite of human begetting in the flesh (94.25–28). Similarly, in Great

---

[1] There is a concern with nakedness in the text in general, not only for human beings but for everything. Thus it must be asserted that Truth did not come into the world naked but in types (ⲚⲦⲨⲠⲞⳞ) and images (Ⲛ̅ⲈⲓⲔⲰⲚ) (67.9–11).

[2] This is similar to Dial. Sav. 143.11–15: one receives the garment when one departs from the decay of the flesh.

Pow., the community describes itself as acting against its fleshly birth,[1] in the creation of the archons, which gives law (48 9–11; see also 42.5–6). They are exhorted to cease from evil lusts and desires (40.5–7).

The theme of body/flesh and sexuality finds its most intense discussion in Thom. Cont. The text holds all things to do with the body and the world, sexuality and the propagation of human life, as totally negative. However, there is no explanation offered as to why the world is evil, and lust and sexual intercourse are evil except that humans involved in the world and in sexual activity are like the beasts and in this way lose their love for the Light. The most consistent theme of the text concerns the fire of the passions which burns in the bodies of those who are not perfect or not striving for the height of perfection. The fire of human lust is linked with the idea of the visible world (= corrupt; 141,14–15) and visible spirits which are in opposition to the invisible pleroma and the truth (138.27–34; 140.1–5, 19–20). Visible bodies, that is human bodies, vessels of flesh (141.6–7), which result from intercourse like the beasts (139.8–11), survive by eating creatures like themselves and so they change. What changes decays and perishes and has no hope of life since such bodies are bestial (139.2–6).

The importance of this theme for this text can be judged from the number of times it appears in the woes uttered by Jesus in the final section of the text. Woes are called down upon:

- those who hope in the flesh (= the prison that will perish), and the world, and who make this life their god (143.10–15);
- those within whom the insatiable fire burns (143.15–16);
- those within the grip of the burning within them (143.18–21);
- those drunk with fire, deranged by the burning (143.21 – 144.2);
- those who live in intimacy with womankind and are polluted by intercourse with them (144.8–10);
- those in the grip of the powers of the body (144.10–12);
- those who beguile their limbs with fire (144.14–19).

2.4 Femaleness[2]

The essential difference which we have noted above between body/flesh and mind/spirit is also expressed within the texts by the use of gender imagery.

---

[1] I have followed Cherix's translation here, although both Fischer's and Wisse's translation of ⲕⲁⲧⲁ as "gemäß"/"according to" is also possible, as he notes (30). The former makes more sense in the context.

[2] See the study of Wisse 1988b.

Maleness and femaleness are equated, for the most part, with mind and body respectively.[1]

The major difficulty with the human body for these texts is that it reproduces itself and thus continues the entrapment of human beings in the world of matter. Because it is the female body which gives birth, femaleness at least under this aspect comes to be used as a shorthand for all that bodiliness entails. Thus, in Dial. Sav., the Lord gives the instruction, "Pray in the place where there is no woman", which Matthew interprets to mean "Destroy the works of femaleness" (= the work of giving birth), not because there are other ways of giving birth but in order that women will cease giving birth (144.15–21; see also 140.12–14: "Whatever is born of truth does not die; whatever is born of woman dies").

The condemnation of femaleness should be understood primarily in terms of the relation of femaleness to the production of matter in human birth, rather than as a condemnation of all female persons. Treat. Seth, which condemns femaleness, nevertheless can name the heavenly triad as Father, *Mother* and Christ, and describe eternal life in fatherhood, *motherhood and rational sisterhood* and wisdom (66.28–32). This triad is changed soon after in the text to fatherhood, motherhood and rational brotherhood and wisdom (67.2–5).[2]

The opposite of femaleness is maleness, which is used as an image for the mind. The struggle of the Gnostic towards salvation against the powers and the passions which come from them is illustrated in a long reflection in Testim. Truth 42.23 – 45.6, where there is an exhortation to become a disciple of one's mind which is male (see also Teach. Silv. 93.5–13; 102.15–16; see the Light in Soph. Jes. Chr. which is also masculine, 107.25 – 108.5). The work of the Saviour Revealer is presented in Soph. Jes. Chr. as the completion of "the masculine multitude" in this earthly realm through his teaching (118.6–7).

From all this we can sum up that, first, the connection between femaleness and bodiliness is not intended to be taken as more than analogous, and one should not go into absurd arguments about the changing of sex to ensure salvation. It is simply maleness as spirit/mind, the rational element in the human being, which is the prerequisite for salvation, and one does this by a movement of the female element of human beings to the male element (1 Apoc. Jas. 41.16–19). As Zost. 131.5–8 puts it, "Flee from the madness and the

---

[1] The only exception I have found to this is in Teach. Silv. 93.7–21 which certainly equates the mind with maleness, but equates the soul with femaleness (see also 92.30–31) rather than the body which is an abortion from the female.

[2] Bethge is less certain: "Ob das hier im Sinne von EvThom (NHC II,2) Logion 114 gemeint ist bzw. mit einer negativen Sicht der Frauen überhaupt zusammenhängt oder nur im Zusammenhang mit dem folgenden Begriff 'gebären' gesagt ist, soll hier offenbleiben" (1979, 167 n.12).

bondage of femaleness, and choose for yourselves the salvation of maleness."
Thus when in Gos. Thom. 114, Jesus suggests he will make Mary male, or
that females should make themselves male in order to become living spirits
and so enter the kingdom, we are not dealing with any concept of changing
sex, but the acquisition of rationality/mind or spirit.[1] In fact the idea in Gos.
Thom. seems to be basically asexual, if one takes the rest of the text into account with its emphasis on becoming a child so as to enter the kingdom (Log.
4, 22, 46, 50). See further discussion in Chapter IX.

The simple analogy of femaleness for human bodiliness is taken a step further when, for example, Treat. Seth describes femaleness as giving birth to
all that the body or matter represents, that is, to evil and its kin (jealousy,
division, anger, wrath, fear, a divided heart, and empty non-existent desire).
These are exactly the opposite of the ideals of unity and friendship (65.24–
31). In the extreme case of Thom. Cont., femaleness and the female body are
equated literally, and the female body is presented as essentially evil, rather
than bodiliness itself (both male and female) as evil. Thom. Cont., which focuses on the evil of sexuality and the fire of the passions, presents women
only in negative terms as those who are the partners in polluting intercourse
(144.8–10), so that I would doubt whether women are included at all among
those addressed in that text by the Saviour.

Although most texts are not as extreme as Thom. Cont., there is certainly a
common view of femaleness as constituting something weak or defective. On
a cosmic level, Tri. Trac. refers to the illness of femaleness which belongs to
the emanations of the Logos before his conversion, who are only likenesses
or shadows of what is in the Pleroma (94.16–20). Within the earthly setting,
in 1 Apoc. Jas., James questions the Lord about the seven women disciples,
commenting "And behold, all women bless you" (38.18–20), adding that he is
amazed how such powerless vessels have become strong by a perception
which is in them (38.20–23). In a rather backhanded way, it is still an unusu-
ally positive statement. In this same text, the Lord explains that he existed
before femaleness, which constitutes an assurance of its place below him in
the order of things (24.26–31).[2]

The defectiveness of femaleness is particularly stressed when a female
character acts without a male partner. Thus in Soph. Jes. Chr. BG 118.15–
16; 114.13–18, Achamoth's (= the female's) productions are said to be both
alien and not alien: alien because she produced them without having inter-

---

[1] *Contra* Meyer who designates one of the five themes of the text as the sexual transformation of Mary (1985, 561–7). I also do not think there is a concern here with the heavenly angelic double. Rudolph writes that the saying may have its basis in the fact that for the heavenly *Urbild* which is frequently female, the returning *Abbild* must be naturally male, for the
union of the two to be accomplished (1979, 25). Others disagree that the angelic double, at
least in Valentinianism, is male (see, e.g., Williams, M. 18).

[2] More specifically it can be inferred that the Lord is prior to the creation of Sophia's offspring Achamoth who is "the female" (34.4; female from a female 35.12–13).

course with the Pre-existent One (see also 1 Apoc. Jas. 34.12–15), not alien because she is from the Pre-existent One (34.4–8).

Conclusion

The major focus of the investigation in this chapter has been the differentiation of humankind usually into three types (pneumatic, psychic and hylic). This information helps in understanding the form in which Jesus makes contact with humans, which will be the subject of the following chapter. Because he comes primarily to the world to act as revealer for the penumatics, his essential form for this relationship must be spiritual, although he must don flesh in order to enter the world governed by the archons.

IV

Being and Nature of Jesus

In this chapter I investigate the manner of Jesus' contact with the earth; that is, in what form he has managed to communicate within this context. If the earthly context is really nothing more than the stage-work for cosmic struggle, even for human beings, then there is no necessity to become involved apart from donning a costume. To the extent that the earthly context is taken seriously, so much the more must Jesus immerse himself in this world.

There is, therefore, a wide range of possibilities for the way in which his being will adapt as he moves into contact with the world: he may take on a form that enables human contact but does not change his essentially heavenly being; he may take on a human form that complements his heavenly being (two natures); he may actually take on a form that necessitates abandoning some (but not all) aspects of his heavenly being so that he is more able to "be" a human being or at least a pneumatic human being.

There are a number of concepts related to the question of the form chosen. The more human-like the form that is chosen, the more he immerses himself in the world; the more immersed in the world, the more he will be in danger from the powers there, and will need to struggle against them in order to free himself and to free others. He will also be in danger from the flesh itself, the more he takes it on as a real form. Some of these ideas will be dealt with when I consider how Jesus closes his contact with the earthly context in Chapter VIII.

I would suggest that it should be possible to contruct a sort of three-dimensional graph with three major axes, along which the texts in the corpus could be plotted in the following way: the more texts affirm the earthly contact of the Jesus figure, the more physical his flesh should be, and the more necessary becomes a split into two natures of heavenly and earthly existing side by side; the more illusory the earthly context which the Jesus figure contacts (= the more cosmic the activity within an earthly setting), the less his need for real flesh, and the less necessity there is for a division of his being into two natures. This could be shown, for example, by a comparison of Tri. Trac. (cosmic setting, spiritual flesh, no division of person) and Treat. Res. (earthly setting, real flesh, division of person into Son of God and Son of Man).

In this chapter, a number of possibilities are considered for the being of the earthly Jesus, with one of the major categories for discussion being whether Jesus takes on flesh or not, along with what other comments the texts might make regarding his person in general. We will also consider at what stage in relation to entry or closure the Jesus figure might be. Initially we will work "downwards", beginning with the earthly Jesus figure understood in a spiritual sense, moving to a more physical Jesus. I will concentrate on that aspect of Jesus which is the focus of the texts, although I must point out that some texts describe a number of different stages of the Jesus figure. One should be careful then to leave a little flexibility when dealing with texts allocated to any of the particular sections below.

Not every presentation of the being and nature of Jesus in these documents is positive. A number of documents view some aspect of the Jesus figure in a negative light, either an aspect that is concurrently associated with the heavenly Jesus (e.g. Apoc. Pet.), or an aspect of Jesus that is manifested in an earlier stage of contact with the earthly region (Ap. Jas.). It is not only that Nag Hammadi texts in general might pay no heed to a real human historical character of Jesus; some in fact present such an aspect and treat it in a negative way in contrast to the heavenly or more spiritual Jesus. This is so in only a minority of cases, but one should still be aware of the phenomenon.

1. The Earthly Jesus as Primarily a Spiritual Heavenly Being

In the discussion subsequent to the paper in Robinson, J.M. 1981, Colpe states: "Wherever one finds the phrase, *ho logos sarks egeneto*, one is certainly not dealing with a Gnostic text!" (663).[1] Yet great care is required. What these texts mean by "flesh" is not always clear, especially with their propensity for using words which can be interpreted in at least two ways. For the most part, the Jesus who is a spiritual being hides his spiritual "flesh" under shapes, likenesses or a human body. With these texts, the unity of Jesus' heavenly existence is preserved within the earthly context. There is no diminishment of his spiritual self by his coming to the earthly context and no progression towards a real complementarity of natures where a multiplicity of forms is attested in his human being.

1.1 The Gospel of Philip

In Gos. Phil. Jesus has flesh and blood, but this does not mean that he is human, although in Chapter II I discuss how this gospel presents his human birth from Mary and Joseph. Perhaps Jesus prior to his becoming the Christ at the Jordan is a human being (there is no real discussion of this in the text), but his transformation there leaves no doubt that thereafter he is a spiritual being. The gospel tells us that his flesh is the Logos (57.6) and his blood is the Holy Spirit (57.6–7).[2]

---

[1] Partrick follows a similar line of thought, especially in his evaluation of the non-docetic nature of many of the texts in which Jesus is said to have flesh.

[2] This is a very different interpretation of eucharistic tradition than that found in the New Testament, and must be understood in conjunction with the later statement in 63.21: "The eucharist is Jesus".

Because Jesus is a spiritual being, he cannot be seen by other beings (including the angels) outside of his usual heavenly context. Consequently his real flesh (the Logos) must hide itself (58.2–3) if he is to be seen by other beings. Thus the text tells us that Jesus took them all by stealth (ⲚⲀ̅ⲒⲞⲨⲈ) for he did not appear as he was but in the way that he would be able to be seen (57.28–32). To the great he appeared as great, to the small as small, to angels as an angel, to men as a man (ⲌⲰⲤ ⲢⲰⲘⲈ) (57.33 – 58.2).[1] This could be related to the earlier statement that Christ has everything in himself, whether man, or angel, or mystery, and the Father (56.13–15). In other words, he has within himself the capacity to take on a variety of likenesses in order to make contact or to communicate with other beings, including human beings in the earthly context, and perhaps even including the Father in the heavenly region.[2]

The theme of hiddenness and deception in this gospel will be discussed further in Chapter IX. It is also related to the activities of begetting and creating which I discuss in relation to the Jesus figure in Chapter VI.

1.2 The Gospel of the Egyptians

In Gos. Eg. also, the flesh or body of the earthly Jesus is associated with the Logos. As has already been noted in Chapter 2, Seth undergoes baptism in a Logos-begotten body (III)/has baptism of the body, through [the] Logos-begotten one (IV), which he prepared in a mystery for himself through the virgin (III 63.11–13/IV 74.25–29). This baptism is established through Jesus, "he whom the great Seth has put on" (III 64.2–3/IV 75.16–17). Jesus is further described as holy (IV only), incorruptible, Logos-begotten (III)/ begotten by a living Logos (IV), the living one (III only) (III 63.24 – 64.3/IV 75.13–24). Thus, although Jesus is the means by which Seth moves from the heavenly to the earthly region, he cannot be considered to have a true human existence.

1.3 The Testimony of Truth

I have already discussed Testim. Truth in some detail in Chapter II. In this text too, Jesus' bodily conception is associated with the Logos and with the virgin. It remains here to reiterate that the description of Jesus' passing through the virgin, taken together with his victory over the carnal powers of the Jordan and John, indicate that his heavenly being is not at all affected by his coming into the earthly context. Moreover, he is a stranger to defilement (30.20) and is sinless (32.27 – 33.2).

---

[1] The reversal of this process is found in 58.5–10 where Jesus makes the disciples great so that they can see him in his greatness.

[2] The Lord is the outer in relation to the Father who is in secret or the inner (67.36 – 68.17).

1.4 Trimorphic Protennoia

Trim. Prot. appears to follow a similar line of thought to Gos. Phil. The text deals with the descent of Protennoia as the Logos or Christ into the region below, the world of mortals (47.31–32), for the purpose of self-revelation within "their tents" (47.13–15). Helderman concludes that the latter phrase is intended as a deliberate re-interpretation of Jn 1:14, in that the revealer Protennoia "eben nicht selber unter/mit den Menschen arteigen wohnt, son-dern nur ihre Umwelt als Szenerie und ihre Körper als Umhüllung braucht um nach Art einer Person sein Wort hören zu lassen, wenn auch in einer kurzfristigen Manifestation" (1978, 207).[1]

The text asserts further that revelation by the Logos, who is perfect (37.4), ineffable, unpolluted, immeasurable, and inconceivable (46.14–15), is made possible by his taking on the likeness (ⲡⲉⲓⲛⲉ) of "their image" (ⲉⲓⲕⲱⲛ)[2] (47.15–16) and wearing everyone's garment, so as to hide within them (47.16–18). This is not simply the human garment of flesh which is the crea-tion of the archons or Demiurge, but refers to everything that has to do in some way with matter: sovereignties and powers, angels, and every move-ment existing in all matter (47.19–22).[3] The various guises or garments of the Logos are described in detail later in the text: he is clothed as the Son of the Archigenetor (49.12–13), as an angel (49.15–16), as a power (49.17–18), as a Son of Man (49.18–19).

Evans also remarks on the difference in concept here to the Johannine pro-logue: "Whereas in the Prologue the Logos takes up residence within one in-dividual, in Protennoia residence is taken up in a series of beings belonging to the various spheres spanning heaven and earth" (1981b, 398). The choice of the phrase, "takes up residence", is unfortunate. The action of putting on clothing described here is simply a series of clothing-changes.[4] Even putting on the human garment of the flesh cannot in any way be considered as a real dwelling in the flesh, or taking on of real humanity, or taking up residence as a human being in the world. In fact the text warns that those who propose to recognise the Logos in these various clothings are in error (49.7–8).

Even the meeting finally with the earthly crucified Jesus does not consti-tute taking on real flesh. As Filoramo comments, for the Protennoia, "Jesus is only one of many manifestations of a revealing power, an illuminating dy-namis, a soteric entity whose names can change, whose epiphanies can vary, but whose substantial reality remains the same in its structure" (116).

---

[1] Perkins also notes this as an allusion to the Johannine Prologue, specifically Jn 1:14 (1981b, 382). See also Evans et al. 411.

[2] Turner, J.D. translates with "shape" (1990, 427).

[3] Those who debate whether the likeness of their image/their clothing refers to the powers (Robinson, G. 45) or to humankind, or more exactly to the pneumatics (Helderman 1978, 186, 201–4) have set up a false debate, since in this case both apply: the human body/clothing is itself a product of the powers. See also in Ep. Pet. Phil. 136.19–20, where Christ comes down into their (i.e. the archons') mortal/dead mould, though it is not the clothing of the ar-chons but rather a human body (the creation of the archons) which is intended.

[4] See also Robinson, G. 41.

1.5 The Interpretation of Knowledge

A similar concept to the taking on of various likenesses may also be found in Interp. Know., though here the term is not "likeness" but "shape" (cxHMa). Although the text is damaged, it appears to speak of Jesus as the new Adam, who has a shape by which he is known and seen by believers (10.25–26, 33), and by which they are taken above (10.32–33), having entered through the rib whence they came (10.34–36). This may be the shape he takes on in his humility, when he becomes very small (10.27–28). The text also speaks of the shape that exists in the presence (of the Father?), the Logos and the height (10.23–24), but since his becoming small is subsequent to this description, I would assume that here we must differentiate between the two.[1] We might also assume that the heavenly shape is the result of the Father's action of clothing the members of the Son in living rational elements (11.35–38).[2]

1.6 The Second Treatise of the Great Seth and the Letter of Peter to Philip

Both Treat. Seth and Ep. Pet. Phil. speak of Jesus coming down into a body. In both cases it is clear that the heavenly being of this character is in no way disturbed by the action and that the body is a mere shell which is filled up by Jesus.

In Treat. Seth, we read that the pre-existent Jesus Christ (44.33–36) came down into a body, first casting out the one who was already within it (51.20–24). As with previous texts described here, this is the final stage of a series of shape-changes[3] which he has undertaken while passing through the places of the archons (56.21–29). He needs no real human connection to those for whom he has come, since they have their origin and destiny in the heavenly assembly as he also is united with this assembly. He is "the one from you who is among you" (65.19–20). Thus he is in the world, the region below, as a stranger (52.8–9), while at the same time united with believers by their shared heavenly aspect. He alone is perfect, existing with all the greatness of the Spirit/greatness of the Fatherhood of the Spirit (49.15–18; 54.17–18) and the community likewise are the perfect and incorruptible ones (69.23–24), fellow spirits and brothers with him (70.8–10).

Ep. Pet. Phil. makes a number of references to the (blessed) Christ when he was in the body (133.17; see also 138.2; 139.11–12). This body is actually a mould (πλαcMa) which is mortal/dead (ετMooYτ), that is, human, by virtue of the fact that it is a creation of the archons (136.19–20). That he himself is not human, but simply occupying the body-mould, is clear from the failure of the archons to recognise him. They err by thinking that he is a

---

[1] *Contra* Pagels and Turner 1990a, 80–1.

[2] Pagels and Turner (1990a, 82), and Colpe (1974, 111) interpret that the Father is clothed in rational elements.

[3] Tröger refers to it as a "Täuschungsmanöver" (1975, 272).

mortal/dead man (ΟΥΡШΜЄ ЄЧΜΟΟΥΤ) (136.20–22).[1] That he is God, at least subsequent to his earthly activity if not beforehand, is attested not only by the title given to him in 133.7–8, but also by the description of the apostles' worship of him (137.13–14), as also by the typical description of theophany in a mountain setting with lightning and thunder (138.3–5).

The text identifies him as the risen Jesus (139.20–21). That it is the risen Jesus prior to ascension/entry into the heavenly sphere is clear from the setting. The major section of the text comprises revelation by Jesus to the apostles on a mountain. When the revelation is at an end, the appearance is taken up to heaven (138.5–7). There is a departure, however, from the usual canonical Synoptic presentation of the chronology of events, with a further auditory revelation by Jesus as the apostles return to Jerusalem (138.21–28), and another (final) appearance in a second type of commissioning scene by Jesus in 140.15–23.[2]

1.7 The Apocalypse of Peter

Perhaps the most complex form of the Jesus figure is to be found in Apoc. Pet. within the vision of the passion provided for Peter. A character is presented here who comprises four forms or aspects. First there is the Saviour himself who is the intellectual Spirit filled with radiant Light (83.8–10), who observes the vision with Peter and explains it to him. The second form is his servant, the living Jesus, who is the incorporeal body of the Saviour (81.15–18; 82.2; 82.27 – 83.3; 83.6–8). The substitute likeness is the third form. This is Jesus' fleshy part, a physical body susceptible to suffering who is crucified (81.18–24; 82.1–2; 82.21–26; 83.5–6). Finally, there is the intellectual Pleroma of the Saviour, the one who resembles the living Jesus and is filled with the Holy Spirit (82.4–9; 83.10–15).[3]

Havelaar refers to the substitute likeness as the "bodily existence" of the Saviour, a negative view of the body but not a denial of its reality (169). I would question whether we should propose actual bodily existence. The body is certainly there, but the connections between this substitute and the living

---

[1] Bethge proposes to find two types of Christians in the text, those who view Jesus as a dead man and those who recognise him as the Illuminator (1990, 279). However, this passage at least appears to refer to the archons who do not recognise the Christ, rather than certain Christians. Apoc. Pet. and Treat. Seth give more definite indication of a second opposing (mainstream) Christian group who preach about a dead man.

[2] See Bethge for a study of the form of the text and a theory regarding the process of composition of various sources and traditions (1990, 276–7; see also Meyer and Wisse 231–2).

[3] Dubois recognises only two figures of the Saviour: "le Saveur rieur, et son substitut, le seul à subir les souffrances de la crucifixion" (1982, 385). Koschorke first refers to a trichotemy of σῶμα/ψυχή/πνεῦμα (1978b, 25; see also Werner 1974, 577), but subsequently moves to suggest a four-part being: "während sein Erdenlebens hat er sich noch mit einem Fleischesleib verbunden". Tröger suggests three levels here: the pneumatic essence of the *sotêr* (Saviour) in heaven; the living *sotêr* (Jesus); and the fleshly body (*sarkikon*) (1991, 218). Havelaar distinguishes three non-material figures [intellectual Pleroma; intellectual or holy spirit; incorporeal body or living Saviour] combined with the fourth element of the material body (86–7).

Jesus are so fluid and lightly held that to postulate bodily existence for the living Jesus seems to make the matter rather too stable.

It is not clear whether the events narrated are to be interpreted as taking place prior to the passion (thus Werner 1974, 575; 1989, 635; and Schenke, H.-M. 1975a, 277) or thereafter. The former seems more likely given the setting of the Saviour seated in the temple, speaking with Peter (70.14–15), although the latter cannot be ruled out, given the question of whether this is the temple of Jerusalem or the heavenly temple (Brashler 131–5; Dubois 1982, 387–8; and Havelaar 55–7).

Dubois presents two major reasons for identifying the Saviour as "le Resusscité"; i.e. Jesus after the passion. On the one hand, he indicates the significance of the use of the term "Saviour" for Jesus, which he states is not used in the canonical gospels for Jesus during his ministry. On the other hand, he points to the use of the further qualification "the living Saviour", which he proposes as an identification of the resurrected or resuscitated Jesus (1982, 386).

Neither of these arguments suffices in itself. First, it is necessary to ask whether the term "Saviour" is used always in *these* texts for the resurrected Jesus, before making a comparison with the use of this term in the canonical gospels. Secondly, as I will argue below with reference to the Gos. Thom., the qualifier "living" does not necessarily indicate the resurrected Jesus but rather a Jesus who is united with the "living" Father, just as in this text the community are called the living ones (80.3–4) because of their relationship to the Father who is life. This does not mean that they are already in glory or resurrected or resuscitated, but that they are in relation to the Father while still living within the earthly context. This also could be said of the Saviour in the earthly context prior to resurrection or some kind of ascension.

1.8 The Apocryphon of John

A further multiplicity of forms is to be found in Ap. John, but here in reference to the heavenly Revealer-Jesus rather than the earthly Jesus. He is a being of light (2.2), a unity of multiple forms: a child (ⲁⲗⲟⲩ) (BG 21.4), an old man (ϩⲗⲗⲟ) (2.4), and a third form which cannot be decided because of the damaged text. In Chapter II, I have already discussed this passage together with the final section of the text where there are a number of self-designations for the revealer (30.11–12, 15 – 31.16). Giversen sums up for this latter section:

> In the tradition of the section with regard to the self-presentation of the redeemer, there is a clear tendency towards emphasizing the heavenly being; there is no room whatever for any image corresponding to the man Jesus of the New Testament, indeed the spiritual is emphatically stressed, and there is a total disregard of anything personal in the account of the redeemer... (1963a, 272).

This is quite correct, but one should also add that the material on Jesus in the first section of the text has little interest in details about the man Jesus as presented in the New Testament, and is only concerned with his origin in the Father (1.22–24) and his return to that place from which he came (1.11–12).[1]

1.9 The Tripartite Tractate

In Tri. Trac., the Saviour comes into being in flesh (ЄⲚ⟨ЄⲚ⟩ⲦⲀⲂ⳰ⲰⲰⲠЄ ⳰Ⲛ ⲤⲀⲢⳉ) (113.38). His flesh is from "all of them"[2] but above all from the spiritual Logos (114.4–7). The Logos conceives the flesh of the Saviour when the Saviour/Light reveals himself to the Logos (114.10–14). Thus the flesh of the Saviour is spiritual and he does not share in the passions of human flesh (116.26–28), even though the text asserts that he let himself be conceived and born as an infant in body and soul (115.9–11). He is eternal (113.36), an unbegotten impassible one from the Logos (ⲚⲀⲦⲀⲠⲟ⳰ ⲚⲚⲀⲦ⳰⳰Ⲕⲁ⳰ ⲚⲦЄ ⲠⲖⲟⲅⲟⲤ) (113.37–38), a unity from which comes impassibility (116.31–33).

1.10 The Gospel of Thomas

In Gos. Thom. Log. 28 Jesus describes his coming into the world: "I stood in the midst of the world, and I appeared to them in flesh" (ⲀЄⲒⲰ⳰Є ЄⲢⲀⲦ ⳰Ⲛ ⲦⲘⲎⲦЄ ⳰ⲘⲠⲔⲟⲤⲘⲟⲤ ⲀⲨⲰ ⲀЄⲒⲟⲨⲰⲚ⳰ ЄⲂⲟⲖ ⲚⲀⲨ ⳰Ⲛ ⲤⲀⲢⳉ). Here again there is the concept of taking on flesh or human form only as an outward appearance so that others may see and communicate with Jesus within the earthly context.[3] He does indeed appear to have flesh and human parents, but his real being is heavenly from his real heavenly mother and father (see also similarly Gos. Phil.).[4]

Jesus' heavenly being is above all referred to by the use of the description "the living Jesus" or "the living one" (Prologue and Log. 52, 59, 111), which attribute he shares with his heavenly Father, "the living one" or "the living Father" (Log. 37, 50). This is clearly a heavenly attribute which links both characters and attests to the relationship of Jesus with the Father and also to Jesus' heavenly nature (see also Log. 61). Further self-references by Jesus supports this: "It is I who am the Light which is above them all. It is I who am the All. From me did the All come forth, and unto me did the All extend. Split a piece of wood, and I am there. Lift up the stone, and you will find me

---

[1] Perkins rightly states in relation to this text, "The manifestation of the risen Lord is not treated as the occasion to confirm his identity with the earthly Jesus. Rather, an ecstatic recognition of Jesus' divinity constitutes the core of the resurrection tradition" (1993a, 123).

[2] Attridge and Pagels interpret this as a reference to the various aeons of the intermediate world (433), but I agree with Thomassen that here the spiritual church (that is, the spiritual offspring of the Logos) in the sphere of the Logos is intended (1989a, 421).

[3] See Gärtner 141–2, whom Ménard generally follows (1975b, 122–3).

[4] See the discussion in Chapter II.

there" (Log. 77). Just as the light shines in all places, so even the material world is imbued with the presence of Jesus who is the All.[1]

At first glance, Log. 24 ("Show us the place where you are...") implies that the disciples who speak with Jesus are not in the same place as he. However, it might be inferred from the reply that the "place" has to do with the hidden interior heavenly nature of Jesus (as the "man of Light") rather than some external location. Interpretations which make the connection to the glorified Christ in the heavenly region of Light (Kasser 1961, 61 and Ménard 1975b, 116) have a difficulty with those passages which imply that Jesus is actually with his disciples and referring to things which they all see and to events happening to him in an obviously earthly setting (for example, Log. 22; 60; 79; 99; 100).

Log. 37 might be interpreted in a similar way. The question from the disciples, "When will you become revealed to us and when shall we see you?", elicits an answer concerning the ability to see properly so that the son of the living one (i.e. Jesus) might be revealed to them. It is not a case of their not being able to see Jesus physically but rather of their not being able to see his true heavenly being (see also Log. 91). Peter might have come close to guessing a heavenly origin for Jesus in his assertion that Jesus is a righteous angel (Log. 13), but even that is not sufficient. Only Thomas has the real insight concerning Jesus' identity from the heavenly fountain which Jesus measures out, and in this way Thomas is equal to him ("I am not your teacher/master...").[2]

If Jesus is actually present within the earthly sphere, the question still remains as to whether it is before or after a possible passion or resurrection. The discussion concerning whether this is a Jesus post-resurrection focuses mainly on the description of him as the "living" Jesus. I have proposed above that the ascription of the term "living" to Jesus implies his heavenly nature and his relationship of union with his heavenly Father. On the other hand, several commentators (Gärtner 98; Kasser 1961, 28; Partrick 114; and Lelyveld 79) take the phrase to identify the risen Jesus. It is also implied in Arai's suggestion that the phrase indicates that there is no sharp distinction between the earthly Jesus and the resurrected Jesus (1964a, 83 fn. 1).[3]

---

[1] A similar combination of Christ as All (and all as Christ) and as Light that shines in every place is found in Teach. Silv. 101.22 – 102.7. Ménard interprets the saying here in Gos. Thom. as referring to the divinity dispersed in matter, as found also in the images of the pearl and the treasure (1975b,177–8). It is not clear, however, whether the saying is intended in a positive sense or negatively with reference to the entrapment of the sparks of Light within the material world.

[2] Patterson's proposal that the text presents Jesus as a wisdom teacher and radical social critic seems to have moved a little too far from Jesus the heavenly revealer (1990, 629–33).

[3] However Arai is against a post-resurrection setting (1963, 57-9). Arai lists those opposed to a post-resurrection setting: F.V. Filson. 1961. "New Greek and Coptic Gospel Manuscripts." *BA* 24: 13ff; Haechen 1961a, 35f and 1961b, 147ff, 316ff, esp. 316ff; and Weigandt 1: 94 (1964a, 81). See also the summary of positions in Fallon and Cameron.

Ménard comments on the Prologue:

> ὁ ζῶν. ...nous ne croyons pas que la question soit de savoir si le Christ est à prendre ici dans son état prépascal ou postpascal. Il est le Vivificateur, le Sauveur, le Christ ressuscité des Apocryphes gnostiques qui transmet un enseignement ésotérique à ses disciples. Il est le Vivant comme le Père... (1975b, 76–7).

Ménard may have set aside the question of a pre- or post-Easter Christ as irrelevant but it must be asked how he would identify the difference between his "Christ réssuscité" and the risen Christ of the other commentators. What event necessitates the resuscitation of Christ?

There is, in effect, no passion story within Gos. Thom. to help in situating the Jesus figure as pre- or post-passion or resurrection, although there is an exhortation to take up one's cross in the way of Jesus (Log. 55) (see the discussion in Chapter VIII). Indeed, Haenchen proposes that some situations exclude the interpretation of the living Jesus as the risen Jesus, such as his request for a comparative description of himself in Log. 13 (1961a, 35). However, the same passage is used by Gärtner to argue for a post-resurrection Jesus (112–3).

Gärtner and Lelyveld study several logia in order to make their case for the glorified Christ. In Gärtner's section "III. The Nature of Jesus" (118–58), there is a long discussion initially of Log. 13 and the revelation to Thomas of the secret unutterable name of Jesus (118–134).[1] Jesus cannot be compared to anything created or belonging to this world, since he belongs to the eternal, heavenly mystery (126).

> ...when in Logion 13a we read that the Apostles cannot compare Jesus with anything whatever, we are dealing with an essential Christological statement. Everything which has to do with this creation shall perish, and hence it is impracticable to compare any part of the kingdom of light with the things of this world (128).

He then moves to consider Log. 61 (134–5) in which Salome inquires after the true nature of Jesus. Gärtner concludes that Jesus comes from the heavenly world, from the Father,[2] and that he resembles the Father in nature (see also Log. 15) (135–6).

> This implies that here in Logion 15 we have an expression of the concept that Jesus, present among men, represents the Father, that he shares his nature and reveals his secrets, and that he who understands this – sees this – will worship Jesus (137).

Lelyveld focuses on Jesus as the angel of judgment in Logia 10 and 11 (65–68). She proposes that Log. 10 be seen in conjunction with Log. 16 (66),

---

[1] See also Ménard, who follows Gärtner on the nature of Jesus (1975b, 31–33).

[2] See also, once again, Ménard 1975b, 33–4.

with its source in tradition from the Old Testament, apocalyptic literature, and Q (66–67).

> Les deux Logia attribuent ainsi à Jésus une action dont il est annoncé qu'elle sera l'oeuvre du Messager, du Maître, de l'Ange de l'Alliance qui va mettre en mouvement le Jugement (67).

There is nothing in the arguments of Gärtner or Lelyveld that necessitates resurrection as an outcome. The focus of both studies is the heavenly aspect of Jesus, something which is entirely possible for the Jesus figure at any stage of his association with the earthly sphere, without demanding that this aspect be the result of a resurrection process.

1.11 The Dialogue of the Saviour

Dial. Sav. is mainly interested in the association of the Lord with the Light of the Father (139.18–20) and the Truth (140.22–23;144.13–14). Mary's statement that the Lord is "fearful and wonderful" (140.24 – 141.1) may imply something of his divinity. However, although the Jesus of the text is a heavenly figure, the opening passage presumes that prior to the present events the Lord has been "labouring" just like the disciples ("the time has come, brothers, for *us* to abandon *our* labour and stand at rest" [my emphasis];120.3–6).

Krause suggests that these words point to the death of Jesus and of the disciples (see also Voorgang 162), whereas the prayer formula later in the text – "Höre uns, Vater, wie du deinen Sohn erhört hast. Und du hast ihn zu dir genommen und hast ihn bei dir Ruhe von vieler Plage gegeben" (121.5–9; Krause has not indicated his additions to the fragmentary text) – speaks for a point in time after the ascension (1977a, 34). It seems to me that it is simpler in the context of the text as a whole to view the labour as the burden of the flesh, the works of the flesh that must be abandoned. In other words it is time for Jesus to leave the flesh without this necessarily implying a passion as Voorgang suggests (see also Koester and Pagels 15).

The opening passage must refer to the final and eternal experience since it is followed by the statement, "For whoever stands at rest will rest for ever" (120.6–8). Perkins proposes this "opening scene has been partly modeled on the farewell discourse of the Fourth Gospel. Jesus is leaving his labors to return to rest. The disciples are enjoined not to fear, since he has opened the way. The Father is glorified through prayer. The disciples are taught how to address the Father. They have believed the truth and learned to know him" (1980, 107; see also 108 and 110 where she suggests the same influence in the commissioning scene at the conclusion of the section 134.24 – 138.2).

The twice repeated statement by the Lord concerning his own difficulty in reaching the path by which one leaves and goes up to the Light (139.6–7; 145.22–24) implies that his power is somewhat less than we might expect of the risen Lord,[1] particularly when one considers that the state of the Lord before he came seems to be one of greater power since he opened the path by his coming (120.23–24).[2]

Although the Lord may have difficulty with the path, he apparently has no difficulty in traversing the space between heaven and earth (the edge of heaven and earth (ⲡⲁⲱⲕ ⲛ̄ⲧⲡⲉ [ⲙⲛ̄] ⲡⲕⲁϩ) (135.1–2) where he takes the disciples for the vision.

2. Texts Which Present a More Human Jesus within the Earthly Context

The reader should keep in mind other more human portrayals of Jesus which have been mentioned within the previous section on the more heavenly Jesus.

2.1 The Second Apocalypse of James

In 2 Apoc. Jas. a key metaphor of garments and stripping is used to refer to Jesus' being within the earthly region. The action of stripping and going about naked (46.14–16) occurs only after he has reached the earthly region, and not during his descent, as he passes through the worlds (46.12–13). Nakedness is equivalent to perishability as we see from the parallel statement ("he was found in a perishable state though he would be brought up into imperishability"; 46.17–19), and I would interpret this as the state of being in the flesh for the Lord.[3] What is implied then is that the Lord strips off his garment of glory and thereby sacrifices some aspects of his heavenly being in order to take his place within the earthly region.[4]

Later in the text, James speaks of seeing the Lord naked with no garment covering him (58.20–23), which in view of the passage above, would seem to indicate James' seeing the Lord without his heavenly garment.[5] This may be

---

[1] Perkins suggests that these passages from the redactor "may even presume that this revelation occurs before rather than after Jesus' resurrection" (1991, 439). She cites Koester and Pagels 14f.

[2] Voorgang sees a reference here to the Passion "die für den Weg zur Erlösung ein schweres Hindernis darstellt" (162).

[3] See Gos. Phil. 56.29–30, where it is said that those who wear the flesh are naked.

[4] One cannot take the metaphor to its logical conclusion without difficulty. If the Lord strips off glory and thus is perishable when naked, the implication is that he actually possesses perishability beneath that garment of glory. He does not put on another garment which is perishable, but simply takes off the garment of glory.

[5] Veilleux proposes that the nakedness of the Lord is either his humanity seen without his garment of glory, or his self without his fleshly covering (177). W.-P. Funk takes the latter interpretation, since if the Lord had been without his garment of glory everyone would have been able to see him and not just James, whose visionary experience may be implicitly referred to in 57.17–19 (1976, 160–1). However, Funk also refers to the scene with the risen Jesus beginning with 50.3, which he understands as a bodily appearance of Jesus in view of the reaction of James' mother.

supported by the use of the same metaphor in 56.7–14 with reference to James.[1] The statement about the Lord's nakedness occurs in a summary passage in 58.2–24. Here we are told that the Lord is life and light (6–8) and the Demiurge did not see (?)[2] him (2–6). This is a reference to the descent of the Lord in his garment of glory, which generally renders the wearer invisible, prior to his reaching the earthly region and subsequently stripping it off to take on perishability.

One assumes a different understanding of the Lord's being after the passion, when he appears to James as someone who is truly present and not a ghost ("Am I not alive?"; 57.1). When commanded to embrace the Lord (an action associated with understanding and knowledge [57.6, 16–17]), James reaches out to touch him but does not find him as he thought he would be (57.12–14). Obviously James assumes that he will embrace the Lord as he has been used to doing, and this must imply that the Lord is in some bodily form that appears similar to his earlier earthly form.[3]

2.2 Melchizedek

In the previous chapter, three references to Jesus Christ in Melch. were noted solely within the heavenly context, and generally within lists of heavenly

---

[1] The Lord speaks to James in 56.7–14:
   For just as you are first having clothed yourself,
   you are also the first who will strip himself,
   and you shall become as you were before you stripped yourself.
   Veilleux writes: "Jacques ayant été le premier à se revêtir du corps spirituel (en recevant la révélation), sera aussi le premier à se dévêtir de son enveloppe charnelle, et il redeviendra comme il était avant qu'il ne se fût dévêtu de sa gloire céleste" (174), and W.-P. Funk interprets somewhat similarly: "Wie du dich als erster mit Erkenntnis bekleidet hast, so bist du auch der erste, der den irdischen Leib ablegen wird", paraphrasing further: "Wie du als erster Offenbarung empfangen hast, so wirst du auch als erster erlöst werden" (1976, 174).
   Neither of these interpretations seems to appreciate the implication of the final clause; that is, that James' final state will be what it was before he stripped himself. If the stripping means indeed taking off the earthly covering of the body, then logically James' final state will be a return to that covering. Veilleux's attempt to solve the problem by giving two different interpretations of the stripping, the first referring to the physical body and the second to the heavenly glory, is ungrounded. Funk approaches the difficulty in a similar way by treating the final clause separately and suggesting that here the stripping is linked to descent (stripping off the garment of Light) while the previous clause refers to stripping during ascent (stripping off the body) (150–1).
   Taking into account what can be understood already of the concept of stripping and nakedness with relation to the Lord, I would rather interpret the passage in the following way: James has already been clothed in the heavenly clothing (perhaps through his knowledge of, or union with, the Lord), but he will have to strip this off, just as the Lord has done, in order to go through the passion which means moving from perishability to imperishability. Having triumphed through the passion, James will return to the state of being clothed in the heavenly garment which he had before.
[2] naγ is a reconstruction.
[3] As in 1 Apoc. Jas. 31, the scene is reminiscent of the post-resurrection scene between Jesus and Mary Magdalene in Jn 20:11–18. Veilleux also refers to the scene with Thomas in Jn 20:26–27 (175; see also Evans et al. 248), although in the latter scene there is no difficulty in being able to touch the body of the risen Lord.

beings. Apart from these, there are two references to a Saviour in Melch. 4.7 and 14.4, who may be the earthly appearance of this character. The line prior to the first reference contains the phrase "holy disciples", and the reference itself may describe revelatory activity of the Saviour. This may also be connected to the material in 5.1–11 although there are some twenty lines either missing or unreadable in between.

5.1–11 is concerned with right teaching about someone who experienced a real human existence. Contrary to the incorrect teaching of some people (not further identified) he was begotten, ate and drank, was circumcised, came in the flesh, came to suffering, and rose from the dead. It seems clear that this is the earthly Jesus, and the statement is an assertion of his real human existence.[1] What is not clear is whether we are to make the link between the earthly Jesus and the heavenly Jesus Christ or whether these are two figures who must be differentiated; that is, the Saviour Jesus who really suffers as the earthly counterpart of the heavenly Christ who does not suffer.

2.3 The Sophia of Jesus Christ

Soph. Jes. Chr. implies that the earthly form of the Saviour is somehow different from his risen form. The resurrected form is described as a likeness resembling a great angel of Light (91.12–14; see further 93.10–11: He knows the Light from which he has come) which no mortal flesh could bear to see but only pure and perfect flesh (91.15–17). We are told that he does not appear in his previous form (ΜΟΡΦΗ) but in the invisible Spirit (91.10–12). It seems that resurrection (90.15–16) has caused some change and that perhaps his earthly form was not in the Spirit. This could imply a more human form for the Jesus figure in the earthly context. Orbe suggests a Jesus who is a complex of three forms: "*uno* intelectivo, de natura angélica... *otro* psíquico, de índole racional... y *tercero*, de barro, terreno..." (1976, 1: 246).

2.4 The Apocryphon of James

In Ap. Jas., Jesus says that he has put himself under the curse that the believers may be saved (13.20–25), which may be a reference to taking on the human condition or a reference to his death. If it is the latter then it also seems to imply the former as well. There is a degree of humility about the Jesus of this text who encourages James and Peter to be better than he, or to arrive at salvation ahead of him. Although he wants to be gone, he can still be held back by the need of the disciples for his assistance. He also affirms that the Father has no need of him (9.11–15) although he has need of the Father (9.14–15), just as the Father has no need of the disciples (9.16–17).

Despite this, the Jesus of this text is not, strictly speaking, the earthly Jesus. There is the contrast made between him and the Son of Man, references to the previous cross and death, and the fact that he appears (ⲁϤⲞⲨⲰⲚⲄ̄; 2.17). This Jesus is between the resurrection and final return to the region whence

---

[1] See also Böhlig and Markschies 185–6.

he came, in a sort of middle ground which is not earthly yet is accessible to earthly creatures, and is not "heavenly" (i.e. above) but obviously has aspects of the "heavenly".[1] There is a small reference to the ascension in 15.35.

2.5 The Acts of Peter and the Twelve Apostles

In Chapter II, I discussed the possibility that the heavenly Jesus in Acts Pet. 12 Apost. retains the marks of crucifixion. This must imply a real death and earthly existence for the Saviour. There are no further details concerning the earthly context of the Saviour as the text is interested only in the heavenly Jesus in an earthly and heavenly setting, and his revelation to the disciples post-crucifixion. The heavenly Saviour, Lithargoel, is the revealer who does not reveal himself to every man (8.30–31), the son of the great king (8.31–32). His name surpasses all riches, as the wisdom of God surpasses gold, silver, and precious stones (10.25–30). The "recognition scene" in 9.19–26 assumes the divinity of the risen Lord, before whom the eleven disciples prostrate themselves and they worship him.

3. Earthly Flesh and Heavenly Nature as Complementary Natures

These texts should be differentiated from those above which may indeed describe two natures, but they are not complementary. Instead, the heavenly being simply takes up residence in a body and this body does not have any effect upon the spiritual nature of the being.

3.1 Treatise on Resurrection

Treat. Res. describes the Lord as a seed of the Truth[2] (ϹⲠⲈⲢⲘⲀ ⲚⲦⲘⲎⲈ) (44.35), who existed in flesh (ⲈϤϢⲟⲟⲡ ⲍⲚ ⲤⲀⲣⲝ) (44.14–15),[3] who lived "in this place" (= the earth) where the believers are (44.17–19). 44.21–33 provides a summary statement concerning the complementarity of his earthly and heavenly natures:

---

[1] *Contra* Koester who writes: "The dialogues themselves do not presuppose a setting after Jesus' resurrection and ascension (2,17–21). As in the Gospel of John, they are farewell discourses in which Jesus explains what he has said before his departure, but neither resurrection nor ascension are presupposed in these discourses" (1990, 200).

[2] "Valentinians regularly describe as 'seeds' entities on one level of reality which have counterparts on a lower and more material level of reality" (Peel 1985b, 154–5).

[3] See the discussion in Peel 1985b, 146–7, concerning the meaning of "flesh" here. "...given the affinities of Treat. Res. with Valentinian Gnosticism and the subtleties of Valentinian reflections on Christ's body, it is probable... that the "flesh" of Christ mentioned in 44.14–15 is not symbolic of His full Incarnation and mortality." Peel refers to Tertullian who states that the Valentinians held that Christ is flesh of a different kind from other mortals. "What is unambiguously clear in Treat. Res. (44.14–15; 47.4–16) is that 'flesh' is assessed as the temporary mode of earthly existence shared by both Savior and Elect" (147). See Strutwolf (167–8) and Partrick (92–5) for a non-docetic interpretation here.

Now the Son of God... was Son of Man. He embraced them both, possessing the humanity and the divinity, so that on the one hand he might vanquish death through his being Son of God, and that on the other through the Son of Man the restoration to the Pleroma might occur...

ΠϢΗΡΕ Ν̄ΔΕ Μ̄ΠΝΟΥΤΕ... ΝΕΥϢΗΡΕ Ν̄ΡѠΜΕ ΠΕ ΑΥѠ
ΝΕϤΕΜΑ2ΤΕ ΑΡΑΥ Μ̄ΠΕϹΝΕΥ ΕΥΝ̄ΤΕϤ Μ̄ΜΕΥ Ν̄ΤΜΝ̄ΤΡѠΜΕ ΜΝ̄
ΤΜΝ̄ΤΝΟΥΤΕ ϪΕΚΑϹΕ ΕϤΝΑϪΡΟ Μ̄ΜΕΝ ΑΠΜΟΥ ΑΒΑΛ 2ΙΤΜ̄
ΠΤΡϤϢѠΠΕ Ν̄ϢΗΡΕ Ν̄ΝΟΥΤΕ 2ΙΤΟΟΤϤ ΔΕ Μ̄ΠϢΗΡΕ Μ̄ΠΡѠΜΕ
ΕΡΕΤΑΠΟΚΑΤΑϹΤΑϹΙϹ ΝΑϢѠΠΕ Α2ΟΥΝ ΑΠΠΛΗΡѠΜΑ...

However, care should be taken with the description "earthly" for the Son of Man. As Borsch points out, the work of restoring the Pleroma refers to "much larger understandings" than mere humanity: "He (the author) would seem to be suggesting that there was an aspect of the pre-existent, upper world saviour which was human-like" (86).

3.2 The Teaching of Silvanus

Although Teach. Silv. contains a similar concept to Gos. Phil. concerning likenesses, it seems to present a different Jesus to Gos. Phil. In 103.32 – 104.1 we find the following statements in succession: "How many likenesses (Ν̄ΕΙΝΕ) did Christ take on (ΑΠΕΧ̄Ϲ ϪΙΤΟΥ) because of you? Although he was God, he [was found] (Α[Υ]6Ι[Ν]Ε) among men as a man (2ѠϹ ΡѠΜΕ)". The likenesses can be interpreted in a similar manner to those in Gos. Phil. and others above, as the forms which the Christ takes on as he passes through the aeons before finally taking on a human form (perhaps including also forms which he takes on in his struggle against the powers of the Underworld).[1]

The question is what relation these likenesses have to the reality of Christ and whether the human form of Christ is to be counted as a likeness. We are also told that Christ has the image of the Father (ΘΙΚѠΝ Μ̄ΠΙѠΤ), for this image reveals the true likeness (ΠΙΝΕ Μ̄ΜΕ) in correspondence to that which is revealed (100.23–31). He is the All (101.22, 24–25; 102.5; 117.11–13), having obtained it from the Father (101.23–24). Thus, on the one hand, he is the image of the true likeness which is the Father, and on the other hand, he takes on likenesses so that he can reveal this true likeness.

Further in the text we read that Christ became man (ΑϤϢѠΠΕ Ν̄ΡѠΜΕ) (110.18–19) or that he put on humanity (ΠΕΤΑϤ6ѠΛΕ Μ̄ΠΡѠΜΕ) (111.4–6). Putting on humanity is the equivalent of being in deficiency, being generated, and being comprehensible (101.33 – 102.5), but the description in this

---

[1] Contrary to this view, Zandee interprets the forms in relation to the various images used of Christ in 106.21–28 (Tree of Life, Wisdom, Word, Life, Power, Door, Light, Angel, and Good Shepherd), and states that Christ takes the forms in order to appear to humankind "as a perceptible figure" (295).

passage seems to imply that although he is these things, they are not aspects of his *actual* being: he is without deficiency even if he is in the deficiency, ungenerated even if he has been generated, both comprehensible but incomprehensible as to his actual being (101.33 – 102.5). It seems at this point as if becoming human has not affected in any way his real divine nature.

Further passages make this statement less certain. We read that the Wisdom of God became a type of fool for the believer so that he might take him up and make him a wise man (107.9–13), that the Life died for the believer when he (the Life) was powerless, so that through his death he might give life to the believer who had died (107.13–17), and that the Christ died for the soul as a ransom for its sin (104.12–13). From these statements at least, it seems that the humanity of the Christ must be taken seriously, so that in this text we have a concept of two natures existing at the one time together in Christ, the human nature not affecting the divine nature in any way detrimentally, but bringing to him all the same the powerlessness of the human condition and death. If he has two natures, nevertheless he is a single being (99.12–14).

For the most part, the text concentrates on the Christ as an exalted figure, subsequent to his earthly sojourn. Of all the Nag Hammadi texts, Teach. Silv. has the richest selection of titles for Christ, most of them to be seen in relation to what the heavenly Christ means for the community, for his creation, or for the Father. He is the King (96.25; 111.15, 17, 18; 117.10[1]), the Logos (106.24; 111.5–6; 112.32; 113.13–14; 115.18; 117.8–9), God (103.34; 110.17, 18; 111.5), Son of the Father (115.9–10, 15–16, 19), who as the creating hand of the Father (115.3–4, 5) is also the Mother of All (115.8–9). He is described above all in images of light[2] and life (98.22–23; 101.19, 30; 106.21–22, 24–27; 107.13; 111.18; 112.10–11, 36–37; 113.6–7, 15), images of guiding or teaching (96.32; 103.25–26; 106.22–23, 26–28; 107.3, 9; 110.18; 112.35–36; 113.14–15), images of greatness (106.25; 112.9) and yet also of intimacy (110.16; 111.13–14, 19; 112.10). The latter are supported by descriptions of him as patient and mild (118.3–4), wishing to have mercy on everyone (117. 11–13), which reiterates what has already been said of the Father (114. 26–30).

4. Heavenly Being

In this final section I note briefly a number of texts which, although presenting a Jesus figure, have no real interest in earthly categories to any extent, and no interest in explaining how Jesus' contact with the earthly realm is or has been carried out. This may apply to a Jesus who is a heavenly revealer or

---

[1] Janssens suggests amending "king of faith" to "door of faith" (ΠΡΟ 𝈻ΤΠΙϹΤΙϹ) (1983, 93). See also Zandee 10.

[2] The image of Christ as light (= reason/Logos; see Janssens 1983, 57) and sun/fire is expanded in 98.22 – 99.15 (see also for further reflection on Christ as the sun, 101.13–15, 29–35).

it may be a heavenly Jesus whom the community still believe in and pray to, subsequent to his earthly sojourn. Generally speaking, there is no interest in the details of the latter.

First there are the texts which have the barest detail on the Jesus figure in general. Here we must include the description of Christ as holy in Pr. Paul B.10; the self-designation of the Saviour, "I am the knowledge of the truth",[1] in Thom. Cont. 138.13 and his indirect self-description, "It is in light that light exists" (139.21–22), after Thomas' confessional statement in 139.20;[2] and the statement in 1 Apoc. Jas. that the Lord is unnameable from Him-Who-Is (although he has been given two names from Him-Who-Is) (24.22–25), and that he "came forth" before femaleness existed (24.31). However one should note that there is a differentiation between two stages of Jesus' experience in this last text. The first part of the dialogue between James and the Lord takes place two days prior to the Lord's "passion" (25.7) and the second after the Lord's passion and prior to James' "passion".[3] The second dialogue is introduced with James deliberating about the events of the Lord's sufferings.

Gos. Truth contains a little more detail with descriptions of Jesus as a guide who is restful and leisurely (19.18), as one who is patient in accepting sufferings (20.11), who is knowledge and perfection (20.38–39), Jesus of the infinite sweetness (24.8–9). It seems possible that the setting may present Jesus in the Middle (19.19; 20.9–10; 26.4–5, 27–28).

I investigated the link between Jesus and the Word/Son in Gos. Truth in Chapter II. I noted that Jesus, the Son and the Word all have imperishable bodily existence (20.29–32; 26.7–8; 30.27–32; 31.4–8), the Word being said to have come in fleshly form, and that perhaps the body which the Father's love made over the Word (23.30–31) might well be the book which Jesus puts on (20.24). Thus the Word may be the body of Jesus as in Gos. Phil. In any case we are not concerned here with a truly physical body for Jesus. On the other hand, the Son can be seen, heard, tasted, smelt and touched (30.27–32; 38.15–16) i.e. perceived by bodily senses.

---

[1] For a study of the "knowledge of the truth" as a technical phrase expressing the sum of Christian teaching and praxis, see Sell 1982.

[2] On one occasion the Saviour appears to speak of himself in connection with some one or some others, "Therefore it is necessary for us to speak to you..." (140.9–11). There is no indication to whom this may refer. Turner suggests a number of possibilities. It may be the royal plural (as, for example, 1 Jn 1:1) or a conscious literary device with reference either to the Saviour and the "truly wise one", or to the Saviour and Thomas (and the author of the tractate) and addressed to the reader of the tractate. Finally it may be simply the case that it was included in a source copied by the scribe (1975, 147–8). H.-M. Schenke says it is strongly reminiscent of Jn 3:11 with its equally astonishing shift from 1st sing. to pl. (1983, 217). Kuntzmann also refers to Jn 3:11, and thereby finds himself more in agreement with the third hypothesis of Turner: "la source copiée par l'auteur est peut-être la formule de réponse des responsables à la confession des membres de la communauté sur l'utilité de la parole du Sauveur des 1.7–8" (1986, 90).

[3] Orbe remarks that it is curious to find the first part of the dialogue before the passion of Jesus (1965, 169).

In Great Pow., the Saviour is a fairly shadowy figure. We read that he will receive the Great Power and will know him (40.28), and that he will drink from the milk of the mother of the work (40.29–30).[1]

5. Titles and Designations

Finally in this chapter the various titles and designations used of Jesus must be considered.[2] While titles can be helpful, great care is needed when drawing conclusions from their use. Even the simple question of which character uses which title is of great importance in understanding what the writer might mean to say about Jesus.

I have divided the information about the titles into two basic groups.[3] The first table (pp. 90–91) gives the titles or descriptions which are used more than once over a number of texts. I have tried to present a workable but comprehensive overview by including separate categories for basic titles and those titles when used in a phrase: thus "Son" is counted separately from "Son of God"; "king" separately from "king of the universe". Exceptions occur where a basic title has a preceding adjective. In this case, all occurences are included under the one title: for example, in Soph. Jes. Chr., "Saviour" includes "Saviour" (6), "the perfect Saviour" (9), "the blessed Saviour" (1) and "the great Saviour" (1). Similarly in Dial. Sav., "Son" covers "Son" (1) and "only begotten Son" (1); in Acts Pet. 12 Apost., "Son of the living God" (1) comes under "Son of God". Where two or more basic titles occur together they have been treated generally as separate titles. Thus "Lord Saviour" in Soph. Jes. Chr. is treated under "Lord" and "Saviour". Finally, titles in damaged text have only been allowed when the conjectures are fairly certain.

---

[1] Cf. Wisse and Williams 307: "...the mother, in fact." It is not clear who is meant by the mother. Cherix interprets as the Great Power, referring to the work of the Power in 39.14–15 (1982, 27). The only other use of the term ⲘⲁⲁⲨ relates to the mother of the fire (40.10).

[2] See also the lists of titles proposed for the texts in Voorgang 120–240. The items in his lists differ quite considerably from those proposed here.

[3] See the Appendix which provides the page and line references for the occurrence of the titles within each text.

Table 1:

	I,1	I,2	I,3	I,4	I,5	II,1	II,2	II,3	II,7	III,4	III,5
King of the aeons	1										
Lord		12	3	3	9			13	10	5	45
Saviour		6	3	4	6			1	14	17	4
Son		4						6		1 ?	2
Teacher		1			1	1					1
Son of Man		2		3			1	7			2
Jesus the Christ			1	2		1		1		1	
Son of God				3	2			1			
Lord (Jesus) Christ				1							
the Christ					4			20			
Redeemer					1 ?						
Logos								1			
Light									1		
God											

I,1 Pr. Paul	I,5 Tri. Trac.	II,7 Thom. Cont.
I,2 Ap. Jas.	II,1 Ap. John	III,4 Soph. Jes. Chr.
I,3 Gos. Truth	II,2 Gos. Thom.	III,5 Dial. Sav.
I,4 Treat. Res.	II,3 Gos. Phil.	

V,3	V,4	VI,1	VII,2	VII,3	VII,4	VIII,2	IX,3	XI,1	Total
					1				2
13	2	5		2		3			125
				7			2	2	66
					3	1		5	22
					2				6
			3	1			11		30
		1	1		1	1			10
		1						1	8
						2			3
					38	1	7	1	71
						1			2
					6				7
					6	1			8
					1	1			2

V,3   1 Apoc. Jas.   VII,2 Treat. Seth   VIII,2 Ep. Pet. Phil.
V,4   2 Apoc. Jas.   VII,3 Apoc. Pet.   IX,3   Testim. Truth
VI,1 Acts Pet. 12 Apost. VII,4 Teach. Silv.   XI,1   Interp. Know.

The second group of titles comprises titles/descriptions used of Jesus once only and titles/descriptions used more than once but only within a single text.

Pr. Paul

   Lord of Lords (1)

Gos. Truth

   The hidden mystery (1)
   The merciful one (1)
   The faithful one (1)

Treat. Res.

   The solution (1)[1]

Tri. Trac.

   Lord of all (1)
   Lord of glory (1)?
   King of the universe (1)

   Names ascribed to the Saviour:
   – the Redemption of the angels of the Father (1)
   – the knowledge of all that which is thought of (1)
   – the treasure (1)
   – the addition for the increase of knowledge (1)
   – the revelation of those things which were known at first (1)
   – the path toward harmony and toward the pre-existent one (1)

Gos. Thom.

   The living one (1)
   Son of the living one (1)

Gos. Phil.

   Messiah (3)
   The Nazarene (6)
   The perfect man (4)
   The heavenly man (1)
   Pharisatha (1)

---

[1] Peel suggests that this is a christological title (1985b, 157), and Puech suggests a personification "en le Christ" (25), but it might just as easily refer to the Word of Truth in the previous verse, especially since it seems that the solution is further referred to as "the emanation of Truth and Spirit, Grace is of the Truth" (ⲦⲠⲢⲞⲂⲞⲖⲎ ⲚⲦⲘⲎⲈ ⲘⲚ ⲠⲈⲠⲚⲈⲨⲘⲀ ⲦⲈⲬⲀⲢⲒⲤ ⲦⲀ ⲦⲘⲎⲈ ⲦⲈ) (45.12–14). This may well be a title if the concept of Christ as seed of Truth can be equated with the Word of Truth.

Soph. Jes. Chr.

The holy one (1)

1 Apoc. Jas.

Rabbi (9)

Treat. Seth

The Son of Light (1)[1]
The perfect blessed one (of the eternal and incomprehensible Father and
   the infinite Light) (1)
a Christ (2)

Teach. Silv.

King (5)
Sun of life (1)
The tree of life (1)
The Life (3)
The idea (NOHCIC) of incorruptibility (1)
The narrow way (1)
Wisdom (of God) (3)
The (great) power (2)
The door (1)
The angel (1)
The good shepherd (1)
The (faithful) friend (1)
Great goodness of God (1)
Great one of the heavens (1)
A great glory (1)
Judge (1)
The hand of the Lord/Father (2)
The mother of all (1)
Image of the Father (1)

Titles used specifically in relation to the Logos:
– the first-born (1)
– the wisdom (2)
– the prototype (1)
– light of the eternal light (1)
– spotless mirror of the working of God (1)
– the image of his goodness (1)
– the eye which looks at the invisible Father (1)

---

[1] "...sicher eine Bezeichnung für Jesus Christus" (Bethge 1979, 163). Gibbons is less
sure what to make of this figure and interprets him as the double of the Saviour "perhaps left
in the world at Sophia's descent there to be rescued by the Savior at his own descent" (1972,
17). The double of the Christ in the world is a parallel perhaps with the "double" of Sophia:
the emanation of Sophia in the world, Sophia Elpis.

– Life (1)
– King of faith (1)
– the sharp sword (1)

Ep. Pet. Phil.

The holy child (1)
Christ of immortality (1)
Saviour of the whole world (1)
Son of the immeasurable glory of the Father (1)
Son of life (1)
Son of immortality (1)
The one who is in the light (1)
Our illuminator (1)

Interp. Know.

Teacher of immortality (1)
The shape (2)
the reproached one/the one who was reproached (6)
the humiliated one (2)
the one who was redeemed (1)
the head (8)

The comparison of the frequency of use of a title is helpful to a limited degree. It may indicate which titles are favoured across the spectrum of less gnosticising to rather more gnosticising texts. However, these titles may be so common as to make the comparison of little worth. One has only to consider in this regard the use of the most common title "Lord" across the majority of texts under study here (129 times + "Lord of lords" [Pr. Paul], "Lord of all" and "Lord of glory" [Tri. Trac.]).

In this case, it seems more interesting to study texts which use this title much more frequently than any other (e.g. the 45 occurrences in Dial. Sav. as opposed to the use of "Saviour" [4], "Son" [2], "Teacher" [1] and "Son of Man" [2]), or vice versa (e.g. 9 uses of "Lord" in Soph. Jes. Chr. in comparison to 19 uses of "Saviour", but contained within these are the four uses of the double title "Lord Saviour"), or not at all (e.g. Testim. Truth which uses "Son of Man" [11] and "Christ" [7] and "Saviour" [2]; and Teach. Silv. which uses "Christ" 38 times, but "Lord" only in reference to the Father). The last example is all the more surprising when one considers the great number of titles used in that text for Jesus.

That one should be careful even with what seems a straightforward process of counting the number of occurrences of a title is well illustrated by Soph. Jes. Chr. As the Appendix shows, the Codex III version of Soph. Jes. Chr. contains nine occurrences of the title "Lord". In almost every case "Christ" has been substituted for "Lord" in the BG 8502 version of the text.

A comparative study of the frequency of a title must take into account the relative length of each work and the number and frequency of other titles used. Gos. Phil. and 1 Apoc. Jas. both record 13 occurrences of the title "Lord". Yet Gos. Phil. is about twice the length of 1 Apoc. Jas. when one takes into account that at least the last six pages of 1 Apoc. Jas. are very fragmentary. On the other hand, the only other title used in 1 Apoc. Jas. is "Rabbi" (9), while for Gos. Phil. "Christ" occurs more frequently than "Lord" (20), and there are a number of other titles which seem important in the context of the gospel, especially "Nazarene" (6), "Son of Man" (7) and "Son" (6). With regard to this last example, it is worthwhile noting that, while frequency may be an indication of importance, one cannot rule out the possibility that important titles may occur only infrequently, perhaps sparingly.

Within the texts which have a unique occurrence of a title, several texts stand out because of the frequency of this unique occurrence: "the Nazarene" in Gos. Phil., and "Rabbi" in 1 Apoc. Jas. as noted above; "King" (5 + "King of faith") in Teach. Silv. and "Head" in Interp. Know. (8). It is also interesting to note the multiplicity of unique titles in Tri. Trac. and especially in Teach. Silv.

When dealing with frequency, it is necessary to bear in mind the genre of the text under study. Texts which have a great deal of dialogue between Jesus and disciples, for example Soph. Jes. Chr. and Dial. Sav., invariably achieve a greater frequency of the use of the title "Lord", as the favoured form of address to Jesus.

In the end each title must be studied within the context of the individual text in which it occurs. In some cases there are a number of levels of use at play. Thus a differentiation must be made between titles used by enemies and titles used by friends, titles used by the Jesus figure of himself rather than titles used by others about him or in addressing him, and so on.

A good example of different levels within one text is provided by Ap. John in relation to the revealer figure. John addresses the revealer directly always as Lord (13.18; 22.10; 25.27; 26.7, 23, 32–33; 27.12, 22, 31–32). When he speaks to the listener/reader, he uses the title "Saviour" (22.10, 12, 21; 25.16). When the writer of the text refers to the revealer in relation to John, the revealer is also referred to as the Saviour (31.32; 32.5).

Self-reference by the Jesus figure does not occur frequently. In Ap. Jas. the title "Son" (in relation to the Father) is used only by Jesus of himself (9.17–18; 10.14; 14.39;15.2), but when referring back to himself in his previous earthly context, he uses the title "Son of Man" (3.14, 17–18). This latter title is also used by Jesus of himself in Gos. Phil. (63.29–30). "Son" may also be used in self-reference by Jesus in Dial. Sav. (145.17–18; 3rd person self-reference) and Soph. Jes. Chr. (108.7). In the latter text, he also refers to himself as the Saviour (94.14) or the great Saviour (107.22).

The use by Jesus of the title "Son of Man" in Ap. Jas. raises the interesting case of a title used in a negative sense, an aspect of Jesus which is viewed by himself in a negative light. I have not included in the list above the phrase "Son of their glory" found in Apoc. Pet. 82.1–2, since it is not clear that it is intended as a title, but this is a similar case where the fleshly substitute, the likeness of the living Jesus, is referred to by the Saviour in a negative way.

We can say in general that those who call Jesus "Lord" are in positive relationship to him. Soph. Jes. Chr. provides many examples of the use of "Lord" or some variation: "Lord" is the form of address to Jesus from Matthew (94.1), Philip (95.19), Mary (98.10), and the disciples (105.4); "Lord Saviour" from Thomas (96.15; 108.17–18), Matthew (100.17–18), and the holy apostles (112.21); and "holy Lord" from Mary (114.9–10).

The categories of positive or negative relationship are not always easy to differentiate since characters like the disciples may play on either side. In this case, it is essential to note those disciples who possess insight and thus may be counted on to use an appropriate title. Of course an appropriate title in one text may not be appropriate in another. One presumes, for example, that the title "Teacher" from Thomas in Gos. Thom. Log. 13 and from James in 1 Apoc. Jas. 31.5[1] is appropriate. In Dial. Sav. the disciples as a group use both "Teacher" (once only, 142.25) and "Lord" (once only, 136.11; but see the conjecture 126.6) so that "Teacher" appears as appropriate, although the other major characters (Matthew, Judas, Mariam) consistently address Jesus as "Lord". However, "Teacher" from the disciples in Ap. Jas. 15.32 seems to show their poorer understanding of Jesus (they are not privy to the revelation as James and Peter are; 2.33–35) who is called "Lord" or "Saviour" by James and Peter. The Pharisee Arimanios who calls Jesus "Teacher" in Ap. John 1.10 is clearly using the title as an enemy, in contrast to John's use of "Saviour" and "Lord".

I will not deal here with the even more confusing situation of the use of the same title for a variety of characters, one of whom may be the Jesus figure. It is less problematical when it is a case of different aspects of the Jesus figure referred to by the same title. In Apoc. Pet., for example, the title Saviour is found in 70.14; 72.26–27; 73.11–12; 80.8; 81.15; 82.8–9, 28. The last two references are to the intellectual Pleroma, the one who laughs on the tree, whereas the other references are to Jesus in his entirety (i.e. to the mixture of aspects which make up that character).[2]

In the following section I investigate further this phenomenon of titles which may mean one thing in one text and quite a different thing in another by a brief outline of the use of the significant title, "Son of Man".[3]

---

[1] "Der Charakter Jesu als Lehrer wird noch dadurch hervorgehoben, daß Jakobus ihn regelmäßig mit 'Rabbi' anspricht" (Böhlig and Labib 1963, 29).

[2] Havelaar notes the difference in form in these two instances – ⲛⲓⲥⲱⲧ̄ⲏⲣ instead of ⲡⲥⲱⲧⲏⲣ – suggesting that here the term "is used as a predicate to denote a spiritual entity" (164).

[3] See Borsch for a detailed study of the Son of Man in Gnostic literature.

5.1 "Son of Man"

The title "Son of Man" occurs with reference to Jesus or some aspect of Jesus in Ap. Jas., Treat. Res., Gos. Thom., Gos. Phil., Dial. Sav., Treat. Seth, Apoc. Pet., and Testim. Truth.

The first differentiation I would make in the use of the title is whether it refers to Jesus in the heavenly or earthly sphere (though not implying there-by a more earthly or a more heavenly Jesus). The earthly sphere is certainly covered by Ap. Jas 3.14, 17–18 (used by heavenly Jesus of the earthly Jesus); Treat. Res. 44.23, 30–31 (the humanity of the earthly Jesus in comparison to the divinity of the Son of God; but see my reference to this as more than mere humanity in earlier discussion in this chapter) and 46.14–15; Gos. Thom. Log. 86 (self-reference?);[1] and Gos. Phil. 63.29–30 (self-reference).

The Son of Man within the heavenly sphere is found in Gos. Phil. 81.14–15, 15–16, 16–17, 17–18, 18–19, 19 (the Lord is called the Son of Man within the discussion about the Son of Man and the son of the Son of Man and their respective actions of creating and begetting; see the discussion, Chapter VI); Dial. Sav. 135.16–17; 136.21 (the term occurs within the vision section: the first usage seems to refer to the Lord, the second is less clear. It is quite possible that this figure was not originally intended to be equated with the Lord but rather as some secondary heavenly interpreting figure);[2] Treat. Seth 64.11–12; 65.18–19; 69.21–22 (the last two references are self-references "I am (Jesus) Christ, the Son of Man", the last adding "who is exalted above the heavens"); and Apoc. Pet. 71.12 (also "who is exalted above the heavens"). In the latter, as Havelaar points out, the Son of Man may be the equivalent of the figure in 82.15–17, i.e. the intellectual Pleroma of the Saviour (1993, 165).

Within the references to Jesus as Son of Man within the earthly sphere, there are several where the title is used negatively. In Ap. Jas. 3.14, 17–18, the earthly Son of Man is a negative figure in comparison to the heavenly Saviour (those who have spoken with the Son of Man and listened to him are to be ashamed and woe is called down on them).

This is also the case in Soph. Jes. Chr. where the one who knows Son of Man in knowledge and love must bring a sign of the Son of Man so that he can go to the dwelling-places with those in the Eighth (117.22 – 118.3). The fate of this person is clearly parallel to that of the person who knows the Fa-ther defectively, who will go to his rest in the Eighth (117.12–15; = the

---

[1] Koester holds that this is a non-titular usage of the phrase (1968, 215). Lelyveld implies the same by the assertion that the only title Jesus possesses in Gos. Thom. is "the living one" (Log. 111) or the "son of the living one" (Log. 37) (35). Although Log. 86 is a parallel text to Matt 8:20//Lk 9:58, it is not clear that it is a self-reference in the context of Gos. Thom., since in Log. 106 the sons of man (ⲚⲰⲎⲢⲈ ⲘⲠⲢⲰⲘⲈ) are obviously the believers. On the other hand, perhaps for Gos. Thom. Jesus is the Son of Man and those who are the Sons of Man are those who have become like him by drinking from his mouth (Log. 108).

[2] See Koester and Pagels 9. Krause relates the figure to the Lord, citing Matt 8:20f and Mk 2:10 (1977a, 25).

ЄKKΛHCIà of the Eighth [BG 110.9–16/III 111.1–8]), in the lesser third Aeon, rather than to the dwelling-places of the generation over which there is no kingdom, which belongs with the Father and the Forefather (BG 108.12–17). In contrast to the person with defective knowledge is the one who knows Immortal Spirit of Light in silence (through reflection [ЄNΘYMHCIC], and consent in the truth [ЄYΔOKIà 2Ñ TMHЄ]), the one who must bring signs of the Invisible One so as to become a light in the Spirit of Silence (117.15–21). I suspect that this is a (polemical) reinterpretation of the tradition one finds in Lk 12:8–9 where acknowledging Jesus brings acknowledgement from the Son of Man before the angels of God.

Finally it should be noted that a study of the titles can be useful in determining structure in some of the texts. In Soph. Jes. Chr., for example, a clear division of the text is indicated by the change of address from "Saviour" to "perfect Saviour" from 95.21–22 onwards. In Ap. Jas., Koester has remarked that the title "Saviour" is used only in the secondary frames apart from one use (2.40) in the dialogues where the title "Lord" prevails (1990, 200).

Conclusion

The subject of Chapter III was the world to which Jesus comes. In this chapter I investigated the being and nature of Jesus, which has implications for the extent to which he needs to be in or of the earthly world. This in turn relates to the way in which Jesus carries out the key activities of liberation and revelation within that world. The processes of revelation and liberation are the subject of the following chapter.

V

Reasons for the Coming of the Saviour:
Jesus as Revealer and Liberator

In order to understand the Saviour, Jesus, as revealer and liberator in the earthly realm, it is necessary to first know what salvation entails for the Gnostic, what sort of Saviour is required. The process of salvation for the Gnostic is dealt with in more depth in Chapter IX. For present purposes this process may be summarised as comprising the recognition of one's self – one's origin, who one is now, one's destiny – and, by corollary, the recognition of one's relationship with heavenly characters like the Father and the Saviour.

If salvation is a process of self-recognition, and that insight is already present *in potentia* within the self, in one sense the Saviour is essentially superfluous, as Filoramo suggests, and we need to rethink what the term "saviour" might mean for Gnostics apart from its more usual Christian definition of the one who redeems from sin.

Moreover, the predisposition of the spiritual substance to be saved and its natural affinity with the substance of the Saviour constitute as many differences between Gnostic and Christian soteriology. The Gnostic Saviour does not come to reconcile humankind with God, but to reunite the Gnostic with himself. He does not come to pardon a sin that the Gnostic cannot have committed, but to rectify a situation of ignorance and deficiency and to re-establish the original plenitude. The Gnostic Saviour comes to save himself (Filoramo 106).

Filoramo illustrates his last point from the Pistis Sophia: "Enlightening his disciples and forming in them the pneumatic reality that represents the Man of Light, the Gnostic Saviour of the Pistis Sophia does no more than recover that part of himself, his spiritual substance that had fallen prisoner to the darkness" (107).

However, for the Nag Hammadi texts, the division between Gnostic and Christian definitions of salvation are not as clear cut as Filoramo suggests, and that lack of clarity is not dependent upon the continuing debate about which texts are Gnostic and which Christian (note my discussion of the unhelpfulness of this strict delineation in Chapter I). There are many associated aspects to the process of self-recognition, as will be illustrated in the final chapter, and some of them come quite close to some aspects of the understanding of salvation in mainstream Christian circles. This can be seen, for example, in Gos. Phil. which relates that Christ came as a saviour: to ransom those who were strangers, making them his own (52.35 – 53.1, 3–4); to save others (53.1–2), specifically the soul (53.10–13);[1] to redeem the good and the evil (53.2–3, 13–14; see also 60.26–28). His work of salvation also entails reconciliation, nourishment of life, and punishment of evil/the world (see the discussion in Chapter VI).

The situation of the Gnostic who requires salvation is also ambiguous. Salvation is the acquisition of self-knowledge, but the Gnostic does not have the power to come to that insight by him/herself. Someone is required to alert the Gnostic to the insight that awaits recognition, to wake him/her up. In this way, the Saviour needs to be primarily a revealer in the sense of one who awakens, rather than someone who gives extra knowledge that is not already possessed. In fact, the revealer is often rather like an older brother, one who already knows, one who was with the Gnostic in the beginning and will be with him/her in the end in the heavenly assembly. That the spiritual power of the Gnostics is in no sense inferior to Jesus' power may also be implied from texts in which he himself requires awakening or liberation from the bonds of forgetfulness (Soph. Jes. Chr. 107.14–15).

In this chapter, I deal almost exclusively with Jesus as a revealer. In general, most of the texts in the Nag Hammadi corpus give the reasons for his coming as revelation or liberation, or both. Of the two, revelation is by far the most important and frequent.

1. Jesus as Revealer

Jesus appears as a revealer figure in a number of contexts.[2] First, there are the texts in which he is a heavenly revealer with no interest in a human setting. This may be so because he does not specifically enter the earthly context or may be that all his activity in the earthly realm is only interpreted in terms of the struggle of cosmic and heavenly powers. Secondly, he may be a heavenly figure in the sense that he has completed his earthly activity *per se* and is not in the earthly setting as he previously was, but he has not yet returned fully to the heavenly region. His connection with the earthly context

---

[1] Wilson suggests that the author is here making allusion to Jn 10:17–18 so that the soul must be interpreted as Christ's (1962, 71; see also Partrick 125–7, 132; and Evans et al. 147). This might be mistakenly implied also from those translations where the 3rd sing. masc. possessive has been used instead of the definite article which appears in the Coptic ("his life" in Catanzaro 37, and in Isenberg [Layton and Isenberg 145], "son âme" in Ménard 1988, 51). If it is the soul/life of Christ then it would be necessary to indicate where this soul/life fell into the hands of robbers (the archons) and was taken captive (53.11–12). Unless this is a reference in some way to the activity of archons in a variation of a passion story for Jesus (although there is no other reference in the text), it seems more likely that this soul is the one which originates in Sophia, and is given to human beings when the Demiurge breathes it into Adam.

[2] As well as the concept of Jesus as revealer, we find in Trim. Prot. the reverse concept of the Word as the one to whom everything is revealed – as the eye of the three Permanences which exist as Voice (= Father, Mother, Son) (46.28–30).

has been changed in some way, although he still has access to it. Finally, he may be described as Jesus in the earthly context who gives revelation.

1.1 Jesus as Heavenly Revealer

A number of texts present two figures, the primary figure being the heavenly Jesus who is giving revelation, and the secondary figure being the earthly Jesus whose prior revelation is referred to by the heavenly Jesus (see, e.g. Ap. Jas. 8.37 – 9.1; Ap. John 1.13–17; Treat. Res. 44.13–17, 21). It is not always clear at which stage the heavenly figure is to be placed, whether prior to or after a final ascent to the heavenly region. Indeed, there may be no interest at all in such categories. Moreover there are texts in which even the earthly activity of the Jesus figure cannot be said to be really "earthly". In Treat. Res., for example, the symbols used to interpret the death and resurrection of the Jesus figure are cosmic symbols. He is a revealer and a mediating figure who, by overcoming death, provides the way of immortality for the elect (see, e.g., 46.25–32) to follow to the heavenly region.

In Ap. John, the heavenly revealer, who appears and disappears within the earthly context, speaks of prior revelatory (waking) activity within the earthly context, but again the activity is couched in cosmic terms: the revealer who appears as an eagle on the tree of knowledge so as to teach Adam/the copy of Adamas and the woman/the copy of Epinoia and to awaken them out of the depth of sleep (23.26–31); who descends into the Underworld to waken the one who hears from his deep sleep (31.5–7).

This final descent of the revealer into the Underworld in a three-part process is in actual fact a descent into the human person: "I went... that I might enter into the middle of the darkness and the inside of Hades... And I entered into the middle of their prison which is the prison of the body..." (30.33 – 31.4). The revealer wakes the one who hears from his deep sleep (31.5–7), raises him up and seals him with the light of the water with five seals so that death will not have power over him (31.22–25). The one who hears is a model for all those who belong to the immovable race, all those who hear the Saviour who calls their names.[1]

In Apoc. Pet., the setting of the text appears to be earthly, with Jesus and Peter sitting in the temple, but the Saviour here has more the role of an interpreting angel as one expects in an apocalypse, so the Jesus figure is better placed in this first category of heavenly revealer.

---

[1] *Contra* Giversen who takes the final section out of its context within the three-part form and suggests that the more likely interpretation of the final action of the revealer is actually the description of how knowledge came to John who wrote the book: "the exclusive character of the treatise has thus also been emphasized" (1963a, 271). It would be unusual to find a descent of the revealer/Saviour into Hades for the explicit purpose of rescue or revelation to just one person.

1.2 Jesus as Revealer between Earth and Heaven

This is by far the most difficult category to define, given all the possibilities for connection between Jesus and the earthly region. In a sense, all the Jesus figures could be situated in this category, since all revelation is somehow heavenly and comes from or through the heavenly figure of Jesus, and all revelation is basically for those within the earthly context to which both the revealer and the receivers of the revelation do not really belong. However, this category is intended primarily as a temporal rather than a spatial category, that is, it is intended to situate the Jesus figure prior to a final return to the heavenly region, but after ending in some way (suffering, death, struggle, resurrection, and so on) a phase of closer physical or apparent physical connection with the earthly region.

Gärtner characterises this time of the "between-worlds Jesus" as the time of Jesus' perfect teaching according to the Gnostics (prepared for in Lk 24:45 and Acts 1:3). The time is anything from eighteen months to eleven or twelve years (Pistis Sophia) (101).

Thom. Cont. and Soph. Jes. Chr. present two good examples of a Jesus who fits this category. In Thom. Cont., the Jesus figure (named twice, 139.21; 144.37) appears prior to ascension (there is no mention of resurrection) to give secret teaching. He reveals the things that Thomas has pondered over (138.4–7) and in this way the revelation is occasioned somewhat in the same way as in Ap. John, where the revealer figure also comes to help John with his ponderings.

Soph. Jes. Chr. presents a Jesus after the resurrection and presumably prior to ascension, given the obvious parallels to the post-resurrection appearances of the Johannine Jesus in the greeting formula, "Peace be to you. My peace I give to you." (91.21–23; see Jn 14:27; 20:19, 21, 26). The teaching itself is introduced by a "heavenly appearance" scene, and takes place in response to the perplexity and questioning of the followers (91.2–10). The reaction of marvelling and fear by the followers is typical of a "heavenly" appearance (91.23–24).

Some texts are not easily categorised. Thus in Ep. Pet. Phil., the Jesus figure might belong to the category of heavenly revealers, or, as I think is more likely, he appears in a changed form but still to a certain extent within the earthly context between resurrection and ascension (see Chapter IV).[1]

---

[1] Meyer indicates the similarities between the conclusions of both appearance sections in the present text and the ascension or commissioning scenes of the canonical gospels. However, he does not locate the risen Christ specifically for this text as pre- or post-ascension (1981, 144, 160, 181 n. 171, 187 n. 233; see, similarly, Bethge 1978, 168 n. 32, 169 n. 57; and Meyer and Wisse 245, 249). Perkins speaks of the risen Jesus who instructs the apostles (1993a, 101). Presumably she means prior to the ascension.

1.3 Jesus as Earthly Revealer

Some texts contain short summaries concerning the revelation given by the earthly Jesus: Tri. Trac. states that while he was a child he had already begun to preach (133.27–29); in Ap. John, Arimanios' accusation implies that Jesus has been a teacher, albeit a false teacher, within Judaism (1.13–17); Ap. Jas. gives a "life summary" in 8.37 – 9.1, where the major work of the earthly Jesus between origin and death is speaking (8.38); Gos. Truth has a more extensive reflection concerning Jesus the Christ who enlightened those who were in darkness through oblivion (18.16–19), and showed them the way of truth which he taught them (18.19–21), who came as a guide and a teacher in schools (19.17–20).

I would add here also Gos. Thom. and Gos. Phil. in which an earthly Jesus gives secret teaching.

1.4 The Difference between Heavenly and Earthly Revelation, Past and Present Revelation, or between Superior and Inferior Revelation

Some texts make a distinction between some prior revelation and the present revelation, often implying or stating directly that the former revelation is somehow incomplete or misunderstood, and therefore requiring something further. In certain cases, there seems to be some polemic directed at some other revelation which the community has received. Thus 1 Apoc. Jas. purports to contain revelation from the one who has no number (i.e. the highest God), which is superior to some other writing that the community is aware of, or perhaps has used, but which has come from someone of limited understanding (26.6–8).

Often the problem with the former revelation is that followers have not believed or have misunderstood. Ep. Pet. Phil. speaks of an earlier revelation which evoked only unbelief in the apostles, so that what has already been spoken to them must be repeated (135.4–8; see also 138.22–23; 139.11–12 [incomplete revelation implied]).

Soph. Jes. Chr. refers to teaching (about pure and perfect flesh) which has been given prior to the present revelation but it is not clear whether the other teaching has been prior to or after the resurrection (91.17–20). We might assume it is prior to resurrection since it did not suffice in stilling the perplexity of Jesus' followers.

There may be problems which continue with the disciples or hearers of the revelation even in the present setting. Thus in Gos. Thom., Jesus states that he did not tell the disciples what they asked about in former times but he desires to do so now and they do not ask (Log. 92).

In the case of Ap. Jas., not only is the understanding of the former teaching faulty but the former teacher, the Son of Man, is presented negatively (unless this is just a curious way of blaming the former listeners for having misunderstood). There is shame and woe for those who have seen the Son of Man and spoken to him and listened to him, and been healed by him, and so on, but life for those who have not (3.11–34), since the former listeners are said to be those who have not listened to the teaching and are therefore outside of the Father's inheritance. They are told to weep (10.11) and to mourn (10.12) and preach what is good (10.13) and to be ashamed (10.21). We are also told in this text that the earthly Jesus spoke in parables as opposed to the Jesus who now speaks openly (7.1–6), but the text is not consistent since the latter Jesus also uses parables (7.24–35; 8.16–23; 12.22–27; 13.3–8).

1.5 Forms of the Revelation

Certain forms of revelation have certainly been influential in the tradition, most especially where the revelation is given through a series of questions and answers. Sometimes these texts are referred to as dialogues but they are really monologues of the revealer with the questions as no more than the means of moving from one point to the next in the monologue.

In Thom. Cont., where at one stage Jesus appears to ask Thomas his opinion on a point (142.5–7), Thomas' response sums up the whole process as a one-way communication: "It is you, Lord, whom it befits to speak, and me to listen" (142.8–9). As Kirchner rightly comments, Thomas has more the role of an "extra" ("Statisten") than a real dialogue partner, indicating that this is a typical situation, with reference to Ap. Jas. and 1 Apoc. Jas. (793).

On the other hand, whereas the Lord takes the major role in Dial. Sav., answering questions or contradicting statements, at least here some other characters make a contribution to the content of the revelation with which the Lord agrees, or at least the dialogue is more than one-sided. On two occasions Judas speaks to Matthew (135.7–8; 143.11–15), and Mary also speaks to the disciples (131. 19).

There are a number of smaller literary forms which are found frequently in the texts.

1.5.1 Parables

There are parables in Gos. Thom. and Ap. John (see Stroker; and Logan and Wedderburn), and in Ap. Jas. (7.24–35; 8.16–23; 12.22–27; 13.3–8). Ap. Jas. also gives a list of parables (The Shepherds, The Seed, The Building, The Lamps of the Virgins, The Wage of the Workmen, The Didrachmae, and The Woman [8.6–10]), and Great Pow. describes the coming saviour who will speak in parables (40.30–31).

In a kind of "parabolic" teaching activity somewhat reminiscent of the Hebrew prophets, Gos. Phil. describes the Lord going into the dye works of

Levi (63.25–30), mirroring in action the saying about God as a dyer (61.12–20), and Dial. Sav. includes the scene in which Jesus takes up the stone in order to answer a question of Judas (132.19 – 134.24).

1.5.2 Beatitudes and Woes

In Thom. Cont., the teaching in the final section of the text is structured formally into a series of woes (143.8 – 145.1: it is not clear where the final [twelfth] woe ends since the text is damaged) followed by three blessings (145.1–8) and a final exhortation which concludes with a confessional formula (145.8–16). Ap. Jas. has a number of beatitudes (11. 14–17; 12.16–17, 37–39, 41 – 13.1, 11–13; 14.37–39, 41 – 15.3) and woes (11.12–13, 13–14; 12.39–40; 13.9–11).

1.5.3 Introductory Formulae or Formulae Used in Teaching

In the teaching section beginning from 96.21 in Soph. Jes. Chr., there are variations on the formula, "Whoever has ears to hear, let him hear" used either as a break within a section of teaching or an interjection (97.19–24; 98.20–22), or as an introduction to a section of teaching (105.9–11; BG 107.18 – 108.1). Ap. Jas. has the introductory formula, "Amen, I say to you..." (6.2–3; see also 13.8–9).

1.6 Content of the Revelation

In general the revelation is concerned with the revealer himself and secret knowledge from him (e.g. Trim. Prot. 37.8–20; 47.13–15) and/or it is revelation from the highest God/Father through the revealer (Apoc. Pet. 70.23–25; 71.9–13; 1 Apoc. Jas. 26.6–8; On Anoint. 40.19–20; Tri. Trac. 114.22–30; Soph. Jes. Chr. 94.5–13).

The revelation is mostly addressed to disciples or followers by an earthly Jesus, and in this way indirectly to the communities of the text. We have already seen that the revelation is not for those "in the flesh", so that it tends generally to be exclusive to pneumatics (see further discussion in Chapter IX). In some cases the latter are referred to as "the seeds", that is, the seeds from Sophia or Protennoia who belong to the Christ who has come to wake them or liberate them (Ep. Pet. Phil. 136.22–24; Trim. Prot. 36.14–16;[1] 40.31; 41.1–2, 27–28; 50.18).

At first glance Trim. Prot. appears to be far more inclusive in that those who receive the revelation comprise the whole spectrum of beings from the

---

[1] Although this passage does not belong strictly speaking to the appearance of the Word, Helderman is right in proposing that the work should not be so strictly divided as to obscure the main theme which flows in the text, i.e. the work of Protennoia for her own (1978, 201–2).

highest heaven to those in the earthly context: those who dwell in Silence with the first Thought (37.12–13), the Aeons (38.16–18), those who dwell in darkness (37.13–14; 46.31–33), those who dwell in the abyss (37.15), those who dwell in the hidden treasuries (37.16), both offspring or orders of the Logos (88.27 – 89.8), and those who became the sons of the Light (37.19–20). However, even here the Light is revealed only to those who are his own.

Much of the teaching makes use of familiar material, albeit differently interpreted, from the canonical writings (see, e.g., Gaffron's excursus on the New Testament citations and allusions in Gos. Phil. [1969, 32–62]). Thus in Dial. Sav. the Lord teaches the disciples how to pray to the Father in the first section of the teaching (121.3 – 122.1) in a passage very reminiscent of Matt 6:9–13.[1] The actual content of the teaching in Interp. Know. (9.28–35) is presented as a mixture of a number of sayings known to us from the canonical scriptures (see Matt 23:9; 6:9; 12:48–50; 16:26 and parallels; Pagels and Turner 1990a, 80; and Evans et al. 381–91).

The teaching covers a broad range of themes, from instruction on how the community should live together and what they should strive towards, through to details about heavenly mysteries, cosmology, the origin and destiny of Gnostics,[2] the origin and working of the Saviour, the revelation of the Father, and so on. In one sense all the teaching is revelation but there is also revelation which is more explicitly of a "heavenly" nature.

There is straightforward information in 1 Apoc. Jas., for example, which tells about the twelve hebdomads/archons and the seventy-two heavens (26.2–30), or in Ep. Pet. Phil. which is concerned with the aeons and archons, and the apostles' place within the scheme of things (134.18 – 135.2). Then there is Ap. John which deals with the nature of the Father, the evolution of the powers in the heavenly region, the development of the human race, and the salvation of souls, and Soph. Jes. Chr. which gives descriptions of various figures of the heavenly realm and relates the process of cosmogonic events, stating that this is the truth to which the normal speculation of humankind does not even come close (92.6 – 93.8). Dial. Sav. is more interested in the end rather than the beginning, the teaching ranging for the most part over details of how one is to be in relation to the world here and details about the time of dissolution (the time for the heavenly journey of the soul), the heavenly garment and the path and so on.

Much more "conventional" teaching is to be found in Ap. Jas. where there is teaching about salvation (11.1–2), emphasis on the kingdom of God/heaven (6.2–8; 7.22–35; 12.22–27; 13.17–19) and the cross and death of Jesus (5.6 – 6.18; "Remember my cross and my death, and you will live" [5.33–35]). There is exhortation to hearken to the word (9.18), to understand knowledge

---

[1] For the relation of other passages to the New Testament, see Krause 1977a, 25–27; and Evans et al. 234–7.

[2] The "classic" question regarding the Gnostic's origin, present situation and destiny can be found, e.g., in Ep. Pet. Phil. 134.23–26. Bethge comments: "So ist gnostisches Gedankengut in EpPt zwar nicht dominierend, hat aber dennoch einen bestimmten Stellenwert" (1990, 278).

(9.19), to love life (9.19–20), to pray to the Father/God (10.32–34), and to repent (10.11–12).

Some teaching is much more focused on the historical circumstances of the community. The instructions of the Saviour in Apoc. Pet., in the context of Peter's visionary and auditory experience,[1] are all in reference to the right understanding of the events of the passion and the threat of heretics to the community. As Koschorke rightly comments, the text has two themes, "die 'Passions'-Geschichte und die Häresiengeschichte" (1978b, 11), and there are clear parallels between those who perpetrate the crucifixion and those who perpetrate the heresies (both groups are deaf and blind, both think that the Saviour has really suffered death, both are under the influence of the archons [12]).

There are a number of texts which focus on the secret nature of the teaching. Thom. Cont. is said to comprise the secret words (138.1–2) or talk about secret things (138.24–25) of Jesus. Ap. John. speaks of secret teaching presented in a mystery (32.2; see also 31.31). Gos. Thom. is characterised as secret sayings (Prologue) given to Thomas by Jesus.[2] In Log. 13 Thomas is taken aside by Jesus to be told three things which he then will not tell the others because of the risk to themselves. The secret teaching is never explicitly revealed, although the rest of the text could perhaps be regarded as secret teaching in its own right.[3] Certainly Log. 62 has a reference to the mysteries which Jesus tells.

Apart from Great Pow., where it is stated that the Saviour will proclaim the Aeon that is to come (40.31 – 41.1),[4] future events are the focus of the

---

[1] On Peter's ecstatic condition as he repeats the revelation from the Saviour to his listeners, see Böhlig 1989c.

[2] Gärtner proposes that "the very term ⲍⲱⲡ, 'to hide', 'to be secret,'... must also be considered to be a technical term for the Divine revelation", used in adjunct to μυστήριον (109–110). See also Ménard 1975b, 30.

[3] Several writers have dealt with the problem that this gospel comprises well-known sayings of Jesus and can hardly be regarded as secret teaching. "We have in a sense, therefore, to admit that the prologue's view of the material does not agree particularly well with the material itself, if we follow our principle – of 'superficial' sayings and their deeper understanding – strictly" (Gärtner 112). However, Gärtner goes on to suggest that the discrepancy is more apparent than real, that the prologue is not from a later editor since so many of the sayings witness to an overall gnostic view (113; see also Ménard 1975b, 31). Lincoln proposes that the text was addressed at the same time to initiates and non-initiates (Log. 2 outlines the various levels of initiation), and that this is the ground of the seeming paradox between secret teaching and a text which was widely circulated and apparently intended to be so (68–9). Lelyveld notes the same problem: "Pourtant une première lecture montre qu'il n'en est rien (paroles secrètes) dans l'EvTh. La plupart des Logia s'addressent à un auditoire anonyme ou bien aux disciples en général. Il y a un seul Logion, le Logion 13, dans lequel Jésus parle en effet séparément à un disciple Thomas" (6–7), but proposes finally that "hidden words" is just a circumlocution for the traditional expression "parables" (7–8). Davies' solution is to suggest that "Jesus is less the revealer than the revelation, less the one advocating a mode of apprehension than the apprehension itself (675).

[4] Wisse and Williams follow with: "...just as he spoke to Noah in the first aeon of the flesh" (41.1–3), i.e. the saviour is pre-existent to the psychic aeon (307). However Cherix has, "...comme Noé avait parlé dans le premier éon de la chair" (14), noting that ⲱⲁⲝⲉ is always constructed with ⲙⲛ̄, ⲛⲙ̄ⲙⲁ̀ (28).

revelation in texts where James has an important role. In 1 Apoc. Jas., the Lord says he will show James the completion of his (the Lord's) redemption (24.12), giving him a sign of these things (24.13), revealing James' own redemption (29.12–13), and in Ap. Jas., Jesus foretells James' sufferings, death and burial (5.9–21) within teaching about disregarding the flesh and not being afraid of suffering and death (5.6 – 6.18).

Major themes and terms used for the activity of revelation include:

– awakening or calling out of ignorance or forgetfulness (Soph. Jes. Chr. 97.19–24; 107.16–20; Ap. John 23.26–31; 31.5–7);

– enlightenment or causing believers to shine in the Light (Soph. Jes. Chr. 114.5–8; Gos. Truth 18.16–19; Ep. Pet. Phil. 133.27 – 134.1; Trim. Prot. 37.7–20; Tri. Trac. 62.33–38);

– revealing the glory (of the Father) (Soph. Jes. Chr. 107.22–23; Treat. Seth 50.22–24);

– bringing knowledge (Soph. Jes. Chr. 107.25 – 108.5; Gos. Truth 19.32–33; On Bap. A 40.32–35; Ap. John 23.26–31; Tri. Trac. 117.28–29);

– speaking, telling, and revealing the truth and all things and the Father or the highest God (Soph. Jes. Chr. 93.10–12; 96.19–21; 106.7–9; 118.17–25; Tri. Trac. 63.17–19);

– showing the way (Gos. Truth 18.19–21);

bringing rest or immortality (Soph. Jes. Chr. 118.6–15; Interp. Know. 9.17–19);

– moving to union with the revealer (Gos. Thom. Log. 108; Trim. Prot. 47.22–23; 49.9–11, 20–23; Tri. Trac. 63.12–13; 65.17–25).

As a result of the revelation, the community may be more than awakened; they too may be revealers in their own right. In Ap. Jas., for example, the ideal disciple speaks or preaches and is awake, as opposed to those who listen and are sleeping (9.29–35; see also 10.12–13; 11.14–17).

2. Jesus as Liberator

While bringing revelation or awakening the pneumatics is by far the most important activity of the Jesus figure, he is often described within this activity as struggling with the powers in some way on behalf of the seeds or pneumatics. Armstrong comments in this regard:

It is the liberation of the Gnostic children of light from the darkness through the saving enlightenment brought by the Redeemer which is the centre of the picture, not the cosmic defeat of the armies of the darkness (44).

It is certainly the case that really nothing more is required in a spiritual sense than the awakening – certainly the pneumatics do not need to be saved in any sense spiritually[1] – but they do need assistance in coming free from the powers which hold them prisoner in this earthly context. Thus, for example, in Gos. Eg., Seth (who is eventually clothed with Jesus) must pass through the three parousias (the flood, the conflagration, and the judgment of the archons and powers and authorities) in order to save the race who went astray (III 63.4–9/IV 74.17–24).

Liberating activity combined with revelation may take the form of a struggle, as in Soph. Jes. Chr. where the Saviour destroys the work of the archons who are opposed to his revelatory activity, and breaks the bonds in which they have imprisoned Immortal Man (107.15–16; BG 121.15 – 122.3). Even more interestingly, in Interp. Know. Christ is said to destroy the Demiurge ([the arrogant teacher], 9.19–20) but also to teach him (10.13–18) who was himself teaching the church to die (9.20–21, 26–27). On the other hand, liberation may be simply opening up the way out of the earthly context into the heavenly region, as in Dial. Sav. (120. 20–26).

Perhaps Gos. Truth contains the clearest statement about liberating activity connected with revelation. In this text, the major work of the "earthly" Jesus is enlightenment, and even his death is allegorised to the extent that the focus is entirely on the enlightenment that it brings, whether by the fruit (18.24–26) or by the living book (20.24–27). The essential point of the whole activity of salvation is to bring the elect out of ignorance into the knowledge of the Father, since if the Father comes to be known, oblivion will cease to exist (18.9–11; 24.30–32).

One important aspect of the work of liberation is that the Jesus figure himself may need some kind of liberating activity.[2] Tri. Trac. relates that everything needs to be redeemed, even the Son who is the redeemer of the Totality (124.32 – 125.1). He became man (ⲉⲧⲉ ⲡⲣⲉϥϣⲱⲡⲉ ⲛ̄ⲣⲱⲙⲉ ⲡⲉ) (125.1–2), "since he gave himself for each thing which we need, we in the flesh, who

---

[1] Even Teach. Silv. makes that clear where believers themselves are exhorted to raise their dead (i.e. those under the influence of the flesh), and give them life (106.17–20); to knock upon themselves as upon a door, walk upon themselves as on a straight road (106.30 – 107.3; see also 117.5–9, 19–23), raise themselves up like eagles, having left their old man behind (114.17–19).

[2] Perkins rejects the idea that the redeemed redeemer is the core element in Gnostic mythologising. Citing 1 Apoc. Jas. she states: "neither the redeemer nor the redeemed is trapped by forgetfulness" (1993a. 96). Although it may not be a core element, it is at least present in texts such as Tri. Trac.

are his church" (ⲉⲁϥⲧⲁⲁϥ ⲙ̄ⲙⲓⲛ ⲙ̄ⲙⲟϥ ⲛ̄ⲟⲩⲁⲛ ⲛⲓⲙ ⲛⲉⲉⲓ ⲉⲧⲛ̄ⲣ̄ ⲭⲣⲓⲁ ⲙ̄ⲙⲟⲟⲩ ⲁⲛⲁⲛ ϩⲛ̄ ⲥⲁⲣⲝ ⲉⲧⲟⲉⲓ ⲛ̄ⲛⲉⲕⲕⲗⲏⲥⲓⲁ ⲛ̄ⲧⲉϥ) (125.2–5).[1]

In other words, the Saviour takes on deficiency and in this sense needs to be redeemed. The Father set deficiency on the Saviour (125.29) which is also paradoxically "a glory for his Pleroma" (125.31). Just as the Father is a cause of ignorance so also is he a begetter of knowledge (126.6–8) and he kept that knowledge to the end (i.e. the Restoration) (126.9–11). The Son is counted among those who are in the flesh (125.11–12; cf. the Father who counts himself with the aeons and the better self of the Logos in the production of the Saviour, 86.31–32) even though he is the Father's first-born, and his love, who was incarnate (125.13–15), one of the Father's powers (127.9). He was given the grace (ⲡⲓϩⲙⲟⲧ) before anyone else (125.23–24).

Further aspects of liberation and struggle are dealt with in the following chapter. It remains here to consider briefly another possible liberating action for the Jesus figure, investigating whether in Exeg. Soul we may understand Jesus to be the bridegroom of the soul who rescues her.

At first glance it appears that the bridegroom is the heavenly Adam. To save the soul the Father sends her man, her brother, the firstborn, the bridegroom who comes down to her in the bridal chamber (132.7–27). This is later explained as Adam and his partner the soul (133.3–6). The marriage between the two is a return to the former unity (133.6–10),[2] which the soul had with the Father, alone and virginal and androgynous (127.22–25).[3]

However, in 134.25–28, the text tells us that the soul becomes young, ascends, praises the father and her brother by whom she was rescued. This is followed by a reference to the Saviour: the Saviour cries out, "No one can come to me unless my Father draws him and brings him to me; and I myself will raise him up on the last day"(134.34 – 135.4). Considering the two passages together, it seems as if the heavenly Adam may indeed be equated with the Saviour who is Jesus.[4]

---

[1] The text also states that the Son received redemption from the word which descended upon him (125.5–7). Both Thomassen (1989a, 439–40) and Attridge and Pagels (470) see this as a possible reference to the baptism of the Saviour.

[2] Krause (1975b) gives an extensive interpretation of the event in connection with the sacrament of the bridal chamber in Gos. Phil., but Wisse disagrees, saying that the imagery here has nothing to do with that sacramental usage (1975, 79–80).

[3] Scopello speaks of the soul leaving God, who is at once father and spouse (66). This seems unusual in the light of the fact that the soul is said to be androgynous *in itself* in the beginning, i.e. it contains within itself both spouses. Sevrin is right therefore to speak of the rapport between the "père/androgyne" or the "père/fille-fils" (1983, 27).

[4] Scopello provides an extensive review of the imagery of the spouse as brother, including Cant. 4:9 (see also 4:12; 5:1, 2; 8:1) and Adv. Haer. I,28,6 in which Christ and his sister Sophia are mentioned, whom the Ophites call the bride and bridegroom (136–7). However she does not identify the bridegroom here as the Christ but rather probably the Spirit (11; see also Ménard 1975a, 65–66). Sevrin too ultimately disagrees with identifying the bridegroom and Christ, though he does not discount the possibility of speaking of the bridegroom-brother as a saviour figure (1983, 29). If the soul here could be seen to have common features with the Valentinian Sophia then it would be possible to see this saviour as the Saviour or Christ of the Valentinians (30). However in considering the exhortation in the text addressed to

Conclusion

This chapter moves from a consideration of the Gnostic understanding of salvation, to explore the primary nature of the Saviour as revealer, and also liberator. While revelation, and to some extent liberation, is the focus of most texts, nevertheless there are other activities important to the process of salvation. These form the subject of the next chapter.

---

concrete individuals to repent with "all their soul", he proposes that in this case the heavenly double of the soul is closer to the angel which is spoken of in Gos. Phil., or the angels of the Saviour, and cannot be identified with the Saviour himself. He concludes that in no case is the spouse-brother linked with the Christ: "on peut même dire que si ce Christ peut se voir assigner un rôle particulier dans le processus de salut décrit par le mythe (ce qui est très conjectural), c'est précisément à propos d'un événement (le baptême) où l'époux n'intervient pas" (30).

VI

Activity of Jesus and Its Setting

The material for this chapter has been divided into three main categories: activity of a human kind, activity of a "more-than-human" kind, activity of a divine/heavenly kind. These categories are only helpful to a certain extent, since activities can be deceptive and what appears to be human activity and not at all extraordinary may conceal another dimension. Miracles may result from a deity working within a human being or may be performed by a divine person. Teaching may be given by a divinely inspired human teacher or by a heavenly teacher come to earth. Sometimes in the description of the action itself nothing appears otherwise than ordinary and human, yet the context of the rest of the text may make it clear that it is anything but a human action.

1. Activity by and towards Jesus of a Human Kind

This section covers activity which would not be extraordinary for the "average" human being.

1.1 Baptism/Chrisming

The only clear references to baptism for the Jesus figure occur in Gos. Phil. First, there is the statement that the Lord did everything in a mystery: a baptism, a chrism, a eucharist, a redemption, a bridal chamber (67.28–30). Secondly, the Lord experiences baptism, chrism and redemption in his rebirth in the bridal chamber from the union of the Father of All and the virgin at the Jordan (70.34 – 71.2).

I have already argued against baptism for Jesus in Paraph. Shem (see Introduction) and Testim. Truth (see Chapter II). Testim. Truth 69.15–17 asserts also that Jesus does not baptise ("the Son of Man did not baptise any of his disciples").

Some see a possible reference to baptism in Tri. Trac. 125.5–7 which speaks of the Son receiving redemption from the Word which descended upon him.[1] In the same text Colpe interprets the damaged section 37.30–33 as a reference to the anointing of the Logos with the Spirit in "eine wohl glossenartig eingelegte völlige Gnostisierung von Gestalt und Taufe Christi" (1974, 120).[2] Partrick also finds allusions to the baptism of Jesus in two passages of Gos. Truth (21.25b – 22.27a and 27.26–31), but the links to the event at the Jordan seem rather tenuous (76–80).

1.2 Eucharistic/Thanksgiving Celebration

Gos. Phil. makes reference to a eucharistic or thanksgiving prayer of Jesus (ϨⲚ ⲦⲈⲨⲬⲀⲢⲒⲤⲦⲈⲒⲀ) (58.11) to the Father to unite the angels with him and his disciples (58.13–14).[3]

1.3 Jesus as Gatherer and Leader of a Group of Disciples

This kind of activity for the Jesus figure may be presumed for many texts but is only explicit in Gos. Thom. where the disciples ask who will be their leader once Jesus departs (Log. 12).

1.4 Commissioning of Disciples

Evans finds an occasional reference in Gnostic gospels to apostolic commissioning resembling that contained in the New Testament (i.e. Matt 28:18–20; Acts 1:8), citing Ep. Pet. Phil. VIII, 140.15–27 and Gos. Mary BG 8502, 18.15 – 19.2 (1981a, 410). In Ep. Pet. Phil., the commissioning of apostles takes place within the present revelation (137.22–28; 140.19–23), but the text seems to know of a prior commissioning ("orders" [ⲈⲚⲦⲞⲖⲎ]; 132.17; 133.7–8).[4] The apostles have been told to come together and to give instruction and preach in the salvation which was promised them by their Lord Jesus Christ (132.19 – 133.1).

---

[1] See Thomassen 1989a, 439–40; and Attridge and Pagels 470.

[2] In relation to this idea, Gos. Phil. 74.12–17 speaks of the chrism which is superior to baptism and notes that the Son has anointed the apostles, just as the Father anointed him.

[3] It is interesting that both this activity and the baptism mentioned in the previous section are situated within the time frame "on that day" (58.10–11; 71.6–7, 9), and that there are no other uses of this phrase in this text. Either it is to be understood for this passage as a reference to the preceding appearance of Jesus in glory to the disciples, or it refers only to its own specific action (i.e. to a day on which the prayer took place), or it is a specific reference to that day of significance at the Jordan, in which case it may be possible to suggest that eucharist be included among the experiences of Jesus at the Jordan. In personal communication with the author, Luise Abramowski suggested a closeness to the Johannine Abschiedsrede.

[4] The commissioning in 137.22–28 repeats, generally speaking, the formula of 132.19 – 133.1.

It is possible to add a number of texts to those cited by Evans. In Soph. Jes. Chr., the Saviour commissions the disciples, "I have given you authority over all things as sons of Light that you might tread upon their power with your feet" (119.4–8). The disciples are then described as beginning to preach the gospel of God, the eternal imperishable Spirit (BG 127.2–10).

Acts Pet. 12 Apost. knows of an appointment of the apostles to ministry by the Lord prior to his appearance to them in 1.10–12. He has given Peter his name previously also (9.10–13; see also the naming of Peter and his commissioning "as a base" for a remnant in Apoc. Pet. 71.15–21; cf. Matt 16:13–19/ Lk 22:31). There is no time-frame specified for these activities, but one assumes they are prior to the closure of the earthly context for the Lord. In the final commissioning scene (9.30 – 12.20), the apostles are commanded to teach and to heal, enduring the hardships of the faith as the Lord has done.

2. Activity of a "More-than-Human" Kind

This is activity which is not generally attributed to an "average" human being, but is not necessarily outside a human being's capabilities with some kind of divine assistance.

2.1 Prophetic Activity and Miracles/Healing

Gos. Thom. Log. 31 could be understood to contain autobiographical statements from the Lord, as he speaks of how no prophet is accepted in his own village and no physician heals those who know him.[1] Perhaps the itinerant prophet's life is also described in Log. 86, which makes reference to the Son of Man who has nowhere to lay his head and rest.

A number of texts mention miracle-working or wonder-working (e.g. Treat. Seth 52.16)[2] by Jesus. Ap. Jas. speaks of the Son of Man who healed people that they might reign (3.25–27). In Testim. Truth, the Son of Man is said to have destroyed the works of the cosmocrators among humankind, so that the lame, blind, paralytic, dumb, and demon-possessed were granted healing (33.2–8).[3] He is also described as having walked on the waters of the sea (33.8–10; also 33.22–24?).

---

[1] Ménard focuses instead on what this saying might mean for the Gnostic, "Le présent logion va illustrer ce caractère d'étranger qu'ont le gnostique et le monde l'un à l'égard de l'autre" (1975b, 126).

[2] Gibbons (1972, 25) and Painchaud (1982, 89) agree that this may be an allusion to the miracle tradition about Jesus. Painchaud refers especially to Jn 2:23; Evans et al. refer to Jn 2:11; 11:47–48 (296).

[3] That the demons are active within humankind is attested later in the text where there is a long passage dealing with the demons associated with David and Solomon, who were released from where Solomon had enclosed them in water jars when the Romans took Jerusalem, and who since then are with the ignorant (70.1–24).

3. Activity of a Divine/Heavenly Nature

Here a distinction must be made between activity of this nature which is carried out by the Jesus figure within his contact with the earthly realm and that carried out by him outside of this context but which still has an effect in this realm.

3.1 Activity within the Context of Jesus' "Existence" within the Earthly Realm

3.1.1 Transfiguration/Christophany

Strictly speaking, in the canonical accounts, the transfiguration is an activity performed *on* Jesus, a vision experienced by him while at prayer. It is experienced on a secondary level as a christophany by the attendant disciples. In the passages that seem to allude to this tradition within the Nag Hammadi texts, it is the aspect of christophany which is stressed, so that the link to the transfiguration story is not totally clear.

Gos. Phil. 58.5–7 comes closest to the canonical transfiguration story with a reference to an appearance of Jesus to his disciples in glory on a mountain. Although Wilson suggests transfiguration as the most obvious allusion here, he also notes that "a mountain is a common place for revelations of the risen Christ in Gnostic documents" (1962, 92).[1] In Apoc. Pet., Peter has a vision of the light greater than the light of day which comes down upon the Saviour (72.23–27). It is possible that this could be an allusion to the canonical transfiguration story.[2] Partrick interprets the revelation given by the Saviour upon a mountain ("of Olives") in Galilee in Soph. Jes. Chr. 91.17–20 as the transfiguration (138). What appears at first glance to be a reference to the transfiguration in Treat. Res. 48.6–10 contains no reference at all to a Jesus figure (*contra* Partrick 93).

3.1.2 Creative Activity

Val. Exp. describes the activity of Jesus who comes to work with Sophia, in forming and saving the seeds which are from her and which have been dwelling in the human form created by the Demiurge (37.32–38). The descent of Jesus occurs subsequent to the description of descent and ascent of

---

[1] Wilson cites, e.g., Soph. Jes. Chr. and Pistis Sophia (Ménard follows with the same references [1988, 146]). Janssens has no hesitation in interpreting the passage as referring to the transfiguration (1968, 90), as Partrick also (129).

[2] See Evans et al. 306. Havelaar mentions the transfiguration passages in the Gospel texts as having similar elements of an epiphany (66 n. 65). See Orbe 1976, 2: 97, 108 on the ethiopic version of Apoc. Pet.

the Christ in the text. After Christ leaves Sophia and ascends to the Pleroma, Sophia receives Jesus. He descends in order to form a pleroma in "that place" (= the world) which is patterned on the pleroma of the Father (35.17–24),[1] with Sophia's help making a creature from the seeds (35.14–17, 30–31),[2] who is a shadow of pre-existing things (35. 28–30). This work of creation involves separating the passions which surround the seeds (35.31–34) into the better ones which go into the spirit (35.35–36) and the worse ones which go into the flesh (35.36–37). (Thus the creature is both spiritual and fleshly, heavenly and earthly [37.25–28].) Those who belong to the Pleroma are brought forth by him then, together with the angels who belong to the syzygy (36.19–24).

Gos. Phil. has a great deal of material about the activities of creating and begetting, related in part to the activity of the Lord. The Lord is the son of man (81.16) who has the ability to beget (58.17–26: the heavenly/perfect man has more sons than the earthly man, and these sons do not die but are always begotten), and God has given him also the ability to create (81.19–23). He passes on this ability to create, since the son of the son of man creates through the son of man (81.17–19).[3]

Apparently the Lord is the exception to the general teaching of the gospel which states that the one who creates cannot beget (81.23–24).[4] In this regard the Lord is different to the Demiurge who has only the power to create.[5] The difference in the two characters is related to the theme of hiddenness. Whoever creates works openly, he is visible (81.28–30) and what is created is a creature (81.25–26). Whoever begets does so in private, he is hidden (81.30–31).[6] The Demiurge can only create, since he is the so-called offspring of the creator, and is merely a creature. His works are manifest, whereas the Saviour's works are hidden.

---

[1] Pagels writes: "Jesus ascends into the Pleroma to bring forth the *typos* of that creation", i.e., the creation of the seeds (Pagels and Turner 1990b, 94). The text clearly refers to the *descent* of Jesus (35.18–19).

[2] Pagels and Turner identify the creature as the Demiurge, who, subsequent to his fashioning, carries out the next activity of separating the passions (1990b, 164). I have interpreted the separating activity as carried out by Jesus, as does Ménard (1985, 77).

[3] Only H.-M. Schenke (1989a, 171) and Isenberg (Layton and Isenberg 205) read ⲡⲉⲧⲥⲱⲛⲧ as active. Elsewhere in the text the sons of the son of man are said to be begotten, not created (58.17–26; see also 69.4–14).

[4] The saying concerning those who can get brothers for themselves but not sons, since those who are begotten cannot beget, should be understood in reference to believers rather than to the Son (*contra* Wilson 1962, 94), since it is quite clear from 81.19–23 that the Son also has the power to beget.

[5] See Wilson 1962, 181–2; Janssens 1968, 124; and Ménard 1988, 238.

[6] The writer uses the analogy of husband and wife to explore this idea further: no one knows when they have intercourse so that human begetting is hidden (so that even this human marriage of defilement has a hidden quality). See also the analogy of human power and rest (72.4–17). A person's power (ⲆⲨⲚⲀⲘⲓⲥ) is the source of his works (creating) but his children (begetting) come from his rest (ⲁⲚⲁⲡⲁⲨⲥⲓⲥ). This can also be linked to the teaching in 63.11–21 that much effort does not bring results nor the ability to see.

3.1.3 Special Case: The Gospel of Philip

By far the most extensive explicit reflection on the divine activity of Jesus within the context of his earthly existence is to be found Gos. Phil. The reasons for his coming into the earthly realm are introduced frequently by a variation of the formula, "Christ came..." (52.19, 35; 55.6; 68.17; 68.20; 70.12–13).[1] Apart from his activity as Saviour which I have already discussed in Chapter V, his earthly operations encompass reconciliation, nourishment of life, and punishment of the world.

Christ came as reconciler and unifier: to unite the above and below, the outside and the inside (67.30–34) and thus ensure access to the heavenly region (68.17–22); to repair the separation (i.e. death) begun with Adam and Eve, so as to give life to those who died as a result of the separation and unite them (70.12–17).

Christ came as nourisher or life-enhancer: as the Perfect Man who brought bread from heaven to nourish humankind (55.12–14), and the food of the truth by which one has life and does not die (73.23–27).

Christ came as punisher of the world: as the one called Pharisatha (= the one who is spread out) who came to crucify the world (63.21–24).[2] This last

---

[1] I have added 52.19, "Since Christ came...", to the list, although the context in which this phrase belongs is disputed. H.-M. Schenke (1960, 39), Catanzaro (36), Janssens (1968, 81), Ménard (1988, 124), and Layton and Isenberg (142–5) all read 52.19 as the introductory statement. An alternative reading, "He who has believed in the truth has found life, and this one is in danger of dying, for he is alive since Christ came" (52.17–19), is found in Wilson 1962, 66; Till 1963, 73; Kasser 1970, 22; Krause 1971, 95; and Schenke, H.-M. 1989a, 155. Although Schenke, H.-M. 1960, 41 has 55.6 as a concluding phrase, this is changed in Schenke, H.-M. 1989a to an introduction.

For further investigation of introductory formulae in this text (not including those mentioned here), see Gaffron 60–2.

[2] This follows the saying concerning Jesus as the eucharist. Van Unnik combines the two, referring to the Syriac use of "pharisatha" for the eucharistic bread, and commenting, "...the eucharist is not primarily thanksgiving for the work of creation and recreation; it is – typically Gnostic – an annihilation and renunciation of the world" (469). My thanks to Luise Abramowski for drawing my attention to the fact that the Syriac term has a *feminine* ending in reference to Christ, indicating a direct transference of the term for the eucharistic bread. Ménard follows Van Unnik, adding that in the Jacobite rite the host was broken in the form of the cross, so that the parts when spread out represented a crucified man, so that here we have the idea of Jesus spread out on the cross and separating the world above from the world below (1988, 169). However, this does not fit so well with the idea of Jesus as the unifier of the above and below. His further suggestion of reading 84.26–34 (Ménard's reference to sent. 125 should be read as sent. 123) as meaning the separation of the physical world of the Demiurge from the Pleroma by the arms of the cross is not as helpful. The reference to the wings/ arms of the cross appears to denote an attitude of mercy, especially in conjunction with the following sentence which presents the cross as the ark of salvation which saves from the flood of water washing over them. Wilson suggests that crucifying the world "means presumably revealing its true character and worthlessness" (1962, 114), and refers to the Book of Jeu, Book 1, Chapter 1 ("The living Jesus answered and said to his apostles: 'Blessed is he who has crucified the world, and who has not allowed the world to crucify him'"; Schmidt 1978, 39, line 15 – 40, line 2).

action is somewhat tempered by the statement that he came to the whole place (= the cosmos) and did not burden anyone (80.1–2).

3.2 Activity within the Context of the Heavenly Realm, Directed towards the Earth

Since the concern of this study is primarily the work of the Jesus figure within the earthly context, I shall deal only briefly with this category of activity.

On the simplest level, heavenly activity directed towards the earth can be presumed in those texts which attest to an ongoing union between the Jesus figure and the believer/community, after he leaves the earthly realm (e.g. Pr. Paul). We will not deal with these texts here, but rather with those which attest to other activity, either prior to the coming of the Jesus figure or after he leaves the earthly realm.

Gos. Phil. describes the activity of the Christ prior to his coming into the world. He laid down the soul not only when he appeared but from the very day the world came into being (53.6–10).

Acts Pet. 12 Apost. tells of the effective working of the risen Lord. Although he is "physically" absent, he has power to affect what happens to the disciples: he provides the opportune moment for their going down to the sea (1.14–16), and the kindness of the sailors is also ordained by him (1.20–23). Peter expects him to give the apostles power to walk the road to the city of Lithargoel (6.11–12), and the apostles ask him (in a prayer-formula) to give them the power to do what he wishes at all times (9.26–29). Lithargoel says of Jesus (i.e. of himself): "He is a great power for giving strength" (6.17).

In a passage which describes the creative and life-giving activity of the Lord, Teach. Silv. speaks of him as the beginning and the end of everyone. He watches over all and encompasses them (113.21–23). He is troubled about those to whom he brings instruction, mourns for those being punished, rejoices over those in purity (113.24–31). He is a judge but really only in a helping capacity for those engaged in the contest of life (114.13–14).

3.3 Activity within the Heavenly Realm or Directed at the Powers

3.3.1 Creation (and Sustaining of Creation/Life)

The heavenly Jesus figure is described in a number of creative activities, very often as the agent of the Father. In Treat. Seth, he is said to have brought forth a word and an imperishable thought to the glory of the Father (49.20–25), and to have produced thought about the Ennoias and about the descent upon the water (50.13–17).[1] In Teach. Silv., as the Word who is the hand of the Father, he has created everything; he is the mother of all from whom the all has come into being (115.3–9, 16–19), and he gives life and nourishes all things, ruling over all and giving life (113.15–20). Interp. Know. describes his part in the continuing creative work of the Father. The Father does not keep the Sabbath but actuates the Son, and through the Son, continues to provide himself with the Aeons (11.33–35).[2]

A similar work is described in Trim. Prot. where the Son/Word is the only-begotten God (38.22–23; or "the God who was begotten" [39.6, 13]) who himself begets the Aeons (38.18; 39.5–6), establishes them (38.33 – 39.5), reveals them, glorifies them and gives them thrones (38.19–20).

Combined with this creative aspect of the Son/Word, one finds him linked with the giving or sustaining of life: he is the one who bears a fruit of life (46.16–17), pouring forth living water from the invisible, unpolluted, immeasurable spring which is the voice of the glory of the Mother (46.17–19). He is the foundation that supports every movement of the Aeons (46.25–26), the foundation of every foundation (46.27–28), the breath of the powers (46.28).

There is a further link with the creation of the Aeons in Tri. Trac., where the heavenly Church which is produced by the unity of the Father and the Son (by kisses?) (58.21–33), itself procreates innumerable Aeons (59.2–7).

There is creative work done by Christ in Val. Exp. (the establishment of Sophia [26.22–24], the work of separating, confirming, providing form and substance [26.23, 31–34; 27.32]), but this figure must be differentiated from Jesus in the text (see the discussion in Chapter II).

3.3.2 Ordering Activity

A number of texts describe work of the heavenly Jesus figure in relation to ordering powers. In Gos. Eg., either Jesus or Seth-Jesus is the one through whom the powers of the thirteen Aeons are nailed down and established and given armour of the knowledge of the truth (III 64.3–9/IV 75.17–24).[3] In Tri. Trac., the Saviour directs the organisation of the universe according to the authority given to him from the first (88.4–6).[4] Testim. Truth describes a

---

[1] This is possibly a reference to Gen 1:2; see Gibbons 1972, 158.

[2] Material creative work (including humankind) on the other hand is attributed to the Womb/Sophia (3.30–32; 12.31–33).

[3] Speaking of the activity of Jesus-Seth here, Böhlig writes, "Zur Ordnung paßt es, wenn er die Welt mit sich selbst (der Welt) versöhnt. Diese Versöhnung geschieht durch die Absage (ἀποταγή) an die Welt und ihren Herrscher, den Gott der dreizehn Äonen" (1989a, 349–50).

[4] The subsequent summary sentence makes it clear that the organisation is associated with the activity of revelation: "Thus he began and effected his revelation" (88.6–8).

kind of creative activity by dividing or separating (of day from night, light from darkness, corruptibility from incorruptibility, males from females, the gnostic from the error of the angels [40.25–29; 41.2–4]) carried out by the Word of the Son of Man.

The Jesus figure may be involved in Gos. Phil., where the perfect man is said to have the powers in submission (wild and tame, good and evil) as he ploughs preparing for everything to come into being (60.23–26). From this ploughing the whole place (= the cosmos) stands, whether good or evil, the right and the left (60.26–28).[1]

3.3.3 Moving Others to Conversion/Correction

Apart from the rescue of the soul in Exeg. Soul which also belongs to this section in a sense (see also Chapter V), the heavenly Jesus may be involved in the conversion of the Logos and Sophia in Tri. Trac. and Val. Exp. respectively.

In Tri. Trac., the Son gives perfection to the Logos (87.3–4; see also 80.11 – 82.9) by a process of putting himself on the Totalities as a garment (87.1–2).[2] The Saviour is described as the light shining on the Logos as a lifegiver (85.29–30). He brings revelation to the Logos, perfecting him, and sowing in him the word which is destined to be knowledge and power (88.8–27).

Val. Exp. speaks of the correction of Sophia, made necessary by her fall from her position in the Pleroma because of acting without her syzygy (34.23–31; 36.32–38). This correction can only occur through her Son, Christ, who alone has the fullness of divinity (33.28–32).[3] To achieve this he

---

[1] The "perfect man" could be a reference to the gnostic (a previous text affirms that the holy ones are also served by the evil powers by the power of the Holy Spirit [59.18–23]), but the effect of the ploughing seems to imply it is the Jesus figure, who is elsewhere referred to as the perfect man. The text moves immediately to describe the Holy Spirit as the one who shepherds and rules all the powers (60.28–31). Thus, two possibilities present themselves – either the images of shepherding and ploughing are meant to refer to the same character (and therefore the Holy Spirit is the perfect man) or they are complementary activities of controlling the powers by two characters (i.e. Jesus and the Holy Spirit). Wilson identifies the "Gnostic Anthropos" with the Holy Spirit (1962, 104), but Ménard interprets as two separate figures, the Christ and the Holy Spirit (1988, 157).

[2] Attridge and Pagels suggest that this action parallels the action of the Son who clothes himself with the aeons (66.30–32) (340). However, the action of clothing and of being clothed are not the same.

[3] It is impossible to know whether the second passage which mentions the cross contains a further description of the correction of Sophia, or whether it is meant to be interpreted as subsequent to the correction. Ménard brings the two passages together and interprets them as referring to the ascent of Sophia to the Pleroma by means of the cross, which is the Limit separating the world below from the world above (1985, 5), but there is nothing in the text which explicitly leads to the conclusion that the sufferings and correction of Sophia are linked in any way to the cross. Moreover, Ménard's interpretation fails to mention the seeds (33.17–18) and how they are involved.

must leave the powers and descend (33.32–34), in order to enlighten her. After he ascends from her, she suffers in knowing where she dwells, what she is and what has become of her (33.35–38; 34.32–34; see the discussion of the identification of Christ as Sophia's son in Chapter II).

3.3.4 Reconciliation or Restoration Work

Tri. Trac. and Val. Exp. deal with a restoration or reconciliation at the end-time. For Tri. Trac. the end will be a unitary existence like the beginning (127.23–24), after the Totality reveals that it is the Son who is the redemption, the way towards the Father, and the return to the pre-existent (123.27 – 124.3). In Val. Exp., the Jesus figure is not so much the one who brings unity and reconciliation at the end, but he is a part of the reconciliation when Sophia receives her syzygy, when he (Jesus) receives the Christ, and when the seeds receive the angels (39.27–35).

Cosmic reconciliation also occurs in Gos. Eg., from the saving work of Seth/Jesus, which is mentioned in conjunction with baptism and Jesus' birth as the body of Seth (III 63.9, 16).[1] That the baptism established through Jesus is connected with the heavenly realm rather than the earthly,[2] is clear from its being one part of the cosmic process directed by Seth. Gos. Phil. treats the theme also to some extent when it describes the activity of Jesus who pulled out the root of wickedness from the whole place (= the cosmos), in order to expose it and cause it to perish (83.16–17).

Havelaar mentions also the work of Jesus in the apokatastasis in Apoc. Pet.: that he is glorified as Christ in this process (74.7f) as the material reality is abandoned and the Gnostic souls return to their heavenly origin (166–7). This is a process that will be concluded at the end of the age, but it takes place also concurrently with the coming of the Christ.

3.3.5 Activity within the "Heavenly City"

Acts Pet. 12 Apost. depicts Lithargoel, the heavenly Jesus, in the heavenly city as a physician in the company of a disciple (8.15–19) and in his ministry of healing (8.33–35).

---

[1] I follow Böhlig and Wisse in taking the text from Codex III (144–5, 191–2). They reconstruct ογ2ωτῆ ("reconciliation"; Crum 725a) in IV 74.24 and treat ϲγωτϐ ("slaughter"; Crum 723b) in IV 75.3 as a phonetic spelling of 2ωτῆ. On the other hand, H.-M. Schenke considers the reading from Codex III to be "ungnostisch", preferring 2ωτϐ from Codex IV. "Die gnostische Taufe ist hier verstanden als ἀπέκδυσις τοῦ σώματος τῆς σαρκός... und entsprechend redet unser Text mit leichten Varianten des konkreten Ausdrucks von der Tötung der Welt an der Welt, die der Täufling in der Taufe vollzieht..." (1979, 22).

[2] "Der transzendente Charakter der Taufe wird im Ägypterevangelium stark betont" (Böhlig 1969, 16).

4. Setting of the Activity

The texts which deal with activity within the earthly realm range from those which give some (little) physical or geographical detail, to those for which the earthly context is no more than the outer stage-work upon which heavenly activity takes place (e.g. Treat. Res.; Tri. Trac.; Treat. Seth). We have already dealt in Chapter IV with the temporal setting of the texts in relation to the question of whether the Jesus figure is still within his earthly "existence" or whether he has closed that context.

Evans summarises the physical locations of the Gnostic literature as usually the Mount of Olives though sometimes Galilee (Soph. Jes. Chr. III, 91.10–24;[1] Ep. Pet. Phil. VIII, 133.12–17),[2] otherwise the desert (Ap. John II, 1.19),[3] or on a walk (Thom. Cont. II, 138.3), or on a boat dock (Acts Pet. 12 Apost. VI, 1.33 – 2.1) (1981a, 408). It is unusual that Evans does not mention Jerusalem or, more specifically, the temple. Although the setting of the temple in Jerusalem may be interpreted in some instances as metaphorical usage (Gos. Phil. 69.14–23; 84.22 – 85.21; cf. also the same usage with other place names, e.g. the city of Habitation in Acts Pet. 12 Apost.), or there is doubt as to whether it is the earthly or heavenly temple that is intended (Apoc. Pet. 70.14–15; see Brashler 131–5; Dubois 1982, 387–8; and Havelaar 55–7), nevertheless the city and its temple appear quite frequently in the texts compared with the Mount of Olives or a mountain in Galilee (Ep. Pet. Phil. 138.21–28; 139.4–10; Ap. John 1.5 – 2.9; 1 Apoc. Jas. 25.15; 2 Apoc. Jas. 60.1 – 61.26; Treat. Seth 58.13 – 59.9).[4] Evans does not mention the Jordan river either, although that occurs less frequently (Gos. Phil. 70.34 – 71.2; Testim. Truth 30.20 – 31.3).

Other texts give a more general reference to the physical circumstances of the revelation. In Gos. Thom., for example, there are references to infants being suckled (Log. 22), a Samaritan carrying a lamb on his way to Judaea (Log. 60); the brothers and mother of Jesus standing outside where he is teaching (Log. 99); Roman coins and taxes (Log. 100). As we have noted in

---

[1] This passage refers to the previous revelation given by the Saviour upon a mountain ("of Olives") in Galilee (91.17–20). Partrick interprets the event as the transfiguration (138). The physical setting of the revelation in the text is a mountain in Galilee called "Place of Season/ the Fullness of Time and Joy" (ⲙⲁ̄ⲛⲧ ⲍⲓ ⲡⲁ̄ⲱⲉ; 90.19 – 91.1 and ⲙⲁ̄ⲧ ⲍⲓ ⲡⲁⲱⲉ; BG 78.1–2). Till translates with "Reifezeit und Freude", noting that ⲙⲁ̄ is used for ⲙⲁ ⲛ̄ as in Codex III (1955, 196–7). Cf. Tardieu with "lieu de moisson et de joie" (167), and Parrott with "Divination and Joy" (1988, 222).

[2] See also the mountain ⲅⲁⲩⲅⲏⲗⲁⲛ in 1 Apoc. Jas. 30.18–21, where the second dialogue takes place.

[3] Evans and Wisse (99) are in agreement here, contra Giversen who interprets the setting as a mountain (1963a, 47), and Till who suggests the Mount of Olives (1955, 37). Waldstein and Wisse conjecture from BG 20.5–6 to "a mountainous and desert place" (15).

[4] For an extensive study on the term "temple" in general and the uses of the metaphor in the Nag Hammadi texts, see Kuntzmann 1993.

the work on teaching and revelation, one of the most common general settings in the texts is a dialogue situation between Jesus and a disciple/disciples.
Sometimes there may also be scribal activity (Ap. Jas.; Thom. Cont. 138.2–
4).[1]

Other "everyday" physical circumstances and their implied setting are
found, for example, in the list in Melch. 5.1–11 of what has really happened
to Jesus, contrary to the incorrect teaching of some people: he has been begotten, eats and drinks, has been circumcised, and so on.

Conclusion

In this chapter I have dealt with all the activity by and towards Jesus which
does not directly involve revelation and liberation (which formed the focus
of Chapter V). Activity by and towards Jesus necessarily involves other persons or powers as objects or agents of the action. The nature and quality of
what takes place depends in part on the positive or negative nature of the relationships between these persons or powers and Jesus. These relationships
are investigated in the following chapter.

---

[1] Kasser also suggests such activity for Thomas in Gos. Thom. (1961, 27).

VII

Positive and Negative Relationships of Jesus

Chapter II dealt briefly with the human parents of Jesus as they are presented in texts from a positive or negative perspective. Reference to relationships between Jesus and a number of heavenly characters are discussed in the same chapter. Neither of these aspects will be considered again in this present chapter.

1. Positive Relationships

The inclusion of characters in this category does not rule out the possibility that there is some friction with the individuals or groups who are so designated. In Ap. Jas., for example, although there is an intimacy between Jesus and the disciples, his reaction to their ignorance goes well beyond friendly chiding to quite heated invective against them. He calls them "wretches", "unfortunates", "pretenders to the truth", "falsifiers of knowledge", "sinners against the Spirit" (9.24–28).[1] Even the key figures of James and Peter do not understand the teaching (7.4–6), and he labours under their stupidity and their inability to stay awake. It appears that the new revelation is eliciting the same response as prior revelation by the earthly Jesus, "Remember me because when I was with you, you did not know me" (12.35–36).

Jesus' speech (at least in the "farewell discourse") swings continually between positive encouragement or exhortation and reproval or invective (see 13.13–17). It is clear however that there is a positive aspect to the invective since accepting reproof from Jesus leads to salvation (11.3–4), and they will be forgiven because of Jesus' intercession with the Father (11.4–6). Despite this encouragement, Jesus' words are said to bring the disciples and James and Peter both joy and sadness (11.6–10; see also 12. 18). Peter sums up the situation well in 13.27–36: "Sometimes you urge us on to the kingdom of heaven, and then again you turn us back, Lord; sometimes you persuade and draw us to faith and promise us life, and then again you cast us forth from the kingdom of heaven." In reply, Jesus suggests that the disciples ignore the apparent rejection from him and simply rejoice in the promise of life and the kingdom of heaven (14.10–14).

---

[1] See also the rather odd saying in which Jesus refers to his ascent: "But you, when I was eager to go, have cast me out, and instead of accompanying me, you have pursued me" (14.22–25).

The kind of ambivalence found in Ap. Jas. can be found elsewhere. On the one hand, the Jesus figure in Gos. Thom. may rail against the ignorance of the disciples (Log. 37, 43, 91, and passim). On the other hand, in the same text, one reads of his suffering or compassion for the ignorance of humanity: "And my soul became afflicted for the sons of men, because they are blind in their hearts and do not have sight; for empty they came into the world, and empty too they seek to leave the world" (Log. 28).

One other point should be noted. Texts which often give an impression of a kind of equality and real friendliness between Jesus and various disciples or other characters, will sometimes qualify that relationship to some extent by an emphasis in the concluding or "farewell" scenes on the "otherness" of the heavenly or divine Jesus figure, as he is worshipped and given reverence by the disciples who bow down and offer praise (Ap. Jas. 15.6–7; Dial. Sav. 131.17–18; 136.1–4, 10–11).[1]

1.1 Groups[2]

In a general way in the earthly context, the most positive and most important relationship of the Jesus figure is with the pneumatics who are united with him and receive revelation from him. They are often aligned with him in opposition to the powers or the hylics. They are usually designated as the perfect or the elect or the church or "his own". A good example of this relationship is found in Tri. Trac. Here the Saviour is the head and the spiritual race of humankind is his body, and the sharing and unity between them of body and essence is like a marriage (122.12–17; 136.1).[3] They are the church, the "election", who have received knowledge and complete salvation (119.16–18), and are united with him in enduring evil and trials from the hylics (122.7–12).

Occasionally it is difficult to differentiate the heavenly and earthly aspects of those related to the Jesus figure as church or "his own". Thus in Treat. Seth, there is the heavenly assembly and the earthly community who have their origin and destiny in the heavenly assembly. The community are called his kindred and his fellow spirits (50.22–24), are exhorted to rest with him (70.8–10). He is from them and among them (65.19–20), and is despised for their sakes (65.21).[4]

---

[1] In Dial. Sav. 136.14–17, the praise is expressed in formal parallel confessional statements:
Through you, all glories exist
ⲈⲢⲈⲚⲈⲞⲞⲨ ⲦⲎⲢⲞⲨ ⲰⲞⲞⲠ [ⲈⲂⲞⲀ] ⲌⲓⲦⲞⲞⲦⲕ
From you, all blessing derives
ⲈⲢⲈⲠⲈⲤⲘⲞⲨ ⲦⲎⲢⳍ ⲚⲎⲞⲨ ⲈⲂⲞ[Ⲁ Ⳙ]ⲘⲞⲕ
[2] This section is dealt with in much more detail in Chapter IX.
[3] It is difficult to delineate between what is associated with the activity of redemption or salvation and what belongs to the unity experienced in an ongoing way with the spiritual race in the earthly realm. There seems to be little interest in clear temporal delineations.
[4] Bethge suggests this statement is not in keeping with the general soteriological view of the work because of its emphasis on the "Heilsbedeutung der Passion" (1979, 170).

Many texts of course refer to the relationship of Jesus to his disciples or followers who are sometimes called "brothers" or "fellow spirits" (e.g. Ap. John 1.10–11; 31.30–32; 32.4; Dial. Sav. 120.2–4; 142.24–25; Gos. Phil. 55.37; 58.5–7; 59.23–27; 63.34 – 64.9).[1] Within the larger grouping there may be a number of levels at work. Thus in Ap. Jas., there is a three-tiered level of intimacy with Jesus: first James as the most important, then James and Peter, and finally the twelve disciples with James and Peter included. Within the total group of followers, a number of individuals and sub-groups are addressed, ask questions, make statements, and are answered or referred to within the teaching (the disciples, Thomas, James, Mary, Salome, the woman in the crowd, Simon Peter, John the Baptist). The secret teaching is not given to all the twelve disciples (1.22–25), but they are "the beloved" (10.29–30) and all are invited to go with him to the place whence he came (2.25–26), and all are certainly saved by him (8.37 – 9.1). He came down for their sakes to dwell with them that they might dwell with him (9.1–4; 10.28–29).

Soph. Jes. Chr. also has a number of levels at work with a group of twelve disciples and seven women from whom come various dialogue partners or questioners of the Saviour: Philip (92.4–5; 95.19–20), Matthew (93.24 – 94.4; 100.16–19), Thomas (96.14–17), Mary (98.9–10; 114.8–12), Bartholomew (103.22 – 104.4), his disciples (106.9–14), Thomas (108.16–19), "they" (BG 107.13–16), holy apostles (112.19–24). There is little positive feed-back from the revealer to those who ask the questions or make statements but the followers are praised in general for Thomas' question in 108.16–19.

Finally it should be noted that in Gos. Phil. the terms "disciples", "apostles" and "apostolic men" occur throughout the text, but that the latter two terms appear to have somewhat negative connotations, especially in 55.28–30 where they are equivalent to the "Hebrews" to whom the virgin Mary is an anathema. However, there is communication between the apostles and the disciples (59.27–29), and Philip the apostle is specifically mentioned (73.8).

1.2 Smaller Groups

As already noted, the small group of James and Peter in Ap. Jas. ask questions to elicit the revelation from Jesus. Peter is found also with John in Acts Pet. 12 Apost. In general, he is the one who speaks with the Lord and the spokesman for the group who are called variously apostles or the eleven disciples, and John appears only in the concluding stages of the text. However,

---

[1] The reference to others is not always explicit. In Thom. Cont., for example, a wider group apart from the key character Thomas must be understood in positive relation to Jesus. Apart from Mathaias' presence as scribe, Thomas' use of a 1st pers. plur. and Jesus' use of both 2nd pers. sing. and 2nd pers. pl. implies a wider concern for a group, which is not defined although one presumes the group of the perfect. Kuntzmann sees Thomas as a prototype of the perfect because of his identification with the Saviour, and the mixture of 2nd pers. sing. and pl. addressed to him as bringing a kind of deliberate confusion between Thomas as interlocutor and the community (1981, 285).

the final two-part commissioning scene presents John in a more favoured position with the Lord than Peter.[1]

James has a prominent role in 1 Apoc. Jas., with others named to whom he should pass on the revelation or give encouragement: Addai (36.13–16), Salome, Mariam, Martha (?) and Arsinoe (40.22–26).

Dial. Sav. presents Judas, Mary, and Matthew in leading roles, questioning the Lord and making statements[2] and also receiving the vision (although it is really only Judas who speaks of what he sees). The Lord addresses Mary as "sister" (131.22) and Matthew as "brother" (132.10; Judas also calls Matthew "brother", 135.8).

In Gos. Phil. 59.6–11, we are told of a group of three women who always walked with the Lord: Mary his mother, her sister,[3] and Mary Magdalene, called his companion (ΤΕϤΚΟΙΝѠΝΟС) (see also the fragmentary text 63.32–34). Despite difficulties with the text, it seems clear that the passage is speaking of three women who are each named Mary. There seems little ground for the continuing speculation over the equivalence of the three characters.[4]

---

[1] The structure of the commissioning scene may be outlined as follows:

A The commission to teach those who have believed in the name of the Lord (9.33 – 10.13)
 – Peter repeats what the Lord has taught them but he is worried about daily food (10.13–21)
 – The Lord rebukes Peter for his misunderstanding (10.22–30)

B The commission to heal the sick who believe in the name of the Lord (10.31 – 11.1)
 – Peter is afraid to say anything a second time and asks John, who is beside him, to do so (11.1–5; cf. Jn 13:23–24; Evans et al. also give the Johannine reference [266]).
 – John's worry about their having no skills as physicians (11.5–13)
 – Jesus commends John for having spoken rightly (11.14–15)

Sell (1979) fails to take this scene into account. He understands 8.35 – 9.15 as strong evidence supporting Peter's importance in the text, yet one could just as easily interpret this passage as an implicit criticism of Peter rather than an elevation of his status, since he fails to recognise the Lord, so that Jesus must make the statement that he is the Son of the Living God rather than Peter (accepting Sell's theory that the text is consciously based upon Matt 16:13–19; see also Evans et al. 265).
[2] Krause gives a detailed summary of the questions (1977a, 17–18). Koester and Pagels suggest that the statements by Mary "seem to serve as summaries and as transitions to new topics" (4).
[3] H.-M. Schenke emends "her sister" to "his sister" ("seine Schwester"), since the following line speaks of Mary as his sister (1960, 44 and 1989a, 159). Either the emendation must be as Schenke proposes or the next line must be emended to read "her sister".
[4] A number of scholars argue for, or assume, the equivalence of the three. I have already noted proposals from Barc (1982, 374–5) and Orbe (1976, 1: 254) in Chapter II. See also Trautmann (1981, 273), Ménard (1988, 150–1) and Klauck (2357). Wilson finds a basis for the argument either in Valentinian speculation, or in a simple deduction from the names, adding that the Virgin Mary and Mary Magdalene are sometimes confused, and that Epiphanius refers to one of Jesus' sisters as Mary (1962, 97). McNeil explains the opposition of the apostles and the apostolic men to Mary the virgin in terms of their opposition to Mary Magdalene (i.e. a confusion between his mother Mary and Mary his companion) (145).

1.3 Individuals

1.3.1 James

In Ap. Jas., revelation is given sometimes to James alone (8.31–32), who is commanded to follow Jesus and has been taught what to say before the archons (8.33–36). The two apocalypses, 1 Apoc. Jas. and 2 Apoc. Jas., present James as the major character related to the Jesus figure (see further discussion in Chapter VIII).[1] In both texts James is called "brother" by Jesus (1 Apoc. Jas. 24.13–16; 2 Apoc. Jas. 50.11–12). In 2 Apoc. Jas., the Lord also calls him "beloved" (56.16; 57.5) and kisses him on the mouth and embraces him (56.14–15; see also 57.10–11, 16–17).[2]

1.3.2 John

At the beginning of the revelation in Ap. John, John is called by name, given reassurance, and told not to be a stranger to the revealer (2.9–12). This implies that the revealer already knows John and that the questions which John has posed for himself about Jesus are perhaps being answered by the same person. The Saviour smiles (22.11–12; 26.25–26) and rejoices (27.15) in response to John's questions, indicating a positive relationship.

1.3.3 Thomas

In a similar situation to James in Ap. Jas., Thomas receives secret teaching not given to the other disciples in Gos. Thom. He surely fits the description given by Jesus in Log. 108: "He who will drink from my mouth will become like me. I myself shall become he, and the things that are hidden will be revealed to him."

For Thom. Cont., the relationship of Jesus with Thomas is the only one of any interest, although a wider group can be presumed. Jesus addresses him as "O blessed Thomas" (139.25) and "brother Thomas" (138.4; see also 138.10, 19). He is the twin and true companion of the Saviour (138.7–8), exhorted to examine himself and learn who he is and how he was and how he will be, since it is not fitting for the brother of the Saviour to be ignorant of himself

---

[1] See Böhlig's short summary of early Christian sources regarding the high position given to James the Just (Böhlig and Labib 1963, 27). Veilleux gives a very helpful summary of the traditions concerning the person and martyrdom of James the Just (1–7).

[2] The focus of 2 Apoc. Jas. is squarely on James. He is a character of great power, who dooms the temple of Jerusalem to destruction, presumably because of the opposition of those within her to him (60.14–22; H.-M. Schenke refers to Eusebius *Hist. Eccl.* II 23,18, Origen's *Commentary on Matt.* 13:55, and also Celsus I 49 and II 13 [1966, 29]). He is a teacher and speaker to the multitude of the people (45.15–25), the one who receives the revelation from the Pleroma of Imperishability (46.8–9), the one first summoned (46.9–10) and the one who is obeyed (46.11). His *gnosis* and understanding are from above (47.7–11) and what is revealed to him has been hidden from everyone else (47.16–19), even the heavens and the archons and the Demiurge (56.20–23). His knowledge will enable him to come forth just as the Lord has (57.6–8).

(138.7–12). In this way he will be called "the one who knows himself" (138.15–16). We may speculate that Thomas' knowledge of himself is also knowledge of his twin, Jesus.

1.3.4 Mary (Magdalene)

Both Dial. Sav. and Gos. Phil. present Mary in a very positive role. In Dial. Sav., she receives praise for the statement in which she quotes sayings known to us from Matt 6:34b; 10:10b, 24; Jn 13:16: "She uttered this as a woman who had understood completely" (139.11–13; this should be linked with her later statement, "I want to understand all things as they are" [141.13–14]). The Lord praises her for another question (concerning whether she has come to this place to profit or to forfeit): "You make clear the abundance of the revealer" (140.17–19).

As noted above, for Gos. Phil., Mary is the companion of Jesus (59.9; 63.32–34). She is the one whom the Lord loved more than all the disciples and he kissed her often. It is implied that he loves her more because she can see, while the disciples are blind and in darkness (63.32 – 64.9). If we take both statements together, it seems that Jesus and Mary may be regarded as a syzygy.

First, the activity of kissing can be seen in relation to the kiss by which the perfect conceive (59.2–6). Mary Magdalene and Jesus conceive (the perfect?) in this way, so that Mary is not barren in comparison to Sophia who is barren and mother of the angels (63.30–32).[1] In relation to this text, there is a further fragmentary text in 59.30 – 60.1 which may well contain a comparison of the barren Sophia and the fruitful Holy Spirit.

Second, the fact that Mary is able to see means that in seeing Jesus rightly she is able to be united with him. Since Jesus and Christ are the one person, there is a certain parallel to be inferred between the syzygy of Jesus-Mary Magdalene and Christ-Holy Spirit (who also give rebirth to the Gnostic in baptism). If we take this into account with the first point, we could make a (very tenuous) connection between Mary Magdalene and the Holy Spirit to further reinforce the parallelism of the syzygies. A second parallel may be suggested at least on the level of activity, if not on the equivalence of characters, to the bride and bridegroom of the great bridal chamber, the Father of All and Sophia.

Mary also appears in Gos. Thom. Log. 21 where she poses a question to Jesus, but her relationship to him is not described. Here, as in other Gnostic texts, it is Peter rather than the Lord who responds negatively to her. In fact, the Lord defends her against Peter in Log. 114.

---

[1] The text is fragmentary. Sevrin proposes that Mary Magdalene is equivalent to Sophia (1974, 161–3).

1.3.5 Peter

In Apoc. Pet., Peter has been chosen by the Saviour as the beginning[1] for the remnant whom he has summoned to knowledge (71.18–21), Peter himself being summoned first to know the Saviour (71.24–26). The text is aware of the canonical traditions regarding Peter's naming and call to be the first or the foundation, as well as his cowardice during Jesus' passion. Regarding the latter tradition, the point is not laboured: the Saviour simply exhorts him not to be afraid (80.32–33). Peter is also given assurance by Jesus that he will be with him so that his enemies might not prevail over him (84.8–10).

1.3.6 Salome

Gos. Thom. Log. 61 makes a brief reference to Salome who has enjoyed tablefellowship with Jesus, relating that he has come up on her couch and eaten from her table.

1.3.7 The Woman from the Crowd

The woman appears in Gos. Thom. Log. 79 and pronounces a blessing upon the woman who bore and suckled Jesus. Although the blessing is judged to be misplaced (as in Lk 11:27), nevertheless this must count as acting in a positive role towards Jesus.

2. Negative Relationships

2.1 Groups

As the spiritual race or pneumatics in Tri. Trac. are associated positively with the Lord, the human material race or hylics are hateful towards him and his revelation, since they shun the light because it destroys them (119.8–16). They are reponsible for the death of the Lord, since they denied him and plotted evil against him (121.10–18; 122.5–6), and they will remain until the end for destruction (137.9–10).

The most powerful negative group against the Jesus figure in the texts consists of the archons (and their subordinates), who are also sometimes named "the robbers". It is from them that Jesus must rescue the soul, and they are usually described as experiencing some distress (troubled and shaken) by his activity or appearing (e.g. Gos. Phil. 53.11–13; 1 Apoc. Jas. 27.13–24; Treat. Seth 51.24–30; 52.10–14). They may also be those referred to in Gos. Truth as the ones who were wise in their own estimation (19.21–22), who put Jesus to the test (19.22–23). They were confounded because in

---

[1] Brown and Griggs translate with "ruler" (139), Brashler and Bullard with "base" (373).

reality they were foolish (19.23–25), and as a result they hated him (19.25–27).

There is some polemic against Jewish groups as negative to the Jesus figure. Gos. Thom. contains sayings against the pharisees and the scribes (Log. 39 and 102), and the Jews as a group are said to lack insight since they obviously do not know who Jesus is (Log. 43).[1] In Apoc. Pet., the enemies who first appear in the vision are the priests and people who are blind and lacking a guide (72.9–17; 73.12–14).[2] Scribes are also included in this group later in the text (73.2–3).

Gos. Thom. also contains some sayings against the earthly family of Jesus. His reply in Log. 99 concerning his brothers and mother negates a relationship with them, in contrast to a positive "familial" relationship with those who do the will of the Father and will enter the Kingdom of his Father (see also Log. 105: "He who knows the father and the mother will be called the son of a harlot").[3]

Apoc. Pet. 77.33 – 78.1 mentions those who do business in the word of the Saviour, and Ap. John 31.34 – 32.1 refers to a person who exchanges the secret teaching for gain of one kind or another. Surely these are to be interpreted as enemies of the Jesus figure as much as enemies of the community.

2.2 Individuals

2.2.1 The Evil One

Both Ap. Jas. and Teach. Silv. refer to a figure under a variety of names but whom we may generally call the evil one or the wicked one. In Ap. Jas., he appears as the agent of the earthly Jesus' suffering and death (5.20). He is also called the evil devil (4.30), and Satan (4.37, 39). In Teach. Silv., the greatest power against which the Jesus figure contends in the Underworld must be presumed to be the wicked one, called variously the adversary, the spirit of wickedness, and the devil (88.9–13; 91.19–20; 95.1). He is mad and bitter, a horror (104.28–29), a tyrant who is lord over evil thoughts or powers (105.27 – 106.9; 110.4–14) which are in opposition to the holy powers (114.3–6). He deceives by tricks and flattery (95.12 – 96.19), and casts down into the abyss (104.24–31), which is his dwelling place beneath the great mire (85.17–20).

---

[1] Ménard also includes Log. 65 (the parable of the owner of the vineyard) as anti-Jewish (1975b, 167).

[2] These people are also described as praising the Saviour (73.10), but the passage presents difficulties. Both H.-M. Schenke (1975c, 131) and Werner (1989, 639 n.22) suggest that some text has been omitted which would refer to heavenly praise which Peter hears at the same time as the cries of the crowd.

[3] With reference to this passage, Klijn (1962) cites Philo's statement that marriage is a rejection of the heavenly Mother and Father (Leg. All. 2, 491).

2.2.2 Various Powers

There are a number of individual powers set in opposition to the Jesus figure: the destruction which is outside the outer darkness (Gos. Phil. 68.5–8); the power of darkness in the Underworld (Ap. John 31.4) which is disturbed by his coming (30.17 – 31.4); death (Treat. Res. 46.17–19); and Error (Gos. Truth 18.21–24), who was angry at Jesus and persecuted him (18.22–23), was subsequently distressed at him (18.23), and was brought to nothing (18.24).

2.2.3 Arimanios

The Pharisee Arimanios[1] in Ap. John 1.13–17 must be counted indirectly as an enemy. He accuses Jesus *in absentia* of having led others astray into error and turned them away from the traditions of their fathers.

Conclusion

In this chapter the broad range of those in positive or negative relationships with Jesus, including individuals and groups, has been outlined. In the following chapter I investigate in more detail the enemies of Jesus who are involved in the process by which he closes his contact with the earthly realm.

---

[1] Giversen sees a connection between Arimanios and the evil spirit set up by Zoroaster (1963a, 152–3).

VIII

The Close of the Earthly Context for Jesus

Chapter V dealt briefly with the question of what constitutes salvation in Gnostic terms. This is also a question relevant to the process of closing the earthly context and the possibility that death or struggle await Jesus within that. The major descriptions of suffering recorded for Jesus, whether real or illusory, occur generally in the context of the closure.

In Chapter II, I outlined a number of possibilities by which Jesus closes his contact with the earthly realm, departing for the first time and then perhaps re-entering one or more times before a final departure. All of these possibilities will be considered in this chapter, but the major focus will be on the first departure.

In this chapter, I divide the material of the texts into a number of major sections: death (suffering and death; death as cosmic struggle and the conquering of death); crucifixion (as a fact; as the cause of death; not as the cause of death or as the death of someone else); resurrection; ascension/final departure; parousia.

Others have divided the material in various other ways.[1] Tröger has five sections: texts which include explicitly or implicitly the passion of a Saviour figure (including Jesus Christ); texts in which the tradition of passion for Jesus Christ is basically foreign to his nature; texts where only the fleshly covering of the Saviour undergoes suffering; texts where another suffers and the Saviour only appears to suffer; texts where no passion tradition is involved (1978, 1: 10–11). Cozby has the following scheme: the crucifixion and the archons (crucifixion as the work of the archons, and crucifixion as the defeat of the archons); the crucifixion and the incarnation (crucifixion as a consequence of the incarnation, and crucifixion as the repudiation of the material world) (317–45).[2]

Tröger has written extensively on the issue of the suffering of the Saviour, pointing out that the Saviour cannot and must not be overcome in reality by suffering, since that would signal the victory of the archons. The Saviour does not come to the world to exorcise its evil or forgive sins, but to collect the Light, awaken humankind from its ignorance, prepare the way, and bring them home.

---

[1] Voorgang's study of all the Nag Hammadi texts is extensive and helpful (120–240), in particular his overview of the various elements of the passion traditions (246–9).

[2] I have relied on Havelaar 170 for this information, since Cozby's text was not available to me.

Dazu braucht es kein Leiden, kein Kreuz, keine Auferstehung. Denn der gnostische Erlöser bedarf zum Erlösungswerk nicht der tiefsten Erfahrung des Menschenseins: der völligen Einsamkeit und Verlorenheit. Er "*muß*" nicht leiden, "für" nichts und "für" niemand (1975, 269–70).

The study in Chapters II and III, especially the sections dealing with the aspect of Jesus' taking on flesh, has implications for the question of suffering and the closure of the earthly context. The power of the archons and Demiurge is above all the power to cause suffering and death to those in the flesh. This is either a present reality for the soul imprisoned in the human body, or a future possibility, or a permanent imprisonment in this world, where a person does not have the necessary means to pass the archons and return to the heavenly place of origin.

With this is mind, the notion of the graph proposed in the introduction to Chapter IV might be extended. The more Jesus has a truly human nature/flesh, the more he will have to struggle against death, or even perhaps undergo death. The more his earthly existence and the flesh are only an illusion, the less he will need to struggle or undergo death in order to leave the earthly context. In the latter situation he may indeed experience a situation of struggle against death but it will be as a powerful figure (two cosmic forces against each other), not as a human being undergoing the reality of a human death. To win against death is to conquer it – we find only rarely in the texts the paradox of a humiliating death as the means of conquering the archons (e.g. Teach. Silv. and Interp. Know.).

As Voorgang notes there are two main ways of dealing with the passion in the texts: either in a docetic fashion (i.e. that Jesus only appears to suffer: perhaps another suffers for him) or within the concept of two natures (i.e. the second worthless fleshly/earthly nature suffers), the latter being the more frequent (241–4). What becomes obvious from the writings are the great number of possibilities for describing the process of closure and the christologies implied thereby. As Tröger writes:

Gnostic christology is not unified. There are gnostic writings that confess the passion of the Savior, Jesus Christ and interpret his crucifixion as a sign of the victory over the powers of darkness. But such writings also understand the 'meaning of salvation' in gnostic ways, e.g., as crucifixion of the sarx, or as the 'separation of what is mingled.' Other gnostic writings report that the Savior did indeed 'suffer,' but his essence had nothing to do with the suffering itself because he was incapable of suffering... Such statements clearly show that gnostic docetism was a specific christological variant (1991, 216).

1. Death

1.1 Suffering and Death

Tri. Trac. and Ep. Pet. Phil. attest to the suffering and death of Jesus as a fact but without a great deal of further detail with regard to the context or setting of that experience.

In Tri. Trac., the Saviour is said to suffer (113.33–34; 114.34–35), having taken upon himself the death (i.e. ignorance) of humankind (115.3–6), since he is a compassionate Saviour (114.31–32). That the suffering is more than an experience of ignorance may be supposed from the description of his persecution by the powers of the left (both men and angels [121.19]), i.e. the hylics, who deny him and plot evil against him (122.5–6), and do wicked things to him including his death (121.10–14), thinking to rule the universe by slaying the one proclaimed as king of the universe (121.14–18). Tri. Trac. also refers to the burial of the Saviour in a tomb as a dead man (133.30 – 134.1). Although the text is corrupt, it seems to emphasise that he is really dead, although the angels thought (ⲚⲈⲨⲘⲈⲨⲈ)[1] that he was alive, and received life from the one who had died.

After the first appearance of the risen Lord in Ep. Pet. Phil., the apostles discuss the question of the Lord's suffering on their account (138.15–16, 18) and the necessity for them also to suffer "on account of our smallness" (138.19–20). This serves as an introduction to the following section in which Peter addresses his disciples, outlining the following summary of the events of the suffering and death of Jesus: the illuminator Jesus came down; was crucified; bore a crown of thorns; put on a purple garment; was crucified on a tree; was buried in a tomb (139.16–20).

Peter follows the summary with the statement that Jesus is a stranger to this suffering (139.21–22), with a further contrasting (chiasmic) statement, "but we are the ones who have suffered through the transgression of the Mother" (139.22–23).[2] The apostles suffer because they are under the influence of what is perpetrated by the Mother, i.e. their smallness, as already stated in 138.20. Jesus suffers because of them, because of their smallness, by taking on their "mortal mould", to which at the same time he is nevertheless

---

[1] Thomassen translates as "comprirent" (1989a, 249), which seems to read more into the text than is there.

[2] Bethge interprets this as the Fall of Eve (1990, 278), but I am more inclined to see it as a reference to the myth concerning Sophia (see also Koschorke 1977, 330; and Ménard 1977, 46), as outlined in 135.8 – 136.5 where the Mother appears in connection with the Arrogant One. Meyer views this as a reference to Sophia, while it is also reminiscent of references to the fall of Eve, proposing that it "may provide another point of contact between the figures of Eve and Sophia in Gnostic literature" (Meyer and Wisse 231).

a stranger.[1] That Jesus is the "author of our life" (139.27–28; also "author of our rest", 140.4) proceeds from the fact that he has undergone the same suffering; he has done everything "in a likeness to us" (139.24–25).

Koschorke is right to stress the nature of the suffering of Christ as the entrance into mortal bodiliness, rather than the crucifixion,[2] at least as far as Peter's interpretation of the "credal" statement is concerned (1977, 330). However, the fact of the crucifixion itself is not denied, so that the reader is left with a sense of some tension remaining in the text concerning how the experience of the suffering earthly Christ is to be understood. Is it impossible for the Christ to suffer really, despite how it seems with his crucifixion, because he is a stranger to suffering? Or has he suffered really, despite the fact that he should not, because he came and took on our bodily condition and suffered the consequences?

Tröger interprets the "strangeness" of death and suffering to Jesus as the result of his having taken on a strange body:

> Für den Erlöser ist das menschliche Leiden im Grunde fremd, so wie der von ihm angenommen Körper ein Fremd-Körper, ein 'totes Gebilde' ist... Gerade deshalb erkennen ihn ja die Archonten nicht; und was diesem Körper auch widerfahren sein sollte, es war ihr Gebilde, das litt, nicht der Erlöser (1978, 2: 157).

1.2 Suffering and Death as Cosmic Struggle, and the Conquering of Death/Hades

Ten texts are considered in this section: 2 Apoc. Jas., 1 Apoc. Jas., Great Pow., Teach. Silv., Soph. Jes. Chr., Testim. Truth, Treat. Seth, Interp. Know., Treat. Res., and Melch. Many of the texts attest to a real struggle for the Jesus figure, yet as Voorgang indicates, the frequent theme of the judgment and overpowering of the archons that is associated with the struggle is an important consideration in the meaning of the passion. It tends to relativise the representation of suffering, with the focus much more on the motif of overpowering and ascending for the Jesus figure (244–6).

---

[1] Bethge writes that "der Erlöser, der sich ja in einem von ihm angenommen Körper, Substanz der Archonten, befindet, insofern gelitten hat, als das den Körper betraf, der ja von dieser Welt stammt, während der Erlöser aus einer anderen Welt kommt und so, strenggenommen, mit dem Leiden nichts zu tun hat" (1978, 163). Ménard proposes "...la doctrine docétiste d'un Christ ne souffrant que dans une chair apparente anticipe sur la doctrine manichéenne du Jesus patibilis, c'est-à-dire d'un Jésus constitué de l'ensemble des parcelles de lumière tombées dans la matière" (1977, 9). Meyer concludes: "The Ep. Pet. Phil. presents a paradoxical portrait of a Jesus who is both invulnerable and vulnerable, both immortal and dying, a Jesus whose body is both a mortal disguise and a body of death" (1981, 156).

[2] Koschorke situates on the same level those who think Christ really underwent the crucifixion and the archons who did not recognise him: both consider him to be merely a mortal man (1977, 332–3).

1.2.1 The Second Apocalypse of James

2 Apoc. Jas. appears at first to belong to the first section above with Tri. Trac. and Ep. Pet. Phil. James characterises the Lord as "that one whom you hated and persecuted" (50.7–10), who has been judged with the unrighteous and put to death by means of blasphemy, having been cast out (47.23–26).[1] However, in a long speech to the judges (of the Lord), James proclaims that it was really the Demiurge ("your Lord") who did these things (59.6–11). The Demiurge is the Lord who has taken them away from the true Lord (60.5–10).[2] Nevertheless they have judged and oppressed themselves and must remain in their fetters and must repent (59.12–16).

1.2.2 The First Apocalypse of James

The passion of both the Lord and James in 1 Apoc. Jas. must be understood as involving physical suffering only in external appearance, the reality of the situation being that the conflict takes place on the cosmic level with the powers. The setting for the confrontation is Jerusalem, the dwelling place of a great number of archons (25.18–19). There the Lord is seized (25.7–9; 29.16–19) by the powers who are armed against him in judgment (27.18–24). He is fearful before their anger (28.3–4), but does not rebuke (ⲥⲟϨⲉ) them (28.1);[3] rather there is within him a silence and a hidden mystery

---

[1] There is a first person reference to death in 48.8, but I consider that it is James who is speaking (see Böhlig and Labib 1963, 58; and Brown 1972, 140–1 and 1975, 8–16) rather than Jesus (see Schenke, H.-M. 1966, 30; Funk, W.-P. 1976, 108–9; Hedrick 1979, 106; and Veilleux 166). Funk explains that, on the one hand, the self-descriptions are typical for the Gnostic redeemer and, on the other hand, there is not a single sentence which James as the speaker could probably say (108; Veilleux follows Funk). Although admittedly the text is difficult at times to reconcile with James, especially as Funk points out with regard to 49.19–23, the two reasons given for not attributing the speech to James can be opposed from the text itself.

James is presented as a redeemer figure in 55.6–27, indeed is called so by the Lord, "you are an illuminator and redeemer of those who are mine" (55.17–19), and there are certainly statements in this section which James could make, such as the self-designations as the just one (see also 44.14–15, 18; 59.22; 60.12–13; 61.14–15), and as the beloved (see 56.16; 57.5) which only occur in this text with reference to James and never to the Lord. In order to find the terms "just one" and "beloved" used of the Lord, Funk and Veilleux must go outside the text, even so far as invoking the canonical texts. Hedrick translates ⲡⲓⲁⲓⲕⲁⲓⲟⲥ in 49.9 as "the righteous one" instead of "the just one", although he uses the latter translation in every other occurrence of the term (1979, 119). He excuses himself with the reason that he has done so "to avoid confusing the speaker with James".

Other sections of the text are easily related to James: his description as a son (cf. 51.19–22), his obedience to the command (cf. 46.11), his speaking of what he has heard (cf. 51.11–13), and his activity of helping (cf. 59.21–24). Moreover, coming forth from the flesh by *gnōsis* would seem to be more in keeping with a description of James than of the Lord (48.6–7).

[2] I agree with W.-P. Funk's interpretation of the first Lord as the Demiurge (1976, 162), *contra* Böhlig who interprets this passage as referring with "Lord" first to the Father and then to Jesus (Böhlig and Labib 1963, 63).

[3] A little further on in the text the Lord is said to have come with knowledge (ⲅⲛⲱⲥⲓⲥ) and recollection (ⲙⲛⲏⲙⲏ) that he might rebuke their forgetfulness and ignorance (28.7–10). See also 30.1–2 where the Lord speaks of appearing as a reproof (ⲉⲩⲥⲟϨⲉ) to the archons.

(28.1–3). The fact that the Lord is fearful, even as James too is fearful, brings an unexpected human dimension to the text.[1]

Despite the Lord's fear before the archons, James clearly indicates that the Lord is not adversely affected in any way. He came down into a great ignorance and mindlessness but was not defiled by it and his recollection remained (28.11–16). He walked in mud but his garments were not soiled, he was not buried in their filth, he was not caught (28.16–20). Much the same thing is said later in the text in a series of statements by the risen Lord:

– I am he who was within me (31.17–18).
– Never have I suffered in any way nor have I been distressed (31.18–20).
– This people (who existed as a type [ΤΥΠΟC] of the archons [31.23–24]) has done me no harm (31.21–23).[2]

It seems that the "earthly" Lord contains within himself the heavenly Lord or at least the one who will be the heavenly Lord after the passion, the earthly Lord who appears to suffer being only an outward manifestation of the heavenly Lord who does not really suffer.[3] There is a further complexity to the concept since the heavenly Lord is also an image of He-Who-Is. The Jews who appear to oppress the Lord are only a type of the archons who are the real opponents of the heavenly Lord. Thus the scheme may be summarised as follows:

THE APPARENT PASSION		THE REAL PASSION
"earthly Lord"	–	heavenly Lord
|		|
the people	–	the powers

Care is required, however, since the boundary between appearance and reality is not totally clear. The Jews in Jerusalem may be a type of the archons, but the archons are not seen as distinct and dwelling apart in the heavenly region. They dwell in Jerusalem, which is not described as a heavenly city. Thus, although the emphasis in the passion of the Lord (and of James) is on

---

[1] There is another such small "human" detail in the picture of Jesus and James sitting together on the rock while Jesus comforts James in his distress (32.13–16).

[2] Böhlig (Böhlig and Labib 1963, 31), Daniélou (1966b, 289), Brown (1972, 87), and Veilleux (10) see this as a statement that the Jews are not guilty of causing the passion of Christ. Brown states that "the acquittal of the 'people' is due to the Christological viewpoint", i.e. a docetic viewpoint. However it is not so clear that the people are acquitted, as it is also possible to interpret that the people have attempted to do the Lord harm but he has not been affected by their attack. Certainly the Lord proposes that as a type of the archons, this people deserves to be destroyed through the archons (31.23–26). Surely this last saying does not suggest, as Brown thinks, that the people are exonerated even as Jerusalem is not (87).

[3] "On remarquera l'idée que ce qui concerne le Christ visible est l'image de ce qui concerne le Christ invisible... De plus il y a là une christologie décidément dualiste, où les événements de la vie de Jésus ne concernent pas le Christ d'en haut" (Daniélou 1966b, 289).

its cosmological aspect, there is nonetheless also an earthly aspect, even if only to a slight degree.

The process of going through the passion, or perhaps the result of the confrontation with the powers, is interpreted in the text as redemption for the Lord (25.7–9; also for James 29.12–13; 32.28), his completion of his destiny (29.16–19), his fulfillment of "what was fitting" (30.12–13). By contrast, his persecutors, "this people", did what was contrary to what was fitting (31.11–14).

1.2.3 The Concept of our Great Power

Great Pow. 41.13 – 42.15 contains a series of statements in the past tense, for the most part concerned with the cosmic struggle between the Saviour and the archons by which the change of the Aeons proceeds (43.14–15; the word of the Saviour abolishes the law of the Aeon, 42.5–6). The statements are not always arranged in a logical sequence, so that it appears that a number of sources have been put together.

The action may be summarised as follows. The Saviour causes a great disturbance, the archons become angry with him, seize him with the help of one of his followers who knows him, and hand him over to Sasabek, the ruler of Hades, for nine bronze coins (41.13–30). Sasabek, however, cannot seize "the nature of his flesh" (ⲡⲧⲣⲟⲡⲟⲥ ⲛ̄ⲧⲉϥⲥⲁⲣⲁ3) (42.1–2), in fact does not know him (42.4–5), and as a result is put to shame by the destruction of his dominion when the Saviour raises the dead (41.7–13; see also 41.30–32). Thus the Saviour is victorious over both the ruler of Hades and the archons who could not rule over him. The archons try to understand what has happened but do not know that the events are a sign of their dissolution and the change of the aeon (42.8–15). The section concludes with a summary which relies on Matt 27:45, 51–53: the sun set during the day and the day became dark (42.15–17); the evil spirits/demons were troubled (42.17–18).

1.2.4 The Teachings of Silvanus

Teach. Silv. emphasises the humiliating death of the Jesus figure, by describing him as the Wisdom of God who became a type of fool for the believer so that he might take him up and make him a wise man (107.9–13), and as the Life who died for the believer when he was powerless, so that through his death he might give life to him who had died (107.13–17; he died for the soul as a ransom for its sin [104.12–13]). The passion of Christ is seen in terms of a struggle with the Underworld, his death being the ransom and means by which the Underworld is overcome and the soul freed.

The first summary of the events in 103.32 – 104.14 is introduced by the general statement that "Christ is oppressed and bears affliction for your sin" (103.26–28). He is described as taking on likenesses and, although God, coming to the world as a man (103.32 – 104.1). He descended to the Underworld, released the children of death there, sealed up the heart of the Underworld, broke its strong bows, and saved the soul from the strong hand of the Underworld (104.2–8,13–14). When he brought the soul up from the Abyss, the powers saw him and fled (104.8–12).[1]

The second summary of the struggle of Christ in 110.18 – 111.6 concentrates not so much on the liberation of the soul as on the humility and weakness of Christ which overcomes the haughty.[2] The one who is God took on humanity "for your sake" (110.18–19; 111.4–6). He broke the iron bars and bronze bolts of the Underworld, attacked and cast down every haughty power (110.19–24, 29–30), loosened his own chains and brought up the poor and the mourners from the Underworld (110.24–29). He put the haughty to shame through his own humility, casting down the strong and the boaster through his own weakness. He scorned what others consider an honour, so that humility might be exalted (110.31 – 111.4; see also 111.7–8), but he received the crown, gained dominion and appeared giving light to everyone and renewing all through the Holy Spirit and the Mind (112.22–27).

Finally, a later passage in the text shows that the death of Christ indeed is the way by which the dead soul is given life, since the Life died for the believer when he (the Life) was powerless, so that through his death he might give life to the believer who had died (107.13–17). I would suggest that the action in both summaries takes place in association with the passion and death of Christ, and I agree with Janssens that Christ descends into the Underworld rather than the material world (1983, 8–9).[3]

---

[1] Zandee suggests that, rather than the death of Christ, the incarnation is meant here by the descent of Christ into the Underworld (= this world; 4, 295; see Poehlmann 177 "the relocation of Hades upon earth"; also Sumney 204), since the death of Christ is mentioned later in the passage in 104.12–13, following the description of the descent into Hades. This interpretation would be correct only if the statements in the summary are meant to be taken in strictly chronological fashion, which is not necessarily the case. The progression of events is as follows: overcoming the Underworld (103.5–8); bringing the soul up from the Abyss (104.10–12); saving the soul from the strong hand of the Underworld (104.13–14) to show, for example, that 104.13–14 is a summary of the action described in the two previous verses mentioned, rather than a new action.

[2] In this second summary also the description of the events does not proceed in a chronological fashion. In fact, when dealing with this second summary, Zandee proposes the same interpretation: that it is the incarnation of Christ in the world represented as descent into Hades. However, he takes 110.24–26 (Christ loosens his own chains), which occurs within the passage *prior* to the bringing up of the poor and mourners from the Underworld, as a reference to the resurrection! To follow the logic of Zandee is to presume that the summaries proceed in chronological fashion: that Christ is incarnated (descends into Hades), rises (within Hades?), then brings the souls out of Hades, and dies thereafter.

[3] *Contra*, e.g., Tröger 1978, 2: 157; and Peel 1979. It is of course entirely possible that the death of Christ and the descent into Hades is meant to be taken on more than one level and to serve also as an analogy for Christ's liberation of the soul from the bodily existence/animal life which equals death, to bring this soul to the fulness of mind which is attained in the bridal chamber. However, this is not explicitly stated in the text.

1.2.5 The Sophia of Jesus Christ

The revelatory or awakening activity of the Lord in Soph. Jes. Chr. occurs after his struggle with the powers, although BG 121.13–15 describes his teaching the followers about Immortal Man within the summary of his struggle with the powers. Since 90.15–16 uses the phrase "after he rose from the dead", we must assume that the struggle involves death.

The events of the Lord's struggle involve:

– escape from the bond of forgetfulness (III 107.14–15);
– cutting off the work of the robbers (= the archons; 107.15–16);
– loosening the bonds of the robbers from Immortal Man (BG 121.15–17);
– breaking the gates of the pitiless ones (BG 121.18 – 122.2);
– humiliating their malicious intent (BG 122.2–3), with the result that they are ashamed and rise (ⲁⲩⲧⲱⲟⲩⲛ) from their ignorance, being joined with the Spirit and the Breath (BG 122.3–9), so that the two might become one, just as in the beginning (III 117.1–2).

1.2.6 The Testimony of Truth

Testim. Truth narrates that the Son of Man clothed himself with the first-fruits of the powers (= their creations; 32.23–24)[1] and went down into Hades and performed many mighty works (32.24–25), and raised the dead who were there (32.26–27).[2] The descent into Hades is above all a struggle with the powers of darkness, of which the text knows many: angels, demons, stars (29.16–18), archons (= fathers of the world [69.12], and fathers of baptism [69.20–21]), powers and demons (42.24–25), the powers of Sabaoth (73.29–30). The power of the Son of Man on the other hand is connected with his sinlessness, and the cosmocrators of darkness envy him because of this (32.27 – 33.2).

The text warns that the death of the Son of Man or his descent into Hades is not to be interpreted in sacrificial terms as those people interpret their death who give themselves to martyrdom. The Father did not desire human sacrifice (32.19–22).

Pearson interprets the descent of the Son of Man into Hades as the descent to the earth, and the "mighty works" as the miracles of Jesus as recorded in the canonical gospels (Giversen and Pearson 1981b, 113, 130). There are two grounds for arguing against this interpretation:[3] first, we have already had the descent of the Son of Man into the world as the coming to the Jordan, where the world is named as ⲕⲟⲥⲙⲟⲥ and not as ⲉⲙⲛ̄ⲧⲉ. Second, the nature

---

[1] Mahé considers this passage an indication of "la réunion de plusieurs éléments hétérogènes dans la personne du Sauveur" (132).

[2] Christ as life-giver or conqueror of death is also to be found in the image used of him as the bronze serpent: those who believe in him have received life (49.7–9).

[3] Tröger agrees that this is a real descent into Hades, although he interprets the descent in Teach. Silv. to be an analogy for the descent into the world (1978, 1: 99).

of the mighty works seems connected to raising the dead, whereas the miracle tradition occurs explicitly in 33.2–8.

Giversen and Pearson also see a reference to the death of Christ in 33.10–11, which they give as: "For this reason he [destroyed] his flesh... (?) (ⲉⲧⲃⲉ ⲡⲁⲓ ⲁϥ[ⲧⲉ]ⲕⲟ ⲛ̄[ⲧⲉ]ϥⲥⲁ[ⲣ]ⲁ3). They propose that this verse concerns Christ destroying his flesh on the cross, the flesh that really belongs to the powers (1981b, 131). The word "cross" occurs within a very damaged section in 40.25.

1.2.7 The Second Treatise of the Great Seth

Four sections of the text in Treat. Seth deal with the events of the passion or crucifixion in summary form (54.23 – 56.17; 56.20 – 57.18; 58.13 59.11; 59.15–26).[1] The action is interpreted in general as persecution and opposition towards the Christ by the heavenly powers (the Cosmocrator and those with him) (52.29–30). From the four sections, the major details of the action may be set out as follows.

Christ comes down into the world, changing shapes as he comes and assuming the likeness of the powers so that he cannot be seen and can pass by their gates (56.23–30). In doing this he subjects the powers to slavery (56.20–30). Because what he does is the will of the Father, it is not shameful for him nor defiling to come into the world (56.30–35; 57.3–7). The fourth summarising passage deals with the descent of Christ for the purpose of destroying the archons, reiterating that it is by the will of the Father (59.15–19), though here the action is presented as a combined effort of Christ with "his own" (= the heavenly assembly). They come forth from their home, down into the world, coming into being in the world in bodies (59.19–22).

Christ proceeds to place the small Ennoia in the world, which results in disturbance to the various heavenly powers and subsequent opposition to him, including attempting to seize him or simply disbelieving that his plan will succeed (54.23–27, 32 – 55.7). Apart from the four summary sections, 65.9–13, 14–18 gives a final brief reference to the ones who are the slaves of law and earthly fear (= the Jews) who erred in judgment and raised their defiled and murderous hands against him. Thus once again the Jews are put together

---

[1] See Gibbons 1972, 26–7, 34–6, 227; 1973, 244–5; and Painchaud 1982, 111–2 for two different views of how various passages are to be interpreted and how they are related. Painchaud's interpretation that the "passion" sections deal with the events of the passion in a chronological progression seems to ask too much of the text, and I am more inclined to agree with Gibbons' view that the sections deal with basically the same material from different perspectives, although my number and identification of sections does not accord *in toto* with Gibbons' outline. Tröger is also generally in agreement with Gibbons (1978, esp. 259, fn. 1), although he too divides the sections differently. Also of interest is Gibbons' outline of the possible sources (1973, 246–54) and his redactional analysis, esp. in the context of this discussion, "The passion insertions in #1" and "The passion references in #2" (248–9).

with the powers as those who persecuted him.[1]

The details of passion and crucifixion in the passages include being re-strained in fetters (58.23–24),[2] being given a crown of thorns (56.12–13), bearing the cross (56.9–11), being given gall and vinegar and struck with a reed (56.6–8), being nailed to death to a tree with four nails of brass (55.34–35; 58.24–26). The effect of the action is that darkness overtakes the archons because their sun has set, and the world is made poor (58.20–22). Christ tears the veil of the temple with his own hands (58.26–28), the chaos of the earth trembles (58.28–30), and the souls who have been sleeping below rise and go about having put on the new man (58.30 – 59.4; cf. "I came to my own and united them with myself", 59.9–11). The third section characterises Christ's crucifixion (= his going up to the height, his "apparent elevation"; see Painchaud 1981, 346 n. 21) as his third baptism (58.13–17) which seems to be connected with the perfection of the believers in the third glory (58.12–13).

The plan against Christ fails, however, and the persecutors condemn them-selves by their action (56.2–4). He is not afflicted even though punished, and he does not really die as people think, but only appears to (ⲉⲘ ⲡⲈⲦⲞⲨⲞⲚⲍ) (55.10–19, 26–28, 30–34; see also 53.24–25); and thus he is not ashamed (55.19–22). His persecutors were blind so they did not see him but only thought they saw and punished him (55.36 – 56.1, 4–6). Instead, they pun-ished their own man, their father,[3] Simon (55.34–35; 56.6–11). Christ's re-action to the persecution is to laugh at the ignorance of his opposers while he rejoices in the height (56.13–17).[4]

Christ's action against the powers results in the liberation of the Son of Megethos (= Majesty, the "double" of the Saviour; see Gibbons 1972, 216–

---

[1] The fourth summary, which concerns the Christ and his own, says that they are hated and persecuted by those who are ignorant and those who think they are advancing the name of Christ (59.22–26). This second group of people are obviously another Christian group, added anachronistically with the Jews (the ignorant ones) as the persecutors, so that here the persecution of the Christ and the persecution of his own begin to overlap, as the continuation of the passage shows.

[2] "He" or "it" is restrained in fetters. If the text should be translated with "it", is this the crucifixion of the world, as Painchaud suggests, following Gos. Phil., so that it is not Simon but the world which is crucified? (1981, 345, 347 n. 21 and 1982, 114). This seems unlikely given the further activity of tearing the temple veil in relation to the "he". Painchaud allocates the tearing of the veil to the archon rather than to the Christ, though he gives no reason for this identification (1982, 115). I agree with Gibbons who interprets the activity with reference to the Christ (1972, 235). Bethge, too, obviously has the Christ in mind since he interprets the veil as that of the heavenly temple (1975, 104; see also 1979, 170).

[3] This is Simon of Cyrene, the father of Alexander and Rufus, according to Bethge (1975, 98) and Tröger (1975, 269 and 1978, 260), with ref. to Mk 15:21 (see also Evans et al. 299). This is not really clear from the text. The action is similar to Apoc. Peter, where the Saviour's enemies mistakenly crucify "the son of their glory" instead of the servant of the Saviour (= Jesus) (82.1–3).

[4] This is in contrast to the earlier description in 55.23–26 where the Christ was about to be overcome by fear but did not become fainthearted.

18)[1] who was hidden in the region below. He is taken up to the height which is where the Christ is (57.7–12), the place of the heavenly bridal chamber which no one has seen or known (57.12–18).[2]

1.2.8 The Interpretation of Knowledge

Interp. Know. presents frequent reflection on the passion and crucifixion of the Saviour which is seen as his being humbled or reproached. The summary in 5.27–38 provides the basic information of the event as his being pursued "in that place" (= the world), his crucifixion (see also 1.21), and death (but not his own death, because he did not deserve to die because of the church of mortals).[3] We are told further that he was nailed, and that he bore the suffering because he is in the likeness of the believer.[4]

The cross is taken up as a specific theme together with the image of the Head and members in 13.25–37. After having descended into the pit, the Saviour, the Head, comes up from the pit. He is bent over the cross so that he is looking down from the height to Tartaros, and as a result those below can look up and are able to go above to where the Head is (13.25–29, 33–36). Thus the cross stretches between heaven and earth (= the pit).[5] The cross is more the vehicle by which the Head enables the transfer of the members from the region below to the heights than an instrument of suffering, although the text also speaks in 13.36–37 of the nailing of the members. The end of the action is glorification of the Head by the Father (21.33–34).

The theme of Jesus' humility or his suffering humiliation is reiterated in 10.30–31 where he becomes very small in order that by his humility he might bring believers back from "this pit" to the great height from which they had fallen.[6] Those who believe in the Saviour are taken above by him through the shape that they see (10.31–33). Their ascent is described in two ways in two different places in the text: they are borne upon his shoulders (10.34) or they enter through the rib whence they came, that is, into the New Adam, in order to hide themselves from the beasts (= archons) (9.34–37). That the Saviour knows the way back to the heavenly region comes from his association with light in contrast to the darkness from the Mother (13.15–

---

[1] Painchaud goes further: "...c'est le Sauveur apparu dans l'ordre de la manifestation dans un corps de chair. Il est en même temps une représentation collective des ennoias qui sont dans les région inférieures et qui habitent elles aussi, dans des corps" (1982, 109).

[2] The reference is obviously to the heavenly union between the Christ and his earthly double. For imagery of the bridal chamber, see esp. Gos. Phil.

[3] Cf. Ep. Pet. Phil. 139.21–22 where Jesus suffers but is also a stranger to this suffering.

[4] This is similar to Ep. Pet. Phil., in which the community is said to suffer because Jesus has suffered, but he suffered because he took on their smallness.

[5] Colpe speaks of "das kosmische Kreuz" (1974, 111).

[6] Liberation of those in the pit is partially explained in the text as the result of the proclamation and publishing of the edict of the Father, by which those who have been enslaved and condemned in Adam, have been brought from death, received forgiveness for their sins and been redeemed (14.34–38). To this end, the great Son is sent after his small brothers (see also 15.23–26), to spread abroad and proclaim the edict, and to remove the old bond of debt which is their condemnation (14.28–33).

17). His feet (?) provide traces which scorch the path of the ascent to the Father (13.17–20).

Above all, reflection on the humility of the Saviour is found in the description in 12.14–29. He appears in flesh, having changed his name (from Son to Saviour, from Christ to Jesus?), and is reproached and humiliated and redeemed so that believers might be glorious and receive the forgiveness of their sins and receive grace.

Within this section, Pagels and Turner (1990a, 27 and 82) propose that the soteriological work of the one who was reproached is contrasted with that of the one who was redeemed; that is, there are two separate figures: the reproached one who brings forgiveness of sins; and the redeemed one who brings grace. They make a comparison with the concept in Irenaeus *Adv. Haer.* I,21,2 of the visible Jesus and the invisible Christ.

The parallelism of the text, as well as its grammar, suggests to me that this is the same character, not two separate characters:

> Now, through him – this one who was reproached
> – we receive the forgiveness of sins;
> And through him – the one reproached
> and the one redeemed
> – we receive grace.

[Ñ]ΔЄ ϨΙΤΟΟΤϤ Ñ[ϬΙ ΠΕΕΙ] ΝΤΑϨΑΙ ΝΑϬÑϬ
    ΤÑΑΙ ϺΠΚ[ϢЄ ΑΒ]Αλ ÑÑΝΑΒΙ
ϨΙΤΟΟΤϤ ÑΔЄ ÑΠ[ЄΝΤ]ΑϨΟΥΝϬΝΟΥϬϤ ·ϺÑ
    ΑΥϢ ΠЄΝΤ[ΑϨΟΥϹ]ΑΤϤ
    ЄΝΑΙ ÑΤΧΑΡΙϹ   (12.25–29)

Even the question which follows in the text, "Who redeemed the one who was reproached?" (12.29–30), implies that the one who was reproached is also the one who was redeemed. However, the answer "the name", implies that the Son is the redeemer of the Saviour (see 12.19–22), so in this way there is a distinction to be made between Saviour and Son, and not between the reproached one and the redeemed one, as Pagels and Turner suggest.

The further description of the flesh of the Saviour which comes from Sophia as the creatress, and receives the majesty (Megethos) that descends so that the Aeon might enter the one reproached (12.33–36), is interpreted by Pagels and Turner as the Father entering the visible manifestation of the Saviour (1990a, 83), but it would be unusual for the Father to take on such a role. I am more inclined to see this as a further reference to the Son's redeeming of the Saviour, who has appeared in the flesh. Tröger interprets the passages to mean that only the flesh of Jesus has been reproached and Jesus is, at the same time, the Saviour (1978, 1: 24).

1.2.9 The Treatise on Resurrection

Treat. Res. presents a composite character of Son of Man and Son of God, Son of Man restoring the Pleroma (44.30–33) and the Son of God vanquishing death (44.27–29). The Saviour then is the Son of God who suffered, rose, and went to heaven (45.25–28). What this entails we are told in more detail in 45.14–23: he swallowed up death (45.14–15), put aside the world[1] which is perishing (45.16–17), transformed himself into an imperishable Aeon[2] (45.17–18) and raised himself up (45.19), having swallowed the visible by the invisible (45.19–22). This experience was to provide a way of immortality for believers (45.22–23).

1.2.10 Melchizedek

Melch. must be treated as a special case within this section. The text is very damaged with only nineteen lines out of approximately 745 completely extant (Giversen and Pearson 1981a, 19), and conjectures must be treated with extreme caution. In 2.5 – 3.11, there is a description of a struggle between some figure and Death, the cosmocrators, archons, principalities, powers, female gods, male gods, and archangels. They call him "impious" ([Ñⲁ]ⲤⲈⲂⲎⲤ) and "lawless" (ⲘⲠⲀⲢⲀⲚⲞⲘ[Ⲟ]Ⲥ) (3.8). Commentators interpret the passage as referring to the struggle of Jesus against Death.[3] Although it is quite possible that the reference is to Jesus,[4] there is really no way of deriving this absolutely from the present text. The second reference to the Saviour in 14.4 may speak of his destroying Death: [ϤⲚⲀⲢ̄]ⲔⲀⲦⲀⲖⲨⲈ ⲘⲠⲘⲞⲨ.

Another later section of the text (25.2–11) deals with violence against a figure who remains unidentified. Once again the text is extremely damaged[5]

---

[1] See Peel's summary on "the world" (1985b, 160–1).

[2] Puech suggests the alternative: "il est parti pour un éon, ou une éternité, impérissable" (27), but see Peel's arguments (1985b, 161).

[3] The interpretation relies considerably on the restorations, e.g. "And [on] the [third] day he [will rise from the] dead" from ⲀⲨⲰ [Ⲍ̄Ⲙ̄] ⲠⲘⲈⲌ [ⲰⲞⲘⲚ̄Ⲧ Ñ]ⲌⲞⲞⲨ Ϥ[ⲚⲀⲦⲰⲰⲚ ⲈⲂⲞⲖ ⲌⲚ̄ ⲚⲈⲦ]ⲘⲞⲞⲨ[Ⲧ... (Giversen and Pearson [1981a, 46–7]; see also Schenke, H.-M. 1980, 115, Colpe 1980, 110, and Gianotto 195). Böhlig concurs with the interpretation as the Jesus figure (Böhlig and Markschies 185). When the editorial signs given here are checked against the Facs. Ed., (1977, 7), I must conclude that the editors have been very generous in their judgment of the degree of readability which they assert for the manuscript. Such conjectures are better placed in footnotes rather than in the main body of the translation.

[4] Note also that 2.1 may contain the phrase "in parables" (ⲌⲚ̄ ⲌⲈⲚⲠⲀⲢⲀⲂⲞⲖ[Ⲏ]).

[5] The editors make restorations in order to identify the figure as Jesus Christ ("There can be no doubt that the speaker here is Jesus Christ..." [Giversen and Pearson, 1981a, 27]); e.g. "And [you crucified me] from the third hour [of the Sabbath-eve] until [the ninth hour.] And after [these things I arose] from the [dead]" (Giversen and Pearson 1981a, 81; see also Schenke, H.-M. 1980, 123; and Gianotto 206) from: ⲀⲨⲰ [ⲀⲦⲈⲦÑⲀϢⲦ] ⲀⲓⲚ ÑⲀ̄ Π ϢⲞ[ⲘⲦⲈ Ñ̄ⲦⲈ ⲠⲠⲢⲞ]ⲤⲀⲂⲂⲀ[Ⲧ]ⲞⲚ ϢⲀ [ⲠⲚⲀⲨ ÑⲀ̄Π ϢⲓⲦ]Ⲉ ⲀⲨ[Ⲱ ⲘⲓÑÑ[ⲤⲀ ⲚⲀⲓ̈ ⲀⲈⲓⲦⲰ]ⲰⲚ ⲈⲂⲞⲖ ⲌⲚ̄ ⲚⲈⲦ[ⲘⲞⲞⲨⲦ]. The danger of introducing the restorations into the main body of the text is well illustrated in the case of Beltz, who writes of the Melchizedek-Christ figure "der nach 25,1ff. mit dem Rohre geschlagen und in das Grab zu den Toten gelegt, gekreuzigt und von den Toten auferstanden ist" (1981, 156). Conjecture has become reality without any hint of the textual apparatus of restoration.

and all that can be gleaned from it is that the person is addressing his attackers, that they have struck him, have thrown him, and that the persecution may have led to death ("corpse" [ΠΤШΜΑ]; 25.4) and that it may have occurred in relation to a Sabbath (25.6).[1] After a fourteen-line break, Melchizedek describes, in the first person, speech which has been directed to him (beginning 26.2). Since the address in 26.2–14 implies a situation of struggle with enemies whom Melchizedek has destroyed, perhaps Melchizedek is also to be interpreted as the recipient of the previous persecution in 25.2–11.

Giversen and Pearson assign 25.2–10 to Jesus Christ (1981a, 28; see also Gianotto 212), and 26.2–14 to Melchizedek, who presents himself as "the suffering, dying, resurrected and triumphant Savior, Jesus Christ!" Melchizedek is to be understood as functioning in the earthly context "as the image, or even 'alter ego,' of the heavenly Christ" (25).[2]

There has been much discussion about the nature of the relationship of Melchizedek to the earthly Jesus in this text (always assuming of course that the unidentified character of the passages above is the earthly Jesus). I accept that some kind of parallel relationship may exist although it makes little difference to the small amount of information which the text might provide concerning the figure of Jesus Christ in the earthly context.

2. Crucifixion

Several of the texts in the section above have mentioned the cross, or nailing, or crucifixion and these texts will not be treated again in this section.

---

[1] H.-M. Schenke divides the passage in 25.1–11 between two characters using the 1st pers.: Jesus Christ in 25.1–10 and Melchisedek in 25.11, the phrase "my eyes" referring to his vision of the Saviour Jesus who will come after him (1980, 127–8). Böhlig refers to the suffering of Jesus in 25,2ff (Böhlig and Markschies 185), thereby giving no indication of whether he sees a division in the passage. It seems unlikely however, since he holds that Melchisedek is a double of Christ (186).

[2] See also Gianotto who proposes that the combined figure, Melchisedek-Jesus/the earthly Saviour, is the "manifestazioni o immagini del Salvatore celeste" (212–4). The initial argument put forward by Pearson for his theory of the relationship between Melchisedek and Jesus lies on shaky ground, since it proceeds from the restoration of ΠΙΝΕ in 15.12 (Giversen and Pearson 1981a, 25, 69): "I am Melchisedek, the Priest of [God] Most High; I [know] that it is I who am truly [the image of] the true High Priest [of] God Most High" from the Coptic: ΑΝΟΚ [ΜΕΛΑ]ΕΙCΕΔΕΚ ΠΟΥΗΗΒ ΜΠ[ΝΟΥΤΕ] ΕΤΑΟCΕ †[ΕΙΜ]Ε ΑΕ Α[Λ]ΗΘШC ΑΝΟΚ ΠΕ [ΠΙΝΕ Μ]ΠΑΡΧΙΕΡΕΥC ΜΜΕ [ΜΠΝ]ΟΥΤΕ ΕΤΑΟCΕ (H.-M. Schenke has "[das Bild (?)]" [1980, 120]; and Gianotto "[l'immagine]" [201]). See Helderman contra Pearson on this point and his further argument (1989, 342–47). Pearson's earlier work was much more cautious regarding the relationship of Christ and Melchizedek: "...Jesus Christ is prominent in this document, apparently standing alongside of Melchizedek as a redeemer figure. It is clear that the roles of Jesus Christ and of Melchizedek are closely intertwined in this text. In fact it is not out of the question that the two are actually identified with one another. Certainty on this question is, unfortunately, not possible" (1975, 201). Colpe is also less certain, writing that the text "das Verhältnis nicht klar und eindeutig ausspricht", but nevertheless holding for some kind of equal standing between the historical Jesus and Melchisedek (1980, 113, 116).

2.1 Crucifixion as a Fact[1]

Acts Pet. 12 Apost., Val. Exp. and Trim. Prot. mention crucifixion but offer little detail or reflection upon the fact. For Acts Pet. 12 Apost., we are simply given the description of Lithargoel who retains the marks of crucifixion (see the discussion in Chapters II and IV).

In Val. Exp., the main summaries with reference to the event of crucifixion occur on pp. 33 and 35. In a very damaged passage, the names Christ (33.17) and Jesus (33.18) occur, with mention also of "seeds" (33. 17–18), "cross" (33.18–19), and nail wound (33.19–20). The one who suffers did not want to consent to it (33.23–24) [but rather was detained (33.25)?]. Ménard interprets the main character as Christ-Jesus, whose cross is the Limit which separates the world of the Pleroma of the syzygies from the inferior world of Sophia and the passions (1985, 74). However, since the text brings the two characters of Jesus and Christ together only in the final action of the restoration to unity and reconciliation of the All, I am inclined here to interpret the action as referring to Jesus as distinct from Christ.[2]

Trim. Prot. 50.12–15 states that the Word puts on Jesus and bears him from "the cursed wood" and establishes him in the dwelling places of his Father. This is the only appearance of Jesus in the text. Helderman comments: "Jesus aber erreicht das Lichthaus, welchem er ja doch gehört ... sei es dann, dass die Protennoia gemeint ist!" (1978, 194). Jesus may well be intended as a manifestation of the Son, given the reference to the dwelling-places of his Father, but the activity of putting on Jesus or being clothed with Jesus, if one interprets it as an action similar to what the Word has done before (clothing as illusion or deceptive device), may not indicate that the Word is actually this character, nor that it could be Protennoia, of whom the Word is a manifestation. However, one also has to be careful, since clothing in the text is not always an illusion as, for example, in the Gnostics' final clothing in Light (= the Thought of the Fatherhood 48.13–14, 15–17; 49.31–32).

It would seem better to take the position of Filoramo who summarises as follows:

> The various metamorphoses of the Protennoia also end in the meeting with the earthly Jesus, whom she impersonates, freeing him from the accursed cross and re-establishing him in the Father's mansion. As in other Sethian texts, this trespassing into the territory of Christian soteriology is deceptive. Jesus is only one of many manifestations of a revealing power, an illuminating <u>dynamis</u>, a soteric entity whose names can change, whose epiphanies can vary, but whose substantial reality remains the same in its structure (116).

---

[1] See the discussion of Paraph. Shem in Chapter I.
[2] Colpe too asserts the difference made by the text between Jesus and Christ (1974, 113).

One also must question who the Father of Jesus is. We cannot assume that it is the highest God. According to G. Robinson, Jesus sits at the right hand of his father Seth in Oroiael, after the resurrection (1990, 44).[1]

2.2 Crucifixion as Death (of the Total Person or of a Part)

2.2.1 The Apocryphon of James

The cross is death for the Saviour in Ap. Jas. ("Remember my cross and my death", 5.33–34), but it is tribulation that leads to a crown for the Saviour and salvation for believers (8.38 – 9.1). The Saviour's foretelling of the suffering and death of James in 5.13–19 followed as it is by "as I myself, by the evil one?" (5.19–20) may actually be more appropriately a description of the suffering and death of Jesus.[2] The passion includes abuse, unjust accusation, being shut up in prison, unlawful condemnation, crucifixion [without] reason, and burial in the sand (but see Schenke, H.-M. 1971, 122: "in <Schande> begraben").[3]

2.2.2 The Gospel of Truth

Gos. Truth interprets the event of crucifixion with two metaphors concerned with revelation and life. The first occurs in 18.22–35, where Error is angry at Jesus, persecutes him, is distressed at him and brought to naught. Jesus is nailed to a tree and becomes a fruit of the knowledge of the Father. Eating of this fruit causes enlightenment and mutual knowing between those enlightened and the one who enlightens.[4]

The nailing to the tree, which is a symbol that one expects will refer to the death of Jesus, is extended as a metaphor to speak of Jesus as the fruit of the tree to which he is nailed, so that the major teaching here is not about death

---

[1] The use of the term "resurrection" by Robinson is unusual. There is no suggestion of resurrection but rather of a direct ascension from the cross. She writes in her earlier commentary, that this verse "ist offentsichtlich eine gnostische Version der urchristlichen, im NT selbst nur noch durchschimmernden Vorstellung der Himmelfahrt Jesu vom Kreuz..." (Schenke, G. 1984, 162).

[2] "Nicht mystische Gemeinschaft im Leiden mit Christus, sondern das Beispiel des Soter wird den Jüngern als Bild und Motiv für Bejahung und Übernahme ihrer Leiden vor Augen geführt" (Scholten 45).

[3] H.-M. Schenke suggests that ϣⲱⲥ has been written as ϣⲟⲩ. He gives Is 53:9, 12 and 1 Cor 15:43 as supporting texts (1971, 129). F.E. Williams follows Schenke with "<shamefully>" (1985b, 15).

[4] This is almost a parallel in the earthly sense of the union which occurs between Father and the All (19.8–10).

so much as about enlightenment.[1] It is not possible to be really sure that there is any talk about death to be inferred. Arai cites van Unnik's suggestion that here the tree is the Tree of Life (1964a, 95).[2] This of course can be linked, as Arai suggests, to the saying in 20.13 that "his death is life for many".[3] If the Tree of Life is meant, then both metaphors associated with the work of the cross have to do with life as well as enlightenment.[4]

The theme of life is taken up in the later passage in 19.35 – 20.27 which focuses on the association of "the living book of the living" with the crucifixion. This book, written in the thought and mind of the Father, could not be taken by anyone, since to take it meant death, but Jesus was patient in accepting his sufferings until he took it, since he knew that by doing so his death would be life for many. Thus he put on the book and was nailed to a tree. This action is interpreted as the publishing of the edict of the Father on the cross. As with the first passage above, once again the point of the nailing is not so much a concern with the physical matter of death but with revelation.[5] It is found again in 20.34–39, where it is stated that he enters the empty spaces of terrors and passes through those stripped naked by oblivion,[6] because he is knowledge and perfection, and he proclaims the things that are in the heart.[7]

---

[1] Though Strutwolf also writes of this as a revelation event, nevertheless I am less inclined to his stress: "Hier wird interessanterweise ohne doketische Abschwächung vom Leiden und Sterben des Erlösers am Kreuz gesprochen" (164; see also Partrick's similar emphasis, 82–3). Arai writes that Christ's death on the cross in Gos. Truth is decisive for "die Offenbarung der Erkenntnis und die Erlösung der Menschen... Jesus füllt und löst den Mangel der Welt auf durch seine Offenbarung, und somit löst er notwendigerweise seine eigene 'Gestalt' ($\sigma\chi\tilde{\eta}\mu\alpha$) auf, d.h. er muß den leiblichen Tod erleiden. Diese Motivierung des Todes Christi ist nur im Zusammenhang mit der gnostischen Kosmologie und Anthropologie, bzw. der Auffassung der Sünde des EvVer zu verstehen. Die Sünde ist hier lediglich Folge des Irrtums, der Negation der Gnosis (32, 35–9). Dementsprechend gilt die Vergebung der Sünde als bloße Befreiung des Licht-Iches, das vom Irrtum in der Materie gefangengenommen ist (35, 25–29)" (1964a, 100, 104–5).

[2] Van Unnik, W.C. 1946. "The 'Gospel of Truth' and the New Testament." *The Jung Codex*. Ed. F.L. Cross. London. 79ff, esp. 116.

[3] F.E. Williams refers to Mk 10:45 (see also Evans et al. 27) and 1 Tim 2:6 (1985b, 58).

[4] Daniélou makes a connection between this passage and Clement's *Strom.* V, 11,72,2. For Daniélou the most remarkable characteristic is that here in both cases we have the identification of the tree of life and the tree of knowledge. He finds the same identification in the *Letter to Diognetus* XXII, 3–8, which belongs to the same Alexandrain milieu prior to Clement. Daniélou sums up, "Ainsi, en même temps qu'il ajoute une pièce au dossier du gnosticisme, l'Évangile de vérité est un précieux document sur les origines du christianisme en Égypte" (1966a, 294).

[5] See also Williams, F.E. 1985b, 58; and Attridge 1986, 245, fn. 36. For Attridge, this continues what is already begun in John where the primary meaning is revelatory: "...at all points where the 'familiar' descriptions of Christ's person and work are given... that familiar presentation is reinterpreted with unfamiliar metaphors" (244–5). Ménard holds that the writer passes from an orthodox and historical (temporelle) interpretation of the cross (18.24) to a Gnostic and ahistorical (atemporelle) interpretation (20.6, 25–34) (1972, 10–11).

[6] Cf. 18.16–17 where the text says that (Jesus the Christ) enlightened those who were in darkness through oblivion.

[7] The living book of the living is manifested in the heart (19.34–36).

The action of undergoing crucifixion is summed up in 20.29–30 as Jesus drawing himself down to death even though life eternal clothes him. Thus the metaphor of clothing with the book or putting on the book is extended in these and the following lines. However, the metaphor is a little complicated. He is already clothed with life eternal (20.29–30) and yet the following line seems to imply that he is clothed also with mortality. There is no interim explanation of his having put off life eternal in the first place in order to be clothed in perishability, which is then stripped off in death so that he is once more clothed in imperishability (20.30–32).

F.E. Williams suggests that the clothing with life eternal is an eschatological clothing with immortality (1985b, 60), but this is not logical in the sequence. Grobel asks in relation to 20.30 whether there is any passage in the NT in which Jesus is already clothed with eternal life and then refers the reader to the Transfiguration or Jn 11:25, but follows both suggestions with a question mark in the text (1960, 67).[1] Of course, the tenses are a problem for those like Grobel who wish to interpret the sense as referring to events in pre-existence as in Phil. 2:6–8.[2]

Arai deals mainly with 31.4–7 but also with ref. to 20.28ff: "Jesus hatte schon bei seiner Erniedrigung, also vor seiner Auferstehung, 'das ewige Leben' angezogen... (ref. to Jn 11:25; 10:18) (1964a, 81). He summarises:

[D]er Verfasser des EvVer verwendet die neutestamentlichen Zeugnisse über den Auferstandenen in seiner Schilderung als Zeugnisse für den historischen Jesus, wie auch zum Teil in kanonischen Evangelien, vor allem im Johannesevangelium, Erzählungen über den Auferstandenen in das irdische Leben Jesu verlegt sind, was dann später in den apokryphen Apostelakten üblich geworden ist. Zu beachten ist allerdings, daß eine scharfe Unterscheidung zwischen dem 'historischen Jesus' und dem 'auferstandenen Christus' dem EvVer ohnehin fernlag (82–83).

2.2.3 The Gospel of Thomas

Gos. Thom. makes one reference to the cross which the believer must take up: "Whoever does not... take up his cross in my way (ⲚⲦⲀϩⲈ) will not be worthy of me" (Log. 55). Ménard interprets this cross as the heavenly cross which separates the spiritual from the world, and the taking up of this cross as the crucifixion of the world, similar to the concept in Gos. Phil. 53 and 1 Jeu 257.18ff; 258.5ff (1975b, 158).

Log. 65 and 66 contain the parable of the son who is sent to the vineyard and killed, and of the cornerstone which is rejected. If these are taken as

---

[1] Evans et al. refer to 1 Cor 15:53–54 and 2 Cor 5:2–4.
[2] Till (1959, 171), Grobel (1960, 66), and Orlandi (49) translate with the past; Arai (1964a, 81), Ménard (1972, 47), Williams, F.E. (1985a, 89), and Malinine et al. (1956, 11) with the present.

autobiographical parables, this may be a reference at least to the death of Jesus. Ménard suggests that Thomas has omitted the assassination of the Son outside the vineyard because "le Christ est un Sauveur, non pas en tant que Rédempteur souffrant, mais en tant que rélévateur" (1975b, 167). However, there is surely suffering implied in the fact that the son is indeed killed. An earlier logion has attested to finding life through suffering (Log. 58).

Log. 104 speaks of the fasting and praying which the followers must do when the bridegroom leaves the bridal chamber. If this is a reference to Jesus as bridegroom, then his departure leaves them in some kind of deficiency but does not necessarily imply his death.[1]

There is some disagreement among scholars as to the presence or otherwise of a passion story or passion references in Gos. Thom. Haenchen states that there is no passion story, that this gnostic Jesus is no real human being, but rather the son of the Living one, that is, the Father. He does not die to atone for sins but is important as the one who speaks the divine word that brings salvation, that is, as a revealer (1973, 222). On the other hand, some scholars see implicit allusions to the passion. Ménard, for example, suggests that Log. 28 ("And my soul became afflicted for the sons of men...") is an allusion to the passion (1975b, 122).

2.3 Crucifixion as a Fact but not as Death, or as the Death of Someone Else

Treat. Seth., in which the person crucified is not the Christ but Simon, and other texts in which the Christ only appears to die or endure the passion have already been discussed. Apart from these texts there are a number which deal with the crucifixion of the world as the event which really happens, even when a crucifixion appears to be described for the Jesus figure.

2.3.1 The Gospel of the Egyptians

The briefest description is found in Gos. Eg. where we are told that Jesus came and crucified that which is in (III) or under (IV) the law (III 65.17–18/IV 77.14–15).[2]

---

[1] Ménard interprets the saying as referring to the individual Gnostic: "De même que le vrai gnostique ne quitte jamais la chambre nuptiale, ainsi il n'a jamais à suivre des prescriptions visant le jeûne ou à prononcer des prières" (1975b, 204). It is difficult to ascertain any pattern for Ménard's interpretation of some sayings in this gospel with reference to Jesus and some with reference to the Gnostic believer. There seems no reason for interpreting the bridegroom as the Gnostic instead of Jesus, even given the sacrament of the bridal chamber.

[2] Böhlig and Wisse refer to Gal 6:14, Eph 2:15, and Col 2:14 for a similar antinomian attitude in connection with the idea that the world was crucified (196). Evans et al. give Rom 7:4; Gal 3:13; Eph 2:15; Col 2:14 (226).

2.3.2 The Gospel of Philip

In Gos. Phil., the resurrection and the cross are named (along with the light
and the holy spirit) as possessions which the Father gave the Son in the bridal
chamber (74.18–21).[1] There is a parallel to be found in the fact that Joseph,
his earthly father, made the cross from the trees which he had planted (73.9–
15; "the planting was the cross", 73.15). That Jesus is crucified seems to be
implicit in the explanation of his name in Syriac as Pharisatha (the one who is
spread out) for he came to crucify the world (63.21–24), and also in the passage which deals with the words from the cross: "My God, my God, why, O
Lord, have you forsaken me?" It was on the cross that he said these words,
for he separated the place..." (68.26–29).[2]

Rather than any "physical" concern with the cross, the focus tends to be
firmly on the experience of the cross as a means both of separation and of re-
unification in the cosmos.[3] This is emphasised by a number of uses of the
image of the tearing of the temple veil of the holy of holies. This action is
somehow associated with the mystery of the bridal chamber and the ascent of
some from below (69.36 – 70.4, text fragmentary). The tearing signifies
both the revelation of what has been within and the desolation or destruction
of the house (of the Jewish God = the Demiurge). That godhead flees the
temple to find refuge beneath the arms/wings of the cross (84.25–34). The
cross is the (new?) ark which is salvation when the flood of water surges
over them (the Hebrews who are becoming Christians?) (84.34 – 85.1). Perhaps this is simply a reference to the signing with the cross in a baptismal
ritual.

2.3.3 The Apocalypse of Peter

There are vague references to the passion by the Saviour (using the 3rd person for the one who experiences it) in 71.27 – 72.4: the rejection which happened to him; the sinews of his hands and feet; his crowning by those of the
middle; the body of his radiance; and the reproof of Peter three times "in this
night". This passage introduces Peter's vision of the priests and people coming with stones as if to kill himself and Jesus (72.4–9), and the text gives full
responsibility for the passion to the Jews (albeit under the influence of the
archons).

What happens to the Saviour is the completion of the will of the incorruptible Father (80.24–26). He himself cannot be touched by those opposed to
him, whose minds are closed (80.29 – 81.3). He appears to be seized (81.3–6)

---

[1] Trautmann interprets the passage as referring to the initiate at baptism (1986, 125). The
cross as an element of the sacrament of the bridal chamber appears to have a power associated
with chrismation and the reception of the names (of the Father, Son and Holy Spirit?). It is
the power which the apostles called "the right and the left" (67.24–25).

[2] Isenberg has "for he had departed from that place" (Layton and Isenberg 179). Perkins
sees a reference to the crucifixion in 53.1–9 where "Christ lays down 'his life for his own'
from the day the world came into being" (1993a, 79).

[3] See Trautmann's (1986) study of the Cross as performing the function of Limit.

but the text clearly differentiates between three figures, or indeed four figures, since the Saviour who speaks with Peter is to be seen as separate from the figures engaged within the description of crucifixion (see the discussion in Chapter IV).

The physical substitute actually experiences the crucifixion. He is taken and his feet and hands are struck, nails are driven into his fleshly part (81.12–14, 18–21). This one is a substitute in the likeness of the Saviour (81.21–23), a physical body susceptible to suffering (83.4–6), the son of the archons' glory (82.1–3).[1] He is further described as the first-born, the home of demons, the stony vessel (?) in whom they dwell, of Elohim, of the cross which is under the law (82.21–26). This substitute may thus be intended as a type of Adam, the first-born of the Demiurge Elohim, the Jewish creator god.

While the substitute is crucified, a second figure is glad and laughing on the tree/cross (81.10–11), laughing at the blindness of those who thought to persecute him, as they are divided among themselves (82.26 – 83.4).[2] He is the living Jesus, the servant of the Saviour (81.17–18; 82.1–3), and the Saviour's incorporeal body (ⲡⲁⲥⲱⲙⲁ ⲡⲉ ⲛ̄ⲁⲧⲥⲱⲙⲁ) (83.6–8). As Havelaar rightly proposes, this crucifixion is really a repudiation of the world, represented by the material body of the Saviour which has been adopted to be conquered, not to be redeemed (170). I would add that, in this sense, it may be the crucifixion of the world rather than the Saviour.

3. Resurrection[3]

There are a number of texts which simply attest to the fact of the resurrection of Jesus from the dead, such as Soph. Jes. Chr. 90.15–16 and Ep. Pet. Phil. 139.20–21. Melch. 5.1–11 includes rising from the dead in the list of what has really happened to Jesus, contrary to the incorrect teaching of some people. There are some texts in which resurrection is probable but it is not referred to specifically, namely Tri. Trac. and 1 Apoc. Jas.

Partrick adduces two passages in Gos. Truth for Jesus' resurrection: 20.30 – 21.8 and 30.16 – 32.4. Certainly the first passage describes the events after the nailing of Jesus, but it does not necessarily refer to resurrection. It is not even clear in the second that the event of raising applies to Jesus. It seems more likely that it is the Spirit who woke the one who is asleep through ignorance, just as Jesus is the one who opens the eyes of the blind (30.14–16). In fact Partrick's conclusions seem to argue against the passage. The agent of resurrection is certainly the Spirit (30.17), yet Partrick identifies the Risen Jesus as the Spirit (85).

---

[1] This seems to be polemic against Paul (1 Cor 2:8).

[2] One cannot speak literally here of resurrection since the Saviour does not undergo death, but the death of the physical substitute does seem to trigger the dissolution of the ties between the physical body of the Saviour and the psychic body, Jesus.

[3] See the general treatment in Robinson, J.M. (1982) of resurrection appearances of Jesus from Gnostic sources.

3.1 The Tripartite Tractate

Although the text of Tri. Trac. 133.30 – 134.1 is somewhat corrupt, it appears to speak of the Saviour who was in the tomb as a dead man. The angels (?) thought that he was alive, and received life from the one who had died. This may well be an implicit reference to the angelic witness to the resurrection.[1]

3.2 The First Apocalypse of James

In 1 Apoc. Jas. 29.16–19, James says that the Lord will complete his destiny and ascend to Him-Who-Is. It is clear that James expects a reappearance of the Lord after "these things" (29.14–15). After his sufferings we are told that "they" await the sign of his coming and he comes after several days (30.16–18). The appearance of the Lord to James is not a vision within the context of James' prayer, since he stops his prayer to greet the Lord and to kiss him (31.3–5).[2] There is no distance between the Lord and James, who surprisingly continues to call him "Rabbi" (31.5).[3] There is no explicit reference to a resurrection for the Lord but one is reminded here to some extent of the post-resurrection scene in Jn 20:11–18 between Jesus and Mary Magdalene where the latter also calls him "Rabbi" but is not permitted to embrace him.

Explicit reference to the resurrection is made in Gos. Phil., Treat. Res., and Ap. Jas.

3.3 The Apocryphon of James

Ap. Jas. describes the appearance of the Saviour 550 days after his resurrection from the dead (2.19–22), the cross and death now far from him (5.36 – 6.1). The brief credal statement of the Saviour about himself in the 3rd person may be concerned both with the event of the resurrection and subsequent glorification, "...when he was proclaimed among the angels, and glorified among the saints" (10.36–38). We are told he is already glorified and is eager to depart, although the disciples are holding him back (7.35–36, 37–38), compelling him to stay on with them for eighteen days[4] for the sake of the parables. Jesus speaks openly now to James and Peter in contrast to the parables of the earthly Jesus which the disciples failed to understand (they also misunderstand at this second stage). Thus in this text, revelation

---

[1] Thomassen finds another probable reference to the resurrection and ascension of the Saviour in the passage about the Saviour as the perfect man (*contra* Attridge and Pagels who think that this is the spiritual race, the election [457]), who received knowledge immediately so as to return "to the place from which he came, to return there joyfully, to the place from which he came, to the place from which he flowed forth" (123.7–11) (1989a, 437).

[2] Veilleux refers to the kiss as a "signe évident de son passage à la Gnose... (une) sorte de sacrement gnostique" (8, 10).

[3] "Der Charakter Jesu als Lehrer wird noch dadurch hervorgehoben, daß Jakobus ihn regelmäßig mit 'Rabbi' anspricht" (Böhlig and Labib 1963, 29).

[4] See the emendation to eighteen months in Williams, F.E. 1985b, 21.

("filling") occurs between the aftermath of the cross and death and the second departure of Jesus from the disciples, and may be the revelation of the risen Lord prior to ascension.

3.4 The Gospel of Philip

Gos. Phil. tells us that the Lord rose up first and died (56.17–18). Resurrection is necessary before death so that one does not end up in the "middle", which is death (66.7–21). The following sentence should read, "If anyone does not first attain the resurrection, he will not die."[1] It is necessary to go back to 52.13–15 to understand the requirement of death after resurrection in order that one live even more thereafter.[2]

3.5 The Treatise on Resurrection

For Treat. Res., the Son of Man who was known to believers is he who rose from among the dead, being the destruction of death (46.14–19). This Lord and Saviour, Jesus Christ, is the one through whom the resurrection has come into being (48.16–19). The text later gives a description of "the symbols and the images of the resurrection" (49.6–7): "For imperishability [descends] upon the perishable, the light flows down upon the darkness, swallowing it up, and the Pleroma fills up the deficiency (48.38 – 49.6)."[3] This may well be in reference to the Christ, given the earlier description of his activity and the use of the terms with regard to perishability or imperishability and swallowing, and given the following summary sentence which Peel (1985a) and Nagel (1995) at least translate with reference to the Christ: "He (Christ) it is who makes the good" (49.8–9).[4]

Finally in this section, I deal briefly with the problem of imprecise terminology which one finds with regard to resurrection in studies of the Nag Hammadi collection (see also the Introduction). Many scholars assume that these texts, and other Gnostic texts, deal with the time between resurrection and ascension: e.g., Jeremias 24; Arai 1964a, 81; Evans 1981a, 407; and Filoramo 16. From the outline of the occurrence of passages dealing with resurrection above, it must be obvious it cannot be assumed that a Jesus, who has ended his earthly context in some sense by passion or by conflict with the archons, is necessarily a Jesus who is thereby risen, i.e. "the risen Jesus".

---

[1] See Catanzaro (40); Till (1963, 17); Janssens (1968, 87); Kasser (1970, 27); Ménard (1988, 57); and Layton and Isenberg (153); *contra* Schenke, H.-M. (1960, 42; 1989a, 157); Wilson (1962, 85); and Krause (1971, 99).

[2] See also the link with baptism in 73.5–8. Wilson interprets this saying as involving "a certain disparagement" of baptism (1962, 153). On the contrary, the author is simply arguing that those who say that baptism leads to life are wrong. It is the same for baptism as with resurrection – people receive it prior to death so that they may more truly live.

[3] This activity is very reminiscent of Gos. Truth.

[4] Peel, however, does not interpret the passage beforehand as referring to the Christ (1985b, 200–1).

There are remarks too about "the risen/resurrected Christ" as the revealer figure in texts where there is absolutely no reference to a resurrection, or to a death prior to a resurrection. Wisse, for example, describes the framework of Ap. John as "a revelation delivered by the resurrected Christ" (1988a, 104). Certainly, the beginning of Ap. John asserts that Jesus has gone back to where he has come from (1.11–12; 31.26–27), and it is probable that this is a Jesus prior to final ascent (see below) but there is no mention of resurrection in the text.

4. Ascension

There are a number of ways of describing the final ascension of Jesus which decisively ends his connection with the earthly context. He may ascend directly from the experience of passion or the cross, as already seen with Trim. Prot. or in Great Pow., where after the cosmic struggle against the ruler of Hades and the archons, he will appear ascending (42.18–19), and the sign of the next aeon will appear (42.20–23). Some texts refer to a departure for the Jesus figure but there is no explicit mention of an ascension. Thus in Gos. Thom. Log. 12, the disciples know that Jesus will depart from them and ask who will be their leader after him.

In Soph. Jes. Chr. also, the Saviour is said to disappear from his followers at the conclusion of the revelation (BG 126.18 – 127.2; the conclusion is clearly marked: "These are the things that the blessed Saviour said" [BG 126.17–18]) but no detail is given of an ascension. However, both the content of the final speech and the setting of the mountain in Galilee is strongly reminiscent of the ascension scene in Matt 28:16–20.

Tri. Trac. relates that everything needs to be redeemed, even the Son who is the redeemer of the Totality (124.32 – 125.1). If the Saviour is also saved, then it seems logical that he should share in the restoration at the end, which is not just release from the domination of powers (124.3–12) but also includes ascent to the Pleroma, an entrance into what is silent where everything is light while they do not need to be illumined (124.12–25).

Ap. Jas. provides the closest narrative to what one finds in the canonical Synoptic accounts of an ascension; but here it is a more complex action with what appear to be two departures from the twelve disciples. The Saviour appears to them firstly after his departure from them while they gazed after him (2.17–19). The dialogue which follows makes it clear that Jesus has not departed finally ("ascending as he should", 10.14–15; 15.35) to the place from which he came (2.22–24; 14.20–22), and the farewell speech from 10.22 onwards is introduced by, "Behold, I shall depart from you and go away..." (10.22–23). The disciples are exhorted to remember him after his departure (12.34), and to follow him quickly (10.26–27).[1]

Later in the text, Jesus describes his second departure and what will result from it. Glory and hymns await him in the heavens (14.26–27, 29–30). He will take his place at the right hand of the Father (14.30–31), he will go up in a chariot of the spirit (14.33–34), and he will strip himself in order to clothe himself (14.35–36). However, the return to the heavens seems to include battle before victory and praises (15.9–22). That this departure is final can be seen in the fact that revelation has now ceased. He has spoken his last word (14.32–33).

Ap. John too follows some of the themes of Ap. Jas. albeit more briefly. Here Jesus has returned to the place he came from, the perfect aeon (1.11–12; 31.26–27), having disappeared once the revelation is completed (32.2–3). If the revealer is the same person as Jesus, then one of two interpretations is possible. Either he has come again from that place for the purpose of the revelation and then returned again to the perfect aeon, or, when the revelation begins, he has not yet finally returned to that place and is in a kind of in-between phase in which the revelation is made, after which the final return is accomplished. I am inclined to the second interpretation, since the final section of the narrative (32.4–5) looks very much like the ending of a canonical post-resurrection revelation story (with commissioning story, 31.28–31).

Thom. Cont. also implies that revelation must be ensured before Jesus' final departure, with Thomas asking for the secret knowledge "before your ascension" (138.23).[2]

5. Parousia

The word "parousia" occurs only five times in the whole Nag Hammadi collection (Siegert 284). Apoc. Pet. simply mentions the parousia with no further detail (the race of immortal souls will be under harsh fate until the Parousia of the Saviour [78.6]), though Havelaar points to 73.30 and 80.28 concerning a final judgment that should be linked with this eschatological activity of the Saviour (167). Soph. Jes. Chr. 117.8 – 118.3 is also reminiscent of a kind of final judgment scene, especially with the necessity of bringing proofs ("signs" [ⲤⲨⲘⲂⲞⲖⲞⲚ]).

Thom. Cont. warns the reader/listener that the end or the day of judgment (ⲪⲞⲞⲨ ⲚⲦⲔⲢⲒⲤⲒⲤ) (143.8) will not be long in coming: "Only a little while longer" (ⲚⲞⲨⲔⲞⲨⲒ̈ ⲚⲞⲨⲞⲈⲒⲱ) (141.14). Those who love the fire (141.29–31), and those who turn away from or sneer at the word of Thomas as he

---

[1] In 2 Apoc. Jas. too, there is to be an ascension for the disciples, since James will make possible a process of redemption for them which includes receiving revelation, coming to rest, reigning as kings, and passing above every dominion (56.2–7; 59.5–6).

[2] Kirchner suggests that the series of woes and blessings in the final section of Thom. Cont. is similar in function to the farewell speech of Moses in Deut. 27 – 28 (794).

preaches the words of Jesus, will be thrown into Hades and imprisoned there and undergo torment (141.32–41; 142.2; 142.26 – 143.5). On the other hand the elect will receive rest and will reign and be joined with the good one/the king (145.12–16).

Conclusion

This chapter concludes the investigation of the various aspects of Jesus' contact with the world: his origin, entrance into the world, his nature and being, his activity within the world, his positive and negative relationships, and the conclusion of the contact. In the final chapter I use the detail of that experience together with detail about the communities of the text and gather both under a paradigm of liminality as a heuristic device towards understanding how the two experiences relate to each other.

IX

The Community of the Nag Hammadi Writings and Its Jesus: Liminal Community, Liminal Jesus

Quispel comments that "Gnostic doctrine in general should be considered as a mythical expression of self experience. The centre and starting point of every system is man, his predicament in this world and his awareness of salvation" (1975, 155). It would have been possible to begin this entire study with a description of the communities which produced and used the Nag Hammadi writings, and abstract from that the Gnostic system of salvation and its Saviour figure. However I chose to begin with an exploration of the Jesus figure in the texts and now want to work backwards in a sense to look at the communities.

The two aspects of the study – about Jesus and about the community – are indissolubly linked. My work on the Jesus figure thus far suggests that we can learn about the communities, not only from what they say about themselves but also from what they say about their Jesus. Not that it is possible to talk about one Jesus for the collection, but the perspectives on any Jesus figure will reflect the needs, fears, and hopes for salvation of a community within a particular socio-historical setting. This principle applies to any (Christian) Gnostic or mainstream Christian community: the Jesus figure will mirror in part the people who construct him.[1]

Rudolph's comments over fifteen years ago remain a key consideration in any attempt to understand the relationship of theology to anthropology within Gnosticism or any religion or worldview:

> Das Menschenbild einer Religion oder Weltanschauung ist keine bloß abstrakte Konstruktion, auch wenn es über den notwendigen Weg der Reflexion in seinen unterschiedlichen Zügen und Ausformungen auf den ersten Blick so scheinen mag, dahinter steckt die sehr konkrete Auseinandersetzung des Menschen mit seiner natürlichen und gesellschaftlichen Umwelt. Ein solches Menschenbild ist daher der Versuch einer Bewältigung von Problemen, die dem Menschen von seiner äußeren und inneren Welt abverlangt wird, eben auch von seinem 'Inneren', das sich ja als ein vermittelter Schnittpunkt von 'Außen' und 'Innen' erweist. Die soziale Welt, die der Mensch bildet und schafft, von der er aber zugleich abhängig und geprägt wird, ist

---

[1] Although the connection between anthropology/psychology and theology is rarely explicit in the texts, Gos. Truth 19.10–14 provides the example of the ordinary human experience of needing to be known and loved used as the basis for understanding the Father's need to be known.

die Wurzel aller Menschenbilder, davon macht auch die Gnosis keine Ausnahme (1979, 19).

I now propose to outline recurrent themes and concepts by which communities in the texts describe themselves. There is no single community of the texts, no ideal community, but nevertheless there are some common features that may be identified. In presenting the outline, I reiterate examples of the activity of the Jesus figure from the previous chapters to show how the experience of this figure interacts with, and frequently mirrors, the experience of the community.

In this final chapter, I organise the material on both the community and the Jesus figure within a paradigm of liminality. I do not want to suggest that it is the only possible viewpoint but it can be useful in that it seems to take cognisance of the various key elements that are to be found for both community and Jesus within the texts. It is necessary to keep in mind also that, as well as presenting only one possible perspective, the paradigm of liminality is not exclusive to Gnosticism.

1. Liminality

Ingvild Gilhus has written an excellent study of the Gnostics as permanent liminal groups (1984). Drawing principally on Victor Turner's outline of the three phases of *rites de passage* as separation, *limen* (margin) and aggregation, Gilhus identifies Gnostics as permanent liminal groups, characterised as those experiencing a period of transformation and danger after separation from the world, while the heavenly region or fullness of salvation is not yet attained. In this liminal stage, the Gnostic receives *gnosis* and experiences *communitas* ("a relatively undifferentiated community of equal individuals under the authority of the elders or the instructors" [119]) which opposes existing social structures and maintains the unity of the group. The anti-structural aspect of this existence finds its expression in such associated elements as revelation through ecstasy, and status reversal.

While I accept Gilhus' basic outline and identification of key elements, I disagree with her identification of the Gnostic's liminal stage as separation from the world prior to entrance into the heavenly region or fullness of salvation. I do not think that this is only or always the case although it may be so with some texts. I suggest that it is possible to see the liminal stage as the stage of being in the world after separation from the heavenly homeland of origin, and prior to the Gnostic's return.

Kurt Rudolph's view of the advent of Gnosticism as a politically and culturally marginal movement on the borderline between the East and Rome supports Gilhus' use of the paradigm of liminality to a certain extent: "Das... Doppelgesicht der gnostischen Mythologie: das hellenistische Gewand über einem orientalisch-jüdischen Körper wird verständlich durch die Situation

der hellenistischen Städte, wo bekanntlich beide Traditionen aufeinanderstie-
ßen und auch einen sozialen Konflikt zum Ausdruck brachten" (1979, 25).

The liminal aspect of Gnostic existence can be found mirrored in many
levels in the texts. The structure of the cosmos and heavenly world with their
various borders and means of access could easily be investigated in more detail, for example:

> ...there is now an intermediate place, destined to perform the func-
> tion of cushion and mediator between two conflicting and apparently
> irreconcilable spheres of reality. It is the 'place in the middle' be-
> tween the world of divine plenitude and the place of deficiency and
> non-being. The pleromatic world, ungenerated in the sense that it de-
> rives generation only from itself, is opposed by the world of genera-
> tion: between the two is an intermediate world bound to Sophia...
> (Filoramo 57).

However, I will be investigating the paradigm only with reference to Jesus
and the communities of believers.[1] I have organised the material into the
headings of key elements of liminality as outlined by Turner and Gilhus. In
the first instance Turner constructed his outline of the liminal phase of *rites
de passage* on the basis of social and religious ritual. Here the focus is life experience rather than ritual in the more formal sense, but I think that the basic
categories that Turner suggests are nevertheless helpful, and certainly Turner
himself used the categories more extensively to look at groups like the Fran-
ciscans whom he considered to be permanent liminal groups (Turner, V.W.
140–54).

2. Separation

> The first phase (of separation) comprises symbolic behavior signify-
> ing the detachment of the individual or group either from a fixed
> point in the social structure, from a set of cultural conditions (a
> 'state'), or from both (Turner, V.W. 94).

Since Gilhus proposes the separation of the Gnostic from the world as the
first key step in the process, I will deal with that point first.

One of the key dualistic pairs for the Nag Hammadi texts comprises the
Lord vs the world (ΚΟϹΜΟϹ). Gos. Phil. states that it is necessary for the
Gnostic to come out of the world (65.27) because he loves the Lord, the Son
of God, rather than the world (78.20–25). According to this text, the spirit
of the world (the Sophia of death, Echmoth [?]; 60.12–15) breathes and

---

[1] As Gilhus rightly points out, there are other figures also, such as Ialdabaoth and Sophia,
who are paradigms of the Gnostics' liminal state (121–4). I would add that the figure of
Adam in some writings, as prototype of the Gnostic, would be worth investigating as a liminal figure.

brings winter while the holy spirit (Sophia, Echamoth [?]; 60.10–11) breathes and brings summer (77.12–15).

For the texts in general, the world is either inherently evil, or imperfectly (perishably) created, or is the domain of the evil powers, or some combination of all of these. The attitude of Acts Pet. 12 Apost. is typical: one must simply endure in the world which is full of apostasy and difficulties (7.3–14).

As a corollary of the evil of the world, the human body, as the means of being in the world, is something evil, a product of the archons, and the means by which the Gnostic is imprisoned or enslaved in the earthly context. This represents the enslavement by the highest authorities within the liminal state (Turner, V.W. 102). Although this is so, the body does not thereby rule the Gnostic, and as we shall see, there is obviously a choice about being in the flesh or repudiating it. This can be so, because the flesh does not really belong to the essential being of the Gnostic. Indeed, the imagery of being clothed in flesh and stripping off the flesh (see Chapter III) suggests that the Gnostic may easily divest him/herself of it. We have already dealt with those texts in which the flesh of the Saviour is no more than a covering for his real spiritual self (see Chapter IV). As Havelaar states, "if the Saviour's flesh is not really part of him, neither is that of the Gnostic really part of his true nature" (171).

It is true that the Gnostics feel separated, at least, from the world in which they live, but I would suggest that this is the case because they have first been separated from their real home in the region above. I would propose, therefore, that the liminal phase be seen on a much broader stage, built on the pattern of descent and ascent, with the place of liminality as the world governed by the archons, and with the "border crossings" through the places of the archons, both descending and ascending, as the key moments of separation and aggregation.

This paradigm is clear for the Jesus figure but perhaps not so explicit for the Gnostics, although we know, or the Gnostics know, that they have come from the heavenly region. In one sense the descent of the Gnostic can be seen as more traumatic than that of the Lord. Interp. Know., for example, speaks of the world as the "pit" into which believers have fallen from the heavenly region, having been brought down (by the Demiurge?), bound in nets of flesh (6.28–29).

The situation of separation is summed up well in Ap. John. The imagery associated with humans in the text is totally concerned with the powers of heaven and the powers of the world of darkness (= the prison which is the body). It seems that these people have little or no interest in the everyday world, all that matters being the outcome of the cosmic struggle that is played out on the small scale within oneself. Most often the works of the community are expressed in terms of battle against the archons, and their interest is in the details of the cosmological system and of the place to which they will proceed for their rest. Even where the activity of the believers is described as missionary preaching whether to a select group or to all (and it is a surprisingly constant theme in the writings), it may be that the activity is seen in terms of cosmic struggle rather than as missioning of the earthly inhabitants.

As Rudolph (above) and Wink point out, language about the heavenly powers "masks a vehement protest against the actual order of the world, in its socio-political as well as its spiritual aspects" (Wink 5), yet that protest is not turned into action for social transformation. Wink laments that the Gnostics, for all their insight into the powers, did not move subsequently to engage them in order to recall them to their divine vocation (25). Gnostics are only biding their time here in the flesh, in this prison, enduring until they can return to the heavenly realm where they really belong. They are a liminal group, neither at home in the world nor yet fully at home in the heavenly region, living constantly here in the in-between, a "world between worlds".

Jesus too inhabits a sort of middle ground by his sojourn in the earthly region. He is a heavenly character outside of his "normal" heavenly context who has somehow made himself accessible within the earthly context, in particular to those pneumatics who are caught there but like himself do not belong there. Like the pneumatics/Gnostics, he is a figure between worlds, and this "between worlds" state is taken a step further in some writings in which he is between heaven and earth in another way; that is, after a first departure from the earthly region but prior to a final departure. He has left the earthly region in a sense but has not finally returned to the heavenly region.

3. *Limen*

During the intervening 'liminal' period, the characteristics of the ritual subject (the 'passenger') are ambiguous; he passes through a cultural realm that has few or none of the attributes of the past or coming state (Turner, V.W. 94).

3.1 Insight *(Gnōsis)*

Above all in the Nag Hammadi texts, there is the conviction that salvation is a matter of insight or recognition which saviour figures like Jesus come to awaken in the Gnostics. It is an individual matter, a recognition of the self, of what the Gnostic already possesses (Gos. Phil. 76.17–22), and thus the revelation given to Gnostics is generally speaking not so much an imparting of knowledge but a process of reminding them of, or waking them up to, what they already know. Ap. Jas. tells us that Jesus' invitation is actually not the way by which people enter the kingdom of heaven, but rather by their own fulness which is of the Spirit (2.28–33) "you yourselves are full" (ΤΕΤΝ̄ΜΗ2 Ν̄ΤΩΤΝ̄) (2.33; see also 3.35–37).

Gnostics possess this insight because of their origin. Gos. Truth tells us that if one has insight then he is from above (22.2–4) and he returns there

(22.4–7) and receives rest (22.12); he has knowledge of where he comes from and where he's going (22.13–15). Knowledge of self is not some abstract notion but rather it comprises knowledge about origin, present circumstances and destiny. In Thom. Cont., Thomas is exhorted to examine himself and learn who he is and how he was and how he will be,[1] since it is not fitting for the brother of the Saviour to be ignorant of himself (138.7–12). In this way he will be called "the one who knows himself" (ΠΡΕϤCOOYN ΕΡΟϤ ṀΜΙΝ ṀΜΟϤ) (138.15–16).

This threefold formula of past, present and future identity is typical of Gnostic insight. In 1 Apoc. Jas., the process of redemption (as reported for James) is described as comprising basic formulae questions (34.19–20). The first question asks about identity and origin: "who are you and where are you from" (33.15–18). The following text is damaged but one assumes that there would be a question concerning the present, since the final question concerns where one is going (answer: "to the place from which one came") (34.17–18).[2]

In Soph. Jes. Chr., Mary's second question uses the classic formula: "Holy Lord, where did your disciples come from and where are they going and (what) should they do here?" (114.8–12). The text tells us that the Gnostic belongs to the heavenly region ("your roots are in the infinities", 108.22–23), to the generation over whom there is no kingdom, who are the sons of the Unbegotten Father. This race is where the Gnostic has come from and where he is returning. For the most part, as in this text, the origin of the Gnostic is described as heavenly, just as Jesus' origin. Jesus may be the first of many brothers or a fellow spirit or he may be higher somehow in the cosmic hierarchy but much of what he is, the Gnostic is also – full of insight, a heavenly being, united with the Father/God/Seth.

The heavenly origin is variously described:

– Trim. Prot. gives the origin of the community (the Sons of Light [41.1, 16], the seeds [40.31; 41.1–2, 27–28; 50.18], who belong to Protennoia) as the Light (47.22–23; 49.9–11, 20–23);

---

[1] In view of what would be more typical of a Gnostic formula concerning self-knowledge, I have followed Krause's reading of a past tense for ΑΚϢΟΟΠ, interpreted as a "mißbräuchliche Verwendung von Perfekt I mit Qualitativ von ϢΩΠΕ", based on Quecke's work (Krause and Labib 1971, 36; see also Böhlig and Wisse 192–3). H.-M. Schenke argues that the past tense could have been unambiguously expressed by ΝΕΚϢΟΟΠ so that the question arises whether ΑΚϢΟΟΠ could not more easily be understood as an "eingefärbtes Präs. II" from another dialect (1975b, 9). Turner finds the basis for the use of the present in the fact that Thom. Cont. does not appear to be interested in origins, either of individuals or of the world of matter (1975, 119), but Kuntzmann suggests that, in using the present, Turner "perd le contact avec toute une tradition inquiète de l'identité présente, passée et future de l'initié" (1986, 59).

[2] Böhlig proposes that the third question asks "wie sein Verhältnis zu den Geschöpfen sei, die ihm doch eigentlich fremd seien" (Böhlig and Labib 1963, 32), referring to Irenaeus' Adv. Haer. I 21,5 and Epihanius Pan. 36,3,2–6 which use the same pieces of tradition.

– for Gos. Thom., the solitary and elect are from the kingdom and they will return to it (Log. 49);

– Val. Exp. describes the community as the seeds who have originated from Sophia and the heavenly region (35.14–17, 30–36);
– for Tri. Trac., the community is the heavenly Church which has existed from the beginning (57.34–35), produced by the unity of the Father and the Son (by kisses?) (48.21–33), and comprising many men who existed before the Aeons (58.29–31);

– in Apoc. Pet., the community are the living ones (80.3–4) who are from the life (70.23–24; 71.3–6), from the height of every word of this Pleroma of truth (70.32 – 71.3), another race who do not belong to this Aeon (83.15–19), having been chosen from an immortal substance which can contain him who gives his abundance (83.19–26), a remnant (ⲡⲓⲕⲉⲥⲉⲉⲡⲉ) whom the Saviour has summoned to knowledge and built on Peter as the first one called (71.18–21, 24–25), the little ones[1] who will rule at the completion of the error (80.8–16);

– for Gos. Eg., they are the seed of Seth sown in the Aeons (III 60.9–10; IV 71.20), the incorruptible spiritual church who increase in the four lights of the great, living self-begotten one (III 55.2–6).

Gnostics may find their true origin in a process of spiritual rebirth. For Gos. Phil., the Gnostic like Jesus must be born again in the bridal chamber (= rising again through the image [resurrection]; and entrance into truth, i.e. restoration [ⲁⲡⲟⲕⲁⲧⲁⲥⲧⲁⲥⲓⲥ] 67.13–18).[2] Water and chrisming are the begetting again through the Holy Spirit and Christ (the mother and father of the Christian) in the union of the bridal chamber (69.4–14).

Very infrequently – and Wink characterises this as a "debasement of the primary religious experience" of insight as "rediscovery of one's own authentic selfhood" (38) – one finds that insight may actually include facts of an apparently practical nature. In 1 Apoc. Jas., where the process of redemption is described as comprising the basic formula questions, we are told that the believer must know the answers in order to pass by the toll-collectors (34.19–20), and being able to number the powers gives one ascendency over them.

That there are levels of insight, perhaps better thought of as a process rather than a *fait accompli*, is suggested by texts which recognise levels of initiation into the community. Thom. Cont. distinguishes two levels by the

---

[1] On the use of Matthew's gospel in this text in general and also on the use of the term "little ones" for the community, see Stanton 1977, passim. "As the whole treatise clearly depends on Matthean traditions, it offers the first direct evidence of an ascetic Judeo-Christian group of 'these little ones' with no bishops or deacons, still experiencing heavenly visions and prophetic auditions" (Schweizer 1974, 216). For the use of the New Testament in the text, see Dubois 1983; and Evans et al.

[2] See my forthcoming (1996) article in *Antichthon*, "The Concept of Rebirth as the Christ and the Initiatory Rituals of the Bridal Chamber in the Gospel of Philip."

terms "labourers", which seems to be the technical term for the perfect, and
the "apprentices", who are those who have not yet attained the height of perfection (138.34–36). The latter may be equal to the "babes", those who are
not yet perfect (139.11–12). Lincoln outlines three levels of initiation in the
community of Gos. Thom., based on Log. 2: novices, senior members who
have attained a level of knowledge, and the fully accomplished perfect, who
had achieved the androgynous state.

Soph. Jes. Chr. presents a set of criteria by which the followers of various
categories will find rest: the one who knows the Father perfectly (in pure
knowledge) will go to the Father and have rest in the Unbegotten Father
(117.8–12);[1] the one who knows him defectively will go to his rest in the
Eighth (117.12–15).[2] The two criteria which follow these seem to be parallel
statements to them, speaking of the one who knows Immortal Spirit of Light
in silence, and the one who knows Son of Man in knowledge and love
(117.15 – 118.3).

Of course the very existence of pneumatics and psychics implies that there
are differing levels of insight or at least different processes by which insight
is gained. Tri. Trac. presumes a more complex path for the psychics than the
pneumatics, since although the Saviour reveals himself to them (134.30) and
they know him as their Lord over whom no one else is lord (134.23–26),
they are not saved immediately. Moreover, they will never be on the same
level as the pneumatics. They are the "calling", who are like the attendants or
wedding guests at the wedding of the spirituals and the Saviour (122.19–24).

The psychics are divided into two groups: the first will be saved completely (119.28 – 120.14); the second are further subdivided into those who
abandon the lust for power and remain forever (120.28–29) and those who
do not abandon it and who will receive judgment (121.5).

3.1.1 Insight Brings Truth and Light

As well as the knowledge of origin, present circumstances, and destiny,
insight has other outcomes for the Gnostic, particularly the reception of the
Light, which seems to imply a degree of ecstasy as part of the experience.
This should not be ruled out for the reception of Truth also, which may well
be an analogy for union with the Lord.

1. *Truth*. While truth is associated with knowing things or facts (e.g. Great
Pow. 42.23–29 speaks of knowing the interpretation of the conflict between

---

[1] This may be resting in the Saviour Revealer himself if he is to be identified here with the
Unbegotten Father. It brings to mind the Gospel of John, especially passages like 14:20 (Tardieu refers to 1 Jn 4:6 [200]). Much of what I find reminiscent of the Gospel of John in the
text comes from Jn 14 in the context of the farewell revelation speech of Jesus to the disciples. Perkins suggests that Soph. Jes. Chr. has included Christ into the system of Eugnostos
"by using Johannine metaphors of Jesus as the revelation of the true God" (1980, 94).
[2] That is, the third Aeon, the ЄΚΚΛΗСΙΔ of the Eighth (BG 110.9–16/III 111.1–8).

the Saviour and the archons; Thom. Cont. 138.26–27 describes the difficulty of performing the truth before people),[1] it is most often associated with Jesus or his revelation in a more abstract way. Thom. Cont. designates Jesus as the knowledge of the truth (138.13; and Thomas is the true companion [138.8]). Soph. Jes. Chr. asserts that the truth cannot be found through philosophical speculation, but only through the Saviour: "Lord, no one will be able to find the truth except through you" (ΠⳈΟΕΙⳞ ⲘⲘⲚ ⲗⲁⲁⲩ Ⲛⲁⲱ 6Ⲛ ⲦⲘⲎⲈ ⲈⲒⲘⲎⲦⲒ ⲈⲂⲞⲗ ⳞⲒⲦⲞⲞⲔ) (94.1–3; 92.6 – 93.8; cf. Jn 14:6); for Testim. Truth, the perfect revelation of the Son of Man is the Truth (31.7–10). That truth is not of this world is attested by Dial. Sav.: "Whatever is born of truth does not die; whatever is born of woman dies" (140.12–14).

2. *Light*. Revelation to the Gnostic may be the Light itself or may lead to the Light. In Trim. Prot., the community receives the revelation of the Light from the Word (47.22–23; 49.20–23; 49.9–11). For Great Pow., knowledge of the revealer/speaker brings entrance into immeasurable light (46.6–12).

In Soph. Jes. Chr., those sent by the Son receive Light so that they might shine in Light more than the created Aeons and what is created later, patterned on what is above (108.8; 114.5–8).

3.1.2 The Opposite of Insight: Ignorance

Ignorance is the opposite of insight (sometimes expressed in terms of foolishness vs wisdom, Teach. Silv. 111.22–29; or error vs truth, Gos. Truth 17.15). Gos. Phil. compares ignorance as a slave, with knowledge as freedom (84.10–11). Other vices may be associated with ignorance. Interp. Know., for example, tells us that ignorance and jealousy are the opposites of the graciousness shown by the Word who gives spiritual gifts to the brothers without jealousy (passim within 17 and 18).

Lack of insight is not simply ignorance, but danger, risk, and liability. Dial. Sav.134.1–24 contains a long exposition on the consequences of a lack of knowledge which can be summed up simply: if one lacks knowledge of something, that thing will overpower him (e.g. fire, wind) or that thing is worthless for him (e.g. baptism) or his fate will be with that thing (e.g. perishing with the body). The final statement picks up a common theme of the Gnostics: one who does not understand how he came will not understand how he will go and is no stranger to this cosmos which will be humiliated (134.19–24). This is the reverse side of the questions of origin and destiny.

Ignorance is often described in images of drunkenness or sleeping (e.g. Gos. Truth 22.16–20; Gos. Thom. Log. 28; Interp. Know. 11.15–24), or as being in darkness, stumbling and led astray (e.g. Interp. Know. 9.35–37). In

---

[1] It seems that this performance is the way by which teaching about the secret things is transmitted, which fits with Sell's (1982) theory on the "knowledge of the truth" as the summary of Christian doctrine.

Thom. Cont., the object of insight (at least the Father, if not the Saviour also) is obscure to those in the world who are ignorant and stumbling (ΕΤΟΥΑΙ ΑΡΟΠ) (138.19–21). In its biblical usage the latter verb refers invariably to those stumbling in the darkness (Prov. 4:19; Jer 13:16; Jn 11:9 [Crum 787a]).

Teach. Silv. provides an extended description of the person who is ignorant. Arrayed against the believer are the powers of the Adversary (91.19–20), and "the fool", the one who is under the power of the Adversary. The fool has gone astray from the divine teaching or is ignorant. He leads people astray (87.19–22), is going himself to destruction rather than knowing his way like the wise person (97.7–10), lives in sleep and forgetfulness or drunkenness (88.24–27; 94.19–22; 107.26 – 108.3), has death for his father, ignorance for his mother and evil counsels for his friends and brothers (90.23–27; 91.1–3). The section 97.7 – 98.21 deals with the difference between the wise and the foolish person with regard to their speech (see also 117.30–32) and their friends.

3.1.3 The Outcome of Separation and Insight: Strangeness

> The knowledge, the Gnosis, of the pyschodrama is the precondition for engaging successfully in the operation of liberating the pneuma in man from its cosmic prison. The imaginative game of liberation derives its momentum from an intensely experienced alienation and an equally intense revolt against it; Gnostic thinkers, both ancient and modern, are the great physchologists of alienation, carriers of the Promethean revolt. (Vögelin 19)

In one sense Vögelin is right, but there are a number of levels to the concept of strangeness or alienation in the texts that should be noted. The basic concept concerns the Gnostics who feel themselves to be strangers, caught in the material world while their real homeland is in the heavenly region. Acts Pet. 12 Apost. makes this clear by describing the setting of the community as the worldly city, Habitation (10.3), in which they are strangers and servants of God (5.10–12).

This situation can be extremely difficult. Treat. Seth. tells us that while in the world, the fleshly cloud overshadows believers (70.1–3; human bodies are "dead tombs", 59.3). In Val. Exp., even though the community are the seeds who have originated from Sophia and the heavenly region, while they are in this earthly context they must dwell in the body which is the creation of the Demiurge (37.32–38). Apoc. Pet. speaks of the difference between immortal souls and mortal souls, and yet the immortal souls resemble the others while they are in the world, since the hour has not yet come (75.26–32).

That there is danger in this kind of strange liminal earthly existence, is attested by the passages dealing with suffering and persecution for Jesus and the community even though they are heavenly beings. Clearly, being away from one's heavenly home is to be in a very vulnerable position. Even the most heavenly of the Jesus figures is not spared some degree of struggle.

However, strangeness of this kind may also be viewed positively. Being strange in relation to the world may be a sign that salvation is assured (e.g. Dial. Sav. 134.19–24). Gos. Thom. Log. 42 seems to issue a warning against thinking otherwise and settling down in this world: "Become passers-by" (ϢⲰⲠⲈ ⲈⲦⲈⲦⲚ̄ⲢⲠⲀⲢⲀⲄⲈ).[1]

Because the Gnostics are strange or alien themselves to this world, there is less chance that they will be contaminated by the things of the world. Ap. John speaks of the community as those on whom the Spirit of life descends (25.23–28) so that they are not affected by anything except that they are still in the state of being (ⲀⲨⲠⲞⲤⲦⲀⲤⲒⲤ) in the flesh (25.33–35). They bear this state while they look expectantly for the time when they will be met by the receivers (25.35 – 26.1). On another level, Gnostics feel that other things and people are strange and must be treated as alien so they are not contaminated or led astray. 1 Apoc. Jas. states that the community are to know what things are theirs and what things are alien (25.3–5).

The concept of strangeness may also be used in a moral sense. Ap. Jas. 11.18–23 first appears to be an exhortation to the disciples to liken themselves to foreigners (ⲨⲘ̄ⲘⲀⲈⲒ) and generally separate themselves from other citizens. In fact it could well be a rebuke that they have turned away as outcasts and fugitives from their real dwelling-place (11.23–29).

Jesus too is a stranger;[2] indeed he is described in Acts Pet. 12 Apost. 3.10–11 as a fellow stranger with Peter (see also Treat. Seth 52.8–9; Testim. Truth 30.20 [he is a stranger to defilement/this world]; Ep. Pet. Phil. 139.21–22 [he is a stranger to suffering]).

3.2 Communitas

Insight into origin and destiny means insight into relationship with God, Christ, and other heavenly characters. This is both the opposite and the complement of the experience of being a stranger in the world. To some extent we have already dealt with this aspect of insight into relationship. It is especially obvious in a text like 1 Apoc. Jas. where the basic formula questions about origin, present circumstances, and destiny are couched in terms of James' relationship to the Father: who are you (a son) and where are you from (from the Father)? (33.15–18); what sort of son and what sort of Father (a son in the Pre-existent One)? (33.21–24).

---

[1] "Aussi faut-il pratiquer une ascèse qui éloigne du monde... Pour Thomas, le parfait est le μοναχός. La condition sociale qui est exigée de celui-ci est celle de prédicateur ambulant" (Ménard 1975b, 143). In somewhat similar vein, Quispel proposes that the logion refers to the Judaeo-Christian wandering preachers and wandering prophets (1967, 21). Baarda summarises a number of possible meanings for the saying and suggests finally that Log. 42 be taken in conjunction with Log. 43 and the exhortation, "Be Hebrews", in the sense that believers be true children of Abraham, the New Israel, as opposed to the Jews (196–7).

[2] For a study of Jesus and Gnostics as "strangers", see Franzmann.

Most commonly, the relationship is described in terms of the Gnostic as son/child of the Father or God (Ap. Jas. 10.39 – 11.1; 1 Apoc. Jas. 33.15–18, 21–24; Teach. Silv. 91.14–16; Gos. Phil. 62.17–26) as son/child or seed of Seth (Melch. 5.17–22), and as brother or fellow spirit of Jesus Christ (Treat. Seth 70.8–10). Teach. Silv. extends the relationship to include the first mother of the Gnostic as Wisdom (91.14–16).

Thus knowledge of self includes knowing to whom one is related by birth or rebirth, whether that be parent or sibling/s. Teach. Silv. includes both relationships. When believers truly know themselves (i.e. their birth, their original substance, race and species, their original divine nature [90.29–31; 92.10–15]), they are able to know God, Christ, the Spirit and the heavenly powers (117.3–5).

In Thom. Cont. relationship is expressed in a more implicit way than the direct parent/sibling model. The one who does not know himself, knows nothing; but the one who does know himself, knows also the depth of the all (ⲡⲃⲁⲑⲟⲥ ⲙ̄ⲡⲧⲏⲣϥ) (138.16–18). According to Kuntzmann, this is the Father (1986, 60).[1] Earlier he had written of the identification of the Gnostic with the Saviour and integration with the knowledge of the All (1981, 280). I think it more likely that here Christ is meant, particularly if we take into account similar terminology in Teach. Silv. The latter text speaks of the Christ who became the all for the sake of believers (106.29–30), and since he is the all, only those who possess the all (i.e. the believers) are able to know him (102.5–7).

As well as the relationship with Jesus as a sibling by virtue of both Gnostic and Jesus being sons of the Father, the relationship may also be expressed as union with him as the Lord who is known or is the source of knowledge, the one who is the Saviour.

This link between insight and union with the Lord is easily seen in texts like Teach. Silv. (knowing who Christ is and acquiring him as friend, 110.14–15), Trim. Prot. (the Word as the Beloved from whom the community receive the revelation of the Light, 47.22–23; 49.9–11, 20–23), and Ap. Jas. (the mutual dwelling between Jesus and those he came to save, 9.1–4).

Teach. Silv. has an extensive outline of what union with Christ entails. The community is exhorted throughout the text to certain activity or attitudes in relation to Christ:

– to live in/with him (88.15–17 [so as to acquire treasure in heaven]; 98.20–21);

– to accept him (90.33 – 91.1 [as a good teacher who loves them very much, 87.24–25; see also 96.32]; 96.19–20);

---

[1] Kuntzmann cites Hippolytus' *Ref.* VI,35,7.

– to accept his wisdom and guard it (118.2–5);

– to keep his commandments (91.25–26 [in order to reign on earth and to
be honoured in heaven, with the angels and archangels as friends and fellow servants, and to acquire places in heaven, 91.26–34]);

– to walk in his way rather than the broad way that leads to the
Underworld/the mire (103.13–26);

– to put him on (109.6–8);

– to let him alone enter their world, the temple within them (109.11–16).

The Gnostic's ability to choose Christ is a gift which Christ himself gives
(104.15–24). He is king, father (96.29–30), and helper (97.1) to believers,
the one who will save them (98.21–22), their Lord (110.8–12), the true vine
which brings joy to the soul and the mind through the Spirit of God (107.33–
35). He alone reveals the Father because he is the image of the Father, revealing the Father's true likeness (100.23–31).

Union may be effected by the ability to truly see, according to Gos. Phil.
In the earthly context one see things but does not become them; in the region
above "you saw the spirit, you became the spirit; you saw the Christ, you became the Christ; you saw [the father, you] shall become the father" (61.20–
35). That union is clearly possible for the Gnostic between the earthly and
heavenly regions is implicit in all the texts, and made explicit in passages
such as Ep. Pet. Phil. 134.17–18: "I am Jesus Christ who am with you forever".

The intimacy of union may be expressed very simply, such as by references to the believers as "his own" or "his seeds", or by the use of possessive
pronouns: *my* Lord, Jesus Christ (Treat. Res. 49.37 – 50.1); *our* Saviour
(Tri. Trac. 114.31). Intimacy is expressed also in a variety of imagery to do
with friendship, marriage, the body, and clothing. In Treat. Res., the believer is embraced by Christ and wears (ϥⲫⲟⲣⲉⲓ) him in this world (45.29–39).
Treat. Seth describes the union of Jesus and the community, in friendship
(67.31–34) and in the heavenly bridal chamber (57.12–18; 67.5–6). For Tri.
Trac., the Saviour is the head and the spiritual race of humankind is his body
(118.28–37). The "election" shares body and essence with the Saviour
(122.12–15), the sharing being like a marriage because of the unity and
agreement (ⲧⲱⲧ) with him (122.15–17; see also 136.1).[1] Both Gos. Thom.
(Log. 75) and Gos. Phil. (see the discussion in Chapter II) also mention the
union between the Saviour and the community in the bridal chamber. Gos.
Phil. includes imagery of clothing: the believer is clothed in Christ (the living man) through the water (75.21–25) or by the chrisming, so that he
becomes Christ (67.26–27); the believer receives the flesh and blood of

---

[1] It is difficult to differentiate here in a temporal sense between what belongs to the activity
of redemption/salvation and what belongs to the unity experienced in an ongoing way with
the spiritual race.

Christ (his Word and the Holy Spirit) which is food, drink and clothing (57.6–8).

Part of the basis for the concept of union can be found in the frequently expressed idea that like attracts like. Those connected to the light or the heavenly region will be attracted one to another and will unite with each other. Treat. Seth speaks of the fellowship which light has with light, darkness with darkness, corruption with what is perishable and what is imperishable with what is incorruptible (69.14–20). Apoc. Pet. uses the analogy of producing fruit – good fruit from good trees, evil fruit from evil trees – in a reflection upon Lk 6:43 (75.7–9; 76.19–23).

3.2.1 Mirroring Christ's Life and Mission, Origin and Destiny; Equality with Christ

Because the Gnostic has the same or similar origin to the Christ, and because the result of insight is expressed in terms of union, one finds frequently that the way mapped out for Gnostic life is a mirror of the life described for the Christ. There is a range of texts:

– texts which state rather simply a resemblance (Apoc. Pet. 76.8–18; Ep. Pet. Phil. 138.15–16, 23–24);

– texts which provide a brief summary (sometimes in a formula) of shared experiences, such as passion and resurrection, or fighting to win the crown of victory, or the cosmic experience of struggle with the powers (Treat. Res. 45.25–28 has: "We suffered with him, and we arose with him, and we went to heaven with him" [ⲁⲛⲱⲡ ⲍⲓⲥⲉ ⲛⲙⲙⲉϥ ⲁⲩⲱ ⲁⲛⲧⲱⲱⲛ ⲛⲙⲙⲉϥ ⲁⲩⲱ ⲁⲛⲃⲱⲕ ⲁⲧⲡⲉ ⲛⲙⲙⲉϥ]; see also 48.35–38; Treat. Seth 58.7–13;[1] On Anoint. 40.14–17; Tri. Trac. 122.7–12; Interp. Know. 21.33–34);

– texts which give a detailed outline of activity of an earthly-cosmic nature.

Soph. Jes. Chr. is a good example of the third type of text. First the community has been given a kind of missionary role by the Son which parallels his own: they were sent by the Son, who himself was sent (108.5–7). Later in the text, we are told that the Saviour has taught them about the Immortal Man (BG 121.13–15) and about the process of liberating him and of vanquishing the robbers (i.e. the archons) and rescuing them too from their ignorance and moving them towards unity so that the followers might yield much fruit (117.2–3) and might rise to Him-Who-Is from the Beginning in joy and glory and honour and grace of the Father of the All (117.4–8). This activity of the followers parallels to a certain extent the activity of the drop of Light/the sons of Sophia in 107.16 – 108.5. A series of final exhortations indicate further works for the followers which parallel the works of the Saviour (see also BG 121.15 – 122.3 and BG 104.11–12): to tread upon their

---

[1] See the comparison in Gibbons 1973, 250.

(the archons') graves;[1] to humiliate their malicious intent; to break their yoke and arouse the Saviour's own (119.1–4; see also 108.15–16).

Perhaps the best example of "mirroring" occurs in 1 Apoc. Jas. Two themes are particularly emphasised: the redemption of the Lord, James and the community; and the relationship of these to Him-Who-Is and to one another.

The purpose of the revelation in 1 Apoc. Jas. is to show James the completion (ⲡⲁⲱⲕ) of the Lord's redemption (ⲡⲁⲥⲱⲧⲉ) (24.12), and to reveal James' own redemption (29.12–13). As the passion of the Lord is his redemption, so the passion of James is James' redemption (29.12–13; 32.28),[2] and both processes are alike: James will be seized like the Lord (25.13–14); his passion is described in strongly cosmological terms (33.5–12; 35.18 – 36.9); James goes to rebuke the twelve (archons) and upset their contentment concerning the way of knowledge (42.20–24),[3] just as the Lord rebukes those who would do him harm.

James can be seen as a type of microcosm of the community, just as he is a kind of mirror of the Lord. Because he is the Just One and because of his relation with the Lord he stirs up opposition against himself (32.3–11). Being just like James and in relationship with the Lord means that the community is likely to stir up opposition to themselves with passion and death to follow (the text contains much comfort for those experiencing persecution). The community and James are exhorted not to be concerned about anything other than their redemption (29.6–8), redemption being identical with a conflict with the archons, there being no other way of achieving the heavenly region than by going through this persecution, by which the perishable goes up to the imperishable (41.15–16).

The text tells us that the Lord is an image of Him-Who-Is (ⲡⲉⲧⲱⲟⲟⲡ) (25.1), and he calls James the Just "my brother", although he is not his biological brother (24.13–16). We must presume that the Lord is also a son of Him-Who-Is if James is also, just as the community of the text are sons (25.3–5). Thus the Lord, James, and the community are sons of Him-Who-Is and are brothers to each other.

The experience of insight is an experience of equality with Christ. As Mack writes concerning Gos. Thom.: "Jesus is a supernatural revealer whose appearance in the world brought enlightenment to his true disciples. Enlightenment is understood as knowledge of one's self as belonging to an other-worldly order of divine origin and self-sufficiency. Thus the boundary

---

[1] This action of treading upon the body is somewhat reminiscent of the treading upon the clothes by the believer in Gos. Thom. Log. 37.

[2] The only passage to speak really in physical terms about James' passion describes the speech of those who do not wish to be involved in seizing him: "We have no part in this blood for a just man will perish through injustice" (43.16–21).

[3] *Contra* Brown who interprets the action as James going to the Twelve "with Jesus' special instruction" (1972, 96).

boundary erodes between Jesus as revealer figure and his true disciples as enlightened ones" (1990b, 11).

Apart from a mirroring of the Lord by certain experiences, there are some texts which say more distinctly that the Gnostic really is equal to the Lord. In Dial. Sav., we receive an idea of this status of the elect when, in the prayer to the Father, they are presented in the same way as the only-begotten Son: "Hear us, Father, just as you heard your only-begotten Son... Again, [hear] us just as you heard your elect" (121.5–7, 18–20). Treat. Res. describes the community as "the All" (47.26–27) which seems to imply an equality with the Christ who is the All in other texts (see also Teach. Silv. and Thom. Cont. in the section above).

Ap. Jas. actually goes further and implies that the Gnostic may even become better than Christ, since he tells the believers, who are sons (16.29–30), to become better than himself (6.19), to hasten to be saved and, if possible, to arrive even before him (7.10–15), for thus the Father will love them (7.15–16). If they do the Father's will, the Father will love them and make them equal to Christ and reckon them as beloved (4.32 – 5.6).

The essential equality between members of the community mirrors the equality of the Gnostic with Christ, although there are levels of initiation into insight to be observed in some communities. Equality may be obvious in the technical terms for believers, for example, "brother" and "sister" in Dial. Sav. 120.3–4. In some cases it is stated quite clearly that the prominent people are essentially the same as the rest of the community. Thus, in 1 Apoc. Jas., the community are sons of Him-Who-Is, just as James is, and in Ep. Pet. Phil., although Peter has a position of prominence (138.17; 139.9–10, 14–15), and his speech is inspired by a holy spirit[1] (139.14), nevertheless, the other apostles too are filled with a holy spirit (140.7–10).[2]

3.2.2 Union of the Group

Emphasis on the individual experience of insight and union with the Lord, and of the community's union with the Lord, does not necessarily preclude a concern for union among the members of the community themselves, but one finds it emphasised rarely. The texts are usually focused on the individual and his/her unity with the Lord, and not so much interested in the unity of these individuals among themselves. Perhaps it is a result of the external circumstances of the group, a sign of the necessity of bringing the group together more strongly because of persecution, that writers turn to the theme of friendship and unity among the members.[3]

---

[1] See Koschorke (1977) for a discussion of Peter's speech as "eine gnostische Pfingstpredigt" and the necessity of the reception of the Holy Spirit for the apostolic proclamation in the world which opposes the archons.

[2] For a brief comparison of the position of Peter in this text with other Gnostic texts, see Ménard 1977, 7.

[3] See Gibbons 1973, 257; Painchaud 1982, 7; and Gaffron 91ff.

The example of Interp. Know. is an extensive one. The text presents the relationship of the Son to his smaller brothers as a pattern for the relationship between the brothers themselves (15.19–38): that he was sent for them (14.28–29), humbled himself on their account (10.27–30; 12.22–23), that he loves them (15.18), and is not jealous but regards himself as a brother and gives grace (15.17–19, 23–26).

Above all, they must not be jealous of one another's spiritual gifts (making progress in the Word [16.31–32], or being adepts of the Word [21.28–29] seem to be especially prized) since by their relationship as members of the same Head, all share in each other's gifts (16.18–38; 18.28–38). This image is extended later in the text to a description of the believers who love abundant life and put forth fruit and are all connected by their roots so that their fruits are undivided, and they have the best of each in common (19.26–36). The members of the Head suffer together and are saved together as members of the one Head (passim within 17 and 18), and if they are to be fit to share in the true heavenly harmony, then they ought to be reconciled with one another in the earthly realm (18.22–27).

This long reflection seems to indicate a considerable degree of friction concerning spiritual gifts and recognition of them within the community ("Why do you despise the one appointed as..." [text damaged]; 18.38 – 19.1). The situation appears to be as drastic as the choice for life or death in the church (19.23–26). The most telling statement is a call to thankfulness: members should just be thankful that they do not exist outside of the body which belongs to the Head (18.33–34).

Koschorke writes of the general scholarly view that the Gnostics are not concerned with community spirit, and the surprise which the discovery of this text brings to such a view, and how close it is to concerns one finds within the Pauline tradition (charismatic gifts connected with the imagery of body and members [1 Cor 12 and Rom 12]; the image of the church as body with Christ as the head [Col and Eph]), although Interp. Know. has its own method of interpreting that tradition (1981, 757–8).

Other texts also are concerned for friendship or harmony within the community. Treat. Seth describes division and enmity as the opposite of friendship and brotherly love, the one who is in friendship being the desire of the Father, the universal and perfect one (62.9–10, 14–27; see also 67.5–19, 32–34; 68.9–13).[1] Christ proclaims: "I was among those who are united in the friendship of friends forever..." (67.32–34).

Gos. Thom. Log. 48 speaks of two making peace with each other in one house,[2] and in Log. 72 the Lord asserts: "I am not a divider...". Log. 25

---

[1] The theme is strongly reminiscent of Johannine material, for example: "It is I who am in you and you are in me, just as the Father is in you in innocence" (49.32 – 50.1; cf. Jn 14:20, 23; 17:21, 23; see also Evans et al. 295).
[2] Ménard interprets this as the Gnostic's return to the unity of the self (1975b, 149–51).

speaks of love for one's brother, and Log. 26 follows with the implications of that in praxis in the saying about the mote in the brother's eye.[1]

3.3 Insight/Revelation for "Others"?

I have already dealt above with different degrees of insight for members of the community and also for psychics and pneumatics. The psychics seem to be in a position to choose insight or not, something really not available to the pneumatics or the hylics by virtue of their predestination, as can be seen in what follows.

There is some ambivalence in the texts as to the status of those who do not belong to the community, both in relation to Jesus and to the community. I have divided the texts below into those which are positive towards others, those which are negative, those which are implicitly negative by virtue of what I would term an "exclusionist" stand, and those which are ambivalent (or at least appear to be so). Within the following sections I will also treat the theme of missionary activity, something which occurs suprisingly often in the texts, since that too makes clear where the ongoing revelatory activity occurs.

3.3.1 Positive Attitude towards Others

Some texts make it clear that being a stranger in the earthly region does not necessarily mean cutting oneself off from others. Gos. Phil. speaks of the free man (the Gnostic) who is actually a slave because of love for those who have not yet been able to attain to the freedom of knowledge (77.25–29). The text exhorts believers to be like Jesus Christ who did not burden anyone, giving comfort rather than distress to the great and small, to the believer or unbeliever (80.1–4). Where the Gnostic cannot help causing distress, it is the wickedness of the other people which is responsible (80.17–20).

Ep. Pet. Phil. characterises Jesus as the Saviour of the whole world (132.18–19). The text emphasises strongly missionary preaching and activity, carried out in the power of the Father, and including a cosmic level as well, since it entails a struggle against the archons (137.22–27). Similarly 1 Apoc. Jas. sees the purpose of the revelation for the faith of the unbelievers/the multitude 29.19–27).

3.3.2 Negative Attitude towards Others

Although believers are urged to speak and preach, some texts mean this obviously only for the community. In a direct polemic against Jn 3:16, Ap.

---

[1] Haenchen says these two logia are against egoism which is the world, and refers further to Log. 27 (1961a, 57). In a later study, he suggests that the use of "brother" here is only meant for the Gnostic companions in the strictest sense (1973, 221).

Jas. asserts that the Father does not love humankind (11.29–32) and later pronounces woe against those for whose sake the Saviour was sent down to the world (13.9–11). Testim. Truth too denies a universal salvation, stating ironically: if only words could effect salvation, the whole world would endure and be saved (32.8–12); if those baptised were headed for life, the world would become empty (69.17–20).

In a strong missionary statement in Thom. Cont., Thomas says that what he hears from the Saviour he will speak about (138.24–26) and he seems to intend to take the teaching farther than the elect, since he asks what to say to blind men and miserable mortals (141.18–25). Jesus replies that he should treat these people as beasts (141.25–29). It seems then that the community is to have no interest in teaching or bringing the revelation to the bestial humans. Thomas continues the theme in a later passage, asking how he and the others can preach the words of Jesus, since they are not esteemed in the world (142.24–26).

Acts Pet. 12 Apost. is not entirely clear on the point of activity for those outside the community. Certainly it differentiates between the rich and poor and the rich fall within a group which is viewed negatively as regards receiving revelation. They cannot see what a treasure the pearl is, in fact cannot even see that the Lord/pearl seller has a pouch. They do not acknowledge the Lord and in return he does not reveal himself to them (3.14–31). The community is to avoid them, not dine with them, nor be friends with them (11.26 – 12.4).

However it is not entirely clear whether the poor are the community or a wider group. We are told that the poor simply want to see the pearl and, although they doubt the Lord's invitation to come to his city where they will be given a pearl free, he repeats the invitation (4.3–34). Peter's question about having enough daily bread in order to provide for the poor brings the response from the Lord that his name surpasses all riches and the wisdom of God surpasses gold and silver and precious stones (10.26–30). Peter then is to feed the poor by preaching the name of the Lord, although he must heal the bodies of the poor first so that people will believe that they can heal the illnesses of the heart also (5.12–14; 11.15–26).

The text also relates that healing is for those who believe in Jesus' name (10.4–6; 10.33 – 11.1), so the poor could be intended as a metaphorical image of the community. This might be inferred also from the teaching of the Lord about renouncing the world and everything in it (5.21 – 6.8; 7.26–30; 10.14–17). As Parrott rightly suggests, the disciplinary journey to the heavenly city is itself a way of becoming poor and being able to respond to Jesus (Wilson and Parrott 200).

Election is a key concept in the texts which often complements the negative view. Gos. Thom. speaks of the election of one out of a thousand, and two out of ten thousand (Log. 23). Haenchen proposes a parallel to this saying in Log. 107, where Jesus does not choose the sinner but rather the one of most worth (1961a, 47). Instructions to preach from the housetops what is heard

(Log. 33), and the prayer for the Lord to send out labourers to the harvest (Log. 73), must be tempered with the instruction not to give what is holy to dogs and not to throw the pearls to swine (Log. 93). Ménard sums up for Log. 62: "Thomas ne permet de transmettre les mystères divins qu'à un petit groupe d'initiés (log. 1, 2)" (1975b, 163).

The negative aspects are often accompanied by concepts of predestination, couched in dualistic imagery. Apoc. Pet., for example, describes two categories of souls: mortal souls whose origins are in evil and who belong to these ages, who have been assigned to death, created for their own desires and their eternal destruction; and immortal souls whose origins are from the truth and immortality, who exist in the Eternal One, in the One of the life and immortality of life which they resemble (75.7–9, 12–24; 76.8–18).

3.3.3 Ambivalent or Unclear Attitude towards Others

Some texts are confusing concerning the possibility of various groups to be saved or to be given the revelation or partake in insight. I will deal here with Teach. Silv., Gos. Truth., Ap. John, and Soph. Jes. Chr.

Teach. Silv. seems first to presume two groups, one of whom will be saved. We are told that Christ comes to this group because of the good which is in them (97.1–3), and that he became the all for the sake of believers (106.29–30), and since he is the all, only those who possess the all (i.e. the believers) are able to know him (102.5–7). Yet later in the text, we are told that Christ has exalted man (111.8–9), so that his becoming like God is the means by which man may also become like God (111.9–13).

Gos. Truth also presents two groups: those whose name the Father has spoken and those whose name is unspoken. The latter are the miserable ones who have no name, since they have not been called (21.38 – 22.2). On the other hand, they must be in the Father since nothing is outside of him (27.34–36). However, it seems they will eventually vanish if the Father does not wish to call them or give them a name (27.26 – 28.4).

Ap. John appears to offer a type of (softened) predestination. There are those on whom the spirit of life increases, who cannot be led astray with works of evil (26.12–19), for no one can stand against the power of the spirit (26.12–14). When these come out of their flesh, they will go to the rest (ⲀⲚⲀⲠⲀⲨⳌⲓⳠ) of the Aeons (or "eternal rest") (26.26–32). Others are drawn by the opposing spirit and they go astray (26.20–22). Nevertheless, even though the latter are cast into prison, it is still possible for them to be liberated from forgetfulness, acquire knowledge, become perfect and be saved (26.36 – 27.11). Those who go to eternal punishment on the other hand are those who do know but turn away (27.24–31).

The command in Ap. John to spread the teaching wider includes the fellow spirits (2.23–25; 31.30–31) for it is a mystery of the immovable race. This suggests teaching for a closed group rather than a wider proclamation. The warning against exchanging the teaching for gain (31.34 – 32.1) and the description of the teaching as a mystery and something secret seems also to imply a closed group of receivers.

Soph. Jes. Chr. speaks of those sent by the Son, who himself was sent (108.5–7). It is unclear whether it is intended that only believers will be the recipients of those sent, who will rescue them and also liberate Immortal Man and vanquish the robbers (BG 121.13–15). The final statement of the Saviour has a distinctively "missionary" tone: "I have given you authority (ⲉϫⲟⲩⲥⲓⲁ) over all things as sons of Light that you might tread upon their power with your feet" (119.4–8).[1] This presumes a cosmic more than a material world setting for the activity, as the Gnostic receives authority for dealing with the archons/powers of the cosmos. Perkins interprets the action of treading as the apostolic preaching of the Gnostics, although also seeing the preaching as linked to the defeat of the powers (1980, 71–2, 85, 94, 180).[2] Certainly after receiving this authority the disciples begin to preach the Gospel of God, the eternal imperishable Spirit (BG 127.2–10).[3]

3.3.4. Exclusionist Attitude

Many texts imply a negative view of other groups, simply by their exclusionist stance: Testim. Truth names the Son of Man as revealer "to us" (31.5–7); Ap. Jas. calls blessed those who ascend to the Father (13.11–13), and thrice blessed those who were proclaimed by the Son before they came to be (14.41 – 15.3); Gos. Eg. describes the community as the incorruptible holy race, those privileged to receive the revelation in the book which Seth wrote (III 68.1 – 69.5/IV 80.15–26); in Dial. Sav. only the true or perfect Gnostics are the solitary (ⲛ̄ⲙⲟⲛⲟⲭⲟⲥ) and elect (ⲛ̄ⲥⲱⲧⲡ̄) (120.26); and in Treat. Res. only the spirit will be raised, the psychic and fleshly elements being excluded (45.40 – 46.8; see also 46.25–32).

3.4 Exclusivity and Deception

Deception and hiddenness serve to strengthen (perhaps in an unhealthy way) intimacy and union. The best example of this theme in the texts is Gos. Phil. and I will deal exclusively with it here. Buckley rightly says of this text: "Throughout, tenets of secrecy and exclusivity prevail..." (1980, 574). We have already seen in Chapter II that Jesus comes by stealth and takes different forms, hiding the Logos "flesh" (58.2–3). The text also tells us that Truth, which is a unity in the heavenly region, can only be manifested or apprehended in the earthly world under many names and many types (54.15–18;

---

[1] Note the interesting parallel in Prayer 344 in the Mandaean Prayerbook where the Great (Life) rejoices that "we have trodden down darkness and have brought to nought the rebellious Voice", a prayer used during the footwashing section of the coronation ritual/ordination to Mandaean priesthood (Drower 1959, 239).

[2] "SJC employs the full imagery of resurrection scenes from the canonical Gospels to associate its Gnostic content with the apostolic mission" (Perkins 1980, 94).

[3] See 104.1 for "gospel" (ⲡⲉⲩⲁⲅⲅⲉⲗⲓⲟⲛ) as a technical term.

67.9–12). Both the names and the types can lead to error unless a person can see rightly. Thus names given in the earthly region – "Father", "Son", "Holy Spirit", "Life", "Light", "Resurrection", "Church" – can easily be deceptive and lead to error (53.23 – 54.5). Thus nothing in this world can be taken at face value: what appears to be good may not be good and apparent evil may not be evil.

If this is so then we must ask about correlating possibilities. Does the community present itself deliberately under different forms and names which can deceive those who cannot really see? The text tells us that the saints (ⲛ̄ⲛⲉⲧⲟⲩⲁⲁⲃ) may appear to be ordinary people even to the evil powers, so that they are actually served by the evil powers (59.18–23). The analogy of the superiority of man over the animals seems to make this same point (the superiority of the person is hidden from view and in this way he has mastery over the animals which are stronger than him [64.12–22]).

The Gnostics' duping of the evil powers continues after death. As sons of the bridal chamber they are clothed in perfect light (they have become the perfect man/the perfect light) and the powers cannot see those so clothed in order to detain them in the middle (70.5–9; 76.22–29; 86.4–5) and cannot torment them even in the world (86.7–11). Thus hiddenness or deception are necessary to remain in life or to retain strength. This is explained further by the statement that the revelation of what is hidden means death; e.g. by exposing the intestines of a man or the roots of a tree (82.30 – 83.5) or exposing the godhead/Demiurge in the temple by rending the veil and subsequently destroying his house (85.15).

Jesus, Truth and the Gnostics are involved in deception, although to see them as engaged in deliberate deception may be putting too negative an interpretation on the use of the concept of hiddenness. More damning is description of the archons who deceive people by names which divert their thoughts from what is established to what is not established (54.18–31). In this way the archons make free men their slaves forever. Those who are not Gnostics are also hidden: they are animals in the world in human form. The disciple throws food to them accordingly, but only the children of the household receive the full instruction (81.7–14).

Gos. Phil. also deals with the theme of self-deception. People may deceive themselves that they have a certain name, and thereby be in error. This teaching especially applies to sacramental praxis. Thus a person can be baptised and be called Christian but in effect he has not really received the name, he has simply borrowed it (as opposed to the true Christian who has received the holy spirit as a gift). The proper reception of the name seems to be linked to a proper understanding of what is happening in baptism. There is a hidden quality to baptism which is known only by the Gnostic. Thus one sees the water and the chrism but there is water hidden in the water, fire hidden in the chrism so that the water and fire purify the whole place (= the world), the visible by the visible, the hidden by the hidden... (57.22–27).

Borrowing the name of Christian is dangerous since payment is demanded from the one who has borrowed the name (by contrast, the one who has received the gift does not have to give it back) (64.22–31). Likewise if one does not acquire names (of the Father, Son, and Spirit?) in the chrisming, then the name (Christian?) will be taken from him (67.21–24). This may also include the idea that the name of Christian itself is a powerful thing not to be treated lightly (i.e. borrowed), since naming oneself as a Christian causes disturbance unlike the name of Jew, Roman, Greek, barbarian, slave or free (62.26–34).

3.5 Results of Insight, Union, and Separation from the World: Conflict with Other Groups

Gilhus sums up succinctly that "*communitas* has two directions: opposition to the existing structure – an anti-structure, and maintenance of the communion upon which it is built" (1984, 119). There is no explicit incitement in the texts to physical violence or persecution against other groups, although there is certainly polemic against them, and there is the added conflict implicit in exclusive and separating behaviour. What is clear is that the texts witness to considerable conflict against the Gnostics, some conflict escalating to real physical persecution. There is often conflict on a cosmic scale, or a mixture of earthly and cosmic conflict, and even though some texts appear to include only earthly adversaries, one can never rule out the possibility that the earthly adversaries are influenced by cosmic forces.

3.5.1 Conflict with Christian and Jewish Groups

1. *The Gospel of Philip*. Gos. Phil. presents the situation of two communities in contention, both of whom are using the same terminology and ritual practice, and both calling themselves Christians. It is clear that the community of the text was once a part of the community they oppose, characterised as Hebrews, orphans with only a mother (52.21–24).[1] The community of the text sees itself as continuing in the line of the apostles ("the apostles who were before us" [62.6–7]; the Father anointed the Son and the Son anointed the apostles and the apostles anointed us [74.16–18]), although even this stage is to be superceded, since the apostles and the apostolic men are Hebrews (= those who have received something other than the Lord [62.6], 55.29–30).

According to the community of the text, only they really have the name of Christian as a gift, the others have borrowed it and do not understand. It would seem certain that the opposing community is not a Jewish community but that the name Hebrew is used metaphorically. However, one has to

---

[1] See Wilson 1962, 68–9. Wilson finds the basis for the statement that the Hebrews have only a mother in the Valentinian theory of Sophia's production of matter without a consort.

account for the strong interest in using such symbolism in the first place.[1] It may be of course that the Jewish roots of this Christian community have been strongly maintained (although note the negative attitude to the Jewish God as the Demiurge)[2] or perhaps in the broader context for the community there is some dialogue or confrontation with Jewish groups, suggesting a social setting of Jews and Christians, and within the Christians at least two opposing groups.[3]

2. *The Second Treatise of the Great Seth.* Treat. Seth presents a similar situation to Gos. Phil., in fact there are many points of contact with Gos. Phil. in the way that the situation is described: there are two groups in opposition to the (Christian Gnostic)[4] community of the text, one Christian and the other Jewish, the latter characterised as the "unseeing ones" (65.2–4; 68.25). The opposing Christians who are not living the true Christian life are under the influence of Adonaios, and have only been given an incomplete revelation (52.5–7) so that they do not know the Christ properly (60.1). They think they are advancing the name of Christ but they are unknowingly empty, not knowing who they are, like dumb animals (59.24–30).

This makes it clear that self-knowledge (the result of being in union with Christ) is necessary for knowing the Christ perfectly. These so-called Christians are not in union because they serve two or even more masters (60.2–3). In fact, they follow false teaching (= slavery), such as believing that they must die with Christ (49.25–27).[5] They have been led astray by the archons who proclaim a doctrine of the dead man, Jesus, which is a lie designed to

---

[1] Jewish symbols in Gos. Phil. are used positively (52.15–17 ["gentile" {ⲉⲑⲛⲓⲕⲟⲥ} used as a negative term may be positive in a relative sense: the Hebrew is therefore better than a gentile, although a Christian is better than a Hebrew]; 82.26–30), neutrally (51.29–32; 69.14 – 70.4), and negatively (52.21–24; 54.31 – 55.5, 29–30; 62.6, 35 – 63.4; 75.2–11; 84.23–29).

[2] 54.31 – 55.5 and 62.35 – 63.4 describe God as a man-eater to whom men are sacrificed as animals. Before men were sacrificed, animals were sacrificed since those to whom they were sacrificed were not gods. I am inclined to agree with Ménard that there is a link intended here from the Demiurge to the God of the Jews (1988, 166; see also Janssens 1968, 97). On the other hand Buckley interprets the passages positively: "God consumes man because man is essentially divine, i.e., fit food for God" (1980, 575), but this does not take account of the fact that the men who are sacrificed are slaves/animals made so by being deceived by the archons (54.18–31). I would also interpret 84.23–29 with reference to the Jewish God (the godhead who controls the creation and flees from the temple when the veil is torn). Wilson interprets the character as the Supreme God, from the parallel in Sophia Jesu Christi (1962, 191–2), while Koschorke (1973, 318), Janssens (1968, 128), and Ménard (1988, 243) see him as the Demiurge. The difficulty in interpretation is compounded by the fact that the text makes no differentiation by the title "God" between the Demiurge and the Father. The passage must be seen in conjunction with 75.2–11 which describes the creation of the world through a mistake. The one who created was not imperishable nor was his creation imperishable although he wanted it to be so (i.e. Jewish God/creator = Demiurge).

[3] Siker characterises the community as Valentinian Gnostic Christians in direct contact with both Jews and non-Gnostic Christians. "Hebrews" does not refer to Jews (who are explicitly mentioned elsewhere in the text) but to non-Gnostic Christians (277, 286).

[4] See Gibbons 1973, 242.

[5] Baptism is affirmed in the text, not as dying in Christ, but rather as making the Ennoia of the Fatherhood perfect through the living water (61.35 – 62.1).

resemble the freedom and purity of the perfect assembly (60.21–25). In a strongly ironical statement, the reader is told that these Christians hate the one in whom they exist, who has control of them, while they love the one in whom they do not exist (60.33–35). On the one hand the position of these people seems somewhat ameliorated by their partial knowledge of Christ, since the one who rules them, Adonaios, also knows him partially; on the other hand, they hate and persecute the ones who have been liberated by Christ (59.30–32).[1]

It seems clear that the community of the text is experiencing persecution from another Christian group and they need to be strongly assured that they will triumph through the persecution. Painchaud is correct in suggesting that the community of the text is being exhorted to make a choice between two Christs and two interpretations of Church (1982, 7). However this is not the only choice to be made: even more basic is the choice to be made against belonging to Yaldabaoth.

The third aspect of choice which is introduced is really a choice for or against Christ, rather than two interpretations of Christ. Those who belong to the archon Yaldabaoth are the Jews, and both he and the Jews are completely ignorant of the Christ. The long "counter-litany" from 62.27 – 64.1 (see my treatment of this section in Chapter III) outlines the entire history of the Jews which has been under the influence of the Hebdomad, Yaldabaoth, with the result that, like the so-called Christians, the Jews too are in slavery. In their case it is a slavery under the doctrine of angels and dietary laws, since they do not know the truth (64.1–6). They will never find a *Nous* of freedom until they come to know the Son of Man (64.8–12). In this latter statement at least there appears to be some hope for the Jews.

3. *The Apocalypse of Peter.* The two major themes of Apoc. Pet. are the passion and the heretics arrayed against the community.[2] There is considerable fear that the community will be misled and destroyed by believing in what people say who speak (falsely) in the Saviour's name (79.31 – 80.7). These have created an imitation remnant in the name of a dead man (Hermas, the first-born of the unrighteousness) so that the little ones do not believe in the light which exists (78.15–19). Thus they are the cause of the immortal ones falling into transgressions, although the latter will be given the Saviour's forgiveness in the end (78.8–11), while the ones who have oppressed them will be punished (79.16–17). It seems that the opponents have already led some members astray and pose a threat to the continuing existence of the community.

---

[1] See also Bethge's comment on 61.23 – 62.3 concerning the possibility of the Christians gaining redemption, albeit of a lesser quality (1979, 168–9).

[2] Koschorke's study of the Gnostic polemic in Apoc. Pet. against the mainstream Christian ("church") tradition is the most important work in relation to this section. See especially "Teil II: Die Polemik der Petrusapokalypse (NHC VII,3) gegen das Kirchliche Christentum" (1978b, 11–90).

The revelation by the Saviour to the community is a process of reminding them that they are built on what is strong (i.e. Peter) (70.25–27), so that they might distinguish righteous words from unrighteous words. Such discernment is important in view of the false teaching by the heretics. Thus the community is reassured that they stem from the beginning, from Peter, and that those in error, and not the community, are the ones who have fallen away since this beginning, under the influence of the Father of their error (73.23–28). They are the ones who come after Peter who are characterised as men who speak falsely, proclaiming the name of a dead man (74.10–14).

Whether the community is set over against another group, or a number of groups is unclear. Koschorke interprets the opposition as one group, suggesting that the structure "some...some...others..." is simply a stylistic device (1978b, 14). On the other hand, Brashler interprets the structure literally and identifies six groups (222–35). Filoramo suggests polemic against "the True Church" and other Gnostic groups (124).

Certainly at first glance, the very confrontational group in 77.22 – 78.1 (those who oppose truth as the messengers of error, who set up their error and law and do business in the word of the Saviour), seem to be a more serious threat than those who are ignorant. They speak of mysteries that they do not understand and are boastful about possessing exclusively the mystery of the truth and they envy the immortal soul (76.27 – 77.3). However, the text makes it clear that ignorance is not a relatively blameless condition: the sons of the Aeon blaspheme the community because they are ignorant of them (73.18–21). I am more inclined therefore to follow Koschorke, taking into account that the "sons of the Aeon" are surely also "those from this place" (= the world) who are completely dead (83.29–34; the opposite of the community who are alive and not from this Aeon).

The heretic group is certainly to be identified as Christian although apostate according to the viewpoint of the community. They are "outside our number", having bishops and deacons who claim their authority from God. This is self-deception on the part of the heretics of course. In reality they are under the judgment of the leaders (archons) and are dry canals (79.21–31). They are the workers who will be cast into outer darkness as opposed to the community who are the sons of light (78.22–26). They are the race of the sisterhood, an imitation who oppress their brothers and rejoice in taking the little ones prisoners, as opposed to the brotherhood (the community), the spiritual fellowship, who are united in community and reveal the marriage of incorruptibility (78.31 – 79.21).

3.5.2 Conflict with Gnostic Groups

Other texts attest to conflict with Gnostic groups, some of which are Gnostic Christian. Testim. Truth contains a great deal of polemic, directed not only against the mainstream church but also against other Gnostic groups.[1] As in Gos. Phil., compared with all of these groups, the Gnostic alone understands what being a Christian means. The most extensive polemic concerns those who confess Christ by martyrdom (31.26 – 32.8, 13–14, 19–22; 33.24 – 34.7) and by baptism (69.7–28),[2] but as Koschorke sums up: "Seine anti-katholische Polemik greift fast alle Fragen auf, die zwischen Kirche und Gnosis zur Debatte standen (Askese, Martyrium, Taufverständnis, Christologie, Auferstehungshoffnung, Schriftverständnis, Vorwurf des Judaismus an die Adresse der Kirchenchristen u.a.)" (1977, 324).

Polemic against baptism is taken further in 69.7–28 where one reads of those who receive baptism as a hope of salvation, calling it the "seal" but who are actually thereby under the power of the fathers of the world (i.e. the archons) (69.7–13), also called the fathers of baptism, who are defiled (69.20–22). This is obviously the same fate as awaits those who give themselves to martyrdom and who hasten to the principalities and authorities. In contrast to these, the Gnostic knows that he is sealed (69.13–15), and his baptism of truth is the renunciation of the world (69.22–24). Only *saying* that one renounces the world is a lie, and one ends up in this way in the place of fear (i.e. the place of the demons) (69.24–28).

Apart from polemic against the mainstream Church, there is general talk of heretics and schism within a damaged section of text at 59.4, 5 where there is polemic against certain groups: specifically the Simonians and another group, both condemned for their sexual practices (58.2–4; 67.30–31). Other characters and groups are mentioned but the damaged nature of the text only allows the conjecture that these also are the subject of polemic: Valentinus and his disciples (56.1–5), and Isidore (57.6–7).

3.5.3 Conflict with Unknown Groups or with Individuals

The community of Great Pow. is in conflict with another unnamed group which is characterised as those who acted according to the creation of the archons and its other archons (48.7–8).[3] By contrast the community describes

---

[1] For an extensive discussion of the polemic against the various groups, see Koschorke 1978b, esp. "Teil III: Die Polemik von Testamonium Veritatis (NHC IX,3) gegen die 'Häresien' der Katholiken und Gnostiker" (91–174).

[2] The text asserts that confessing Christ/one's belief in word and not in power does not bring salvation (31.22–26; 32.8–12), and neither does giving oneself over to death/martyrdom for the sake of the Name (31.26–29; 34.1–7). The Father, the God of Truth does not want human sacrifice (32.19–22). The people who do these things are in error and ignorance (31.26–28; 32.6–8, 13–14). Those who choose martyrdom are bearing witness only to themselves. They are sick and not able to raise themselves (33.24 – 34.1). They do not know where they are going and do not know who Christ is. They think that they will live but in reality they hasten towards the principalities and authorities (31.26 – 32.8). Connected with this is the erroneous view of those who think they will rise on the Last Day (34.26 – 35.4...). The text is damaged so that the reason for the error is not learnt, but later it is stated that carnal resurrection is destruction (36.30 – 37.1).

[3] Wisse and Williams suggest that the text makes reference to the Anomoeans, whose evil heresies have no basis (40.7–9), and that the reference provides the identification of this

itself as acting against its fleshly birth, in the creation of the archons, which gives law (48.9–11; see also 42.5–6). That this concept of law may be a reflection on the new law of Christ over the old law of the Jews could be implied in the statement that the true people are those who are uncircumcised (45.20–22).

A number of other texts mention conflict with an individual. Apoc. Pet. speaks of those in error who will fall into the hand of an evil craftsman (ⲟⲩⲣⲉϥⲣ̄ⲧⲉⲭⲛⲏ)[1] with a dogma of many forms (74.18–20), who may well be identified as Paul.[2] In Testim. Truth also there appears to be specific polemic against Paul's teaching in Gal 1:8 (73.17–22). The text is damaged but it seems to emphasise the freedom of the soul contrary to this teaching (73.22–24). Teach. Silv. describes the believer opposed by the powers of the Adversary (91.19–20). The one under the power of the Adversary is "the fool" who constantly appears in the text set over against the believer.

Apart from groups and individuals, there are also familial or kinship conflicts to be found in Gos. Thom., where there are sayings about hatred of father, mother, brothers and sisters (Log. 55), the redefinition of familial ties to refer to those who do the will of the Father (Log. 99), and the distinction made between an earthly father and mother and a heavenly father and mother in Log. 101 (see also Log. 105).

3.5.4 Violent Conflict

One receives the impression that the community of Thom. Cont., which clearly leads a very ascetical life-style, is labouring under hard times, perhaps confrontation, perhaps even persecution from another group or other

---

group (292). However, cf. Fischer ("und dem, was eurem Wesen nicht entspricht! Schlechte Spaltungen haben keinen Bestand" [1973, 172]) and Cherix ("Rompez... ces [énergies] disparates, inclinations malignes sans fondements" [14]) who disagree with Wisse's translation. Cherix suggests that the masculine form ⲁⲛⲍⲟⲙⲟⲓⲟⲥ would have been used instead of the neuter if the Anomoeans were meant, and that for "heresies" one would have ⲙⲛ̄ⲧⲍⲉⲣⲉⲥⲓⲥ rather than ⲍⲉⲣⲉⲥⲓⲥ.

[1] Krause and Girgis have "Handwerker" (161), and Brown and Griggs have "artificer" (140). Siegert has "Handwerker [wie technitês]" although giving the reference incorrectly as 76,18 (312). Werner (1974, 579 and 1989, 639) and Koschorke (1978b, 39) have "Betrüger", and Brashler has "an evil cunning man" (35; see also Brashler and Bullard).

[2] If a connection can be made between this character and the false proclamation of the name of a dead man, this may well be a reference to Paul, given his preaching (e.g. in Rom 4:24–25; 1 Cor 1:17–18; 2:2; Gal 3:1), and the description of him in Acts 18:3 as a craftsman/tentmaker having the same craft as Aquila and Priscilla διὰ τὸ ὁμότεχνον εἶναι ἔμενεν παρ᾽ αὐτοῖ". Although the pair in 74.27–34 might be interpreted as Simon and Helena (see Werner 1974, 576; and Schenke, H.-M. 1975a, 281–3), it may well be, as Koschorke suggests, that the author has used Simon as a paradigm of "the heretic", as a code for Paul (1978b, 41). Koschorke concludes: "Ptr als die ἀρχή wahrer Gnosis und der nach ihm kommende Paulus als der Stammvater der 'Häresie', des Glaubens an den 'Toten': in diesen Chiffren scheint ApcPt die Polemik gegen das kirchliche Christentum zu führen" (42).

groups.[1] That these groups comprise or include Christians is implied by the statement about those who have lost their first love[2] and the slight against the sacrament of baptism as practised by the opponents.[3] These still have the ability to see the invisible things and the Gnostics must separate themselves from these people (141.2–4).

Gos. Thom. seems to know a situation of persecution: pronouncing a blessing on those hated and persecuted (Log. 68) and those who have been persecuted within themselves (Log. 69). There is also the blessing of the womb which has not conceived (Log. 79), and the fortunate man who knows where the brigands will enter and arms himself before they invade (Log. 103).

For Ep. Pet. Phil., the community suffers because Jesus himself suffered (138.15–16, 23–24). The powers (= the lawless ones, 139.28–30) fight against the inner man (137.22), and detain believers because they do not want them to be saved because they belong to Jesus and have rest (137.4–6, 10–13). The community suffers also from earthly opponents, first unidentified (134.8–9), but later in the text described as the power of the synagogue and the governors of this world (138.24–27; cf. Matt 10:17–18; Lk 21:12). Bethge suggests as well an *Auseinandersetzung* with the Great Church (1978, 165), but this is not as clear as in some of the previous texts. Obviously by its very nature as a document of a Gnostic group, this could be presumed, but the text does not speak explicitly of such opposition or disagreement.

The text of 1 Apoc. Jas. contains much comfort for those experiencing persecution (29.6–8; 41.15–16). Some have identified the opponents – the twelve archons or hebdomads and their subordinates, the seventy-two heavens (27.13–17) – as "the Twelve" and the seventy-two disciples of the canonical tradition.[4] However I must conclude that there is no evident connection

---

[1] See Perkins 1980, 103–7 for possible description of the opponents. She summarises: ...we must conclude that the opponents were probably orthodox Christians who also revered traditions that were said to have come from the Risen Jesus through Thomas. By the time ThCont is written, the ascetics seem to have withdrawn to their own sect, 'resting among their own.' But there is still enough interaction among the two groups to produce converts to one side or the other. One must admit, however, that ThCont reads as though the opponents are having more success in winning converts for their version of Christianity than are the ascetics (106–7).

[2] Perhaps a lack of ascetical practice leads them to destruction (140.39f). See the comments by Kuntzmann, who relies on Perkins (1980, 103–7): "les dialogues entre Thomas et le Sauveur sont l'echo des discussions entre les ascètes et leurs opposants, qui ont sans doute rejeté l'ascétisme exagéré tout en restant fidèles aux paroles que Thomas auraient reçues de Jésus ressuscité. Ces opposants ont perdu le 'premier amour'..." (1986, 91).

[3] The opponents are drunk with fire, in the darkness and deranged by the burning. They have baptised their souls in the water of darkness (ⲁⲧⲉⲧⲛ̅ⲱⲙⲥ̅ ⲛ̅ⲛⲉⲧⲛ̅ⲯⲩⲭⲏ Ϩⲙ̅ ⲡⲙⲟⲟⲩ ⲙ̅ⲡⲕⲁⲕ[ⲉ]) (144.1).

[4] Daniélou identifies the seventy-two heavens as the seventy-two disciples of the mainstream Christian tradition (1966b, 289), but does not go further to equate the twelve archons with "the Twelve", as Veilleux does (10). Schoedel interprets the twelve in Jerusalem as the twelve disciples (Brown has "the Twelve" [1972, 96]), but differentiates this twelve from the "darker powers of the universe" associated with Jerusalem and Judaism because "the twelve (and thus catholic Christianity) move within the more beneficent spheres of the activity of Achamoth, the lesser Sophia" (Schoedel and Parrott 261).

between the heavenly powers and the figures of the mainstream tradition.[1] The question of a polemic against the mainstream tradition is another matter. One might suggest such a polemic in the description of the inferior interpretation concerning seven hebdomads rather than twelve which is found in the scriptures (ⲛⲉⲅⲣⲁⲫⲏ), since the one who spoke concerning this scripture had limited understanding (26.6–8). However it is not clear whether the use of ⲅⲣⲁⲫⲏ here is a reference to canonical Christian texts.

Other texts too speak about persecution. It seems that the community of Interp. Know. is under violent persecution. There are enemies (who exist in the flesh [20.30–31] and are senselessly mad [20.36–37]) who are persecuting them to death (20.24–26), tearing apart what appears to be them (their bodies) as if they could hope to find them, but all in vain (20.33–36), since they live by the Spirit (20.32–33) and thus they (i.e. their spiritual life) cannot be seen (20.31–32).

3.6 Dualism

Imagery of dualism is prevalent in the Nag Hammadi texts, mirroring the situation of the group in conflict with the world and with all others who are strangers to them.[2] I have already dealt above with the polar opposites of insight vs ignorance (with their associated binaries of wisdom vs foolishness, truth vs error, wakefulness vs sleep or drunkenness). Here I shall simply

---

[1] The text makes it clear that James rebukes the twelve in Jerusalem (42.20–24). I would argue that these twelve are equivalent to the previously mentioned twelve archons who most probably have their dwelling-place in Jerusalem since we are told that it is the dwelling-place of a great number of archons. Certainly the passion of Jesus and of James takes place in Jeru salem and, since it is a struggle between them and the powers, one assumes that the twelve archons opposed to them are also in this place. Added to this is the similar action of rebuke described for Jesus and James (Jesus' rebuke is against his persecutors, who are a type of the archons) and the fact that elsewhere in the text James is clearly in opposition to the twelve ar chons (28.20–24).
However, a further question concerns whether the twelve archons are meant to represent the Twelve/the twelve apostles. The text describes the people (the Jews) as a type of the archons. If the twelve archons are also to be interpreted as the Twelve/the twelve apostles, then it is necessary to suggest how these Twelve and the people are connected. The only possible connection I can think of is not found in this text but in Gos. Phil. where the apostles and the apostolic men are referred to as Hebrews, i.e. those who have not attained perfection in the Christian community and do not have the full knowledge of the revelation. However, this seems to necessitate going too far afield to find a connection between the two groups for the present text.
[2] As Couliano points out, and as I would make clear for a number of aspects of Gnosticism including this, dualism does not identify Gnosticism, but "gnostic myth is a particular transformation that belongs to a vast series of myths known as 'dualistic'" (xiv). Couliano dismisses the idea of starting from a perspective which sees dualistic imagery and thought processes as arising out of a situation of conflict or crisis (240), although he does recognise the counter-cultural aspect of Gnosticism and all Western dualistic trends which he analyses (xv). Couliano's concept of dualism as an "ideal object" which originates in the human mind as a logical process or game of binary decision-making is intriguing (see esp. Chapter 1: Dua lism: A Chronology; Chapter 10: The Tree of Gnosis; and the Epilogue: Games People Play).

summarise a number of other possiblities out of the many available,[1] and then concentrate on the dualism of freedom vs slavery.

A simple list of binary opposites with examples noted from a number of texts will suffice to show the range:

the world/region below	vs	heaven/region above (Gos Truth 24.20–26)
deficiency, envy and strife	vs	unity and perfection (Gos. Truth 24.20–26)
multiplicity	vs	unity (Gos. Truth 25.10–19)
terror	vs	imperturbability (Gos. Truth 42.7)
emptiness	vs	fulness (Gos. Truth 36.21–34; Ap. Jas. 4.6–22)
ignorance, sleep, nightmare, terror	vs	wakefulness, dawn (Gos. Truth 28.32–30.14; 32.26–34; Ap. Jas. 9.29–35)
drunkenness, deception	vs	sobriety (Ap. Jas. 3.9–10; 8.29)
listening	vs	speaking/preaching (Ap. Jas. 9.29–35; 10.12–13; 11.14–17)
impermanence	vs	stability (Ap. John 25.23)
transcience	vs	eternity (Dial. Sav. 137.9–11, 14–15)

Gos. Truth is the richest in examples of polar opposites, but the opposition does not extend to the Father, since there is nothing outside of him (26.9–10). Deficiency and its associated elements are a result of the Father's incomprehensibility.

3.6.1 Slavery vs Freedom

The dualism of slavery and freedom is related in a plethora of ways to major concepts and themes in the Gnostic thought-world. It relates to questions of power within the liminal experience of the "kingless race" and the limitation of enslaved earthly existence within fleshly bodies produced by the archons;[2] to questions about status reversal for those whose origin is in the heavenly

---

[1] A number of these dualities also occur in Turner's list of liminality contrasted with status systems (Turner, V.W. 106–7).

[2] Rudolph describes the typically sharp anti-political polemic in the Gnostic texts which use political nomenclature within the teaching about the enslavement of human beings by over-worldly powers. The other side of the polemic is the Gnostics' self-description as the kingless race, their "Brüderethik", and the (qualified) equality of the sexes (1979, 22–25).

region, now strangers and aliens in the land of Habitation and under the threat of earthly and heavenly powers, but who are nevertheless free by virtue of their origin and insight.

In the world, the archons are the slave masters who constrain the community through cares and fear (Treat. Seth 61.21–24; Interp. Know. 6.36–37). The community may be enslaved by virtue of their bodies, but in fact they are free because of their insight into the truth, while others are slaves of sin through ignorance (Gos. Phil. 77.15–19; 83.18–22; 84.10–11). They are free too because they do not belong to this world or this age and do not love their enslaving bodies (Apoc. Pet. 75.15–26).

The opposite of slavery is not simply to be free, it is also to rule. Teach. Silv. tells us that wisdom, education and holy teaching are crown and robe and throne (87.11–14; 89.10–12, 20–24; see the fool by comparison, 89.26–34). The Wisdom who is Christ is highly prized: it is a holy kingdom, a shining robe, much gold and brings great honour (107.3–8). 2 Apoc. Jas. promises rest (ⲘⲦⲞⲚ) (see also Soph. Jes. Chr. 117.8–12), kingship, and perhaps a god-like compassionate nature like the Father (56.2–7).[1] Testim. Truth describes a future for the one who knows himself and God who is over the truth: this one will be saved and will be crowned with an unfading crown (44.30 – 45.6).

As noted above, the only positive use of the concept of slavery is in Gos. Phil., where the free man (the Gnostic) is paradoxically a slave because of love for those who have not yet been able to attain to the freedom of knowledge (77.25–29).

3.7 First Steps to Aggregation: Salvation even in the Present World

The Gnostic experience is somewhat unusual in relation to the liminality paradigm since aggregation already begins in a sense while the Gnostic is within the liminal phase, so that one could say that there is a kind of "proto-aggregation". Nevertheless, the strangeness of the present realm remains and there is still a completion of sorts to come with the return to the heavenly region. This sort of imagery and approach to the world fits well with the idea of a liminal group; that is, those who are neither at home in the world nor yet fully at home in the heavenly region.

Thus salvation does not necessarily refer to something experienced in the heavenly homeland. Even where resurrection is part of the process of salvation, it does not necessarily refer to an event after physical death and on the way to the heavenly homeland. As seen in Gos. Phil., resurrection must come before death, to give just one example.

---

[1] See also 53.21–24; cf. Ex 33:19.

In this way, life for the Gnostic, post-revelation and pre-return to the heavenly region, is a little like the life of Jesus in some texts, where Jesus has struggled with the powers of Death, or has experienced the passion or resurrection or both, but has not yet returned completely to the Father (although the texts do not tell us where he goes between appearances). Complete salvation has already occurred for the Gnostic (e.g. Tri. Trac. 119.16–18: the spiritual race have complete salvation in every way; see also Dial. Sav. 121.20 – 122.1), so that sometimes the line between the Gnostics and heavenly community becomes quite fluid. In Gos. Truth, for example, the delineation between the Aeons and the elect is very unclear, possibly because the elect are already enjoying some kind of existence in the region above while still waiting in the region below (42.17–39). Great Pow. asserts that the community has already found rest in the heavens (42.30–31) and has come to be in the unchangeable Aeon (48.12–13).

Similar ideas of a heavenly existence of some kind while still living in the earthly realm can be found in Tri. Trac. 135.9–18; Treat. Seth. 57.31 – 58.4; and Treat. Res. 47.26–27. Believers in Ap. Jas. are urged to pay heed to the glory that awaits Jesus above and to listen to the heavenly hymns even now (14.26–29).

It is not always possible to be perfectly clear about whether the texts are speaking of this world or the heavenly world. Gos. Phil. states that: "you saw the spirit, you became the spirit; you saw the Christ, you became the Christ; you saw [the father, you] shall become the father" (61.20–35). Buckley proposes that the text means to abolish the separation of subject and object, with the past tense implying that the one addressed "has already seen the vision and has entered into the other realm by ritual means" (1988, 4171). However, the highest goal of identification with the Father is still to be achieved.

The question remains as to whether the other realm has in fact been entered, if the Father has been seen but the believer has not become the Father. Can it be that everything is a type of the Truth, even the Christ, so that when believers receive the Christ for example, they are still only receiving the Truth under one of its types? (The text asserts that when the Gnostic leaves the world he has already received the truth in images [86.11–12]). The final reception of Truth and becoming the Truth will only happen when the Father is truly seen and the believer unites with him in the Pleroma. This eschatological aspect must be kept in mind, although the text also states "the world has become the Aeon, for the Aeon is the Pleroma for him... it is revealed to him alone, not hidden in the darkness and the night, but hidden in a perfect day and a holy light" (86.13–19).

Treat. Res. too is somewhat ambivalent. The believer is embraced by Christ until his setting (i.e. death), and then he is drawn to heaven by him like beams by the sun, not being restrained by anything (45.31–39). "This is the spiritual resurrection which swallows up the psychic in the same way as the fleshly" (ΤΕΕΙ ΤΕ ΤΑΝΑϹΤΑϹΙϹ ÑΠΝΕΥΜΑΤΙΚΗ ΕϹШΜÑΚ ÑΤΨΥΧΙΚΗ 2ΟΜΟΙШϹ ΜÑ ΤΚΕϹΑΡΚΙΚΗ) (45.39 – 46.2). Christ brings rest (ΜΤΑΝ) for the true believer (43.35–37), and the text asserts that the believers rose with him, and went to heaven with him (ⲁⲚⲦⲰⲰⲚ ⲚⲘ̄ⲘⲈϤ ⲁⲨⲰ ⲁⲚⲂⲰⲔ ⲁⲦⲠⲈ ⲚⲘ̄ⲘⲈϤ) (45.25–28). Yet the text also speaks of the resurrection which is lived in this world, where rest is already received (43.34 – 44.3), and Christ is worn in this world (= immortality?) (44.28–31).

Those united with the Lord here are frequently said to have received life or that they will not experience death (e.g. Gos. Thom. Log. 1 and 18; Gos. Eg. III 66.4–8/IV 78.6–10; Soph. Jes. Chr. 97.24 – 98.9; 2 Apoc. Jas. 58.6–7; 57.1; 62.19; 63.5–10, 13 [life related to the Lord is a key theme in this text]). Perhaps this is very close to the concept of receiving the resurrection even here in this life, which has occurred in some of the texts above.

3.8 Transformation

The transformation process for the Gnostic takes place obviously during the awakening that occurs with the revelation by the Saviour figures, and the way that this implies a whole new aspect for the believer. There is a good example of this concept in Gos. Thom. where the strict delineation of normal earthly categories are smudged: what Jesus offers is nothing known to the human senses (Log. 17). Interestingly the process is positively described in terms of human anatomy, and is related to a question concerning the disciples entering the kingdom as children. The new person is a child, perhaps born again (?). There is to be no distinction between inside and outside, above and below, male and female, and the believer has new eyes, hands, feet, and likeness to replace the old in entering the kingdom (Log. 22).

This transformation of the whole person described by means of the body metaphor should be seen in relation to those other body metaphors used frequently in the texts:[1] i.e. about androgyny or asexuality. The rejection of differentiated gender, of the physical body, and the rejection of femaleness are linked of course to the human potential for sexual relations and reproduction. In the first instance, many texts reject sexual relations because sexuality is seen to derive from an animal nature, and in the second instance, they are rejected because they lead to the reproduction of human beings, and this simply means that more human beings are trapped in the earthly context. In relation to this, femaleness or the female gender is used as the metaphor for passion and animal lust and the deficiency of the rational aspect in human beings (see the section on "femaleness" in Chapter III).

The deficiency of femaleness is clear in Teach. Silv. which describes the fall of the mind which is male (see also 102.15–16) into a male-female entity which, having cast out the mind, became female (i.e. became psychic [the soul is the wife of the mind, 92.30–31]). When this element was cast out, the result was something not human, something of a fleshly, animal nature (93.7–21).

---

[1] See also the extensive section on body and flesh in Chapter III.

At first glance, texts seem to offer a number of possibilities for Gnostics: to reject femaleness/the works of femaleness, to reject femaleness by becoming male, or to become a child. These are not mutually exclusive, although they may not be correlative.

When it is suggested that Mary must become male in order to become a living spirit and thus enter the kingdom of heaven (Gos. Thom. Log. 114; see also 1 Apoc. Jas. 41.16–19), this should not be read as Mary needing to experience a change of sex. Rather two related things are being suggested: first, she must renounce the deficiency within her (a human deficiency rather than a deficiency she has because she is female) and take on rationality; and second, she must return to Eden.

The return to Eden is a return to the innocent state of Adam as the First Man, the complete human being prior to separation and death, as Gos. Phil. would put it. The return to Adam is not a return to maleness literally or even indeed to androgyny, since androgyny is implicitly bisexual. Adam is not a divided human being, he is not "bi" anything, simply the complete human being.

Returning to Gos. Thom., I would suggest that not only is Mary to become male but she is also presumably to become a child if the other messages of that gospel are taken seriously. The image of the child also presumes asexuality or presexuality (in terms of the culture in which the image is first used) rather than androgyny.

A number of logia in Gos. Thom. use the image of the child (Log. 4, 21, 22, 37, 46, 50) and the image is related to other key images and themes like the single one (Log. 4, 22), life (Log. 4, 18, 50), the kingdom (Log. 22, 46), the beginning and the end (Log. 18, 50), the first and the last (Log. 4), and undressing (Log. 21, 37).

There are various activities related to being a child:

– seeking the place of life;
– becoming one/a single one;
– undressing in order to let the owners of a field which has been squattered on have it back, or undressing to tread upon the garments;
– becoming one by collapsing the binary oppositions and becoming a new person;
– becoming acquainted with the kingdom.

To become a child means to return to the unity of the self as it was in the beginning (the end is as the beginning, the way one was as the first shall be the way one is as the last), by divesting oneself of the world/the flesh and impugning it and then becoming a new spiritual person. By doing this one enters the kingdom, the place of life and light, which is the place of origin and where there is rest for the children of the living Father.

There has been much speculation as to what the child actually represents, especially the seven-day-old child of Log. 4.[1] Most scholars refer to the androgynous Adam before the Fall in order to interpret the figure of the child and the "single one" (oүa oүwт), who represent a spiritually transformed being, returned to the unity and innocence of the beginning (e.g. Klijn 1962, 272–8; Kee 1963, 309; Ménard 1975b, 83; and Lelyveld 27–32),[2] but there is often confusion between the concepts of androgyny and asexuality, with some scholars seeming to assume the equivalence of the two. I agree with Meyer that Gos. Thom. is concerned with asexuality rather than androgyny when referring to the child and the single one, especially when one takes Log. 22 into account (1985, 559–61; see also Klijn 1962, 273, 276–8).

Kee goes further to suggest that the undressing of the children in Log. 21 is the stripping off of sexuality rather than the stripping off of the body (1963, 311), but this seems a little too influenced by modern Western differentiations between body and sexuality. However, I would agree with his general statement that "becoming as a child, and entering the kingdom, and achieving a state of asexuality are very nearly interchangeable terms" (313).

There is paradox in the use of the image of the child, who is surely the most powerless individual in most communities and societies. Yet in Gos. Thom. it becomes a focusing and primary image for a group of grown adults who would be a law unto themselves as the kingless race against the powers. The paradox is extended in Log. 46, where it is asserted that no human being is superior to John the Baptist but anyone who becomes a child will be acquainted with the kingdom and will become superior to John (i.e. greater than the greatest human being). Further ordinary social and personal lines of identity and power are smudged in the images of women renouncing female-

---

[1] Kee interprets the child of seven days as "living in the perfect week, and therefore before the fall", citing Log. 37 as making the connection between becoming as a child and return to the primordial state of innocence (1963, 309, 313; see also Smith 1965/66). Meyer describes the child of seven days as unspoiled, unworldly, because he is not yet circumcised, and generally sums up the attributes of children as innocence, sinlessness, sexual naïveté and purity (Logs. 4, 21, 22, 37, 46) (1985, 558–9; see also Haenchen 1961a, 52). Lelyveld proposes to understand the infant of seven days from 1 Hen 93,3 or Jub 2,14 and 3,8 (in the first week of the creation Adam is one, single, androgynous; in the second week he enters into the duality of male-female), or from the Targums or Philo, for whom Gen 1 and 2 speak of two different men, the first being a unity and androgynous and made in the image of God. Of the associated theme of the first and last, she writes that this is not hierarchical language but eschatological: "...il apparaît comme l'enfant de la semaine parfaite, étant un, non pas l'enfant de l'origine des temps, mais de la fin des temps, quand tout aura retrouvé l'ordre et le sens primitif" (27–32). Klijn also refers to the concept of Adam as originally androgynous in late Talmud sources, Ephrem, and especially Philo (*Leg All.* 1,31; *Opif. mundi* 151–153 [where the first Adam is asexual]; and *Leg All.* 2, 491 [where as soon as a man marries he leaves his heavenly Father and Mother]) (1962, 275–8).

[2] See also Krause who writes of the *monachos* as the perfect Gnostic who has united the female and male aspects of his soul to come back to his original unity (1977a, 29). Morard links "the solitary and elect" in defining the *monachos*: "il est bien l'élu qui, détaché du monde matériel de la chair où il était tombé, a retrouvé, par le mystère de sa réunification intérieure, les privilèges de sa condition première au sein du royaume de la lumière dont il était issu" (397).

ness to become male, and both women and men returning to an ungendered state as children. All these metaphors are concerned with serious status reversal.

Finally I deal with one aspect of transformation which is not often emphasised in scholarly works on the Gnostics, and may be a bit surprising when passages are grouped together on certain of these themes. I refer here to a concept about having to work for transformation as well as being wakened into it. There is not just the insight given, but also hard work to be done! In this section I will sum up briefly a number of recurring themes: renunciation, faith, fighting the good fight, love, prayer and good works.

3.8.1 Renunciation

Testim. Truth sums up the whole process of salvation as resting on the two foundations of knowledge (of oneself and of Imperishability) and renunciation (of the world and the Law which rules there). Transference to the heights by the Christ follows the renunciation of foolishness and the advance to knowledge (36.3–7, 26–28). Renunciation is seen by Gos. Truth to be repentance and turning back to the Father (*metanoia*) (35.22–23).

Generally the believer renounces ignorance or all that is associated with it and moves to insight or its associated elements. Thus a believer may renounce the forgetfulness of the archons brought on by sexual activity for wakefulness (Soph. Jes. Chr. 97.23; 108.8–10; 101.10–13). Other aspects of ignorant life to be renounced are: lust and what is visible (Thom. Cont. 140.1–5, 19–20); drunkenness (Gos. Truth 22.16–20); blind thought, which is the bond of flesh which encircles the believer (1 Apoc. Jas. 27.1–6); the world and its riches[1] and everything in it (Gos. Thom. Log. 110; Acts Pet. 12 Apost. 5.21 – 6.8; 7.26–30; 10.14–17). Apoc. Pet. 75.34 – 76.4 simply mentions a general attitude of renunciation.

This list gives the impression that the elements to be renounced are not basically part of believers but rather put on them by the power of the archons or they exist around the believer in the world. Gos. Phil. has a slightly different concept in that what is renounced seems to be from the person themselves. Each man has to dig down after the root of evil which is within him and pluck out the root from his heart by recognising it (ⲤⲞⲨⲰⲚ) (83.18–22). Interp. Know. too speaks of surmounting sin (21.33–34). That it is not simply sinfulness by virtue of being in the flesh, but that the believer may also sin, is attested in the warning that to sin against the Word is to sin more than the Gentiles (21.29–30).

---

[1] Ménard interprets all the sayings about riches in a metaphorical sense. In Logia 63 and 64, e.g., the riches are the *pneuma* of the gnostics, fallen into matter, and the buyers and the sellers are those who have not practised poverty and will not participate in heavenly rest (1975b, 163–4). On the other hand, Patterson interprets these logia as radical social teaching (1990, 629–33).

Most texts speak of renunciation in terms of turning away from something. A few texts speak in more drastic terms. Melch. mentions the self-sacrifice (as opposed to animal sacrifice) involved in baptism (6.25 – 7.3; 16.7–12). In Ap. Jas. the Lord states that the kingdom belongs to those who put themselves to death (6.17–18). Believers are urged to become seekers for death (6.7–8), since death will teach them election (6.13–14). That life will come from death is summed up in the small credal formula: "Remember my cross and my death, and you will live" (ⲁⲣⲓ ⲡⲙⲉⲉⲩⲉ ⲙ̄ⲡⲁⲥⲧⲁⲩⲣⲟⲥ ⲁⲩⲱ ⲡⲁⲙⲟⲩ ⲁⲩⲱ ⲧⲉⲧⲛ̄ⲛⲁⲱⲛ̄ⲍ̄) (5.33–35).

Even in these texts, however, there is cautionary note about being prudent, that one should not overdo renunciation. As Bethge rightly points out with relation to the ethic in Treat. Seth, certainly the Gnostics have freedom (61.7–11) but this should not lead to libertinism, nor to asceticism at any price, but rather to responsible living and behaviour, i.e. following the inner law (61.12–14) (1979, 166–7).

3.8.2 Faith

For Acts Pet. 12 Apost., those who endure the burden of the yoke of faith will be included in the kingdom of heaven (7.15–19) and Interp. Know. states that it is good for a person to have faith, because the world is the place of unbelief (1.33–37). For Gos. Phil., faith and love are two necessary elements of the believer's life (61.36 – 62.6). In the analogy of God's farming with its four elements of faith, love, hope and insight, faith is likened to the earth (ⲕⲁⲍ) in which one takes root (79.22–20).

There are various foci of the faith of the believer: the truth (Thom. Cont. 142.10–11 [ⲛ̄ⲕⲣ̄ⲡⲓⲥⲧⲉⲩⲉ ⲍⲛ̄ ⲧⲙⲏⲉ]); the secret teaching or revelation (Ap. Jas. 1.26–28; Dial. Sav. 136.1–4; 142.11–15); Jesus (Val. Exp. 36.15–17; Gos. Phil. 61.36 – 62.6) and his cross (Ap. Jas. 6.2–7); and the names of the Father, Son and Holy Spirit (Tri. Trac. 127.32–34).

Believers themselves may be a source of faith. Soph. Jes. Chr. speaks of those who are visible here, who belong to the Unbegotten Father, who can be the source of faith in the invisible things (98.13–20).

3.8.3 Fighting the Good Fight; Winning the Spiritual Contest

The life of the believer is sometimes presented in images of striving in the fight or the contest. Ap. John 26.3–7 states that all that is needed is endurance to finish the good fight; Interp. Know. 21.33–34 speaks of surmounting sin in order to win the crown of victory.

Teach. Silv. provides the best examples of exhortation to fighting the good fight. The text describes human life as a type of contest of which Christ is the judge who crowns the winners and teaches the believer how to contend (112.19–22; see also 112.10–19; 114.1–15; 117.17–19). In more forceful imagery of war rather than contest, the person is likened to a military camp or fortified town which must be guarded against the enemy (84.26 – 86.23; see also 108.3–14; 113.31 – 114.1). A "quiet life" within the city is the opposite of being a captured desolate city (85.6–10). One must not flee like an animal but rather fight and be on the watch. 84.26 – 86.23 ends with a prayer for God to dwell in the camp, the Spirit to protect the gates, the mind of piety to protect the walls, holy reason to be a torch in the mind to burn the wood which is sin.

3.8.4 Love, Prayer, Good Works, . . .

For Gos. Phil., love is like the wind through which one grows in the spiritual life (79.28–29). Treat. Seth assures believers that they will be victorious in everything (60.3–7) since they have upright love, innocence, purity, goodness, and a mind of the Father in an ineffable mystery (60.7–12).

The idea that prayer is not just the simple line of communication with the heavenly region, but necessary for intercession can be found in Ap. Jas. 11.29–32; Melch. 8.28; Ep. Pet. Phil. 133.21–26; 134.3–9; and Pr. Paul.

In Dial. Sav. 121.20 – 122.1 we are told that the elect have saved their souls by the sacrifice of the Father and their good works.

4. Aggregation

> In the third phase (reaggregation or reincorporation), the passage is consummated. The ritual subject, individual or corporate, is in a relatively stable state once more and, by virtue of this, has rights and obligations vis-à-vis others of a clearly defined and 'structural' type... (Turner, V.W. 94–5)

4.1 The Movement to Aggregation: Passage out of the World and the Return to the Region Above

The return journey to the heavenly place of origin is the liminal situation *par excellence*, or perhaps the intensification of the experience of liminality. Although I suggest that the entire experience of being in the world for the believers is one in which they are liminal and the figure who provides the revelation is also liminal, the revelation or awakening is crucial for that final phase of the liminal state between this world and the heavenly world after death. The return to the place of heavenly origin is a *rite de passage* in itself, and the danger of the final transitional state is apparent for Jesus and for the Gnostics, in the struggle with the powers which most often accompanies that return.

Of course the paradigm for the return is contained in the descriptions of Jesus' coming to the earthly region (see the study in Chapter II). His descent involves shape or "clothing" changes, a concern for the necessity of hiding from the archons or at least duping them by assuming a shape like theirs, and shaking or disturbing the archons by passing through their territory. This aspect of the descent should not be forgotten, just because there is more attention paid to the ascent and the struggle involved, by virtue of the importance of this event in the canonical passion narratives.The return/ascent both of Jesus and the Gnostics mirrors this descent, and there are many references to clothing, putting off one body for another, and contending with the archons.

That heaven is the final destination is quite clear. What awaits the believer there is variously described. Attaining the kingdom may entail being given a crown and the power to rule, or being received into the Light. Often it means receiving rest (e.g. Gos. Phil. 66.7–23). Treat. Seth. describes the souls of believers taken to the heavenly region to stand before the Father without weariness and fear (57.31 – 58.4).

I have already noted some ambiguity or unclearness for the accounts of the Gnostic experience of resurrection, (i.e. whether it speaks of this world or the next), and care should also be taken with the accounts of the return. This process may not actually always be associated with a time after physical death. It may be that return takes place within the experience of insight or within some ritual experience while the body is yet within the earthly context. I would judge the texts which follow to have some degree of unclearness, especially Trim. Prot. and Ap. Jas.

I begin with two texts which seem to imply that the believer gets ready here or even sets out on the path while in the earthly context; that is, instructions about the path read rather like instructions for the daily life of the believer in this world. Acts Pet. 12 Apost. advises believers to follow renunciation as the way to reach the heavenly city. They are counselled to forsake everything, to fast daily from stage to stage of the journey, because there are robbers (= the archons?) and wild beasts (the powers in general?) on the road (5.21 – 6.8; 7.26–30). Teach. Silv. exhorts believers to walk in Christ's way rather than the broad way that leads to the Underworld/the mire (103.13–26).

Dial. Sav. has extensive descriptions, instructions and advice about the path for the return. The path belongs to the Father and the Son (145.17–18), and the beginning of it is love and goodness (142.4–6). It leads to the Pleroma where the Gnostics belong, even though they presently live in the place of deficiency (139.16–18). They have known the path (145.19–20) and are more aware of it than any angel or authority (145.14–16, text damaged). Even if the archons become great (Ⲉ[Ⲩ]ⲱ[ⲁ]Ⲛ̅Ⲡ̅Ⲛⲟ6) they will not be able to reach the path (145.20–22).

The crossing itself is quick, the good taken up to the Light quickly like a visible voice and a flash of lightning (136.6–10; see also 136.17–19). The Gnostics are not to be afraid of what will meet them on the path (e.g. the first power of darkness? [text fragmentary], 122.4), for if they are afraid it will engulf them (122.17–19).[1] Nevertheless, the crossing place (ⲡⲙⲁ ⲛ̄ⲁ̅ⲓⲟⲟⲡ) is fearful (123.23 – 124.1), and the Gnostic must pass over with singleness of mind (ⲙ[ⲛ̄ ⲟⲩ]ϩⲏⲧ ⲛ̄ⲟⲩⲱⲧ) (124.2–3; another aspect of the theme of unity vs multiplicity).

Even though the archons dwell above the Gnostics and thus should logically be their rulers (138.12–13), the Gnostics will rule over the archons when they clothe themselves in light, and enter the bridal chamber (138.14–20; see also 146.18–24). The clothing in light seems to be a way of becoming invisible to the archons as in 145.8–14, so that the passage back may be made without interference from them (cf. Gos. Phil. 86.4–11). The one who knows the path by which he is to leave is given the garments of life (ⲛ̄ϩⲃⲥⲱ ⲙ̄ⲡⲱⲛϩ) (139.4–6), and these garments are in contrast to the transient garments of the archons and the administrators which do not last, in which the sons of truth are not to clothe themselves (143.15–22).

Although this brings to mind the ritual of the bridal chamber, nevertheless other passages would seem to imply that we are really speaking about the actual passage after death. In 143.6–10, Mary speaks of the disciples having taken their stand in the mystery of truth with the result that they are transparent to the cosmos. Her statement is immediately followed by Judas speaking to Matthew about wanting to understand the garments in which they are to be clothed when they depart the decay of the flesh (143.11–15; = the blessedness attained after stripping oneself [143.22–24]). At least in the vision the soul receives the garment on the journey to the heavens (136.22), rather than during life in the earthly region.

Trim. Prot. has a stronger ritual tone than Dial. Sav., with the return described as an element within the baptism ritual (or is the baptism ritual used as metaphor for the return?) The ascent of the seeds to the heavenly region is described in 48.6–35 and 49.23–36: the process involves baptism with the Water of Life (48.6–7, 18–21), which means to be stripped of what belongs to the Chaos and the bodily and psychic [the garments of ignorance; 49.30–31] (48.7–12) and to be clothed in Light (= the Thought of the Fatherhood 48.13–14, 15–17; 49.31–32), to be enthroned (48.21–24) and glorified (48.24–26; cf. the similarity to the Aeons who are established, glorified and given thrones [38.19–20, 33 – 39.5]), to be taken to the Light and to receive the Five Seals (48.30–32).

Ap. Jas. presents a good description of the return of Jesus (his second departure?) to the heavenly region: glory awaits him (14.26–27); as do hymns up in the heavens (ϩⲛ̄ ⲙ̄ⲡⲏⲩⲉ) (14.29–30); he will take his place at the right hand of the Father (14.30–31); he will go up in a chariot of the spirit (14.33–34); he will strip himself in order to clothe himself (14.35–36).

---

[1] This is reminiscent of Gos. Phil. 66.4–6 which states that the flesh is not to be feared (which leads to its mastery) nor to be loved (which leads to being swallowed by it and paralysed).

Part of his return seems to include battle and a victory followed by praises (15.9–22). That it will be similar for the disciples may be assumed from Jesus' constant urgings for them to follow quickly after him to the heavenly region. (12.16–17). Yet the blessing pronounced in 12.17 on the one who has seen himself as a fourth one (ⲙⲁⲁϩⲧⲁⲩ) in heaven seems to imply a contemporaneous existence in heaven while one is on the earth.

4.2 The Movement from Multiplicity to Unity

Since in the Gos. Phil. unity is the characteristic not only of Truth but of everything in the heavenly region (those exalted above the world are indissoluble and eternal [53.21–23]), one would only expect that the return to the heavenly region would be a return from multiplicity to unity, above all in the experience of the bridal chamber. All the apparent (but deceptive) dualisms of the earthly region – light and darkness, life and death, right and left , good and evil – are really brothers of one another and inseparable, and each one will dissolve into its earliest origin (ⲁⲧⲉϥⲁⲣⲭⲏ ⲝⲓⲛ ⲱⲟⲣⲡ) (53.14–21). There is a future aspect to this activity of union, which may also include a wider group than the Gnostics: with the revelation of wickedness, perfect light will flow out of everyone, slaves will be free, captives ransomed, those separated will reunite (85.21–31).

Similarly, for Tri. Trac. the process of redemption is an escape from multiplicity of forms, inequality and change (132.16–28), by the Saviour who is a unity from which comes impassibility (116.31–33). Gos. Truth presents the cosmos as a place of deficiency, a place of envy and strife in contrast to the place of unity and perfection (24.20–26). Unity is reached by the attainment of oneself, purification from multiplicity, the consuming of matter by fire, darkness by light, death by life (25.10–19). Val. Exp. states that the community will experience reconciliation and unity when they are finally united with their angelic forms, which appears to be parallel to the union of the Church and the Man (the second syzygy of the second tetrad, which consists of Logos-Life, Man-Church, 29.30–37). Finally Gos. Thom. and Dial. Sav. both speak of those already in unity by the figure of the solitary one. These are the perfect (Dial. Sav. 120.26) who will find the kingdom/enter the bridal chamber (Gos. Thom. Log. 49 and 75).

4.3 Completed Salvation/Union in the Heavenly World

I have already dealt with this theme of salvation and union within the previous section and noted it as possibly proto-aggregation. In this final section I simply outline a number of texts which speak more explicitly of events that will happen in the heavenly world associated with the process of salvation. Thus Thom. Cont. tells us that the elect will receive rest and will reign and be joined with the good one/the king (145.12–16). For Gos. Truth too, the believer who knows he is from above will return there (22.2–7) and receive rest (22.12). Testim. Truth asserts that the one who knows himself and God who is over the truth will be saved and will be crowned with an unfading crown (44.30 – 45.6). In Ap. Jas. the mutual dwelling between Jesus and those he came to save (9.1–4) seems to imply that those he saved will dwell with him in the region above. Perhaps they will live with him in the heavens in the house that he is building for them (13.3–8).

Conclusion

This final chapter takes up the concept of the relationship of the communities which produced and used the texts and the type of Jesus which one finds in them. I have only scratched the surface of this aspect of Jesus research, and extended the work of Gilhus into a more detailed outline. This material could provide the basis for a study in its own right.

Epilogue

This study has produced a simple outline of major events and relationships in the experience of Jesus within the earthly context as found within the collection of texts from Nag Hammadi. Every text which mentions Jesus has been included as a valid source of information for the study. No judgment has been made as to the relative worth of individual texts based on how early they might be dated nor on how close they might be to an "orthodox" position. The texts studied are considered to be Christian, for the most part Gnostic Christian, and the collection as a whole is considered to have belonged to a Christian community which would have seen itself somehow within the broad range of groups calling themselves Christian in the early centuries CE.

No single portrait of Jesus emerges from the study, nor any type of composite christology. Rather it is a summary of portraits, organised within major themes and concepts about Jesus that occur in the majority of the texts. Thus the study is more of a descriptive handbook than a work which analyses the figure of Jesus across the texts. I have not written an analysis with a focus on similarities and inconsistencies and tried to make comparisons between the individual portraits in all the texts. I have simply dealt with the spectrum of approaches to the figure to be found in the collection of the texts.

I believe the study to be immensely important for understanding the origin, historical development and ongoing identity of Christianity as one of the world religions. It represents a study of the founder of this religion according to one of the numerous strands of tradition which developed about him. In that sense it is a valid historical study of interpretations of the historical Jesus.

Appendix: Titles

This appendix gives the page and line numbers for the occurrence of the titles. They are arranged in order, according to their first appearance in the text.

Pr. Paul

  Lord of Lords (A.14)
  King of the aeons ([ⲡⲢ̄ⲢⲞ Ⲛ̄ⲚⲀⲒⲰⲚ] A.14)

Ap. Jas.

  Lord (1.12; 4.23, 31; 5.36; 6.1, 22, 28, 32, 35; 13.31, 36; 16.29)
  Saviour (1.23, 32; 2.11, 17, 40; 16.24–25)
  Son (9.17–18; 10.14; 14.39;15.2)
  Teacher ([ⲡⲤⲀ?] 15.32)
  Son of Man (3.14, 17–18)

Gos. Truth

  The hidden mystery ([ⲡⲒⲘⲨⲤⲦⲎⲢⲒⲞⲚ ⲈⲐⲎⲠ] 18.15)
  Jesus the Christ (18.16)
  The merciful one, the faithful one ([ⲡⲒⲰⲀⲚ?ⲎⲦ ⲡⲒⲡⲒⲤⲦⲞⲤ] 20.10)

Treat. Res.

  Saviour (43.36–37; 45.14; 48.18–19)
  Lord Christ (43.38)
  Lord (44.13; 48.18; 49.38 – 50.1)
  Son of God (44.16–17, 21–22, 29)
  Son of Man (44.23, 30–31; 46.14–15)
  Jesus (the) Christ (48.19; 50.1)
  The solution ([ⲡⲂⲰⲀ] 45.5)

Tri. Trac.

  Christ (122.18; 132.18; 134.13; 136.1)
  Saviour (121.2, 11; 122.5; 138.21–22)
  Lord (119.15; 121.30; 138.21)
  Lord of all (121.1)
  The Lord of glory? (120.26)

Son of God (120.36; 133.18–19)
King of the universe (121.17)
The Redeemer? (138.22)

Names of the Saviour:
– the Redemption of the angels of the Father (125.19–20).
– the knowledge of all that which is thought of (127.12–13)
– the treasure (127.13–14)
– the addition for the increase of knowledge (127.14–15)
– the revelation of those things which were known at first (127.15–16)
– the path toward harmony and toward the pre-existent one (127.17–19)

Ap. John

Teacher (1.10)
Lord (13.18; 22.10; 25.27; 26.7, 23, 32–33; 27.12, 22, 31–32)
Saviour (22.10, 12, 21; 25.16; 31.32; 32.5)
Jesus Christ (32.6)

Gos. Thom.

Teacher (Log. 13)
Son of the living one (Log. 37)
Son of man (Log. 86)
The living one (Log. 111)

Gos. Phil.

Christ (52.19, 35; 55.6, 11; 56.4, 7, 9, 13; 61.30, 31; 62.9, 10, 12, 15;
    68.17, 20; 69.6–7; 70.13; 71.19; 74.15–16)
Son (54.7, 8; 74.17 [x 2], 23 [x 2])
The perfect man (55.12; 58.20–21 [in contrast to Adam]; 60.23–24; 80.4)
Lord (55.34, 37; 56.16; 59.7, 24; 62.6; 63.25; 64.9–10; 67.27; 68.6–7;
    74.25; 78.22, 24)
Messiah (56.8–9; 62.8, 11)
The Nazarene (56.12; 62.8, 9, 11, 14–15, 16)
The heavenly man (58.17)
Son of man (63.29–30; 81.14–15, 15–16, 16–17, 17–18, 18–19, 19)
Saviour (64.3)
Son of God (78.20–21)
Jesus Christ (80.1)
Logos (80.4–5; unclear passages concerning Jesus as the Logos: 57.7;
    58.34; 78.29–30; 78.34 – 79.1; 79.5–10; 83.11–13; 84.8)
Pharisatha (63.21–24)

Thom. Cont.

Saviour (138.1, 4, 27, 37, 39; 139.25, 32; 140.8; 141.4, 25; 142.6, 10, 26; 143.8)
Lord (138.21; 139.13, 20, 22; 140.6; 141.3; 142.3, 8, 19; 145.5)
Light (139.20)

Soph. Jes. Chr.

Jesus the Christ (90.14 [title of the work])
Saviour (91.7, 10, 24; 92.6; 94.4, 14)
The perfect Saviour ([ⲡⲧⲉⲗⲓⲟⲥ ⲛ̄ⲥⲱⲧⲏⲣ] 95.21–22; 96.18; 98.12; 100.19–20; 105.8–9; 106.14–15; 108.19–20; 114.13; also BG 107.17–18)
The great Saviour ([ⲡⲛⲟϭ ⲛ̄ⲥⲱⲧⲏⲣ] 107.22)
The blessed Saviour ([ⲡⲙⲁⲕⲁⲣⲓⲟⲥ ⲛⲥⲱⲧⲏⲣ]; BG 126.17–18)
Lord (94.1 [ⲡⲉⲭ̄ⲥ̄ BG 83.1]; 95.19 [ⲡⲉⲭ̄ⲥ̄ BG 86.7]; 98.10 [ⲡⲉⲭ̄ⲥ̄ BG 90.1–2]; 105.4 [ⲡⲉⲭ̄ⲥ̄ BG 100.4]; BG 102.8 has ⲡⲉⲭ̄ⲥ̄ but there is no title in III, 106.9–14)
Lord Saviour (96.15 [ⲡⲉⲭ̄ⲥ̄ ⲡⲥⲱⲧⲏⲣ BG 87.9]; 100.17–18 [no title in BG]; 108.17–18 [ⲡⲉⲭ̄ⲥ̄ ⲡⲥⲱⲧⲏⲣ BG 106.11–12]; 112.21 [ⲡⲉⲭ̄ⲥ̄ ⲡⲥⲱⲧⲏⲣ BG 114.14])
Holy Lord ([ⲡⲁⲟⲉⲓⲥ ⲉⲧⲟⲩⲁⲁⲃ] 114.9–10 [ⲡⲉⲭ̄ⲥ̄ ⲉⲧⲟⲩⲁⲁⲃ BG 117.13–14])
Holy One ([ⲡⲉⲧⲟⲩⲁⲁⲃ] 104.5)
Son (108.7)?

Dial. Sav.

Saviour (120.1 [title of the work], 2; 125.1, 18)
Only begotten Son ([ⲡⲙⲟⲛⲟⲅⲉⲛⲏⲥ ⲛ̄ϣⲏⲣⲉ] 121.6–7)
Lord (125.4, 10; 126.18, 21; 127.20, 22; 128.16; 129.3, 20; 131.18, 22; 132.6, 10, 12, 15, 21, 23; 137.7; 138.8, 14, 22; 139.21; 140.1, 11–12, 15, 17, 20, 22, 24; 142.4–5, 9, 11, 17, 22; 143.3, 7–8, 15; 144.3–4, 8, 15, 23; 145.8; 146.1, 9, 12)
Son of Man (135.16–17; 136.21)
Teacher (142.25)
Son (145.17–18)?

1 Apoc. Jas.

Lord (24.11; 26.6, 16; 29.4, 19; 30.10, 12; 31.14; 32.17, 23, 28; 38.24; 40.9)
Rabbi ([ϩⲣⲁⲃⲃⲓ] 25.10; 26.2, 14; 27.14; 28.5; 29.14; 31.5; 40.4; 41.20)

2 Apoc. Jas.

  Lord   (46.20; 60.7)

Acts Pet. 12 Apost.

  Lord (1.12, 16; 10.14–15, 22; 11.7)
  Jesus Christ, Son of the living God (9.11–12)

Treat. Seth

  The Son of Light (51.2–3)
  a Christ (52.3–5)
  The perfect blessed one (59.5–8)
  Son of Man (64.11–12)
  a Christ, the Son of Man (65.18–19)
  Jesus Christ, the Son of Man (69.21–22)

Apoc. Pet.

  Saviour (70.14; 72.26–27; 73.11–12; 80.8; 81.15; 82.8–9, 28)
  Son of Man (71.12)
  Lord (81.8, 26)

Teach. Silv.

  Christ (88.16, 29; 90.33; 96.20; 98.21, 26; 99.4, 13; 100.25; 101.14, 17,
      22, 25, 29, 33; 102.2, 5, 7; 103.14–15, 25, 33; 104.19; 106.22; 107.27;
      108.32; 109.7, 10, 11, 31; 110.12, 14; 111.15; 112.19; 115.5; 116.25,
      30; 117.18; 118.3)
  Jesus Christ (91.26)
  King (96.25; 111.15)
  The divine teacher (96.32)
  The (true) light (98.22–23; 101.19, 30; 106.26–27)
  Sun of life (98.23)
  The idea (NOHCIC) of incorruptibility (101.28–29)
  The narrow way (103.25–26)
  God (103.34; 110.17, 18; 111.5)
  The tree of life (106.21–22)
  Wisdom (of God) (106.22–23; 107.3, 9)
  The life (106.24–25; 107.13; 112.10–11)
  The (great) power (106.25; 112.9)
  The door (106.26)
  The angel (106.27)
  The good shepherd (106.27–28)
  The (faithful) friend (110.16)
  Teacher (110.18)

Great goodness of God (111.13–14)
King of every virtue (111.17)
King of life (111.18)
King of the aeons (111.18)
Great one of the heavens (111.19)
A great glory (112.10)
Judge (112.19–20; 114.13–14)
The hand of the Lord/Father (115.3–4, 5 [= the mother of all]; 115.8–9)
Son (115.9–10; 115.19)
The divine Son (115.15–16)
Image of the Father (115.19)
The (divine) Logos (106.24; 111.5–6; 112.32; 113.13–14; 115.18; 117.8–9)

Titles specifically in relation to the Logos:

– the first-born (112.35)
– the wisdom (112.35–36; 113.14–15)
– the prototype (112.36)
– the (first) light (112.36–37; 112.36–37)
– Light of the eternal light (113.6–7)
– spotless mirror of the working of God (113.3–5)
– the image of his goodness (113.5–6)
– the eye which looks at the invisible Father (113.7–9)
– life (113.15)
– king of faith (117.10)
– the sharp sword (117.10–11)

Ep. Pet. Phil.

Saviour of the whole world (132.18–19)
Lord Jesus Christ (133.1; 139.8)
God Jesus (133.7–8)
Blessed Christ (133.16–17)
The holy child Jesus Christ (133.25–26)
Son of life (134.3–4)
Son of immortality (134.4–5)
The one who is in the light (134.5–6)
Son (134.6)
Christ of immortality (134.6–7)
Redeemer (134.7)
The light (138.12–13)
Lord Jesus (139.11, 26; 140.12–13)
Our Illuminator Jesus (139.15)
Son of the immeasurable glory of the Father (139.26–27)

Testim. Truth

Son of Man (30.18; 31.6–7; 32.22–23; 37.27–28 [?]; 38.4 [?]; 41.2–3; 60.6
[?]; 67.7–8; 68.11 [?]; 69.15 [?]; 72.25–26 [?])
Christ (35.4; 36.4; 45.9, 14; 49.7; 50.3 [?]; 74.4)
Saviour (45.17; 67.8)

Interp. Know.

Saviour (3.26; 21.23)
Teacher of immortality (9.19)
The shape (10.23, 33)
Son (11.33–34, 34; 12.22 [?]; 13.11 [?]; 14.28)
the reproached one/the one who was reproached (12.15, 15–16, 25–26,
27–28, 30, 36)
the humiliated one (12.19 [?], 23)
the one who was redeemed (12.28)
the Head (13.25, 33, 35–36; 16.28; 17.31; 18.28–29, 35; 21.33)
Son of God (14.21–22)
Christ (15.16–17)

Bibliography

The bibliography contains only those works cited in the study, plus editions of the Nag Hammadi texts.

Abramowski, Luise. 1983. "Nag Hammadi 8,1 'Zostrianus', das Anonymum Brucianum, Plotin, Enn.2,9 (33)." *JAC.E* 10, 1–10.

Aland, Barbara, et al., eds. 1978. *Gnosis. Festschrift für Hans Jonas*. Göttingen: Vandenhoeck & Ruprecht.

Altheim, Franz and Ruth Stiehl. 1973. *Christentum am Roten Meer. Zweiter Band*. Berlin/New York: de Gruyter.

Arai, Sasagu. 1963. "'Jesus' im Thomasevangelium." *Journal of Christian Studies* 10: 57-9.

Arai, Sasagu. 1964a. *Die Christologie des Evangelium Veritatis: Eine religionsgeschichtliche Untersuchung*. Leiden: Brill.

Arai, Sasagu. 1964b. "Jesusverständnis in der Gnosis." *Das Problem des historischen Jesus*. Biblische Studien 2. Tokyo. 87-9.

Armstrong, A.H. 1992. "Dualism: Platonic, Gnostic, and Christian." Wallis 33–54.

Attridge, Harold W., ed. 1985a. *Nag Hammadi Codex I (The Jung Codex). Introductions, Texts, Translations, Indices*. NHS 22. Leiden: Brill.

Attridge, Harold W., ed. 1985b. *Nag Hammadi Codex I (The Jung Codex). Notes*. NHS 23. Leiden: Brill.

Attridge, Harold W. 1986. "The Gospel of Truth as an Exoteric Text." Hedrick and Hodgson 239–55.

Attridge, Harold W. and George W. MacRae. 1985. "The Gospel of Truth: I,3:16.31–43.24." Attridge 1985a, 55–122.

Attridge, Harold W. and Elaine H. Pagels. 1985. "The Tripartite Tractate: I,5:51.1–138.27." Attridge 1985b, 217–497.

Aune, David E. 1987. *The New Testament in Its Literary Environment*. LEC. Philadelphia: Westminster.

215

Baarda, T. 1983. "Jesus said: Be Passers-by. On the meaning and origin of Logion 42 of the Gospel of Thomas." *Early Transmission of Words of Jesus: Thomas, Tatian and the Text of the New Testament.* Amsterdam: VU Boekhandel/Uitgeverij. 179–205.

Barc, Bernard. 1980. *L'Hypostase des Archontes. Traité gnostique sur l'origine de l'homme, du monde et des archontes (NH II,4).* BCNH.T 5. Québec/Louvain: Les Presses de l'Université Laval/Éditions Peeters. v–147.

Barc, Bernard, ed. 1981. *Colloque international sur les textes de Nag Hammadi (Québec, 22–25 août 1978).* BCNH.E 1. Québec/Louvain: Les Presses de l'Université Laval/Éditions Peeters.

Barc, Bernard. 1982. "Les noms de la Triade dans l'Évangile selon Philippe." Ries et al. 361–76.

Barry, Catherine. 1993. *La Sagesse de Jésus-Christ (BG, 3; NH III, 4).* BCNH.T 20. Québec: Les Presses de l'Université Laval.

Batdorf, Irvin W. 1984. "Interpreting Jesus Since Bultmann: Selected Paradigms and Their Hermeneutical Matrix." *SBL.SP* 23: 187–215.

Bauckham, Richard. 1992. "Gospels (Apocryphal)." *Dictionary of Jesus and the Gospels.* Eds. Joel B. Green and Scot McKnight. Downers Grove, IL: Intervarsity Press. 286a–91b.

Bauer, Walter. 1909. *Das Leben Jesu im Zeitalter der neutestamentlichen Apocryphen.* Tübingen: Mohr (Siebeck). (Unaltered and photographically reproduced by the Wissenschaftliche Buchgesellschaft [Darmstadt], 1967.)

Baumotte, Manfred, ed. 1984. *Die Frage nach dem historischen Jesus. Texte aus drei Jahrhunderten.* Reader Theologie. Gütersloh: Mohn.

Beltz, Walter. 1974. "Bemerkungen zur Adamapokalypse aus Nag-Hammadi-Codex V." Nagel 1974, 159–63.

Beltz, Walter. 1981. "Melchisedek – eine gnostische Initiationsliturgie." *ZRGG* 33: 155–8.

Berger, Klaus. 1984. "Gnosis/Gnostizismus I. Vor- und außerchristlich." *TRE* 13: 519–35.

Bertrand, Daniel Alain. 1975. "'Paraphrase de Sem' et 'Paraphrase de Seth'." Ménard 1975c, 146–57.

Bethge, Hans-Gebhard. 1975. "'Zweiter Logos des großen Seth'. Die zweite Schrift aus Nag-Hammadi-Codex VII." *ThLZ* 100: 97–110.

Bethge, Hans-Gebhard. 1978. "Der sogennante 'Brief des Petrus an Philippus'. Die zweite 'Schrift' aus Nag-Hammadi-Codex VIII." *ThLZ* 103: 161–70.

Bethge, Hans-Gebhard. 1979. "Anthropologie und Soteriologie im 2 LogSeth (NHC VII, 2)." Nagel 1979, 161–71.

Bethge, Hans-Gebhard. 1990. "Der Brief des Petrus an Philippus." Hennecke and Schneemelcher 1990⁶, 1: 275–84.

Bethge, Hans-Gebhard, Bentley Layton and the Societas Coptica Hierosolymitana. 1988. "On the Origin of the World (II,5 and XIII,2)." Robinson, J.M. 1988³, 170–89.

Bethge, Hans-Gebhard, Bentley Layton and the Societas Coptica Hierosolymitana. 1989. "On the Origin of the World." Layton 1989, 2: 28–134.

Bethge, Hans-Gebhard and Orval S. Wintermute, trans. 1984. "On the Origin of the World (II,5 and XIII,2)." Robinson, J.M. 1984², 162–79.

Betz, Otto. 1990. "Der Name als Offenbarung des Heils (Jüdische Traditionen im koptisch-gnostischen Philippusevangelium." *Jesus der Herr der Kirche. Aufsätze zur biblischen Theologie II.* WUNT 52. Tübingen: Mohr (Siebeck). 396–404.

Blair, Harold A. 1982. "Allegory, Typology and Archetypes." Livingstone 1982, 263–7.

Böhlig, Alexander. 1967. "Die himmlische Welt nach dem Ägypterevangelium von Nag Hammadi." *Muséon* 80: 5–26, 365–77.

Böhlig, Alexander. 1969. "Christentum und Gnosis im Ägypterevangelium von Nag Hammadi." *Christentum und Gnosis.* Ed. Walther Eltester. BZNW 37. Berlin: Topelmann. 1–18.

Böhlig, Alexander. 1989a. "Das Ägypterevangelium. Ein Dokument des mythologischen Gnostizismus." Böhlig 1989b, 1: 341–70.

Böhlig, Alexander. 1989b. *Gnosis und Synkretismus. Gesammelte Aufsätze zur spätantiken Religionsgeschichte.* 2 vols. WUNT 47/48. Tübingen: Mohr (Siebeck).

Böhlig, Alexander. 1989c. "Zur Apokalypse des Petrus." Böhlig 1989b, 2: 395–8.

Böhlig, Alexander and Pahor Labib. 1962. *Die koptisch-gnostische Schrift ohne Titel aus Codex II von Nag Hammadi im Koptischen Museum zu Alt-Kairo.* Deutsche Akademie der Wissenschaften zu Berlin, Institut für Orientforschung 58. Berlin: Akademie.

Böhlig, Alexander and Pahor Labib. 1963. *Koptisch-gnostische Apokalypsen aus Codex V von Nag Hammadi im Koptischen Museum zu Alt-Kairo.* WZ(II) Sonderband.

Böhlig, Alexander and Christoph Markschies. 1994. *Gnosis und Manichäismus. Forschungen und Studien zu Texten von Valentin und Mani sowie zu den Bibliotheken von Nag Hammadi und Medinet Madi.* BZNW 72. Berlin: de Gruyter.

Böhlig, Alexander and Frederik Wisse. 1975. *Nag Hammadi Codices III,2 and IV,2: The Gospel of the Egyptians (The Holy Book of the Great Invisible Spirit).* NHS IV. Leiden: Brill.

Borg, Marcus J. 1991. "Portraits of Jesus in Contemporary North American Scholarship." *HTR* 84: 1–22.

Borg, Marcus J. 1994a. *Jesus in Contemporary Scholarship.* Valley Forge, PA: Trinity Press International.

Borg, Marcus J. 1994b. "Reflections on a Discipline: a North American Perspective." Chilton and Evans 9–31.

Borsch, Frederick H. 1970. *The Christian and Gnostic Son of Man.* SBT (2nd series) 14. London: SCM.

Brashler, James. 1977. *The Coptic "Apocalypse of Peter": A Genre Analysis and Interpretation.* Diss., Claremont Graduate School.

Brashler, James and Roger A. Bullard. 1988. "Apocalypse of Peter (VII,3)." Robinson, J.M. 1988³, 372–8.

Brown, Scott Kent. 1972. *James: A Religio-Historical Study of the Relations between Jewish, Gnostic, and Catholic Christianity in the Early Period through an Investigation of the Traditions about James the Lord's Brother.* Diss., Brown University, USA. Ann Arbor, MI: University Microfilms International.

Brown, S. Kent. 1975. "Jewish and Gnostic Elements in the Second Apocalypse of James (CG V,4)." *NT* 17: 225–37.

Brown, S. Kent and C. Wilfred Griggs. 1975. "The Apocalypse of Peter: Introduction and Translation." *Brigham Young University Studies* 15: 131–45.

Bruce, Frederick F. 1974. *Jesus and Christian Origins outside of the New Testament.* London/Grand Rapids: Hodder & Stoughton/Eerdmans.

Buckley, Jorunn J. 1980. "A Cult-Mystery in *The Gospel of Philip.*" *JBL* 99: 569–81.

Buckley, Jorunn J. 1988. "Conceptual Models and Polemical Issues in the Gospel of Philip." *ANRW* II 25.5: 4167–94.

Bullard, Roger A. 1970. *The Hypostasis of the Archons. The Coptic Text with Translation and Commentary.* PTS 10. Berlin: de Gruyter.

Bullard, Roger A. and Joseph A. Gibbons. 1988. "The Second Treatise of the Great Seth (VII,2)." Robinson, J.M. 1988[3], 362–71.

Burridge, Richard A. 1992. *What are the Gospels? A Comparison with Graeco-Roman Biography.* MSSNTS 70. Cambridge: Cambridge UP.

Callan, Terrance. 1990. "Sayings of Jesus in the Gos. Thom. 22, 2 Clem 12, Gos. Eg. 5." *JRSt* 16: 46–64.

Cameron, Ron, ed. 1982. *The Other Gospels: Non-Canonical Gospel Texts.* Philadelphia: Westminster.

Cameron, Ron. 1990. "Introduction." *Semeia* 49: 1–5.

Cameron, Ron. 1991. "The *Gospel of Thomas* and Christian Origins." Pearson 1991a, 381–92.

Cantwell, L. 1981. "The Gospels as Biographies." *SJTh* 34: 193–200.

Carlston, Charles E. 1994. "Prologue." Chilton and Evans 1–8.

Catanzaro, C.J. de. 1962. "The Gospel According to Philip." *JThS* 13: 36–71.

Charlesworth, James H. 1987. *The New Testament Apocrypha and Pseudepigrapha: A Guide to Publications, with Excurses on Apocalypses.* ATLA 17. Metuchen/London: ATLA.

Charlesworth, James H. 1988. *Jesus within Judaism: New Light from Exciting Archeological Discoveries.* ABRL. N.Y.: Doubleday.

Charlesworth, James H., ed. 1992. *The Messiah: Developments in Earliest Judaism and Christianity.* The First Princeton Symposium on Judaism and Christian Origins. Minneapolis: Fortress.

Charlesworth, James H. and Craig A. Evans. 1994. "Jesus in the Agrapha and Apocryphal Gospels." Chilton and Evans 479–533.

Cherix, Pierre. 1982. *Le Concept de Notre Grande Puissance (CG VI, 4). Texte, remarques philologiques, traduction et notes.* OBO 47. Fribourg, Suisse/Göttingen: Éditions universitaires/Vandenhoeck & Ruprecht.

Chilton, Bruce and Craig A. Evans, eds. 1994. *Studying the Historical Jesus: Evaluations of the State of Current Research*. NTTS 19. Leiden: Brill.

Colpe, Carsten. 1974. "Heidnische, jüdische und christliche Überlieferung in den Schriften aus Nag Hammadi III." *JAC* 17: 109–25.

Colpe, Carsten. 1980. "Heidnische, jüdische und christliche Überlieferung in den Schriften aus Nag Hammadi IX." *JAC* 23: 108–27.

Corley, Bruce, ed. 1983. *Colloquy on New Testament Studies: A Time for Reappraisal and Fresh Approaches*. Macon, GA: Mercer University Press.

Couliano, Ioan P. 1992. *The Tree of Gnosis. Gnostic Mythology from Early Christianity to Modern Nihilism*. N.Y.: HarperSanFrancisco.

Cozby, J. 1985. *Gnosis and the Cross. The Passion of Christ in Gnostic Soteriology as Reflected in the Nag Hammadi Tractates*. Diss., Duke University.

Craig, William L. 1993. "From Easter to Valentinus and the Apostles' Creed Once More: A Critical Examination of James Robinson's Proposed Resurrection Appearance Trajectories." *JSNT* 52: 19–39.

Crossan, John D. 1988. "Divine Immediacy and Human Immediacy: Towards a New First Principle in Historical Jesus Research." *Semeia* 44: 121–40.

Crossan, John D. 1991. *The Historical Jesus: The Life of a Mediterranean Jewish Peasant*. N.Y.: HarperSanFrancisco.

Crum, W.E. 1939. *A Coptic Dictionary*. Oxford: Clarendon.

Dahl, Nils A. 1991. *Jesus the Christ: The Historical Origins of Christological Doctrine*. Minneapolis, MN: Fortress.

Daniélou, Jean. 1966a. Rev. of Arai 1964a. *RSR* 54: 293–4.

Daniélou, Jean. 1966b. Rev. of Böhlig and Labib 1963. *RSR* 54: 285–93.

Dart, John. 1988. *The Jesus of Heresy and History. The Discovery and Meaning of the Nag Hammadi Gnostic Library*. San Francisco: Harper & Row. (Revised and expanded 2nd ed. of *The Laughing Savior*. 1976)

Davies, Stevan. 1992. "The Christology and Protology of the *Gospel of Thomas*." *JBL* 111: 663–82.

Dihle, Albrecht. 1991. "The Gospels and Greek Biography." Stuhlmacher 1991a, 361–86.

Doresse, Jean. 1966. "'Le livre sacré du grand Esprit invisible' ou 'L'Évangile des Égyptiens': texte copte édité, traduit et commenté d'après le codex I de Nag'a-Hammadi/Khénoboskion." *JA* 254: 316–435.

Doresse, Jean. 1968. "'Le livre sacré du grand Esprit invisible' ou 'L'Évangile des Égyptiens': texte copte édité, traduit et commenté d'après le codex I de Nag'a-Hammadi/Khénoboskion." *JA* 256: 289–366.

Dormeyer, Detlev. 1989. *Evangelium als literarische und theologische Gattung.* EdF 263. Darmstadt: Wissenschaftliche Buchgesellschaft.

Dormeyer, Detlev and Hubert Frankemölle. 1984. "Evangelium als literarische Gattung und als theologischer Begriff. Tendenzen und Aufgaben der Evangelienforschung im 20. Jahrhundert, mit einer Untersuchung des Markusevangeliums in seinem Verhältnis zur antiken Biographie." *ANRW* II 25.2: 1543–704.

Downing, F. Gerald. 1994. "A Genre for Q and a Socio-Cultural Context for Q: Comparing Sets of Similarities with Sets of Differences. *JSNT* 55: 3–26.

Drower, E.S. 1953. *The Haran Gawaita and the Baptism of Hibil-Ziwa. The Mandaic Text Reproduced Together with Translation, Notes and Commentary.* Città del Vaticano: Biblioteca Apostolica Vaticana.

Drower, E.S. 1959. *The Canonical Prayerbook of the Mandaeans.* Leiden: Brill.

Drower, E.S. 1960. *The Thousand and Twelve Questions (Alf Trisar Šuialia). A Mandaean Text edited in Transliteration and Translation.* VIOF 32. Berlin: Akademie.

Drower, E.S. 1962. *The Mandaeans of Iraq and Iran: Their Cults, Customs, Magic Legends, and Folklore.* Leiden: Brill. (Reprint of Oxford, 1937.)

Dubois, Jean-Daniel. 1982. "Le préambule de l'Apocalypse de Pierre (Nag Hammadi VII,70,14–20)." Ries et al. 384–93.

Dubois, Jean-Daniel. 1983. "L'*Apocalypse de Pierre* (Codex VII) et le Nouveau Testament." CBCo 1: 117–25.

Dubois, Jean-Daniel. 1986. "Contribution à l'interprétation de la Paraphrase de Sem." Rosenstiehl 150–60.

Dunkerley, Roderic. 1957. *Beyond the Gospels: An Investigation into the Information on the Life of Christ to be Found outside the Gospels.* Harmondsworth: Pelican.

Dunn, W. 1961. "What does 'Gospel of Truth' mean?" *VigChr* 15: 160–4.

Eckardt, A. Roy. 1992. *Reclaiming the Jesus of History: Christology Today.* Minneapolis, MN: Fortress.

Elliott, James K. 1991. "The Apocryphal Gospels." *ET* 103: 8–15.

Emmel, Stephen. 1977. "Unique Photographic Evidence for Nag Hammadi Texts: CG II 2–7, III 5 and XIII 2*." *BASPap* 14: 109–21.

Emmel, Stephen, ed. 1984. *Nag Hammadi Codex III,5: The Dialogue of the Savior.* NHS XXVI. Leiden: Brill.

Epp, Eldon J. and George W. MacRae, eds. 1989. *The New Testament and Its Modern Interpreters.* BIMI 3. Philadelphia/Atlanta, GA: Fortress/ Scholars.

Evans, Craig A. 1981a. "Jesus in Gnostic Literature." *Bib.* 62: 406–12.

Evans, Craig A. 1981b. "On the Prologue of John and the *Trimorphic Protennoia.*" *NTS* 27: 395–401.

Evans, Craig A. 1989. *Life of Jesus Research: An Annotated Bibliography.* NTTS 13. Leiden: Brill.

Evans, Craig A. 1995. *Jesus and His Contemporaries: Comparative Studies.* AGJU 25. Leiden: Brill.

Evans, Craig A. et al., eds. 1993. *Nag Hammadi Texts and the Bible: a Synopsis and Index.* NTTS 18. Leiden: Brill.

The Facsimile Edition of the Nag Hammadi Codices. Published Under the Auspices of the Department of Antiquities of the Arab Republic of Egypt in Conjunction with the United Nations Educational, Scientific and Cultural Organization. Codices I/II/III/IV/VII/VIII/XI, XII and XIII. 1972/ 1974/1976/1975/ 1972/1976/1973. Leiden: Brill. (abbrev. Facs. Ed.)

Fallon, Francis T. and Ron Cameron. 1988. "The Gospel of Thomas: A Forschungsbericht and Analysis." *ANRW* II 25.6: 4195–251.

Fieger, Michael. 1991. *Das Thomasevangelium. Einleitung, Kommentar, Systematik.* NTA 22. Münster: Aschendorff.

Filoramo, Giovanni. 1990. *A History of Gnosticism.* Trans. Anthony Alcock. Oxford: Blackwell.

Finegan, Jack. 1969. *Hidden Records of the Life of Jesus.* Philadelphia: Pilgrim.

Fischer, Karl Martin. 1973. "Der Gedanke unserer großen Kraft (Noêma). Die vierte Schrift aus Nag-Hammadi-Codex VI." *ThLZ* 98: 169–76.

Fischer, Karl Martin. 1975. "Die Paraphrase des Seem." Krause 1975a, 255–67.

Frankemölle, Hubert. 1994. *Evangelium – Begriff und Gattung. Ein Forschungsbericht.* 2nd ed. SBB 15. Stuttgart: Verlag Katholisches Bibelwerk.

Franzmann, Majella. 1990. "Strangers from Above: An Investigation of the Motif of Strangeness in the Odes of Solomon and Some Gnostic Texts." *Muséon* 103 (1990): 27–41.

Fredriksen, Paula. 1988. *From Jesus to Christ: the Origin of the New Testament Images of Jesus.* New Haven/London: Yale UP.

Funk, Robert W., Hoover, Roy W. and The Jesus Seminar. 1993. *The Five Gospels: the Search for the Authentic Words of Jesus.* N.Y.: Polebridge Press (Macmillan).

Funk, Wolf-Peter. 1975. "'Die Lehren des Silvanus'. Die vierte Schrift aus Nag-Hammadi-Codex VII." *ThLZ* 100: 7–23.

Funk, Wolf-Peter. 1976. *Die zweite Apokalypse des Jakobus aus Nag-Hammadi-Codex V.* TU 119. Berlin: Akademie-Verlag.

Funk, Wolf-Peter. 1989. "1. Koptisch-gnostische Apokalypse des Paulus." Hennecke and Schneemelcher 1989[5], 2: 628–33.

Gaffron, Hans-Georg. 1969. *Studien zum koptischen Philippusevangelium unter besonderer Berücksichtigung der Sakramente.* Bonn: Rheinische Friedrich-Wilhelms-Universität.

Gager, John G. 1974. "The Gospels and Jesus: Some Doubts About Method." *JR* 54: 244–72.

Gamble, Harry Y. 1989. "The Canon of the New Testament." Epp and MacRae 201–43.

Gärtner, Bertil. 1961. *The Theology of the Gospel of Thomas.* London: Collins.

Gero, Stephen. 1988. "Apocryphal Gospels: A Survey of Textual and Literary Problems." *ANRW* II 25.5: 3969–96.

Gianotto, Claudio. 1984. *Melchisedek e la sua tipologia. Tradizioni giudaiche, cristiane e gnostiche (sec. II a.C.–sec. III d.C.).* SRivBib 12. Brescia: Paideia Editrice.

Gibbons, Joseph A. 1972. *A Commentary on "The Second Logos of the Great Seth".* Diss., Yale University. Ann Arbor, MI: University Microfilms International.

Gibbons, Joseph A. 1973. "The Second Logos of the Great Seth: Considerations and Questions." *SBL.SP* 12: 242–57.

Gilhus, Ingvild S. 1984. "Gnosticism – A Study in Liminal Symbolism." *Numen* 31: 106–28.

Gilhus, Ingvild S. 1985. *The Nature of the Archons: A Study in the Soteriology of a Gnostic Treatise from Nag Hammadi (CG II, 4).* StOR 12. Wiesbaden: Harrassowitz.

Giversen, Søren. 1959. "Evangelium Veritatis and the Epistle to the Hebrews." *StTh* 13: 87–96.

Giversen, Søren. 1963a. *Apocryphon Johannis: The Coptic Text of the Apocryphon Johannis in the Nag Hammadi Codex II with Translation, Introduction and Commentary.* AThD 5. Copenhagen: Munksgaard.

Giversen, Søren. 1963b. "Nag Hammadi Bibliography: 1948–1963." *StTh* 17: 139–87.

Giversen, Søren, and Birger A. Pearson. 1981a. "NHC IX,1: Melchizedek." Pearson 1981, 19–85.

Giversen, Søren, and Birger A. Pearson. 1981b. "NHC IX,3: The Testimony of Truth." Pearson 1981, 101–203.

Gnilka, Joachim. 1994. *Theologie des Neuen Testaments.* HThK.S 5. Freiburg: Herder.

Goehring, James E. et al., eds. 1990a. *Gnosticism & the Early Christian World: In Honor of James M. Robinson.* Forum Fascicles 2. Sonoma, CA: Polebridge.

Goehring, James E. et al., eds. 1990b. *Gospel Origins & Christian Beginnings: In Honor of James M. Robinson.* Forum Fascicles 1. Sonoma, CA: Polebridge.

Good, Deirdre J. 1987. *Reconstructing the Tradition of Sophia in Gnostic Literature.* SBL.MS 32. Atlanta, GA: Scholars.

Grant, Robert M. 1990. *Jesus after the Gospels: The Christ of the Second Century.* London: SCM.

Green, Joel B. and Max Turner, eds. 1994. *Jesus of Nazareth: Lord and Christ. Essays on the Historical Jesus and New Testament Christology.* Grand Rapids, Michigan: Eerdmans.

Grobel, Kendrick. 1960. *The Gospel of Truth: A Valentinian Meditation on the Gospel.* London: Adam & Charles Black.

Grobel, W.K. 1962. "How Gnostic is the Gospel of Thomas?" *NTS* 8: 367–73.

Guelich, Robert. 1991. "The Gospel Genre." Stuhlmacher 1991a, 173–208.

Haardt, Robert. 1967. Rev of Böhlig and Labib 1963. *WZKM* 61: 153–9.

Haenchen, Ernst. 1961a. *Die Botschaft des Thomas–Evangeliums.* TBT 6. Berlin: Töpelmann.

Haenchen, Ernst. 1961b. "Literatur zum Thomasevangelium." *ThR* 27: 147–78, 306–38.

Haenchen, Ernst. 1973. "Die Anthropologie des Thomas-Evangeliums." *Neues Testament und christliche Existenz. Festschrift für Herbert Braun zum 70. Geburtstag am 4. Mai 1973.* Eds. Hans D. Betz and Luise Schottroff. Tübingen: Mohr (Siebeck). 207–27.

Havelaar, Henriette W. 1993. *The Coptic Apocalypse of Peter (Nag Hammadi Codex VII,3). Text Edition with translation, Commentary and Interpretative Essays.* Diss., Rijksuniversiteit, Groningen.

Hedrick, Charles. 1979. "NHC V,4: The (Second) Apocalypse of James." Parrott 1979, 105–49.

Hedrick, Charles W. 1981. "Christian Motifs in the *Gospel of the Egyptians*: Method and Motive. *NT* 23: 242–60.

Hedrick, Charles W. 1986. "Introduction: Nag Hammadi, Gnosticism, and Early Christianity – A Beginner's Guide." Hedrick and Hodgson 1–11.

Hedrick, Charles W. 1988. "Introduction: The Tyranny of the Synoptic Jesus." *Semeia* 44: 1–8.

Hedrick, Charles W., ed. 1990. *Nag Hammadi Codices XI, XII, XIII.* NHS 28. Leiden: Brill.

Hedrick, Charles W., and Robert Hodgson, Jr., eds. 1986. *Nag Hammadi, Gnosticism, and Early Christianity.* Peabody, MA: Hendrickson.

Helderman, Jan. 1978. "'In ihren Zelten...'. Bemerkungen bei Codex XIII Nag Hammadi p. 47: 14–18, im Hinblick auf Joh i 14." *Miscellanea Neotestamentica.* Eds. T. Baarda et al. NT.S 47. Leiden: Brill. 181–211.

Helderman, Jan. 1989. "Melchisedeks Wirkung. Eine traditionsgeschichtliche Untersuchung eines Motivkomplexes in NHC IX, 1,1–27,10 (*Melchisedek*)." *The New Testament in Early Christianity. La réception des écrits néotestamentaires dans le christianisme primitif.* Ed. J.-M. Sevrin. BEThL 84. Leuven: University Press/Peeters. 335–62.

Hennecke, Edgar, and Wilhelm Schneemelcher, eds., 1989⁵/1990⁶. *Neutestamentliche Apokryphen in deutscher Übersetzung.* 2 vols. Tübingen: Mohr (Siebeck).

Hoffmann, Paul. 1982³. *Studien zur Theologie der Logienquelle.* NTA NF 8. Münster: Aschendorff.

Hoffmann, R. Joseph. 1986. "Other Gospels, Heretical Christs." *Jesus in History and Myth.* Eds. R. Joseph Hoffmann and Gerald A. Larue. N.Y.: Prometheus Books. 143–55.

Hofius, Otfried. 1978. "Agrapha." *TRE* 2: 103–10.

Hofius, Otfried. 1991. "Unknown Sayings of Jesus." Stuhlmacher 1991a, 336–60.

Hollenbach, P.W. 1983. "Recent Historical Jesus Studies and the Social Sciences." *SBL.SP* 22: 61–78.

Hollenbach, P.W. 1989. "The Historical Jesus Question in North America Today." *BTB* 19: 11–22.

Horsley, Richard A. 1989. *Sociology and the Jesus Movement.* N.Y.: Crossroad.

Horsley, Richard A. 1991. "Logoi Prophētōn? Reflections on the Genre of Q." Pearson 1991a, 195–209.

Horsley, Richard A. 1994. "Wisdom Justified by All Her Children: Examining Allegedly Disparate Traditions in Q." *SBL.SP* 33: 733–51.

Jacobson, Arland D. 1987. "The History of the Composition of the Synoptics Sayings Source, Q." *SBL.SP* 26: 285–94.

Jacobson, Arland D. 1992. *The First Gospel: an Introduction to Q.* Sonoma, CA: Polebridge.

Janssens, Yvonne. 1968. "L'Évangile selon Philippe." *Muséon* 81: 79–133.

Janssens, Yvonne. 1978. *La Prôtennoia Trimorphe (NH XIII, 1).* BCNH.T 4. Québec: Les Presses de l'Université Laval.

Janssens, Yvonne. 1983. *Les Leçons de Silvanos (NH VII, 4).* BCNH.T 13. Québec: Les Presses de l'Université Laval.

Jeremias, Joachim. 1963. *Unbekannte Jesusworte. Dritte, unter Mitwirkung von Otfried Hofius völlig neu bearbeitete Auflage.* Gütersloh: Mohn.

Johnston, R.K. 1992. "Biblical Authority and Hermeneutics: The Growing Evangelical Dialogue." *SWJT* 34: 22–30.

Kasser, Rodolphe. 1961. *L'Évangile selon Thomas. Présentation et commentaire théologique.* BT(N). Neuchâtel (Suisse): Delachaux & Niestlé.

Kasser, Rodolphe. 1965. "Textes gnostiques. Remarques à propos des éditions récentes du Livre de Jean et des Apocalypses de Paul, Jacques et Adam." and "Textes gnostiques. Nouvelles remarques à propos des Apocalypses de Paul, Jacques et Adam." *Muséon* 78: 71–98, 299–306.

Kasser, Rodolphe. 1970. "L'Evangile selon Philippe." *RThPh* 20: 12–35, 82–106.

Kasser, Rodolphe, et al., eds. 1973. *Tractatus Tripartitus. Pars I. De Supernis. Codex Jung F. XXVI^r – F. LII^v (p. 51–104).* Bern: Franke.

Kasser, Rodolphe, et al., eds. 1975. *Tractatus Tripartitus. Pars II. De Creatione Hominis. Pars III. De Generibus Tribus. Codex Jung F. LII^v – F. LXX^v (p.104 – 140). Oratio Pauli Apostoli. Evangelium Veritatis: Supplementum Photographicum.* Bern: Franke.

Keck, Leander E. 1971. *A Future for the Historical Jesus: The Place of Jesus in Preaching and Theology.* London: SCM.

Kee, Howard C. 1963. "'Becoming a Child' in the Gospel of Thomas." *JBL* 82: 307–14.

Kee, Howard C. 1977. *Jesus in History: An Approach to the Study of the Gospels.* 2nd ed. N.Y.: Harcourt Brace Jovanovich.

King, Karen L., ed. 1988. *Images of the Feminine in Gnosticism.* StAC. Philadelphia: Fortress.

Kirchner, Dankwart, ed. 1977. "'Das Buch des Thomas'. Die siebte Schrift aus Nag-Hammadi-Codex II. Eingeleitet und übersetzt vom Berliner Arbeitskreis für koptisch-gnostische Schriften." *ThLZ* 102: 793–804.

Kirk, Alan. 1994. "Examining Priorities: Another Look at the Gospel of Peter's Relationship to the New Testament Gospels." *NTS* 40: 572–95.

Klauck, H.–J. 1992. "Die Dreifache Maria. Zur Rezeption von Joh 19,25 in EvPhil 32." Van Segbroeck et al., 2343–58.

Klijn, Albertus F.J. 1962. "The 'Single One' in the Gospel of Thomas." *JBL* 81: 271–8.

Klijn, Albertus F.J. 1977. *Seth in Jewish, Christian and Gnostic Literature.* NT.S 46. Leiden: Brill.

Kloppenborg, John S. 1987. *The Formation of Q: Trajectories in Ancient Wisdom Collections*. StAC. Philadelphia: Fortress.

Kloppenborg, John S. 1990. "'Easter Faith' and the Sayings Gospel Q." *Semeia* 49: 71–99.

Kloppenborg, John S. 1993. "The Sayings Gospel Q: Recent Opinion on the People behind the Document." *CR.BS* 1: 9–34.

Kloppenborg, John S. and Leif E. Vaage. 1991. "Early Christianity, Q and Jesus: The Sayings Gospel and Method in the Study of Christian Origins." *Semeia* 55: 1–14.

Koester, Helmut. 1957. "Exkurs: Der Gebrauch des Wortes εὐαγγέλιον in nachapostolischer Zeit." *Synoptische Überlieferung bei den apostolischen Vätern*. TU 65 (= 5. Reihe, Bd. 10). Berlin: Akademie. 6–12.

Koester, Helmut. 1968. "One Jesus and Four Primitive Gospels." *HTR* 61: 203–47.

Koester, Helmut. 1980. "Apocryphal and Canonical Gospels." *HTR* 73:105–30.

Koester, Helmut. 1983. "Formgeschichte/Formenkritik II. Neues Testament." *TRE* 11: 286–99.

Koester, Helmut. 1984. "Überlieferung und Geschichte der frühchristlichen Evangelienliteratur." *ANRW* II 25.2: 1463–542.

Koester, Helmut. 1986. "Gnostic Sayings and Controversy Traditions in John 8:12–59." Hedrickson and Hodgson 97–110.

Koester, Helmut. 1988. "The Extracanonical Sayings of the Lord as Products of the Christian Community." *Semeia* 44: 57–77. (Revised form of "Die ausserkanonischen Herrenworte als Produkte der christlichen Gemeinde." *ZNW* 48 [1957]: 220–37.)

Koester, Helmut. 1990. *Ancient Christian Gospels: Their History and Development*. London/Philadelphia: SCM/Trinity Press International.

Koester, Helmut. 1991. "Epilogue: Current Issues in New Testament Scholarship." Pearson 1991a, 467–76.

Koester, H. 1994a. "The Historical Jesus and the Historical Situation of the Quest: an Epilogue." Chilton and Evans 535–45.

Koester, H. 1994b. "Written Gospels or Oral Tradition?" *JBL* 113: 293–7.

Koester, Helmut and Elaine Pagels. 1984. "Introduction." Emmel 1984, 1–17.

Koschorke, Klaus. 1973. "Die 'Namen' im Philippusevangelium. Beobachtungen zur Auseinandersetzung zwischen gnostischem und kirchlichem Christentum." *ZNW* 64: 307–22.

Koschorke, Klaus. 1977. "Eine gnostische Pfingstpredigt. Zur Auseinandersetzung zwischen gnostischem und kirchlichem Christentum am Beispiel der 'Epistula Petri ad Philippum' (NHC VIII,2)." *ZThK* 74: 323–43.

Koschorke, Klaus. 1978a. "Der gnostische Traktat 'Testimonium Veritatis' aus dem Nag-Hammadi-Codex IX. Eine Übersetzung." *ZNW* 69: 91–117.

Koschorke, Klaus. 1978b. *Die Polemik der Gnostiker gegen das Kirchliche Christentum. Unter besonderer Berücksichtigung der Nag-Hammadi-Traktate "Apokalypse des Petrus" (NHC VII,3) und "Testimonium Veritatis" (NHC IX,3)*. NHS XII. Leiden: Brill.

Koschorke, Klaus. 1981. "Gnostic Instructions on the Organization of the Congregation: The Tractate Interpretation of Knowledge from CG XI." Layton 1980/81, 2: 757–69. [This is by and large a translation of Koschorke's article in *ZThK* 76 (1979): 30–60].

Krause, Martin. 1964. "Das literarische Verhältnis des Eugnostosbriefes zur Sophia Jesu Christi. Zur Auseinandersetzung der Gnosis mit dem Christentum." *Mullus. Festschrift Theodor Klauser*. JAC.E 1. Münster, Westfalen: Aschendorffsche Verlagsbuchhandlung.

Krause, Martin. 1971. "Erster Teil. Koptische Quellen aus Nag Hammadi." Krause and Rudolph 5–170.

Krause, Martin. 1973. "Die Paraphrase des Sêem." Altheim and Stiehl 2–105.

Krause, Martin, ed. 1975a. *Essays on the Nag Hammadi Texts in Honour of Pahor Labib*. NHS 6. Leiden: Brill.

Krause, Martin. 1975b. "Die Sakramente in der 'Exegese über die Seele'." Ménard 1975c, 47–55.

Krause, Martin. 1975c. "Zur Bedeutung des gnostisch-hermetischen Handschriftenfundes von Nag Hammadi." Krause 1975a, 65–89.

Krause, Martin. 1977a. "Der *Dialog des Soter* in Codex III von Nag Hammadi." Krause 1977b, 13–34.

Krause, Martin, ed. 1977b. *Gnosis and Gnosticism. Papers Read at the Seventh International Conference on Patristic Studies (Oxford, September 8th–13th 1975)*. NHS 8. Leiden: Brill.

Krause, Martin. 1983. "The Christianization of Gnostic Texts." Logan and Wedderburn 187–94.

Krause, Martin and Viktor Girgis. 1973. "Die Petrusapokalypse." Altheim and Stiehl 152–79.

Krause, Martin and Pahor Labib, eds. 1962. *Die drei Versionen des Apokryphon des Johannes im koptischen Museum zu Alt-Kairo.* ADAI.K 1. Wiesbaden: Harrassowitz.

Krause, Martin and Pahor Labib. 1971. *Gnostische und hermetische Schriften aus Codex II und Codex VI.* ADAI.K 2. Glückstadt: Augustin.

Krause, Martin and Kurt Rudolph. 1971. *Die Gnosis. Bd. II: Koptische und mandäische Quellen.* BAW.AC. Zürich/ Stuttgart: Artemis.

Kuntzmann, Raymond. 1981. "L'identification dans le *Livre de Thomas l'Athlète.*" Barc 1981, 279–87.

Kuntzmann, Raymond. 1986. *Le Livre de Thomas (NH II,7).* BCNH.T 16. Québec: Les Presses de l'Université Laval.

Kuntzmann, Raymond. 1993. "Le Temple dans le Corpus copte de Nag Hammadi." *RevSR* 69: 15–37.

Kümmel, Werner G. 1965/66. "Jesusforschung seit 1950." *ThR* 31: 15–46, 289–315.

Kümmel, Werner G. 1975. "Ein Jahrzehnt Jesusforschung (1965–1975)." *ThR* 40: 289–336.

Kümmel, Werner G. 1981. "Jesusforschung seit 1965: Nachträge 1975–1980 (Teil 1 und 2)." *ThR* 46: 317–63.

Kümmel, Werner G. 1988. "Jesusforschung seit 1981, I. Forschungsgeschichte, Methodenfragen." *ThR* 53: 229–49.

[The Kümmel articles from 1965–1982 are collected in Kümmel, Werner Georg. 1985. *Dreißig Jahre Jesusforschung (1950–1980).* Ed. Helmut Merklein. BBB 60. Bonn: Hanstein; second edition, 1994. *Vierzig Jahre Jesusforschung (1950–1990).* Ed. Helmut Merklein. BBB 91. Weinheim: Beltz Athenäem Verlag.]

Lampe, G.W.H. 1961. *A Patristic Greek Lexicon.* Oxford: Clarendon.

Lampe, Peter, and Ulrich Luz. 1991. "Overview of the Discussion." Stuhlmacher 1991a, 387–404.

Lattke, Michael. 1978. "Bibliographie." Leroy, Herbert. *Jesus: Überlieferung und Deutung*. EdF 95. Darmstadt: Wissenschaftliche Buchgesellschaft. 139–54.

Lattke, Michael. 1979. "Neue Aspekte der Frage nach dem historischen Jesus." *Kairos* NF 21: 288–99.

Layton, Bentley. 1974. "The Hypostasis of the Archons, or *The Reality of the Rulers*." *HTR* 67: 351–425.

Layton, Bentley, ed. 1980/1. *The Rediscovery of Gnosticism: Proceedings of the International Conference on Gnosticism at Yale, New Haven, Connecticut March 28–31, 1978*. SHR 41. 2 vols. Leiden: Brill.

Layton, Bentley, ed. 1987. *The Gnostic Scriptures*. Garden City, N.Y.: Doubleday.

Layton, Bentley, ed. 1989. *Nag Hammadi Codex II,2–7 together with XIII,2*, Brit. Lib. Or.4926(1), and P. Oxy. 1, 654, 655*. NHS 20. 2 vols. Leiden: Brill.

Layton, Bentley, ed. and Wesley W. Isenberg, trans. 1989. "The Gospel according to Philip." Layton 1989, 1: 142–215.

Leipoldt, Johannes. 1967. *Das Evangelium nach Thomas. Koptisch und Deutsch*. TU 101. Berlin: Akademie.

Lelyveld, Margaretha. 1987. *Les logia de la vie dans l'Évangile selon Thomas. À la recherche d'une tradition et d'une rédaction*. NHS 34. Leiden: Brill.

Liddell, Henry George and Robert Scott. 1925–40⁹. *A Greek-English Lexicon*. Revised and augmented by Henry Stuart Jones. 2 vols. Oxford: Clarendon.

Lidzbarski, M. 1915. *Das Johannesbuch der Mandäer*. Giessen: Töpelmann.

Lidzbarski, M. 1925. *Ginzā. Der Schatz oder das grosse Buch der Mandäer*. Göttingen/Leipzig: Vandenhoeck & Ruprecht/Hinrichs'sche Buchhandlung.

Lincoln, Bruce. 1977. "Thomas-Gospel and Thomas-Community: A New Approach to a Familiar Text." *NT* 19: 65–76.

Livingstone, Elizabeth A., ed. 1976. *Studia Patristica. Vol. XIV. Part III*. TU 117. Berlin: Akademie-Verlag.

Livingstone, Elizabeth A., ed. 1982. *Studia Patristica. Vol. XVII in Three Parts. Part One*. Oxford: Pergamon.

Logan, Alistair H.B. and A.J.M. Wedderburn. 1983. *The New Testament and Gnosis: Essays in Honor of Robert McL Wilson.* Edinburgh: T. & T. Clark.

Lührmann, Dieter. 1969. *Die Redaktion der Logienquelle.* WMANT 33. Neukirchen-Vluyn: Neukirchener Verlag.

McDonald, James I.H. 1980. "New Quest – Dead End? So What about the Historical Jesus?" *Studia Biblica 1978. II. Papers on the Gospels. Sixth International Congress on Bibical Studies, Oxford 3–7 April, 1978.* Ed. Elizabeth A. Livingstone. JSNT.S 2. Sheffield: JSOT Press. 151–70.

Mack, Burton L. 1988. *A Myth of Innocence: Mark and Christian Origins.* Philadelphia: Fortress.

Mack, Burton L. 1990a. "All the Extra Jesuses: Christian Origins in the Light of the Extra-Canonical Gospels." *Semeia* 49: 169–76.

Mack, Burton L. 1990b. "Lord of the Logia: Savior or Sage?" Goehring et al. 1990b, 3–18.

Mack, Burton L. 1991. "Q and the Gospel of Mark: Revising Christian Origins." *Semeia* 55: 15–39.

Mack, Burton L. 1992. "The Christ and Jewish Wisdom." Charlesworth 1992, 192-221.

Macklin, Robert. 1990. *The Secret Life of Jesus.* Sydney/London: Pan Books.

McLean, Bradley H. 1995. "On the Gospel of Thomas and Q." Piper 321–45.

McNeil, Brian. 1978. "New Light on Gospel of Philip 17." *JThS* 29: 143–6.

MacRae, George W. 1965. "The Coptic Gnostic Apocalypse of Adam." *HeyJ* 6: 27–35.

MacRae, George W. 1979. "NHC V,5: The Apocalypse of Adam." Parrott 1979, 151–95.

Mahé, J.-P. 1983. " ʾΟΜΟΛΟΓÍΑ: Témoignage et martyre dans le valentinisme et dans le *Témoignage de Vérité.*" *CBCo* 1: 126–39.

Malinine, Michel, et al., eds. 1956. *Evangelium Veritatis. Codex Jung f. VIIIᵛ–XVIᵛ (p. 16–32) / f. XIXʳ–XXIIʳ (p. 37–43).* Zürich: Rascher.

Malinine, Michel, et al., eds. 1963. *De Resurrectione (Epistula ad Rheginum). Codex Jung F. XXIIʳ–F. XXVᵛ (p. 43–50).* Zürich/Stuttgart: Rascher.

Meier, John P. 1991/1994. *A Marginal Jew: Rethinking the Historical Jesus.*
2 Vols. ABRL. N.Y.: Doubleday.

Ménard, Jacques-É. 1972. *L'Évangile de Vérité.* NHS 2. Leiden: Brill.

Ménard, Jacques-É. 1975a. "L''Évangile selon Philippe' et l''Exégèse de
l'âme'." Ménard 1975c, 56–67.

Ménard, Jacques-É. 1975b. *L'Évangile selon Thomas.* NHS 5. Leiden: Brill.

Ménard, Jacques-É, ed. 1975c. *Les textes de Nag Hammadi. Colloque du
Centre d'Histoire des Religions (Strasbourg 23–25 octobre 1974).* NHS 7.
Leiden: Brill.

Ménard, Jacques-É. 1977. *La Lettre de Pierre à Philippe.* BCNH.T 1. Québec: Les Presses de l'Université Laval.

Ménard, Jacques-É. 1983. *Le Traité sur la Résurrection (NH I,4).* BCNH.T
12. Québec: Les Presses de l'Université Laval.

Ménard, Jacques-É. 1985. *L'Exposé valentinien. Les Fragments sur le baptême et sur l'eucharistie.* BCNH.T 14. Québec: Les Presses de l'Université
Laval.

Ménard, Jacques-É. 1988[2]. *L'Évangile selon Philippe: introduction, texte –
traduction, commentaire.* Gnostica. Paris: Cariscript.

Meyer, Marvin W. 1981. *The Letter of Peter to Philip. Text, translation and
commentary.* SBL.DS 53. Chico, CA: Scholars.

Meyer, Marvin W. 1985. "Making Mary Male: The Categories 'Male' and
'Female' in the Gospel of Thomas." *NTS* 31: 554–70.

Meyer, Marvin W. 1990. "The Beginning of the Gospel of Thomas." *Semeia*
52: 161–73.

Meyer, Marvin W. and Frederik Wisse. 1991. "NHC VIII,2: *Letter of Peter
to Philip.*" Sieber 227–51.

Migne, J.-P., ed. 1863. *S. Cyrillus Alexandrinus. Opera quae reperiri potu-
erunt omnia.* T. 7. PG 74. Paris: Migne.

Morard, Françoise. 1980. "Encore quelques réflexions sur Monachos."
VigChr 34, 395–401.

Mortley, Raoul. 1992. "'The Name of the Father is the Son' (Gospel of Truth
38)." Wallis 239–52.

Mueller, Dieter. 1985a. "Prayer of the Apostle Paul: I,1:A.1–B.10." Attridge 1985a, 5–11.

Mueller, Dieter. 1985b. "The Prayer of the Apostle Paul: I,1:A.1–B.10." Attridge 1985b, 1–5.

Murdock, William R. and George W. MacRae. 1979. "NHC V,2: The Apocalypse of Paul." Parrott 1979, 47–63.

Nagel, Peter, ed. 1974. *Studia Coptica*. BBA 45. Berlin: Akademie-Verlag.

Nagel, Peter, ed. 1979. *Studien zum Menschenbild in Gnosis und Manichäismus*. Wissentschaftliche Beiträge, Martin-Luther-Universität, Halle-Wittenberg 39 (K 5). Halle (Saale).

Nagel, Peter. 1995. "Die Abhandlung über die Auferstehung." Draft translation with notes, given by Nagel to the author, 8.8.95.

Orbe, Antonio. 1965. Rev. of Böhlig and Labib 1963. *Gr.* 46: 169–72.

Orbe, Antonio. 1976. *Cristología Gnóstica. Introducción a la soteriología de los siglos II y III*. BAC 384. 2 vols. Madrid: Biblioteca de Autores Cristianos.

Orlandi, Tito. 1992. *Evangelium Veritatis*. Testi del Vicino Oriente antico 8/2. Brescia: Paideia.

Pagels, Elaine H. 1979. *The Gnostic Gospels*. N.Y.: Random House.

Pagels, Elaine H. 1988. "Pursuing the Spiritual Eve: Imagery and Hermeneutics in the *Hypostasis of the Archons* and the *Gospel of Philip*." King 187–206.

Pagels, Elaine H. and John D. Turner. 1990a. "NHC XI,1: The Interpretation of Knowledge." Hedrick 1990, 21–88.

Pagels, Elaine H. and John D. Turner. 1990b. "NHC XI,2: A Valentinian Exposition with 2a: On the Anointing; 2b,c: On Baptism A and B; 2d,e: On the Eucharist A and B." Hedrick 1990, 89–172.

Painchaud, Louis. 1981. "La polémique anti-ecclésiale et l'exégèse de la passion dans le *Deuxième Traité du Grand Seth*." Barc 1981, 340–51.

Painchaud, Louis. 1982. *Le Deuxième Traité du Grand Seth (NH VII, 2)*. BCNH.T 6. Québec: Les Presses de l'Université Laval.

Parrott, Douglas M., ed. 1979. *Nag Hammadi Codices V,2–5 and VI with Papyrus Berolinensis 8502,1 and 4*. NHS 11. Leiden: Brill.

Parrott, Douglas M. 1988. "Eugnostos the Blessed (III,3 and V,1) and The Sophia of Jesus Christ (III,4 and BG 8502,3)." Robinson, J.M. 1988³, 220–43.

Parrott, Douglas M., ed. 1991. *Nag Hammadi Codices III,3–4 and V,1 with Papyrus Berolinensis 8502,3 and Oxyrhynchus Papyrus 1081: Eugnostos and the Sophia of Jesus Christ*. NHS 27. Leiden: Brill.

Partrick, Theodore Hall. 1969. *Jesus of Nazareth in Second-Century Gnosticism*. Diss., University of Chicago.

Pasquier, Anne. 1988. "Prouneikos. A Colorful Expression to Designate Wisdom in Gnostic Texts." King 47–66.

Passow, Franz. 1970. *Handwörterbuch der griechischen Sprache*. (Photographic reproduction of Leipzig 1852.) Darmstadt: Wissenschaftliche Buchgesellschaft.

Patterson, Stephen J. 1990. "The Gospel of Thomas and the Historical Jesus: *Retrospectus* and *Prospectus*". *SBL.SP* 29: 614–36.

Patterson, Stephen J. 1991. "Paul and the Jesus Tradition: It Is Time for Another Look." *HTR* 84: 23–41.

Patterson, Stephen J. 1992. "The Gospel of Thomas and the Synoptic Tradition: A Forschungsbericht and Critique." *FF.F* 8: 45–97.

Patterson, Stephen J. 1993. *The Gospel of Thomas and Jesus: Thomas Christianity, Social Radicalism, and the Quest of the Historical Jesus*. FF.RS. Sonoma, CA: Polebridge.

Pearson, Birger A. 1975. "The Figure of Melchizedek in the First Tractate of the Unpublished Coptic-Gnostic Codex IX from Nag Hammadi." Eds. C. Jouco Bleeker et al. *Proceedings of the XIIth International Congress of the International Association for the History of Religions*. SHR 31. Leiden: Brill. 200–8.

Pearson, Birger A., ed. 1981. *Nag Hammadi Codices IX and X*. NHS 15. Leiden: Brill.

Pearson, Birger A. 1986. "The Problem of 'Jewish Gnostic' Literature." Hedrick and Hodgson 15–35.

Pearson, Birger A., ed. 1991a. *The Future of Early Christianity: Essays in Honor of Helmut Koester*. Minneapolis, MN: Fortress.

Pearson, Birger A. 1991b. "Pre-Valentinian Gnosticism in Alexandria." Pearson 1991a, 455–66.

Peel, Malcolm L. 1979. "The 'Descensus ad Inferos' in 'The Teachings of Silvanus' (CG VII, 4)." *Numen* 26: 23–49.

Peel, Malcolm L. 1985a. "The Treatise on the Resurrection: I,4:43.25–50.18." Attridge 1985a, 123–57.

Peel, Malcolm L. 1985b. "The Gospel of Truth: I,4:43.25–50.18." Attridge 1985b, 137–215.

Perkins, Pheme. 1971. "The Soteriology of Sophia of Jesus Christ." *SBL.SP* 10: 165–77.

Perkins, Pheme. 1980. *The Gnostic Dialogue: The Early Church and the Crisis of Gnosticism*. Theological Inquiries. New York: Paulist.

Perkins, Pheme. 1981a. "Gnostic Christologies and the New Testament." *CBQ* 43: 590–606.

Perkins, Pheme. 1981b. "Logos Christologies in the Nag Hammadi Codices." *VigChr* 35: 379–96.

Perkins, Pheme. 1990. "John's Gospel and Gnostic Christologies: The Nag Hammadi Evidence." *AThR.S* 11: 68–76.

Perkins, Pheme. 1991. "New Testament Christologies in Gnostic Transformation." Pearson 1991a, 433–41.

Perkins, Pheme. 1992. Rev. of Grant 1990. *CBQ* 54: 153–4.

Perkins, Pheme. 1993a. *Gnosticism and the New Testament*. Minneapolis: Fortress.

Perkins, Pheme. 1993b. "Jesus before Christianity: Cynic and Sage?" *CCen* July 28–August 4. 749–51.

Pétrement, Simone. 1990. *A Separate God: The Christian Origins of Gnosticism*. Trans. C. Harrison. San Francisco: Harper.

Piper, Ronald A. 1995. *The Gospel behind the Gospels: Current Studies on Q*. NT.S 75. Leiden: Brill.

Poehlmann, William R. 1974. *Addressed Wisdom Teaching in The Teachings of Silvanus: A Form Critical Study*. Diss., Harvard University.

Poirier, Paul-Hubert. 1983. "La *Prôtennoia Trimorphe* (NH XIII, 1) et le vocabulaire du *Descensus ad inferos*." *Muséon* 96: 193–204.

Polkow, D. 1987. "Method and Criteria for Historical Jesus Research." *SBL.SP* 26: 336–56.

Polotsky, Hans J. 1987. *Grundlagen des koptischen Satzbaus: Erste Hälfte.* ASP 28. Decatur, GA: Scholars.

Porcarelli, Andrea. 1993. "Immagini di Gesù Cristo nello gnosticismo antico." *Sette e Religioni* 12: 59–91.

Puech, Henri-Charles. 1963. "Notes critiques." Malinine et al. 1963, 19–48.

Quecke, Hans. 1962. "Eine mißbräuchliche Verwendung des Qualitativs im Koptischen." *Muséon* 75: 291–300.

Quispel, Gilles. 1967. *Makarius, das Thomasevangelium und das Lied von der Perle.* NT.S 15. Leiden: Brill.

Quispel, Gilles. 1975. "Genius and Spirit." Krause 1975a, 155–69.

Reumann, John. 1989. "Jesus and Christology." Epp and MacRae 501–64.

Rewolinski, Edward T. 1978. *The Use of Sacramental Language in the Gospel of Philip (Cairensis Gnosticus II,3).* Diss., Harvard University.

Richardson, Cyril. 1973. "The Gospel of Thomas: Gnostic or Enratite?" *Heritage of the Early Church: Essays in Honor of Georges Vasilievich Florovsky.* Eds. David Neiman and Margaret Schatkin. OrChrA 195. Rome: Pont. Institutum Studiorum Orientalium. 65–76.

Ries, Julien, et al., eds. 1982. *Gnosticisme et monde hellénistique. Actes du Colloque de Louvain-la-Neuve (11–14 mars 1980).* PIOL 27. Louvain-la-Neuve: Université Catholique de Louvain, Institut Orientaliste.

Roberge, Michel. 1992. "La crucifixion du Sauveur dans la paraphrase de Sem (NH VII,1)." *Actes du IVe Congrès Copte, Louvain-la-Neuve, 5–10 septembre 1988. II. De la linguistique au gnosticisme.* PIOL 41. Louvain-la-Neuve: Université Catholique de Louvain, Institut Orientaliste. 381–7.

Roberge, Michel and Frederik Wisse. 1988. "The Paraphrase of Shem (VII,1)." Robinson, J.M. 1988[3], 339–61.

Robinson, Gesine (see also Schenke, Gesine).

Robinson, Gesine. 1990. "The Trimorphic Protennoia and the Prologue of the Fourth Gospel." Goehring et al. 1990a, 37–50.

Robinson, James M. 1975. "Jesus as Sophos and Sophia: Wisdom Tradition and the Gospels." Wilken 1-16.

Robinson, James M. 1979. "Getting the Nag Hammadi Library into English." *BA* 42: 239–48.

Robinson, James M. 1981. "Sethians and Johannine Thought: The *Trimor-phic Protennoia* and the Prologue of the Gospel of John." Layton 1981, 2: 643–63.

Robinson, James M. 1982. "Jesus: From Easter to Valentinus (or to the Apostles' Creed)." *JBL* 101: 5–37.

Robinson, James M., ed. 1984[2]/1988[3]. *The Nag Hammadi Library in English*. Leiden: Brill.

Robinson, James M. 1986. "On Bridging the Gulf from Q to the Gospel of Thomas (or Vice Versa)." Hedrick and Hodgson 127–75.

Robinson, James M. 1988. "The Study of the Historical Jesus after Nag Hammadi." *Semeia* 44: 45–55.

Robinson, James M. 1991. "The Q Trajectory: Between John and Matthew via Jesus." Pearson 1991a, 173–94.

Robinson, James M. 1994. "Die Bedeutung der gnostischen Nag-Hammadi Texte für die neutestamentliche Wissenschaft." *Religious Propaganda and Missionary Competition in the New Testament World. Essays Honoring Dieter Georgi*. Eds. Lukas Bormann et al. Leiden: Brill. 23–41.

Rosenstiehl, Jean-Marc, ed. 1986. *Deuxième Journée d'Études Coptes (Strasbourg 25 mai 1984)*. CBCo 3. Louvain/Paris: Peeters.

Rouleau, Donald, and Lucien Roy. 1987. *L'épître apocryphe de Jacques (NH I,2). L'acte de Pierre (BG4)*. BCNH.T 18. Québec: Les Presses de l'Université Laval.

Rudolph, Kurt. 1965. Rev. of Böhlig and Labib 1963. *ThLZ* 90: 359–62.

Rudolph, Kurt. 1969. "Gnosis und Gnostizismus, ein Forschungsbericht." *ThR* 34: 121–211, 358–61.

Rudolph, Kurt. 1971. "Gnosis und Gnostizismus, ein Forschungsbericht." *ThR* 36: 1–61, 89–124.

Rudolph, Kurt. 1972. "Gnosis und Gnostizismus, ein Forschungsbericht." *ThR* 37: 289–360.

Rudolph, Kurt. 1973. "Gnosis und Gnostizismus, ein Forschungsbericht." *ThR* 38: 1–25.

Rudolph, Kurt. 1975. "Coptica-Mandaica. Zu einigen Übereinstimmungen zwischen koptisch-gnostischen und mandäischen Texten." Krause 1975a, 191–216.

BIBLIOGRAPHY 239

Rudolph, Kurt. 1979. "Zur Soziologie, soziologischen 'Verortung' und Rolle der Gnosis in der Spätantike." Nagel 1979, 19–29.

Rudolph, Kurt. 1983. "'Gnosis' and 'Gnosticism' – the Problems of Their Definition and Their Relation to the Writings of the New Testament." Logan and Wedderburn 21–37.

Rudolph, Kurt. 1985. "Die Nag Hammadi-Texte und ihre Bedeutung für die Gnosisforschung." ThR 50: 1–40.

Rudolph, Kurt. 1990. "Die Gnosis: Texte und Übersetzungen." ThR 55: 113–52.

Sanders, E.P. 1993. The Historical Figure of Jesus. London: Allen Lane, The Penguin Press.

Sato, Migaku. 1987. Q und Prophetie: Studien zur Gattungs- und Traditionsgeschichte der Quelle Q. WUNT 2/29. Tübingen: Mohr (Siebeck).

Schenke, Gesine. 1984. Die dreigestaltige Protennoia (Nag-Hammadi-Codex XIII). TU 132. Berlin: Akademie.

Schenke, Hans-Martin. 1959a. Die Herkunft des sogenannten Evangelium Veritatis. Göttingen: Vandenhoeck & Ruprecht.

Schenke, Hans-Martin. 1959b. "Vom Ursprung der Welt. Eine titellose gnostische Abhandlung aus dem Funde von Nag-Hamadi." ThLZ 84: 243–56.

Schenke, Hans-Martin. 1960. "Das Evangelium nach Philippus. Ein Evangelium der Valentinianer aus dem Funde von Nag-Hamadi." Leipoldt and Schenke 1960, 31–65 (cf. ThLZ 84 [1959]: 1–26).

Schenke, Hans-Martin. 1962a. Der Gott "Mensch" in der Gnosis: Ein religionsgeschichtlicher Beitrag zur Diskussion über die paulinische Anschauung von der Kirche als Leib Christi. Göttingen: Vandenhoeck & Ruprecht.

Schenke, Hans-Martin. 1962b. "Nag-Hamadi Studien II: Das System der Sophia Jesu Christi." ZRGG 14: 263–78.

Schenke, Hans-Martin. 1966. Rev. of Böhlig and Labib 1963. OLZ 61: 23–34.

Schenke, Hans-Martin. 1971. "Der Jakobusbrief aus dem Codex Jung." OLZ 66: 117–30.

Schenke, Hans-Martin. 1973. "'Die Taten des Petrus und der zwölf Apostle'. Die erste Schrift aus Nag-Hammadi-Codex VI." ThLZ 98: 13–19.

Schenke, Hans-Martin. 1975a. "Bemerkungen zur Apokalypse des Petrus." Krause 1975a, 277–85.

Schenke, Hans-Martin. 1975b. "Sprachliche und exegetische Probleme in den beiden letzten Schriften des Codex II von Nag Hammadi." *OLZ* 70: 5–13.

Schenke, Hans-Martin. 1975c. "Zur Faksimile-Ausgabe der Nag-Hammadi-Schriften." *ZÄS* 102: 123–38.

Schenke, Hans-Martin. 1979. Rev. of Böhlig and Wisse. *OLZ* 74: 17–23.

Schenke, Hans-Martin. 1980. "Die jüdische Melchisedek-Gestalt als Thema der Gnosis." *Altes Testament – Frühjudentum – Gnosis. Neue Studien zu 'Gnosis und Bibel'.* Ed. Karl-Wolfgang Tröger. Gütersloh: Mohn. 111–36.

Schenke, Hans-Martin. 1983. "The Book of Thomas (NHC II. 7): a Revision of a Pseudepigraphical Letter of Jacob the Contender." Logan and Wedderburn 213–28.

Schenke, Hans-Martin. 1989a. "Das Evangelium nach Philippus." Hennecke and Schneemelcher 1989⁵, 1: 148–73.

Schenke, Hans-Martin. 1989b. "Die Taten des Petrus und der zwölf Apostel." Hennecke and Schneemelcher 1989⁵, 2: 368–80.

Schenke, Hans-Martin. 1989c. *Das Thomas-Buch (Nag Hammadi-Codex II,7). Neu herausgegeben, übersetzt und erklärt.* TU 138. Berlin: Akademie.

Schmidt, Carl, ed. 1978. *The Books of Jeu and the Untitled Text in the Bruce Codex.* Trans. Violet Macdermot. NHS 13. Leiden: Brill.

Schoedel, William R. and Douglas M. Parrott. 1988. "The (First) Apocalypse of James (V,3)." Robinson, J.M. 1988³, 260–8.

Scholer, David. 1971. *Nag Hammadi Bibliography 1948–1969.* NHS 1. Leiden: Brill.[1]

Scholer, David. 1990. "Q Bibliography Supplement I: 1990." *SBL.SP* 29: 11–13.

Scholten, Clemens. 1987. *Martyrium und Sophiamythos im Gnostizismus nach den Texten von Nag Hammadi.* JAC.E 14. Münster, Westfalen: Aschendorffsche Verlagsbuchhandlung.

---

[1] See the ongoing work by Scholer in the Supplements to the bibliography which appear each year in *NT*, beginning from 13, 1971.

Schrage, Wolfgang. 1964. *Das Verhältnis des Thomas-Evangeliums zur synoptischen Tradition und zu den koptischen Evangelienübersetzungen. Zugleich ein Beitrag zur gnostischen Synoptikerdeutung.* BZNW 29. Berlin: Töpelmann.

Schulz, Siegfried. 1972. *Q: Die Spruchquelle der Evangelisten.* Zürich: Theologischer Verlag.

Schweizer, Eduard. 1974. "The 'Matthean' Church." *NTS* 20: 216.

Schweizer, Eduard. 1987. "Jesus Christus I. Neues Testament." *TRE* 16: 671–726.

Schwertner, Siefried M. 1992². *IATG²: Internationales Abkürzungsverzeichnis für Theologie und Grezgebiete.* 2nd ed. Berlin/N.Y.: de Gruyter.

Scopello, Maddalena. 1985. *L'Exégèse de l'âme. Nag Hammadi Codex II,6. Introduction, traduction et commentaire.* NHS 25. Leiden: Brill.

Seeley, D. 1992. "Jesus' Death in Q." *NTS* 38: 222–34.

Sell, Jesse. 1979. "Simon Peter's 'Confession' and *The Acts of Peter and the Twelve Apostles.*" *NT* 21: 344–6.

Sell, Jesse. 1982. *The Knowledge of the Truth – Two Doctrines: The Book of Thomas the Contender (CG II,7) and the False Teachers in the Pastoral Epistles.* EHS.T 194. Frankfurt am Main/Bern: Peter Lang.

Sevrin, Jean-Marie. 1974. "Les noces spirituelles dans l'Évangile selon Philippe." *Muséon* 87: 143–93.

Sevrin, Jean-Marie. 1975. "A propos de la 'Paraphrase de Sem'." *Muséon* 88: 69–96.

Sevrin, Jean-Marie. 1983. *L'Exégèse de l'âme (NH II,6).* BCNH.T 9. Québec: Les Presses de l'Université Laval.

Sevrin, Jean-Marie. 1985. *Le dossier baptismal séthien. Études sur la sacramentaire gnostique.* DGMFT Ser. 4, T. 5. Louvain-la-Neuve.

Sieber, John H., ed. 1991. *Nag Hammadi Codex VIII.* NHS 31. Leiden: Brill.

Siegert, Folker. 1982. *Nag-Hammadi-Register. Wörterbuch zur Erfassung der Begriffe in den koptisch-gnostischen Schriften von Nag-Hammadi mit einem deutschen Index.* WUNT 26. Tübingen: J.C.B. Mohr (Paul Siebeck).

Siker, Jeffrey S. 1989. "Gnostic Views on Jews and Christians in the Gospel of Philip." *NT* 31: 275–88.

Smith, Jonathan Z. 1965/66. "The Garments of Shame." *HR* 5: 217–38.

Smith, Jonathan Z. 1982. "Sacred Persistence: Towards a Redescription of the Canon." *Imagining Religion*. Chicago Studies in the History of Judaism. Chicago: University of Chicago. 36–52.

Smith, Jonathan Z. 1990. *Drudgery Divine: On the Comparison of Early Christianities and the Religions of Late Antiquity*. London: School of Oriental and African Studies.

Stanton, Graham N. 1977. "5 Ezra and Matthean Christianity in the Second Century." *JThS* 28: 67–83.

Stanton, Graham N. 1989. *The Gospel and Jesus*. Oxford Bible Series. Oxford: University Press.

Stegemann, Viktor. 1934. *Die Gestalt Christi in den koptischen Zaubertexten*. Quellen und Studien zur Geschichte und Kultur des Altertums und des Mittelalters 1: Reihe D, Untersuchungen und Mitteilungen. Heidelberg: Bilabel.

Stroker, W.D. 1988. "Extracanonical Parables and the Historical Jesus." *Semeia* 44: 95–120.

Stroumsa, Gedaliahu A.G. 1984. *Another Seed: Studies in Gnostic Mythology*. NHS 24. Leiden: Brill.

Strutwolf, Holger. 1993. *Gnosis als System. Zur Rezeption der valentinianischen Gnosis bei Origenes*. FKDG 56. Göttingen: Vandenhoeck & Ruprecht.

Stuhlmacher, Peter, ed. 1991a. *The Gospel and the Gospels*. Grand Rapids, Michigan: Eerdmans. (originally published as *Das Evangelium und die Evangelien. Vorträger vom Tübinger Symposium 1982*. WUNT 28. Tübingen: Mohr [Siebeck], 1983).

Stuhlmacher, Peter. 1991b. "The Theme: The Gospel and the Gospels." Stuhlmacher 1991a, 1–25.

Sumney, Jerry L. 1992. "The *Teachings of Silvanus* as a Gnostic work." *SR* 21: 191–206.

Talbert, Charles H. 1988. "Once Again: Gospel Genre." *Semeia* 43: 53–73.

Tardieu, Michel. 1981. "'Comme à travers un tuyau'. Quelques remarques sur le mythe valentinien de la chair céleste du Christ." Barc 1981, 151–77.

Tardieu, Michel and Jean-Daniel Dubois, eds. 1986. *Introduction à la littérature gnostique. I. Histoire du mot 'gnostique', Instruments de travail, Collections retrouvées avant 1945.* ICA. Paris: Éditions du CERF/Éditions du C.N.R.S.

Telford, William R. 1994. "Major Trends and Interpretive Issues in the Study of Jesus." Chilton and Evans 33–74.

Thatcher, Tom. 1994. "The Gospel Genre: What Are We After?" *RestQ* 36: 129–38.

Thomassen, Einar. 1989a. *Le Traité Tripartite (NH I,5). Texte établi, introduit et commenté par Einar Thomassen. Traduit par Louis Painchaud et Einar Thomassen.* BCNH.T 19. Québec: Les Presses de l'Université Laval.

Thomassen, Einar. 1989b. "The Valentinianism of the Valentinian Exposition (NHC XI,2)." *Muséon* 102: 225–36.

Thomassen, Einar. 1993. "Gnostic Semiotics: The Valentinian Notion of the Name." *Tem.* 29: 141–56.

Till, Walter C. 1955. *Die gnostischen Schriften des koptischen Papyrus Berolinensis 8502.* TU 60 (= 5. Reihe, Bd. 5). Berlin: Akademie-Verlag.

Till, Walter C. 1959. "Das Evangelium der Wahrheit: Neue Übersetzung des vollständigen Textes." *ZNW* 50: 165–85.

Till, Walter C. 1963. *Das Evangelium nach Philippos.* PTS 2. Berlin: de Gruyter.

Trautmann, Catherine. 1981. "La parenté dans l'*Évangile selon Philippe.*" Barc 1981, 267–78.

Trautmann, Catherine. 1986. "Le schème de la croix dans l'Évangile selon Philippe (NH II,3)." Rosenstiehl 123–9.

Trevijano, Ramón. 1989. "La Madre de Jesús en el Evangelio de Tomás (Logg. 55, 99, 101 y 105)." *RCatT* 14: 257–66. (?)

Tröger, Karl-Wolfgang. 1975. "Der zweite Logos des großen Seth: Gedanken zur Christologie in der zweiten Schrift des Codex VII." Krause 1975a, 268–76.

Tröger, Karl-Wolfgang. 1978. *Die Passion Jesu Christi in der Gnosis nach den Schriften von Nag Hammadi.* 2 vols. Diss. (Habil.), Humboldt-Universität, Berlin.

Tröger, Karl-Wolfgang. 1991. "Jesus, the Koran, and Nag Hammadi." *ThD* 38: 213–18.

Tuckett, Christopher M. 1982. "Synoptic Tradition in Some Nag Hammadi and Related Texts." *VigChr* 36: 173–90.

Tuckett, Christopher M. 1984. "Synoptic Tradition in the Gospel of Truth and the Testimony of Truth." *JThS* 35: 131–45.

Tuckett, Christopher M. 1986. *Nag Hammadi and the Gospel Tradition: Synoptic Tradition in the Nag Hammadi Library.* Edinburgh: T. & T. Clark.

Tuckett, Christopher M. 1991. "Q and Thomas: Evidence of a Primitive 'Wisdom Gospel'? A Response to H. Koester." *EThL* 67: 346–60.

Turner, John D. 1975. *The Book of Thomas the Contender from Codex II of the Cairo Gnostic Library from Nag Hammadi (CG II,7): The Coptic Text with Translation, Introduction and Commentary.* SBL.DS 23. Missoula, Montana: Scholars Press and the Society of Biblical Literature.

Turner, John D. 1990. "NHC XIII,1: Trimorphic Protennoia." Hedrick 1990, 371–454.

Turner, John D. 1994. "Ritual in Gnosticism." *SBL.SP* 33: 136–81.

Turner, Victor W. 1969. *The Ritual Process: Structure and Anti-Structure.* London: Routledge & Kegan Paul.

Van Segbroeck, F. et al., eds. 1992. *The Four Gospels, 1992. Festschrift Frans Neirynck.* BETL 100. 3 vols. Leuven: University Press/Peeters.

Van Unnik, W.C. 1963/64. "Three Notes on the 'Gospel of Philip'." *NTS* 10: 465–9.

Veilleux, Armand. 1986. *La première apocalypse de Jacques (NH V,3). La seconde apocalypse de Jacques (NH V,4).* BCNH.T 17. Québec: Les Presses de l'Université Laval.

Vögelin, Eric. 1974. *Order and History. Vol. 4: The Ecumenic Age.* Baton Rouge: Louisiana State University Press.

Voorgang, Dietrich. 1991. *Die Passion Jesu und Christi in der Gnosis.* EHS.T 432. Frankfurt: Peter Lang.

Waldstein, Michael and Frederik Wisse, eds. 1995. *The Apocryphon of John. Synopsis of Nag Hammadi Codices II,1; III,1; and IV,1 with BG 8502,2.* NHMS 33. Leiden: Brill.

Wallis, Richard T., ed. 1992. *Neoplatonism and Gnosticism.* Studies in Neoplatonism: Ancient and Modern 6. Albany: SUNY.

Walter, Nikolaus. 1989. "Paul and the Early Christian Jesus-Tradition." *Paul and Jesus: Collected Essays.* Ed. A.J.M. Wedderburn. JSNT.S 37. Sheffield: JSOT Press. 51–80.

Weidinger, Erich. 1990. *Die Apokryphen: Verborgene Bücher der Bibel.* Augsburg: Pattloch.

Weigandt, P. 1961. *Der Doketismus im Urchristentum und in der theologischen Entwicklung des zweiten Jahrhunderts.* 2 vols. Diss., Evang.-Theol. Fakultät der Ruprecht-Karl-Universität zu Heidelberg.

Wenham, David, ed. 1985. *The Jesus Tradition Outside the Gospels.* GoPe 5. Sheffield: JSOT.

Werner, Andreas. 1974. "Die Apokalypse des Petrus: Die dritte Schrift aus Nag-Hammadi-Codex VII." *ThLZ* 99: 575–84.

Werner, Andreas. 1989. "Koptisch-gnostische Apokalypse des Petrus." Hennecke and Schneemelcher 1989[5], 2: 633–43.

Widengren, Geo. 1946. *Mesopotamian Elements in Manichaeism (King and Saviour II). Studies in Manichaean, Mandaean, and Syrian-Gnostic Religion.* UUA 1946: 3. Uppsala/Leipzig: Lundequist/Harrassowitz.

Wilken, Robert L., ed. 1975. *Aspects of Wisdom in Judaism and Early Christianity.* University of Notre Dame Center for the Study of Judaism and Christianity in Antiquity 1. Notre Dame/London: University of Notre Dame Press.

Williams, Francis E. 1985a. "The Apocryphon of James: I,2:1.1–16.30." Attridge 1985a, 13–53.

Williams, Francis E. 1985b. "The Apocryphon of James: I,2:1.1–16.30." Attridge 1985b, 7–37.

Williams, James G. 1989. "Neither Here Nor There: Between Wisdom and Apocalyptic in Jesus' Kingdom Sayings." *FF.F* 5,2: 7–30.

Williams, Michael A. 1988. "Variety in Gnostic Perspectives on Gender." King 2–22.

Wilson, Robert McL. 1962. *The Gospel of Philip: Translated from the Coptic Text, with an Introduction and Commentary.* New York/Evanston: Harper & Row.

Wilson, Robert McL. 1978a. "Apokryphen II. Apokryphen des Neuen Testaments." *TRE* 3: 316–62.

Wilson, Robert McL., ed. 1978b. *Nag Hammadi and Gnosis. Papers read at the First International Congress of Coptology (Cairo, December 1976).* NHS 14. Leiden: Brill.

Wilson, Robert McL. 1978c. "Slippery Words. II. Gnosis, Gnostic, Gnosticism." *ET* 89: 296–301.

Wilson, Robert McL. 1982. "Nag Hammadi and the New Testament." *NTS* 28: 289–302.

Wilson, Robert McL. 1989. "New Testament Apocrypha." Epp and MacRae 429–55.

Wilson, Robert McL. and Douglas M. Parrott. 1979. "NHC VI,1: The Acts of Peter and the Twelve Apostles." Parrott 1979, 197–229.

Wink, Walter. 1993. *Cracking the Gnostic Code: The Powers in Gnosticism.* SBL.MS 46. Atlanta, GA: Scholars.

Winkler, Gabriele. 1994. "Die Licht-Erscheinung bei der Taufe Jesu und der Ursprung des Epiphniefestes. Eine Untersuchung griechischer, syrischer, armenischer und lateinischer Quellen." *OrChr* 78: 177–229.

Wisse, Frederik. 1970. "The Redeemer Figure in the Paraphrase of Shem." *NT* 12: 130–40.

Wisse, Frederik. 1975. "On Exegeting 'The Exegesis on the Soul'." Ménard 1975c, 68–81.

Wisse, Frederik. 1988a. "The Apocryphon of John (II,*1*, III,*1*, IV,*1*, and BG 8502,2)." Robinson, J.M. 1988[3], 104–23.

Wisse, Frederik. 1988b. "Flee Femininity: Antifemininity in Gnostic Texts and the Question of Social Milieu." King 297–307.

Wisse, Frederik and Francis E. Williams. 1979. "NHC VI,4: The Concept of Our Great Power." Parrott 1979, 291–323.

Zandee, Jan. 1991. *The Teachings of Sylvanus (Nag Hammadi Codex VII, 4).* Egyptologosche uitgaven 6. Leiden: Nederlands Instituut voor het Nabije Oosten.

Indexes

1. Modern Authors

Pagels and Turner 1990a: 75 n.1, n.2,
    106, 147
Pagels and Turner 1990b: 32 n.1, n.2,
    n.3, n.4, 33, 33 n.3, 34, 62 n.1, 117
    n.1, n.2
Painchaud 1981: 145, 145 n.2
Painchaud 1982: 39 n.1, 115 n.2, 144
    n.1, 145 n.2, 146 n.1, 178 n.3, 187
Parrott 1988: 123 n.1
Partrick: 19, 49 n.3, 50, 51 n.4, 72 n.1,
    79, 85 n.3, 100 n.1, 114, 116, 116
    n.1, 123 n.1, 152 n.1, 156
Pasquier: 39 n.2
Passow: xviii n.3
Patterson 1990: 21 n.3, 79 n.2, 199 n.1
Patterson 1991: 3 n.1
Patterson 1993: 21 n.3
Pearson 1975: 149 n.2
Pearson 1986: 16 n.5
Pearson 1991b: 17 n.1
Peel 1979: 142 n.3
Peel 1985a: 158
Peel 1985b: 85 n.2, n.3, 92 n.1, 148 n.1,
    n.2, 158 n.4,
Perkins 1971: 17, 20, 43, 43 n.2, 44, 44
    n.1,
Perkins 1980: 45 n.1, 81, 170 n.1, 183,
    183 n.2, 191 n.1, n.2
Perkins 1981a: 43 n.1
Perkins 1981b: 74 n.1
Perkins 1990: 30
Perkins 1991: 7, 13 n.1, 21 n.3, 82 n.1
Perkins 1992: 21 n.1
Perkins 1993a: 34 n.3, 78 n.1, 102 n.1,
    109 n.2, 155 n.2
Perkins 1993b: 13 n.3
Pétrement: 15 n.1
Piper: 11 n.4
Poehlmann: 142 n.1
Poirier: 59
Polkow: 14 n.1
Porcarelli: 19
Puech: 92 n.1, 148 n.2

Quecke: 168 n.1
Quispel 1967: 173 n.1
Quispel 1975: 163

Reumann: 2 n.1
Rewolinski: 34
Richardson: 15 n.1
Roberge 1992: xviii, xviii n.3, xix
Roberge and Wisse: xvii–xviii, xviii n.2,
Robinson, G: 31 n.5, 74 n.3, n.4, 151,
    151 n.1
Robinson, J.M.: 5 n.1
Robinson, J.M. 1975: 12 n.5
Robinson, J.M. 1979: 19 n.1

Robinson, J.M. 1981: 72
Robinson, J.M. 1982: 19, 156 n.3
Robinson, J.M. 1984: 6 n.2
Robinson, J.M. 1986: 13 n.2
Robinson, J.M. 1988: 3, 5, 6 n.2, 13
Robinson, J.M. 1991: 13 n.1
Robinson, J.M. 1994: 14 n.1, 21 n.3
Rudolph 1965: xvi n.1
Rudolph 1969: xiii n.1
Rudolph 1971: xiii n.1
Rudolph 1972: xiii n.1
Rudolph 1973: xiii n.1
Rudolph 1975: 53 n.4
Rudolph 1979: 68 n.1, 163–5, 167, 193
    n.2
Rudolph 1983: 15 n.1
Rudolph 1985: xiii n.1
Rudolph 1990: xiii n.1

Sanders: 7
Sato: 12 n.3
Schenke, G.: 151 n.1
Schenke, H.-M. 1959a: 30 n.1, n.2
Schenke, H.-M. 1959b: 47 n.1
Schenke, H.-M. 1960: 50–1, 118 n.1,
    128 n.3, 158 n.1
Schenke, H.-M. 1962b: 42
Schenke, H.-M. 1966: xvi n.2, xvii n.1,
    129 n.2, 139 n.1
Schenke, H.-M. 1971: 151, 151 n.3
Schenke, H.-M. 1973: 28 n.1
Schenke, H.-M. 1975a: 77, 190 n.2
Schenke, H.-M. 1975b: 168 n.1
Schenke, H.-M. 1975c: 132 n.2
Schenke, H.-M. 1979: 40 n.2, 122 n.1
Schenke, H.-M. 1980: 148 n.3, n.5, 149
    n.1, n.2
Schenke, H.-M. 1983: 88 n.2
Schenke, H.-M. 1989a: 35, 117 n.2, 118
    n.1, 128 n.3, 158 n.1
Schenke, H.-M. 1989b: 28 n.1
Schoedel and Parrott: 191 n.4
Scholer 1971: xiii n.1
Scholten: 151 n.2
Schweizer 1974: 169 n.1
Schweizer 1987: 12 n.1
Schwertner: xxiii
Scopello: 110 n.3, n.4
Seeley: 12 n.1
Sell 1979: 128 n.1
Sell 1982: 88 n.1, 171 n.1
Sevrin 1974: 50–1, 130 n.1
Sevrin 1975: xviii, xviii n.1, xix
Sevrin 1983: 110 n.3, n.4
Sevrin 1985: 40, 40 n.2, 41, 41 n.3
Siegert: xviii, 160, 190 n.1
Siker: 186 n.3
Smith 1965/66: 198 n.1

2. Nag Hammadi Texts

3. Ancient Authors and Texts

Acts of the Apostles

1:3	102
1:8	114
18:3	190 n.2

Alf Trisar Šuialia II,32
53 n.1

Apostolic Fathers
11 n.3

Book of John 115,10–18
53 n.1

Canticles

4:9	110 n.4
4:12	110 n.4
5:1	110 n.4
5:2	110 n.4
8:1	110 n.4

Celsus

I 49	129 n.2
II 13	129 n.2

Clement of Alexandria
3 n.3

Strom. V,11,72,2
152 n.4

Colossians   179

2:14   154 n.2

Coptic Magical Papyri
50 n.1

1 Corinthians

1:17–18	190 n.2
2:2	190 n.2
2:8	156 n.1
2:9	3
12	179
15:43	151 n.3
15:53–54	153 n.1

2 Corinthians

5:2–4   153 n.1

Cynics   12 n.5

Cyril of Alexandria

Commentary on John Bk XII, 1046
xviii

Deuteronomy

27 – 28   160 n.2

Deutero-Paul 16 n.1

1 Enoch

93,3   198 n.1

Ephesians   179

2:15   154 n.2

Epiphanius   128 n.4

Pan. 36,3,2–6
168 n.2

4. Subject Index

God of Truth 29
godhead 184
Good 28
good/goodness 60, 100, 121, 158, 161,
    176, 182, 184, 202, 204
  good one 204
  good works 201
gospel/s 2, 7–8, 11, 15
  formation 11
  genre 6–8
    birth legends 9
    catechisms 8
    miracle stories 9
    parable source 9
    passion narrative 8, 11–12, 22
    passion-resurrection narrative 11
    sayings of Jesus 8
  gospel of God 115, 183
governors of this world 191
grave (of the archons) 63, 177
Great Church 191
Great Mind 30
Great Power 26, 64, 89
Great Sophia 45

Habitation 123, 172, 194
Hades/Hell 59, 101, 138, 141, 143, 161
  ruler of Hades 159
healing 115, 181
heart 68
  ears of the heart 60
heavenly region/region above 26–7, 47,
    58–9, 62, 73–6, 79, 85, 101–2, 106,
    117–19, 122, 126, 132, 140, 146, 160,
    164–9, 171–2, 175–7, 183, 193–6,
    201–5
  heavenly realm of Sabaoth 47
  seventh heaven xvi
  seventy-two heavens 29, 106, 191
heavenly army/bodyguards 36–7
heavenly beings 47, 83, 85, 99, 105–6,
    168, 173
heavenly interpreter 97
heavenly journey 106
heavenly Paradise 28
heavenly triad 67
Hebdomad 39, 57, 187
  seven hebdomads 192
  twelve hebdomads 29, 106, 192
Hebrew 127, 155, 185
  Hebrew prophets 104
Hermas 187
heterodoxy 4, 17, 20, 28, 107, 187–9
He-Who-Is 29, 88, 140, 157, 176–7
hiddenness 73, 117, 129, 139, 146, 183–
    4, 195, 202
historical Jesus research 1–23, 207
  quests 1–2, 6, 19

holy of holies 155
Holy Spirit/holy spirit xvi, 28, 30, 35,
    49–52, 54, 65, 72, 76, 130, 142, 155,
    166, 169, 175, 178, 184, 200
human beings 60–9, 73, 106, 163–4, 166,
    181, 184, 197
  human condition 37, 59, 74, 136
  human form 78, 116, 184
  three races 62
  three types 62, 69
  three-part: mind, soul, body 61
  three-part: spirit, soul, body 60
  two types 62
  two-part: soul, body 61
humiliation 171, 177
hylic 37, 59, 69, 126, 131, 137, 180
hymn 160, 203
  heavenly hymns 195

Iesseus-Mazareus-Iessedekeus 40
ignorance 30, 58, 61, 63–4, 99, 108–10,
    125–6, 129, 135, 137, 140, 143, 145,
    156, 168, 171–2, 176, 187–8, 192–4,
    199, 203
illumination 65, 74, 137, 150, 159
image 26, 29, 32–3, 36–8, 44, 62, 74,
    86, 93, 149, 169, 177, 195
immortality 58, 101, 108, 148, 182, 196
  immortal ones 187
imperishability 29, 52, 60, 82, 115, 158,
    176–7, 183, 199
incorruption 59, 121, 155, 169, 176
  incorruptible ones 75
Ineffable one 32–3
Infinite/infinities 26, 168
initiation 169–70, 178, 182
insight 79, 96, 99, 130, 132, 167–78,
    180, 182, 184–5, 191–2, 194, 199,
    200, 202
  gnōsis 164, 167, 172, 189
invisibility 59, 66, 83–4, 148, 203
  Invisible One 28–9, 98
  invisible things 191, 200
Isidore 189

James 48, 57, 68, 82–4, 88, 96, 108,
    125, 127–9, 140, 157, 168, 177–8
  burial 108
  his father 48
  his mother 48
  Just One 177
  microcosm of the community 177
  mirror of the Lord 177
  passion 88, 139, 177
  redemption 108, 177
  relationship with the Father 173
  relationship with Jesus 177
  sufferings and death 108, 151